THE STORY OF THE HUGUENOTS

A UNIQUE LEGACY

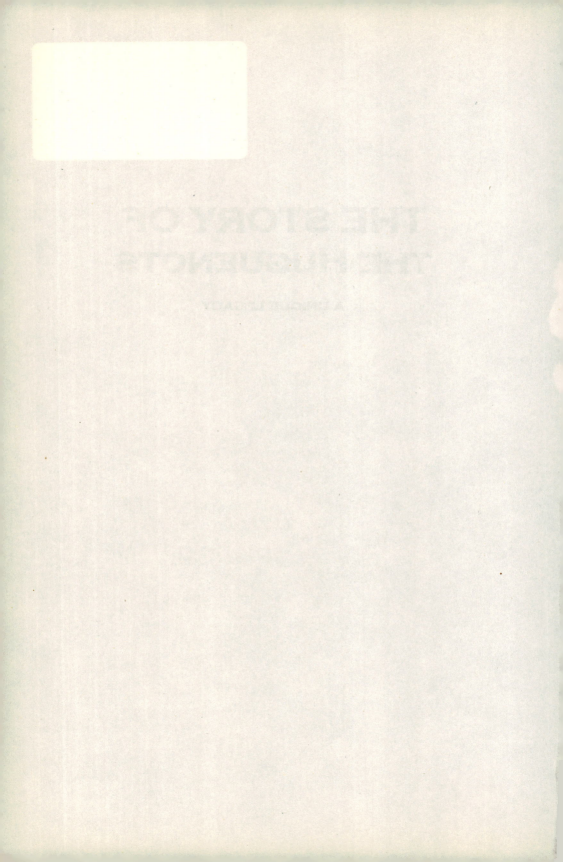

THE STORY OF THE HUGUENOTS

A UNIQUE LEGACY

NOT JUST ANOTHER BOOK

First Published in 2018 by NotJustAnotherBook
Copyright © Joyce Hampton
(for not just another book)
Email: hampton.joyce14@yahoo.com

All rights reserved. No part of this publication may be reproduced, stored in a retrieval system, or transmitted in any form or by any means, electronic, mechanical, photocopying, recording, or otherwise, without prior permission in writing from the publisher.

The copyright holder has asserted the moral right to be identified as the author of this work.
Cover Design and copyright © Joyce Hampton

Main Text Set in Times New Roman 12.0
Published by not just another book

ISBN: 978-0-9935665-2-3

Pageset Limited, High Wycombe, Bucks
Printed and bound in Great Britain by Berforts Limited

Contents

List of Illustrations viii

Preface xi

Acknowledgements xiii

Timeline of Major Events xv

Introduction xix

Part One

The Beginnings of French Protestantism .... - 1 -

   - 1 - A Question of Faith .... - 2 -

   - 2 - The Road to the Wars of Religion .... - 15 -

   - 3 - The First Three Wars 1562-76 .... - 25 -

   - 4 - The St Bartholomew's Day Massacre and the final Five Wars 1572-88 .... - 36 -

   - 5 - The Wars of the League 1589-98 .... - 49 -

   - 6 - From the Edict of Nantes to the Succession of Louis XIV ...... - 57 -

   - 7 - The Fronde to the Revocation 1648-85 .... - 68 -

   - 8 - Post-Revocation: Persecution and Punishment ..... - 81 -

   - 9 - Decisions and Harsh Realities .... - 90 -

Part Two

The Exodus and the Way Forward .... - 99 -

   - 10 - Time to Start Again .... - 100 -

   - 11 - Protestant England's Welcome .... - 113 -

   - 12 - Assimilation, Integration and Discord during the Tudor and Stuart Eras .... - 121 -

   - 13 - England's Huguenot Churches .... - 134 -

   - 14 - England: Aid & Legal Status .... - 149 -

   - 15 - To Aid One's Fellow Man .... - 158 -

The Story of the Huguenots – a Unique Legacy

- 16 - London Settlements ....- 166 -

- 17 - Spitalfields and Silk Weaving...............................- 176 -

- 18 - Huguenot European Emigration..........................- 191 -

- 19 - To Explore the Furthest Reaches........................- 214 -

- 20 - Riots, Justice and Retribution............................- 227 -

- 21 - The Glorious Revolution and the Huguenot Regiments....- 236 -

- 22 - Citizenship, Faith and Loyalty............................- 247 -

- 23 - French Inheritances..- 251 -

Part Three

Huguenot Enhancement of Life in the United Kingdom – A Legacy . - 255 -

- 24 - Commerce, Benevolence and The Word..........................- 256 -

- 25 - Science and Service ....- 281 -

- 26 - The Quality of the Huguenot Artisan ....- 297 -

- 27 - Architecture and Creativity ....- 312 -

- 28 - The Arts ....- 320 -

Part Four

France and England to the Present Day ....- 331 -

- 29 - France – Injustice and Enlightenment................- 332 -

- 30 - The early 20th Century ....- 338 -

- 31 - To the end of the 20th Century ....- 351 -

- 32 - Revolution and Recognition, Apology and the Future ....- 362 -

Appendices

1. The Edict of Nantes

Including its secret Articles and Brevets................- 375 -

2. The Edict of Fontainebleau (Revocation) ....- 401 -

3. The Huguenot Cross...- 405 -

4. The Huguenot Refugee's Four-part Song ....- 406 -

The Story of the Huguenots – a Unique Legacy

Tables ....- 407 -

Huguenot Societies...- 410 -

Notes ....- 412 -

Bibliography ....- 447 -

Index ....- 465 -

List of Illustrations

Book cover	*The Flight of the Protestants from France,* part of the engraving by Jan Luyken, 1696, reproduced courtesy of the Huguenot Museum, Germany.

Between Parts 1 and 2

Fig 1	The Flight of the Protestants from France (The Huguenot Museum, Germany).
Fig 2	Map of France and its borders in the 16th century (The Huguenot Museum, Germany).
Fig 3	Martin Luther (author's collection).
Fig 4	John Calvin (author's collection).
Fig 5	The tomb of Odet Coligny, Canterbury Cathedral (author's collection).
Fig 6	Montauban, important Huguenot stronghold (author's collection).
Fig 7	Le Château d'Arques-la-Bataille (author's collection).
Fig 8	La Rochelle harbour entrance (Janet Williams).
Fig 9	The Black Prince's Chantry, Huguenot Chapel, Canterbury Cathedral, French biblical inscription (author's collection).
Fig 10	The Constance Tower, Aigues Mortes (author's collection).
Fig 11	Portrait of Guillaume Guion (Guion family archive).
Fig 12	Map showing Huguenot escape routes in the 17th and 18th centuries. (Map drawn by the author.)

The Story of the Huguenots – a Unique Legacy

Between Parts 2 and 3

Fig 1 A méreau token (Huguenot Museum, Rochester, Kent).

Fig 2 The French Hospital, Victoria Park, Hackney (private collection/©Look and Learn/Illustrated Papers Collection/Bridgeman Images).

Fig 3 Jean Dupen's indenture of apprenticeship (Dupen family archive).

Fig 4 Residents of the French Hospital (The Huguenot Society).

Fig 5 Silk design for John Rondeau (Rondeau family archive).

Fig 6 Huguenot houses of Spitalfields, London (author's collection and family archive).

Fig 7 The Bank of England, Threadneedle Street, London (author's collection).

Fig 8 Bobbin on display on a Spitalfields house (author's collection).

Fig 9 Intricate carving, exterior of a house in Spitalfields (author's collection).

Fig 10 Franschhoek, Western Cape, South Africa (author's collection).

Fig 11 The Bethnal Green mulberry tree (The Gentle Author).

Fig 12 An original Jacquard weaving loom in Lyon (author's collection).

Fig 13 Memorial to the Huguenots of Wandsworth (author's collection).

Between Parts 3 and 4

Fig 1 Houblon Almshouses, Richmond, south-west London (Richmond Charities).

Fig 2 Portrait of Sealy Fourdrinier (Nicole Wood née Guillermoprieto, descendant of Henry Fourdrinier).

Fig 3 Baptismal entry for Catherine Elizabeth Guion, 1705 (Guion family archive).

Fig 4 The Calas family house, Toulouse (author's collection).

Fig 5 Portrait of Mary Blaquiere (Guion family archive).

The Story of the Huguenots – a Unique Legacy

Fig 6	Glasses manufactured by Huguenot craftsmen (The Huguenot Museum, Rochester, Kent).
Fig 7	Guilbauld cabinet at the Geffrye Museum, London (supported by the Heritage Lottery Fund and MLA/V&A Purchase Grant Fund).
Fig 8	The signed pledge to rebuild the Luneray Temple, Normandy (author's collection).
Fig 9	The rebuilt Temple of Luneray (author's collection).
Fig 10	Plaque in honour of the Huguenots, Spitalfields (author's collection).
Fig 11	The French Hospital, Rochester, Kent (author's collection).
Fig 12	Interior of the Soho Church, 500th anniversary service (author's collection).

Preface

The 31 October 2017 was a truly historic moment as on that date we were able to celebrate the five-hundredth anniversary of Martin Luther sparking the beginning of the Reformation.

During the intervening years an immense struggle took place across Europe as men and women began to openly question the long-held doctrines of the Catholic Church, but during this conflict-ridden half-millennium, it has been more than just religious beliefs that have changed.

In celebration of this quincentenary, and also of the tricentenary of the foundation of the French Hospital in London in 1718, it seemed a most appropriate time to publish a new book on the subject of the Huguenots and their amazing legacy across the world.

When we say 'The Huguenots', we are not talking of just a group of historical people from long ago who have left their mark upon countless countries. Even viewed distantly, the trials and tribulations they suffered – as the following pages will reveal – were arguably but a means by which to forge and temper them into robust individuals almost inured to the cruelty of ethnoreligious persecution, and it is no accident of history that down the generations their strong genetic imprint still manifests itself through their descendants, who continue to demonstrate their worthy values, and who themselves are also a fascinating and intrinsic part of the Huguenot story and journey.

I have been privileged to have been given access to, in some instances, previously unpublished family records of those Huguenots forced to flee their homeland in order to somehow overcome what must have seemed a mountainous struggle to firstly survive and then rebuild their shattered lives again in a new country. Yet, there are countless Huguenot families who have become famous through their illustrious ancestors' entrepreneurial expertise in the many and diverse areas of trade at which they excelled.

There are of course a greater number of lesser-known Huguenot families who in their own quiet way also contributed immensely to their chosen land of adoption, and I felt a sensible cross-section of these families should similarly be included so that a broader range of the history of the Huguenots is provided, and to hopefully encourage people to research their family histories to possibly discover if they too have a Huguenot heritage. Due to the large numbers of Huguenots who settled in the United Kingdom and over time married into British families, there is a reasonable probability that a link to a Huguenot ancestor may indeed be found, and I believe the inclusion of stories of both the famous and the humble serve to supply those indispensable twin qualities of richness and diversity to this book in such a way that the reader will share my enthusiasm for including Huguenots from all walks and stations in life.

Family histories have been woven into the book at the appropriate historic timeline, and thus some families in possession of well-documented records will appear in several passages of the book as their story unfolds.

I have also been fortunate to have been offered help and encouragement by a number of organisations, as well as individuals, not only from England but also from France and beyond whose input has enhanced this book, and for which I am profoundly grateful.

It is truly exciting that a number of Huguenot Societies have during this period been established across the world; accordingly, a list of their contact details can be found at the end of this book.

Joyce Hampton   **31 October 2017**

Acknowledgements

This book has taken a great deal of time to research and write, and I am deeply indebted to the following for their help and encouragement, which is just a small selection of the many organisations and individuals who have helped make this book possible:

John Hampton for his patient dedication of many, many hours of editing, professional proofreading and valued advice.

The following members of the Huguenot Society of Great Britain and Ireland for their encouragement and valued input with family records: David Guyon (Guion), Stanley Rondeau, Victorine Martineau, Mimi Romilly, Glynda Easterbrook (Gaucheron), Peter Duval and Sarah J Ellis (Dupont).

Additionally, the Huguenot descendants who gave me unlimited access to their family archives, including: June Lawrence née Whitfield (Agombar), Anne Dupen-Hopkins (Dupen), Lynwen Clark (Mallandain) and finally the Ouvry family.

The Huguenot Societies of: Great Britain and Ireland, South Africa, Australia, Germany and the Société Jersiaise.

The many organisations that have been of great assistance and encouragement to me, which include: The Spitalfields Institute, The London Metropolitan Archives, The Bancroft Library, The Public Records Office, Kew, together with the Museum of London.

Lastly, but by no means least, the many individuals both in France and in England who have assisted me in my research, in particular

Robert Mallet (France) and Marilyn McIvor (England) with a special thanks to Gerald Cort and Rachael Cort-Bekaert for their encouragement and hospitality in France.

A percentage of net book sales will be donated to the Huguenot Museum, Rochester, Kent, which is working to ensure the memory of the Huguenots and their legacy to us all is never forgotten, and I would strongly advise people to visit to see some of the Huguenot treasures housed in the museum.

All books cited have been referenced to this work, and in many cases downloadable PDF documents have also been fully referenced, but web citations have not been referenced due to, in some cases, the lengthy address although they have naturally been included in the bibliography.

Timeline of Major Events

1517	Martin Luther posts his Ninety-Five Theses to the door of the cathedral of Württemberg challenging the Catholic Church, and thus beginning the Protestant Reformation.
1522	First Protestant French refugee flees to Geneva.
1523	First French Protestant martyr burnt at the stake in Paris.
1536	Calvin leaves France for Geneva.
1534	The initial protection provided by Francis I for Huguenot 'dissidents' (from Parlementary measures seeking to exterminate them) ends with the *Affair of the Placards*.
1550	French and Dutch Churches established in London.
1551	Persecution of Protestants increases with passing of *Edict of Châteaubriant*, which calls upon the civil and ecclesiastical courts to detect and punish all heretics.
1555	First Protestant preacher leaves Geneva for France.
1559	Huguenots organise their first national synod in Paris.
1559	*Peace of Cateau-Cambrésis* concludes Italian Wars.
1559	Succession of Francis II, whose wife, the Queen Consort Mary Queen of Scots, encourages rounding up French Huguenots on charges of heresy, employing torture and burning as punishments.
1560	*Conspiracy of Amboise.* First known instance of the term 'Huguenot' being applied, in this case to conspirators (all of whom are aristocratic members of the Reformed Church) involved in Amboise plot of 1560 - the foiled attempt to wrest power from the influential House of Guise.
1561	*Edict of Orléans* declares toleration to be French government policy, thereby giving Huguenots official protection.
1562	*Edict of Saint-Germain* formally recognises Huguenots for first time amidst growing tensions between Protestants and Catholics.

The Story of the Huguenots – a Unique Legacy

1562	Huguenot numbers peak at an estimated two million, concentrated mainly in the southern and western parts of France. An estimated 1,400 Reformed churches are operating in France in this decade.
1562	Massacre of Protestants at Wassy (1 March) begins French religious wars. Huguenots destroy tomb and remains of Saint Irenaeus (died 202), an early Catholic Church father and bishop.
1562-3	First major arrival of French Huguenots in England.
1564	Death of John Calvin.
1566	First uprising against Philip II of Spain In the Spanish Netherlands.
1567	The Duke of Alva, on the orders of Philip II, arrives to instigate suppression of uprising.
1570	*Peace of St Germain* ends the third war of religion in France.
1572	St. Bartholomew's Day Massacre (24 August) results in tens of thousands of Huguenots being killed. Massacres continue throughout France until 3 October.
1572	Spanish Netherlands rises up again in revolt.
1589	Henri III of France assassinated by Jacques Clement, a Catholic monk.
1593	Henri IV abjures his faith and adopts Catholicism in order to be accepted as King of France.
1598	*Edict of Nantes* awarded by Henri of Navarre grants religious and civil liberties to Huguenots, promising protection. Marks end to open hostilities.
1603	Dutch and French Churches hold their first synod in England.
1610	Henri IV King of France assassinated by Francois Ravaillac, a Catholic zealot.
1622	Massacre of Protestants at Negrepelisse by royal forces leads to eventual loss of Huguenot military and political privileges.
1628	Richelieu oversees fall of Huguenot stronghold of La Rochelle.
1629	*Peace of Alès* brings Wars of Religion in France to a conclusion.
1634	William Laud, Archbishop of Canterbury, attacks foreign churches in England creating fear and unease among Huguenot refugees.
1642	Death of Cardinal Richelieu.
1642	Beginning of the English Civil War.
1643	Louis XIV accedes to the French throne.
1648-53	The Fronde, a series of civil wars in France, heralds open rebellion against the policies of Cardinal Mazarin.
1660	Restoration of the monarchy as Charles II accedes to the English throne.
1660	Louis XIV of France starts to legally pressurise Huguenots to abjure their faith. Huguenot population drops to 856,000 by mid-decade, most of whom, by now, live in rural areas.

The Story of the Huguenots – a Unique Legacy

1676	Pressure intensifies on Huguenots to conform to Catholicism. Inception of the *Caisse des conversions*.
1681	Increasing waves of Huguenot refugees arriving in England leads to first financial collection (brief) to assist them.
1681	Inception of the Dragonnades in France: ill-disciplined Catholic soldiers brutalise Protestants in order to force their abjuration of faith.
1685	Louis XIV revokes the *Edict of Nantes*.
1686	Royal Bounty to raise funds for the refugees is implemented.
1688	Amidst fears of a return to Catholicism in England, William of Orange is invited to accede to the English throne on behalf of his wife Mary, only accepting to jointly rule with her, and prepares an invasion fleet.
1689	Start of Nine Years' War between France and the 'Grand Alliance' including England.
1690	Battle of the Boyne (Ireland) results in victory for Protestant William.
1694	Bank of England is founded to help fund spiralling costs of war with France.
1697	*Peace of Ryswick* ends war with France.
1702	Regional group in Cévennes, known as the Camisards, rise up against Catholic Church. Government troops eventually destroy them, but revolt forces more moderate approach to anti-Protestant repression.
1702	War of the Spanish Succession brings England into war with France.
1713	*Peace of Utrecht* finally ends War of the Spanish Succession.
1718	The French Protestant Hospital is founded in London.
1762	Final execution of Huguenot minister in France occurs near Toulouse, where Jean Calas is tortured and killed, both events leading to Voltaire's intervention, which succeeds in the annulment of sentence and posthumous exoneration of Calas.
1787	*Edict of Toleration* is signed following efforts of Voltaire and fellow Enlightenment writers, and the brother of Louis XVI.
1789	Declaration of the Rights of Man and of the Citizen gives Protestants equal rights as citizens.
1789	French Revolution begins, bringing about the execution of Louis XVI, a radical change of government, and the Napoleonic Code.
1790	Descendants of Huguenots encouraged to return to France. French citizenship is offered in the *Right of Return*.
1793	National Assembly passes the *Civil Constitution of the Clergy*, subordinating the Catholic Church in France to the French Government.

xvii

The Story of the Huguenots – a Unique Legacy

1794	Following Robespierre's death, churches in France are re-opened.
1802	Napoleonic Code gives official recognition to Protestant Churches.
1852	Foundation of the French Protestant Historical Society in Paris.
1883	Foundation of the American Huguenot Society in New York.
1885	Foundation of the Huguenot Society of London, later becoming the Huguenot Society of Great Britain and Ireland.
1889	Modification made to the *Right of Return* of 1790.
1985	Tri-centenary celebrations of the revocation of the *Edict of Nantes*.
1890	Foundation of the German Huguenot Society.
1905	French Government passes law (9 December) to divide church and state.
1945	Foreign descendants of Huguenots lose automatic right to French citizenship.
1953	Foundation of the Huguenot Society of South Africa.
1985	Formal apology publicly given by French President, Francois Mitterrand, to descendants of French Protestants on the 300th anniversary of the revocation of the *Edict of Nantes*.
2003	Foundation of the Huguenot Society of Australia.
2014	The Huguenot Museum established as a trust in Rochester, Kent.
2017	500th anniversary of Martin Luther beginning Protestant Reformation with the Ninety-Five Theses. Celebrations organised for every month of the year in many villages, towns and cities across the world.

Introduction

Throughout history many different nationalities have arrived on the shores of the British Isles. Down the ages they have come: Romans, Vikings and Normans, to conquer; others, such as Fleming and Jewish communities, to trade. Each of these groups have naturally left a vestige of some description that has illustrated their settling here, but the impact of some, such as the Huguenots, has gone further and has left such a wonderfully rich and varied legacy on the histories of their new homelands that it still today enhances all our lives – and few places have benefitted from that impact more than here in Great Britain.

When Huguenot refugees brought their skills and their religious faith to our shores, it was of course initially to escape the cruel realities of religious persecution. But this desperation quickly led to the realisation by government and people that these poor, destitute individuals could reimburse our ancestors' granting of asylum tenfold with the sheer measure of their diligent industriousness, invaluable professional skills, rational forward thinking and unrelenting hard work – and the only demand they made of our own ancestors was the right to practice the 'new' faith without fear of tyrannical oppression.

There is an old saying, 'your loss is my gain', and that is certainly true of the Huguenot exodus from France whose rulers realised only too late and at such cost that the loss of so many invaluably skilled resources was going to hurt the French economy

The Story of the Huguenots – a Unique Legacy

for years to come. If they gave it serious thought, more worrying for the French king and government was that such prized skills were now in the hands of France's enemies – established countries, who were more than willing to utilise this remarkable new asset in favour of warring successfully on these refugees' former homeland, and it is without doubt that France's loss was most definitely the Huguenots' adopted countries' gain.

The Huguenots were the first 'refugees'[1] – the word became part of the English language in the 1680s to describe the French-speaking Calvinists who came to these shores. Their arrival spanned a long period of time starting in the reign of Henry VIII, and it was a peaceful invasion in which they were for the most part welcomed – remarkable when one considers the tumultuousness of those times.

The origin of the term 'Huguenot' is uncertain[i] although there are several suggestions, one plausible explanation being that it may derive from the German word 'Eidgenosse', meaning 'companion, comrade or partner who has sworn an oath'. In Swiss-German, Eidgenosse seems to have translated into 'Eignot', and thereon translated into French as 'Huguenot', the term now being applied to French Protestants. Other possible contenders for the source of Huguenot include a derivation of the name of the Swiss politician Besançon Hugues, who was one of the leaders of the Geneva Eidgenossen. And a yet further option is that the name was taken from the famous King Hugo, whose haunted tower in Tours was a popular meeting place for Huguenots.

Perhaps it is one of the enduring mysteries of History that we shall never know for certain, and perhaps that is how it should be left.

In the meantime, I have proceeded to apportion this book into four parts. The first tells the story of how the Protestant religion grew in France during the chaos and bloodshed of the eight wars

---

[i] Noel Currer-Briggs & Royston Gambier, *Huguenot Ancestry* (Chichester, 1985) p4.

of religion, the League Wars, and the discrimination, maltreatment and killings inflicted on Huguenots simply for defying the prevailing religious orthodoxy.

The second part then focuses on the Huguenot exodus from France, particularly those who came to Great Britain (including the Channel Islands[2]) with special reference to the many who eventually settled in London. Importantly for future world history, it was not only to these shores that the Huguenots came, choosing as some did to travel further afield to start new lives in many other countries and territories, such as South Africa, America, Canada, Holland, Germany and Belgium, and some into eastern Europe - all part of the great journey of Calvinism, and all included in this part of the book.

The third part describes their story of innovation and integration within British society that impacts upon the many fields in which the Huguenot legacy continues to enrich our daily lives.

The final part offers a more up to date look at the Huguenot ethos on both sides of the English Channel (or La Manche).

In 1517, Martin Luther had nailed his immense scholastic work, known to history as *The Ninety-Five Theses*, to the door of the castle church in Württemberg in direct response to Pope Leo X having issued a further set of 'indulgences' that would financially assist the rebuilding of St Peter's Basilica. Copies of this document were soon widely circulated thanks to the new invention of the printing press, thus paving the way for the means by which this Reformation would spread so quickly across the continent. Luther had also been the first to translate the Bible into German so that ordinary people, for the first time, were able to have a chance of reading the scriptures in their own language. Yet, he was not the only man to question the Catholic Church's doctrines[ii]. Zwingli was another of those early, important – and extremely courageous

---

[ii] Cecil Jenkins, *France: People, History and Culture* (London, 2011) p47.

– reformers. In France, in the same year, Jacques Le Fevre wrote *Sancti Pauli Epistolae* – a doctrine that would become a cornerstone of the future French Protestant faith. And it was this new faith that now quickly spread across many regions of France.

The early years of the burgeoning new faith known as 'Protestantism' caused many people of many different walks of life – from the titled nobility to the skilled artisan – to freely choose to adopt this new form of worship, and as their numbers grew, Huguenots rapidly became an influential group within France. It was no surprise, perhaps, that such growth of so defiant a challenge to the established order could not be allowed to continue. Retaliation to the perceived threat could be seen within just a few years when the new religion claimed its first martyr in 1523 with the burning at the stake of Jean Valliere in Paris for 'heresy' – his crime apparently being blasphemy against the Virgin Mary. In the year before his martyrdom the first Protestant refugee, Lambert of Avignon, had fled across the border to Switzerland[iii]. This was a time when a person's priorities in life were their soul and how, during their lifetime, they could prepare for, and attain, salvation at the end of their life. Unstoppably, or so it seemed, more people were beginning to question the Catholic Church and its teachings just as others before them had done.

The French king, Francis I, having alliances with Protestant German princes, was assumed to be tolerant of this new religion even though he had given no clear indication of his support at that time. Many high-ranking members of the nobility were in favour of tolerance, including the king's sister, Marguerite, Queen of Navarre, but, in an ominous foreteller of things to come, there were numerous, powerful voices raised against the spread of Protestantism.

To endeavour to persuade Francis I to take a tolerant attitude towards the new religion and its followers, Zwingli dedicated his

---

[iii] Robin Gwynn, *Huguenot Heritage: The History and Contributions the Huguenots of Britain* (London, 1985) p8.

On True and False Religion to the king as did John Calvin with his *Christianae Religionis Institution*[iv].

Thus, Francis I was often swayed towards leniency and then, through the actions of others, away from it. Tragically, two seismic events in 1534 caused him to give his whole-hearted support to the Catholic faith. The first was an agreement with the Pope whereby France, hitherto mired in a series of wars since 1494 known as the Italian Wars, would be allowed to recover Milan from the Holy Roman Emperor if the French king agreed to stamp out heresy, i.e. Protestantism, in France. The second, of a very different nature, was the nailing of one of the Huguenots' infamous placards to the bedroom door of the king, so angering him that he resolved to deal severely with the non-conformists.

In our modern world it is perhaps hard to understand how an individual's choice of faith could have such a profound effect on the society they lived in, but in order to understand how mediaeval and renaissance Europe became divided by religion we need to go back to an earlier era….

[iv] Robin Gwynn, *Huguenot Heritage: The History and Contributions the Huguenots of Britain* (London, 1985) pp.8-9.

Part One

The Beginnings of French Protestantism

Long before Protestantism had begun to establish itself in France, there had been many who had openly questioned Catholic doctrine, and who were consequently expected to recant their 'heretical' beliefs. Should this expectation be defied, they would be required to pay the ultimate price of death. This was the uncompromising status quo that preceded the birth of Protestantism, yet it is worthy of reviewing because how such earlier questioning of the Catholic Church in many parts of Europe was perceived by the Church and other ruling authorities did much to lay the foundations for understanding how the Huguenots themselves both came into being and suffered under such prevailing ultra-religious tyranny.

And we should also bear in mind the struggles of other Protestant groups, such as the Walloons; and of the many 'protest' groupings and factions that developed in similar ways across Europe, including England. Some of these were not just brutally persecuted; they were mercilessly extinguished, and if it were not for the careful recording of a few brave men and women, their courageous struggle for the simple freedom to worship as they saw fit would have been lost without trace, and our knowledge of human history would be that much poorer as a result.

The story of all these peoples to survive and live according to what we see today as the most basic of all 'human rights', whilst heart-breaking at times, must be told for many good reasons, but most importantly because if it is not, then we are all that much poorer and less well-equipped in those ways that truly matter – *if* religions and races are ever to co-exist peacefully with each other.

- 1 -

- 1 -

A Question of Faith

In southern France during the 12th century the Cathars had raised their voices to question religious doctrine as interpreted by the Catholic Church. For over a century, Cathars and Catholics in the Languedoc region of France had lived side by side in relative harmony; nevertheless, over time the papacy had begun to feel the power of the Catholic Church being eroded – along with the lucrative taxes it had become accustomed to receiving. The Church at first tried military expeditions, then preaching campaigns, to persuade a return to the 'true' faith, but without success. The Cathars, essentially dualists[3], stubbornly held firm. And, so it was that Pope Innocent III resorted to calling for a crusade against them.

The Albigensian Crusade, beginning in 1209, lasted for 20 years and was in fact a series of battles designed to completely eradicate Catharism. Despite the harsh realities of facing well-equipped and trained soldiers, the Cathars stood their ground as best they could. Yet in 1216 this established pattern of resistance and retaliation began to change when the Dominican friars, with the authority and approval of the papal court, created the first papal inquisition – a powerful institution ruthless in its desire to root out any form of perceived heresy. For those who chose to stand firm against the inquisitors, ultimately there was life imprisonment or the fires of the inquisition as Cathar beliefs, the polar opposite to Catholic doctrine, were seen as a threat that might persuade people to rise up against the Church[v]. The Inquisition[4] thus created had as its base remit the objective of seeking out all non-believers, such as Cathars.

Yet, prior to the Cathars, there had arisen earlier religious groups challenging Catholic doctrine, amongst which were the Waldensians[5], also known as the 'Poor Men of Lyon'. They too had disputed the Church's teachings, declaring that the Bible was the sole source from which salvation could be found. In many of their beliefs the Waldensians were the first Protestants in France given that they too rejected papal authority along with indulgences, purgatory and the belief of transubstantiation – all key objections that were to be raised in later centuries by those French Protestants known to history as the Huguenots[vi].

In England, during the second half of the 14th century, John Wycliffe, a theologian and teacher at Oxford University, began to question Catholic teachings and the excessiveness of the Church's wealth; he was supported by no less a figure than the influential Duke of Lancaster, John of Gaunt, third son of King Edward III. Wycliffe was a man who pressed for reform of the Church, and he built a sizeable following amongst the ordinary people of England, but he inevitably became an enemy and therefore a target of the Church as he continued to defend his belief that it should give up its wealth and that its clergy should live in poverty. The Pope consequently issued no fewer than five papal bulls against Wycliffe during 1377-78.

Ignoring these missives from the very highest level of the Catholic Church, Wycliffe decided to return to Oxford University to fulfil his long-held desire of seeing the Latin Bible translated into English for all to read, and by 1381 this task had been completed. Wycliffe had by now already set up an Order of Poor

---

[v] O'Shea Stephen, *A Perfect Heresy,* (London, 2001) pp.17-20.
[vi] Ibid, p8.

Preachers, who were now told to go amongst the poor people and distribute the Word of God as written in the Bible. 1381 was incidentally the same year as the Peasants' Revolt. Wycliffe's preachers had no doubt stirred up an already angry populace, who now rose up against yet another royal tax. During the revolt, Archbishop Simon Sudbury was murdered and his successor, a determined man, threw his full weight behind condemnation of not only Wycliffe but also what he stood for. Against such odds, with many of his followers deserting him, his works were banned in May of the following year. Wycliffe died in 1384, succumbing to a series of strokes[vii].

This was not the end of the story of Wycliffe, however; he had angered and troubled the mediaeval Catholic Church whose view of things can only be gleaned through the prism of its overwhelming power, and its tremendous fury towards Wycliffe and his Bible would now be felt in all its immensity. In 1415 at a Church Council, it was ordered that all versions of his Bible be burned; Wycliffe was proclaimed a heretic, and his body exhumed and burnt.

In 1440, a German goldsmith by the name of Johannes Gutenberg invented the first printing press; ten years later – and very significantly – he had built a working prototype of a machine capable of producing large numbers of sheets of the printed word at a speed far greater than any number of scribes could produce by hand. Ironically, his first commercial orders were from the Catholic Church itself, which required thousands of sheets of indulgences; yet by 1455 Gutenberg had progressed further and produced the very first 42-line Bible in modern Europe on a moveable type press. The printing press itself, and Gutenberg's progressive development of it, was of course to hugely catalyse the rate at which ideas, arguments and counter-arguments would now spread within kingdoms and across frontiers, throughout Europe

---

[vii] G. Elmore Reaman, The Trail of the Huguenots in Europe, the United States, South Africa and Canada (London, 1964) p23.

and possibly beyond as it swept in, amongst its subject matter, a relative clamour of debate, doubt and deliberation on 'new' knowledge to a greater audience than had known of such things before. With a now proven method of producing written material quickly, cheaply and on an increasingly large-scale, the range of subjects inevitably emanated from, and led back to, the central themes of the times as felt by the people of those times. Religion was naturally at the forefront of the subject matter, and the new debate swirling around it made its impact on the escalating challenge being made by Huguenot's, some of whom must have seized on this extraordinary opportunity to communicate their new, exciting and simultaneously defiantly disobedient thoughts and ideas in the intensifying questioning of established dogma, which now took a great leap forward, and not just in France.

Often Scotland is overlooked in the history of the Huguenots, but France and Scotland had for many years enjoyed a close relationship, known as 'The Auld Alliance'. The first Protestant martyr in Scotland was Paul Crawar, who was charged with bringing heretical documents produced by Wycliffe and Huss into the kingdom. For this crime, he was burned at the stake. If this was meant to deter others, the Catholic Church failed. It was merely the start for Scotland as from then on numerous incidents were recorded of individuals as well as of groups questioning the Church and its prescribed method of worship. In 1523 Luther's articles began to enter the country and a Scottish translation of Wycliffe's New Testament began to be distributed; people reading this crucially began to ask why Faith was not based solely upon the Bible's teachings[viii].

The famous leader of the Protestants in Scotland was John Knox. Born to lowly parents sometime between 1505 and 1515, he went to Glasgow to study before being ordained. He vehemently preached against the Catholic Church and joined a band of men

---

[viii] G. Elmore Reaman, *The Trail of the Huguenots in Europe, the United States, South Africa and Canada* (London, 1964) p84.

who killed the Cardinal of St Andrews. Knox was caught by the French fleet when it took St Andrews and for 19 months was a galley slave in France, only being released following the request of Edward VI of England, whose chaplain he later became.

When the king died, and his Catholic half-sister Mary became Queen of England, Knox fled and eventually spent time in Geneva, where he espoused Calvinism, and then went on to preach, in French, for two years in Dieppe. Knox, a gifted orator, must surely have felt a deep empathy with the Huguenots. He returned to Scotland in 1559 and because of his passionate and persuasive rhetoric, people hearing him speak began destroying Catholic churches and monasteries, and it is undeniable that Knox helped shape the future Protestant Church in Scotland[ix].

Yet the previous century had witnessed another courageous challenger of religious orthodoxy: Erasmus. Born in Rotterdam on 27 October 1469, he travelled extensively throughout Europe and was well known in England, France, Italy and Germany. Perhaps because he had been forced into a monastery as a child after his parents died, and perhaps through being blessed with great intellect, Erasmus had started at an early age to question religious doctrine. He began to delve into the Church's teachings and found enlightenment from within the Bible itself. He escaped the monastic life when he accepted a position as a Latin secretary to the Bishop of Cambrai, then for many years went from country to country, from post to post. He concluded that a corrected Latin version of the New Testament was required as the existing edition, although updated over the years, now contained many inaccuracies. In 1516 his translation of the Greek version of the Bible into Latin was printed, followed by a revised version a year later. But Erasmus was not happy to rest on his laurels – he wanted his version of the New Testament to be read and understood by all,

---

[ix] G. Elmore Reaman, The Trail of the Huguenots in Europe, the United States, South Africa and Canada (London, 1964) p87.

including the common man, who unfortunately was unable to read or speak Latin[x].

These must have been times of relatively deep and widespread unease within the Catholic Church as it was becoming increasingly aware that the centuries-old rigid adherence to the doctrines of the Church were being increasingly questioned throughout Europe. Much as the Renaissance period had given the opportunity to rediscover a purer, earlier time in other spheres such as art and architecture, so did the Protestant Reformation seem to allow people to doubt, disengage with or openly defy the practices that had grown over time within the Church, and amid such feelings, there began the desire to return to a simpler form of religious practice.

In England, Henry VIII had begun the Reformation in order to divorce Katherine of Aragon and marry Anne Boleyn in 1533, becoming the Supreme Head of the Church of England by Act of Parliament in 1534 following the break with Rome. Here, the challenge seemed to be against change as far from all of Henry's subjects approved of this new form of religion nor the dissolution of the monasteries, and risings such as that in the north known as the 'Pilgrimage of Grace' constituted his subjects' attempts at persuading the king to return to the 'old' ways. The Catholic Church, especially the monasteries, was still extremely robust and resilient with friends in high places, and a treasury of its own that had grown wealthy on the backs of the poor.[6]

Across just 21 miles of water, the first burgeoning of reformation in France was recorded in the town of Meaux where many of the town's inhabitants were skilled artisans, and, living in such close proximity to the Flemish border they often heard at first-hand, from cities such as Bruges, Brussels and Antwerp, of the multitude of new ideas fresh from the innovation of the printing presses of these towns. And it was from Meaux that the

---

[x] G. Elmore Reaman, *The Trail of the Huguenots in Europe, the United States, South Africa and Canada* (London, 1964) p27.

posters known as the *Affair of the Placards* was to be later conceived. French people were beginning to choose which faith they would follow.

An example of one of the earlier converts to the new faith was Bernard Palissy – a famous potter who rose to become a renowned philosopher and writer. His attitude towards the new religion typifies many of his countrymen. He had been born in 1510 in the Périgord region of France. Due to his father being an artisan and Bernard's bourgeoning artistic talents, Bernard served an apprenticeship as a painter of glass. He travelled across France as well as Luxembourg and Flanders as he plied his trade, meeting fellow artisans who had begun to observe the teachings of Luther. He returned to France in 1539 at a time when restrictions of religion and in particular the publication of religious pamphlets were being supressed; perhaps for this reason, he chose to live in the quiet province of Saintonge, south-western France. He listened to the teaching of Philibert Hamelin[7], one of John Calvin's disciples, and became a founder of the Huguenot church in Saintes from where Calvinism was spread to La Rochelle and Bordeaux. At first, Palissy continued in his trade as a glass painter, but gradually he learnt the craft of enamelling, his skill bringing him to the attention of the Duke de Montmorency, who had recently commissioned his new chateau near Paris, and who now placed a substantial order with Palissy for tiles to embellish the planned structure.

His patron was, however, unable to protect him from being put on trial as a follower of the new religion although the duke was able to save his life by arranging for his transfer from Bordeaux to the jurisdiction of Paris. Undeterred, Palissy set up a new factory in Paris at the Tuileries[8] from where his reputation gained him many influential patrons including no less a personage than the king, but in the end his creative renown did not spare him; his admirable steadfastness to the new religion unfortunately resulted in his arrest and imprisonment in the Bastille. He died there a year later aged 78 still true to his beliefs[xi].

Those in society with an education, such as lawyers, artisans and merchants, were more likely to be drawn to Protestantism with its simple faith unadorned with what they perceived to be superstition, whereas the Catholic priest could easily intimidate and convince the less-educated that divine retribution could not be appeased without the intervention of saints or penances. The walls of Catholic churches clearly depicted painted visions of Purgatory and Hell[9] for those who did not either buy indulgences, pay for Masses for the dead, or pray for intervention through the saints to avert any disaster that might befall them, or for it to be mitigated in some merciful way, such as crop failure or animal disease. This does not imply a lack of education amongst Catholics of all classes but perhaps a greater conservatism inherent in their faith. The Catholic Church continued to hold sway over much of arable France where the conditions of basic existence were arguably hardest of all, and where, therefore, the poor agricultural classes were more influenced by the possibility of divine intervention as told to them by the accepted Church, whereas the towns and cities – populated increasingly with skilled professional people – were more inclined towards what they saw as the enlightened logic of Protestantism.

In 1530, a scholar by the name of Jacques Lefevre of Etaples, north-west France, completed his translation of sections of the Bible into simple French, teaching others that:

> *True repentance consists of a change of heart, a conversion, a return to God – a movement initiated by the Holy Spirit and not stemming from any bodily fear, chastisement or sacrifices....*

[xi] Noel Currer-Briggs & Royston Gambier, *Huguenot Ancestry* (Chichester, 1985) pp.5-6.

His translations were to become the foundation of all future versions of the French Bible. It was the Biblical Reformation message that was central to the emerging, intellectually-based challenge: 'Justification is by faith, not by works'. Yet, far from everyone applauded his message – the Catholic Church continued to adhere to a religion of 'works'. Lefevre, although persecuted by the Catholic Church, had a profound influence on his students, among them a figure who would become famous throughout Europe and beyond – John Calvin.

Calvin was born in July 1509 in the small town of Noyon near Paris. His mother died young, leaving her small son to be raised by a nobleman's family. His father was secretary to the Bishop of Noyon, and he was able to influence his 11-year-old son's employment to the position of a cathedral chaplain. The income from this position gave him the means to study French, Latin, law and theology. Calvin was first acquainted with the Protestant religion through his nephew, Pierre Olivetan, who had in 1533 converted to the reformed (Protestant) faith. Gradually, John Calvin became an active and respected member of the reformed faith, but his views were not so pleasing to the Catholic Church and one speech he wrote and sent to his friend Nicholas Cop was to infuriate the Church authorities to such a degree that both men were forced to flee Paris.

Calvin took up residence in Strasbourg, where he married the young widow Idelette van Buren before settling in Basle; it was while resident here in 1536 that he published his *Christianae Religionis Institution*. He sent a copy of this publication with a preface to Francis I, king of France.

Travelling back to Strasbourg via Geneva, John Calvin met Guillaume Farel, who asked for his help with the attempted reformation of religion. At first Calvin refused as he wanted to continue his studies, but he was so taken with Farel's passion he decided to abandon his own plans to further his education and instead chose to stay and write a new Bible translation. The

The Story of the Huguenots – a Unique Legacy

Christian Academy in Geneva trained hundreds of pastors who were then sent all over Europe to spread the word; many of the pastors were from the French nobility, who assisted immensely in spreading the word, particularly in France[xii]. Calvin went on to write *The Confessions of Faith* in 1558, followed in the next year by his writing of church ordinances that banned dancing, masquerades, gambling, taverns, cabarets, and idleness[10].

The French Protestant Church (Huguenot) was by 1561 made up of approximately 2,500 congregations, led by pastors trained at the Genevan-based academy.

In the same year as Calvin's *The Confessions of Faith* was published, the first Reformed Church was established in Toulouse for the by then already large Protestant population in the city. Just a few years earlier on 7 February 1562, 5,000 Huguenots had gathered for an open-air service, guarded by 100 militia men; they had become accustomed to this military presence and the frequent tension that these gatherings caused between the two faiths. Catholic preachers often whipped up feelings against Protestants, who had only recently taken control of several towns near to Toulouse itself. Protestants held dear the psalms that had been translated into French and despised the Catholic Church's public processions with public prayers and fasts. On several occasions, tensions spilled over into aggression that often ended in at least one fatality[xiii].

On 4 April 1562, nearly two months of violence on the streets of Toulouse began with what should have been a sombre event – the burial of a woman. The mourners were halted when the woman's confessor and her parents stood firmly in the way and stated that she had died a Catholic. An unseemly wrangle broke out over where the woman should be buried – in a Catholic or Protestant cemetery. The alarm was raised, rallying Catholics to

---

[xii] H. G. Koenigsberger and G. L. Mosse, *A General History of Europe: Europe in the Sixteenth Century* (London, 1968) p250.
[xiii] Robert Schneider, *A Public Life in Toulouse 1463-1789: From Municipal Republic to Cosmopolitan City* (New York, 1990) pp.93-7.

The Story of the Huguenots – a Unique Legacy

begin a slaughter of Protestants, and within a short space of time many lay dead or dying on both sides[xiv].

The next day a truce was called, but it was soon broken as fighting re-erupted. Parlement[11], whose members were formed from a Catholic majority, watched in horror at the escalating daily violence. The Huguenots reinforced the Hôtel de Ville whilst the Catholics seized the power stores and encamped in the parlementary palace. By 13 May, the city had turned into a Huguenot fortress, but the Catholics began to fight back with an assault on the Huguenot stronghold, having first issued orders that all Catholics should wear a white cross on their arm as well as placing a white cross in the window of their homes. The Huguenot army contained up to 1,000 able-bodied men, but as more and more Catholics poured into the city they were eventually, inevitably, overwhelmed. When the riots finally subsided, and after several more truces followed each time by renewed hostilities, many people had been murdered – the majority of them Protestants.

By the time the riots finally ceased, up to 4,000 victims had succumbed to the slaughter, and numerous acts of desecration had been enacted by both Huguenots and Catholics. Finally, a truce led to the expulsion of all Huguenots from the city on 17 May, but the killing did not stop there – a further 120 Huguenots were later sentenced to death[xv] by the Catholic-controlled authorities. Protestantism was gaining in strength, but it had colossal mountains in its path. It lacked the infrastructure and established power-base that Catholicism had in great measure – and which it would not yield without a fight to the death.

Part of that infrastructure were the places of worship themselves. There had been only a limited number of Protestant

---

[xiv] Mark Greengrass, *The Anatomy of a Religious Riot in Toulouse in May 1562: The Journal of Ecclesiastical History* (Cambridge, 1983) pp.367-91.
[xv] Robert Schneider, *A Public Life in Toulouse 1463-1789: From Municipal Republic to Cosmopolitan City* (New York, 1990) pp.93-7.

temples built in France before the *Edict of Nantes* because some Catholic churches had already been taken over and refurbished to comply with Huguenot beliefs.

Thus, by the summer of 1560, the method of seizure of buildings by Huguenots was becoming commonplace. The Huguenot community of Nantes was even bold enough to suggest that the Collegiate Church of Notre Dame should be divided so that Huguenots could worship in the nave while Catholics could continue to worship in the choir[xvi].

However, sometimes it was financial gain that was sought as wars are expensive. An example of this relates to the small town of Condom near Toulouse, when, in 1559, Huguenots captured the church – then demanded a ransom of 30,000 livres from the congregation – otherwise, they threatened, they would demolish it.

The government of France viewed this growing problem warily partly because France was still at war with Spain over control of Italy[12] ,and could not therefore devote its full attention to dealing with the growing threat of the Huguenots, but on 3 April 1599 the *Peace of Cateau-Cambrésis* was signed between France and Spain, leaving the government of France at last free to turn its attention to, as they perceived them, its increasingly troublesome Huguenots.

Throughout France in the years 1560-1 there were frequent bloody clashes between Catholics and Protestants, but on 19 November 1561 the massacre at Cahors was to go down in history as one of the most violent outrages against Protestants, a group of whom had gathered at the house of the Seigneur de Carbréres to worship. When the Catholics challenged them, they advised that the king had given approval for them to worship inside the city walls. Within a short time 40-50 people lay dead. It was later stated by a Protestant native of Cahors that the attack had been planned and carried out by prominent local Catholic churchmen[xvii].

[xvi] Raymond A. Menzer (Ed.) and Andrew Spicer (Ed.), *Society and Culture in the Huguenot World 1559-1685* (Cambridge, 2007) p183.
[xvii] Philip Benedict, *Graphic History: The Wars, Massacres and Troubles of Tortorel and Perrissin* (Renaissance Quarterly 61, no. 2 (Summer 2008) p260.

The Story of the Huguenots – a Unique Legacy

We shall never know for sure, but the pattern of escalating tensions that were themselves increasing in violence, revealing fear and hatred on both sides, points to the massacre at Cahors being pre-orchestrated by Catholics, furious at the seemingly relentless nature, and the unlimited extent, of Protestantism and all that this meant for the future of the Catholic Church in France and beyond.

- 2 -

The Road to the Wars of Religion

The French Wars of Religion began in 1562 and did not cease until the *Edict of Nantes* in 1598, although there were some pauses in the clashes between Catholics and Huguenots. The wars were a series of eight conflicts that were to have a profound impact on several generations of people at a time when religion and politics were inextricably socially intertwined. Although this was just as true in Protestant England as it was in Catholic France, tellingly in France there was a maxim, taken from a painting of Louis XII's coronation, which eventually became a heraldic device: 'une foi, un loi, un roi'[13].

This was to firmly bind these three concepts together in France, whereas in Protestant England such ideals were less rigidly linked.

Since the time of Clovis, who acceded to the throne in 481AD and who became the first king to rule over a united Frankish Kingdom, the monarchy in France had closely tied itself to religion, and in return for the monarchy's protection the Church gave the monarchy its blessing.

The Coronation Act itself is derived from the teachings of St Paul, Romans 13:1: '*Non, est enim potestas nisi a Deo, quae autem sunt, a Deo sunt*[14]'.

The concept of 'one faith' was considered essential to law and order within society. Furthermore, without the right faith surely

God would punish the people rather than bless them? The earlier French coronation ceremonies had been fairly simple affairs, but as time passed, events such as the Cathar rebellion caused additional oaths to be included in the ceremony, and thus from the 13th century onwards an oath against heretics was encompassed within the formal rites[xviii].

By the time of the accession of Francis I in 1515, the coronation oath taken by the king as he stood at the altar, on which was placed the gospels and a reliquary of the true cross, was to promise to promote peace in Christendom, to protect Christians against injuries, to dispense justice fairly and mercifully, and to expel heretics from his dominions[xix]. Francis was at first tolerant towards Huguenots and their faith – partly because his sister, Marguerite of Navarre, had sympathies towards Protestantism and allowed non-conformists a measure of protection at her court. Marguerite, Queen of Navarre and Duchesse of Alençon, was an immense help to those of the new religion; she was an educated woman who appreciated the works of Lefevre d'Etaples and offered her protection to the preachers of this new doctrine; including Aime Maigret, who had preached in Rouen in 1522[xx].

Marguerite had *Le Miroir de l'ame Percheresse* published, which in 1548 the young Elizabeth Tudor herself translated into English.

But, not everyone welcomed Luther's challenge to the Church's teachings. Luther's *Ninety-Five Theses* had naturally been very coolly received in Rome. A papal bull – *Exsurge Domine* – had been issued by Pope Leo X in 1520, affirming the banning of the preaching of Lutheran beliefs and the distribution

---

[xviii] Sandra Sider, *Handbook to life in Renaissance Europe* (New York, 2005) p51.
[xix] R. J. Knecht, *French Renaissance Monarchy: Francis I and Henri II* (Abingdon, 2014) p61.
[xx] Pierre Lheureux, *Les Protestants de Luneray et leur Église en pays de Caux*, (Luneray, 1937) p2.

of Lutheran literature. The same year that Leo X had issued this papal bull, Luther's evangelical teachings had begun to find support in France, but by 1523 these early 'heretical' Protestants (as seen from the Catholic viewpoint) began to face penalties. The Sorbonne University, the Church and Parlement levied fines, or imprisoned them; the harshest penalties were saved for monks or priests: life imprisonment or burning at the stake.

From the start of Francis' reign, he was engrossed in foreign matters, but the growing power of the Emperor Charles, who ruled vast swathes of Europe[15], encouraged Francis to align himself with those in opposition to Charles, particularly the Lutherans in Germany. Over time, though, the king and later his son Henri II made sustained attempts to stem the flow of Protestant ideas through various decrees[xxi].

The king's mild toleration, however, did continue, and perhaps would have continued for longer, had it not been for one notorious incident in October 1534, which came to be known in France as the *Affaire des Placards,* and which tragically served to sweep away his open-mindedness. Suddenly, posters fiercely condemning the Mass and the Catholic Eucharist were being nailed up all over Paris, Orléans and Blois – incredibly, even including the door of the royal bedchamber at Amboise. The king's attitude towards Protestants immediately hardened when he heard of this particular placard as he perceived it to be an attack not just on his own faith but also on his royal person. The *Affaire des Placards* had suddenly enraged the king's perception of the reformed religion and galvanised him into taking a firmer stance towards Huguenots, following the years of unrest and uncertainty that preceded it; now, that unrest would explode into open warfare and the all-out struggle for supremacy and survival – involving tyrannical persecution that from now on would have the king's personal stamp of approval.

[xxi] H. G. Koenigsberger and G. L. Mosse, *A General History of Europe: Europe in the Sixteenth Century* (London, 1968) p250.

The Story of the Huguenots – a Unique Legacy

Many leading Protestants including John Calvin fled abroad as the repressive measures came into force. In 1536, whilst living in Switzerland, John Calvin, a figure who was nothing less than inspirational to those following the new religion, had his book – now famously dedicated to Francis I – first published, and from this, French Protestantism gained its ideological basis.

Thus, Francis I, while on the one hand keen to form alliances with the Protestant princes of Germany, began in 1540 to persecute the people of the Vaudois[16] Evangelist Church, ordering numerous burnings at the stake in Dauphiné, Vivarais, Paris and the valleys of Provence. In 1545, he demanded a 'crusade' against the Vaudois of Cabrieres and Merindol, who were particularly hated by the Catholic clergy[xxii].

The historian De Thou noted that:

Everything was horrible and cruel in the sentence denounced against them; and everything was still more horrible and cruel in its execution. Twenty-two villages were plundered and burned, with an inhumanity of which the history of the most barbarous people scarcely affords an example. The unfortunate inhabitants, surprised during the night, and pursued from rock to rock by the lurid light of the fires which consumed their dwellings, only avoided one ambuscade to fall into another. The piteous cries of old men, of women, and of children, far from softening the hearts of the soldiery, as mad with rage as their chiefs, only served to indicate the track of the fugitives and mark their hiding-places, to which the assassins carried their fury.[xxiii]

In 1546 in the town of Meaux, 14 Lutherans including a pastor were burned at the stake. Henri II vigorously opposed Protestantism, and in 1547 created the infamous *Chambre Ardente*

[xxii] Dr Jules Bonnet, *Letters of John Calvin. Vol I* (Gutenburg, E-book) p187.
[xxiii] Martin, W. Carlos., *A History of the Huguenots.* (1866) p83.

within the Paris Parlement specifically for the persecution and trial of Protestants[xxiv]. Parlement in the next two years was to sanction no fewer than 500 prison sentences. Some Protestants, faced with this discrimination and tyranny, appear to have reluctantly returned to the Catholic faith, but many more chose to pursue their beliefs in secret. Eventually this oppression culminated in the Wars of Religion – deeply scarring the country's soul for centuries to come.

* * * * * *

On 24 July 1550, the first Protestant Church was founded in England, just four years after the first Protestant Church in France had been established in Meaux, but from 1555 Protestant temples, as they became known, were gradually being founded in various parts of the country especially in Paris, Angers and Valence, and even more so in Provence, the Garonne valley and the Languedoc. By the late 1550s, Protestantism was becoming prominent in society, mainly through the influence of John Calvin, who had by then returned from Geneva to set up a structure for training pastors to spread the word of Calvinist Protestantism. The first preacher left Geneva in 1555 to return to sermonise the word in France. These teachers were passionate and well educated, ably spreading the word far and wide especially in the south and south west of France where the ideals of the reformed faith were enthusiastically embraced. A further influence on the rise of this new faith was that many noble families were happy to convert to this 'reformed' faith due, it appears, to their enlightenment through education and bible studies.

In France, the concept of 'reformation' was viewed by many as troubling and divisive. Following the death of Francis I, his son succeeded as Henri II; he had, as a child, been held prisoner

---

[xxiv] Norman Davies, *Europe: A History* (London, 1997) p506.

with his brother in Catholic Spain as hostage for their father. Henri II was a devout Catholic who pursued a policy of enhancing the powers of Catholic persons within the Court, and through the inception of a sequence of edicts leading to the *Edict of Chateaubriand* in 1551 and the *Edict of Écouen* in 1559, he ensured the continued persecution of Protestants[xxv]. However, when he died in 1559 following a freak jousting accident[17], a power vacuum developed within French society as nobles both Catholic and Protestant jostled for position behind the new, somewhat sickly 15-year-old king, Francis II. Considered by all to be technically still a minor[18], therefore necessitating the appointment of a Regent, his mother, Catherine de Medici, was duly chosen. Francis had nevertheless been married to Mary Queen of Scots the year before, and his wife and her mother Marie belonged to the Catholic House of Guise. Marie's brother, Francois, Duc de Guise, was not only head of that House, he was also a military hero, whilst their brother the Cardinal of Lorraine was a redoubtable scholar and statesman. Unsurprisingly, and much to the detriment of the Protestant people, these men held considerable power in the land during the brief reign of Francis II.

Other noble houses, such as the ancient House of Montmorency, had similarly held considerable political power including the office of Constable of France during this time. The head of this House was Anne de Montmorency, a Catholic, but his nephews the Chatillon brothers, which included Admiral Coligny, were Protestants. The House of Bourbon were Protestants and, as first princes of the blood, held the right of tutorship over a king until he came of age to govern. They were led by Antoine de Bourbon, King of Navarre, and Louis de Bourbon, Prince de Condé. Thus, the noble houses of France were fundamentally divided by a common factor – religion – and from this division

---

[xxv] Thomas M. Lindsay MA, *A History of the Reformation* in two volumes (Oregon, 1999) p161.

sprang alliances within the Catholic and Protestant groupings. A similar division in England had occurred when the country split into the Houses of York and Lancaster during the period known as the Wars of the Roses with many of the followers of each House giving their allegiance to the head of the House, or to their immediate superior, simply because their leader had made a choice to follow York or Lancaster. This was probably akin to why, in the early years of religious unrest, some French people had chosen to convert to Protestantism – because their superiors had chosen that particular path.

1559 was to be a pivotal year for the Huguenots: with large numbers of trained pastors spreading their message far and wide, Huguenot influence was notably increasing across France. In response to this, Pope Paul IV issued the first *Index Expurgatorius,* setting out all books banned by the Catholic Church[19]. This document also banned specific printers, stating that all printed matter from these named printers were consequently prohibited [xxvi]. That same year, the Huguenots prepared for their first synod, which was held in Paris and attended by 72 members drawn from all the provinces. Significantly, their first Article stated: *'no church can claim principality or dominion over another'.*

This ideal had been greatly influenced by John Calvin, and led to the Huguenots becoming known as those of the 'reformed faith', as distinct from those who followed the ideals of Lutheranism. That same year also saw the inception of provincial synods to oversee Huguenot interests, and although there was no central synod to which these provincial synods were answerable to, Genevan guidance ensured they all followed roughly the same path. As events unfolded in France, so religious unrest favouring Protestantism reached its peak in the neighbouring Low Countries, while England had only the year before witnessed the start of the reign of the Protestant Queen Elizabeth I.

[xxvi] Samuel Smiles, *The Huguenots Their Settlements, Churches and Industries in England and Ireland (1889)* (London) p21.

The Story of the Huguenots – a Unique Legacy

In March 1560, the Huguenots formulated a plan which became known as the *Conspiracy of Amboise* – to capture King Francis II – but which disastrously resulted in the deaths of all the plotters except Louis, Prince de Condé. The plot had been hatched by a needy Perigord nobleman, Le Renaudie, although the agents of Louis, Prince de Condé, were the real instigators of the plot, and it was subsequently assumed that Calvin and Beza had given support to the plan[xxvii]. The Guise family, informed of the plot while the Court was at Blois, took the decision to move the king and court to a safer place, choosing the town of Amboise. When news of the relocation became known, La Renaudie postponed the planned kidnapping of the king, and with his followers moved to a new encampment in the woods surrounding Amboise. Their plans, however, had again been made known to the Guises, and many of the conspirators were captured alive, although La Renaudie was slain following an abortive attempt to storm the chateau. For a week or more the Guise faction wreaked vengeance on the remaining plotters – torturing, quartering and hanging anyone whom they believed to be implicated in the plot, before tossing the bodies into the Loire. It is believed that approximately 1,200 people were executed during this time, their deaths being swiftly followed by the *Edict of Romorantin* in May 1560.

Condé protested loudly against this edict, which deprived freedom of conscience to all but Catholics, leading to a special commission being convened on the orders of the Guise family to bring Condé to trial. Fate, however, spared the prince due to a postponement ordered by the Chancellor, Michel de l'Hopital[20], and the death of Francis II in December 1560.

On 28 January 1561, the *Edict of Orléans* was signed, suspending persecution of the Huguenots; it prohibited officers of the king from entering Protestant homes ostensibly under the guise of any previous edicts, which had banned unlawful assemblies.

[xxvii] S. K. Barker, Dr, *Protestantism, Poetry and Protest: The Vernacular Writings of Antoine de Candieu c1534-1591* (Farnham, 2009) p97.

The edict also demanded that any Protestants who had been arrested as being involved in 'unlawful assemblies' should be released, but with the important caveat that from then on they had to live as good Catholics[xxviii]. As this edict was felt to be in favour of the Protestants, the Catholic clergy resisted its implementation. But this edict had at last given Protestants the confidence to stand firm against any actions designed to limit their freedom of worship. But serious riots broke out in Paris. In some areas, Protestants seized Catholic churches, and, in several cases, Church property was destroyed.

1561 was also the year that Odet de Coligny (the admiral's brother) converted to the Huguenot faith; at the time of his conversion he was the Bishop of Beauvais as well as Cardinal-Archbishop of Châtillon, but he resolutely declined to resign these powerful offices and became known among Huguenots as the 'Protestant Cardinal'[21]. The Huguenots were rapidly increasing in numbers not least, it seemed, due to those who had converted and become preachers of the reformed religion. They must surely have begun to feel a new-found confidence through such increase in numerical strength as well as a soaring conviction of their faith, and some now unwisely turned to attacking Catholic churches, evicting the clergy and stripping these places of worship of all Catholic relics and icons. In an ominous portent of the future, they also began to gather in fields in many parts of the country to form their own army – training to become good soldiers of the faith, should the need arise.

Reacting to these events, the House of Guise, together with Anne de Montmorency and Jacques d'Albon de Saint-André, Maréchal de France, formed the Catholic Triumvirate. Antoine de Bourbon, King of Navarre, later abandoned his Protestant faith and joined this league whilst his wife Jeanne D'Albret, Queen of Navarre[22], remained a staunch Protestant.

[xxviii] Eugène Bersier, translated by Annie H Holmden, *Coligny: The earlier life of the great Huguenot* (London, 1884) p247.

The Story of the Huguenots – a Unique Legacy

Meanwhile, the king's mother, Catherine de Medici, attempted diplomacy to bring peace to the two faiths by issuing the *Edict of Toleration* in January 1562[23]. This edict legalised the practice of Protestantism although there were noteworthy restrictions such as only preaching in open fields outside of the towns or within the private estates of Protestant nobles. This was obviously not attractive to Catholics who felt that the over-assertive Protestants were gaining far too much ground due to such excessive religious tolerance, and thus an uneasy peace existed until broken later in the same year.

The Wars of Religion that were to plague France for 36 years would shortly begin, and perhaps some of the protagonists could foresee that many atrocious acts were going to be carried out by both sides of the religious divide, but there was clearly no going back for Protestantism. On both sides, men and women were prepared to fight for, and if necessary, die for, their faith.

- 3 -

The First Three Wars 1562-76

The spark that lit the flame of conflict was the massacre at Wassy[24], a small town in north-eastern France. On 1 March, Francois, Duc de Guise, and his entourage stopped at Wassy on his way to his estates, and during this unplanned halt he decided to hear Mass in the local Catholic church. While he attended Mass, some of his servants decided to stroll around the town and came upon a group of local Huguenots holding their own Protestant service in a nearby building, possibly a barn. What began as a minor heckle between Catholics and Huguenots quickly became extremely serious as Catholic soldiers now opened fire on unarmed Huguenot worshippers, killing many of the congregation and then setting fire to the building. The Huguenots' response to this massacre was to call a Synod to formulate appropriate counter-measures; their decision was to request that Condé assume the role of Protector of the Churches and give a call to God and to arms, the Synod unequivocally stating there was no other choice if they were to retain their rights to worship freely as Protestants. The spark at Wassy had ignited the ardour of righteousness.

* * * * * *

The First War (1562-3)

On 12 April 1562, the Huguenot leaders signed the manifesto which affirmed that as loyal subjects they had been forced by circumstances to take up arms for liberty of conscience – from this time on, having agreed to their plea, the leadership of the Huguenots came under the supervision of the nobles and thus took on a more militant resonance. The Prince de Condé speedily mobilised his retainers and was able to decisively capture towns along the waterways, highways and crossroads of France although some had already declared for the Huguenot cause, such as Tours, Blois, Angers, Beaugency, Poitiers, Lyon and Bourges, and additionally the town of Orléans, where he established his headquarters.

The prince prudently decided to make contact with Protestant leaders in Germany and England and asked them if they would supply troops and money to help defend the Protestant faith in France. The royal Catholic forces had until then been permanently garrisoned along the Habsburg frontiers, but the swift action of the Huguenot forces in capturing so many towns alarmed the dowager queen Catherine de Medici, who called upon the Guise family and their associates to come to the Crown's aid. A request for assistance was sent to the Pope and to Philip II of Spain by the Guise faction. In July 1562, the royal army rode out of Paris marching south. Poitiers was the first town to fall; after a short siege, Bourges surrendered on 31 August.

On 20 September, Queen Elizabeth of England proclaimed the *Treaty of Hampton Court*, whereby she agreed to lend the Huguenots 140,000 gold crowns. The Huguenots' part of the deal was to guarantee they would surrender Calais to the English if they won the war; in the meantime, Le Havre was to be occupied by the English as surety.

The Catholic army advanced on Rouen, which fell on 26 October. During this siege, Antoine de Bourbon had been fatally wounded, and he died on 17 November. There followed several prolonged sieges of towns by both Catholics and Protestants, with just one pitched battle being fought at Dreux, resulting in the capture of Anne de Montmorency, but which nonetheless ended in a Catholic victory. Even worse than this defeat for the Protestants was the loss of the Prince de Condé who was captured. After this, Admiral Coligny and most of the Huguenot forces withdrew to their headquarters at Orléans, which came under siege by the Catholic army during the winter of 1562-3. During this siege, the sole-remaining first generation Catholic leader met his death when an assassin mortally wounded Francois, Duc de Guise, on 24 February.

With large areas of the south of France still staunchly Huguenot and the royal treasury virtually empty, Catherine de Medici urgently proposed a solution by issuing the *Edict of Amboise* on 19 March 1563, more widely known as the *Edict of Pacification*. This allowed the Huguenot nobility to practice their religion on their estates, but the rest of the Huguenot population now had their choices curtailed as this latest edict restricted their worship to outside the walls of only one town per *bailliage* [25].

Far from having the desired effect of lasting peace that had been looked for, the *Edict of Pacification* instead added to the tension and resentment experienced by both sides in many towns, but the peace held for four years during which time England and France signed the *Peace of Troyes* in 1564, and Elizabeth accepted a payment of 120,000 gold crowns – thus recouping most of the money she had loaned the Huguenots (money which the French royal treasury could ill afford) – for giving up any claim to Le Havre.

The Catholics in the meantime again tried to suppress the printing presses, this time with a decree dated 10 September 1563 signed by Charles IX, specifically relating to the town of Lyon, that stipulated:

It is forbidden to publish or print any work or writing, in rhyme or prose without the previous authorisation of our lord the King, under pain of being hanged or strangled.

The year after this first war finished, the life of the great reformer John Calvin also ended. He had returned to Geneva a few years earlier where he worked tirelessly to promote reformation including the creation of an academy to train preachers. Worn out by his tireless efforts to further the spread of the reformed religion, his health began to deteriorate, and he died in Geneva on 27 May 1564.

* * * * * *

The Second War (1567- 1568)

The House of Guise remained powerful even with the death of its head, Francois, Duc de Guise. His brother, the Cardinal de Lorraine, set about consolidating his power by lobbying for greater repression of the Huguenot religion following the Protestant uprising in the Spanish Netherlands[26]. Spain had firmly put down the rebellion against the Catholic Church and brought an end to the breaking up of religious statues that Huguenots vehemently maintained were unnecessary for true worship.

Not long after the end of the First War of Religion, Charles IX was declared to be of age, but to the dismay of the Huguenots his court was very much under the control of the Guise family. Unsurprisingly, Huguenots became increasingly concerned by the immense power being wielded by Catholics for their own advantage, and the apparent, unhurried implementation of the *Edict of Amboise*. Catherine de Medici began a two-year tour of the provinces with her son Charles IX in an effort to establish unity with all the nobility, but when she met with the Duke of Alba, the very man who had been sent in 1567 to carry out the repression of Calvinism in the Low

Countries[xxix] on behalf of the King of Spain[27], the Huguenot nobility became uneasy and suspicious of Catherine's intent. There was a growing belief that the French and Spanish courts had arranged to jointly destroy all heretics within their respective borders, although this was never proven. But, further alarm set in when it became known that Spanish troops had marched along the Spanish Road[28] from Italy to Flanders on the eastern borders of France.

In the summer of 1567, after lengthy deliberations, the Huguenot leaders agreed a plan. They gathered together a sizable group of cavalrymen to seize control of the inadequately protected court at the Chateau of Monceaux. The nearest royal garrison was 30 miles away at Chateau Thierry. The plot, however, was uncovered on 24 September just as it was about to be implemented, by which time the court had moved to the more secure Chateau de Meaux. Alarmed at the news that horsemen were assembling at Rosay-en-Brie, Catherine de Medici requested that the Swiss guards escort the court to Paris immediately, and they left Meaux just a day after the plot was discovered, arriving at the Louvre in Paris in the early evening of 25 September. Their journey had not been without incident though, as they encountered an armed band of Huguenots on the journey, but the Swiss guards were militarily better trained and equipped, and capably defended their escort.

In the south of France, numerous towns were captured by Huguenot forces, including Nimes where on 30 September 1567, St Michael's Day, a massacre of leading local Catholics took place, known as *The Michelade*. Passions were running high on both sides of the religious divide, but the events that led up to this particular massacre were probably a combination of factors ranging from a harvest stolen from a gardener by the garrison to Catholic tyranny and their appropriation of the consulate; the

---

[xxix] Derek Wilson, *A Brief History of the English Reformation* (London, 2012) p364.

plan devised by the Prince de Condé to arm Protestants; a quarrel between two prominent families (one Huguenot, the other Catholic); the Huguenots' intelligence-gathering of a planned Catholic counter-offensive, as well as a deep-rooted desire for vengeance by Huguenots for the previous massacres of their brethren[xxx]. Because religion and politics in that era were closely allied, Huguenots were genuinely afraid of Catholic supremacy – and for good reasons: fearfulness for the future of their own beliefs and mindful of previous massacres carried out by Catholics. In all, 192 Catholic persons were killed that day either in Nimes itself or in the surrounding area, and several Catholic churches and religious houses were either damaged or razed to the ground. The Nimes massacre was no less bloody than that of Wassy, and Francis de Beaumont, the Baron de Andrets, who led the massacre at Nimes, justified his actions with these words:

> *Nobody commits cruelty in repaying it – the first are called cruelties, the second justice. The only way to stop the enemy's barbarities is to meet them with retaliation.*

Similar sentiments had previously been uttered earlier by the Catholic Blaise de Monluc in Guyenne[29].

The only major battle of this second war was the *Battle of St Denis*, where a small Huguenot band was forced into conflict with the larger royal army north of Paris. The plan was to cut off royalist supplies in order to force them to negotiate. Shortly after the arrival of Condé at St Denis, the Huguenots set out their demands for peace: Charles IX was to dismiss all foreign troops, confirm the *Edict of Amboise* (which had ended the First War of Religion), call the Estates General, and remove a number of specific taxes. Charles' response was to issue a proclamation requesting Condé, Coligny and fellow leaders to lay down their

---

[xxx] Allan Tulchin, *That Men Would Praise the Lord: The Triumph of Protestantism in Nimes 1530-1570* (Oxford, 2010) p172.

arms. Perhaps realising they had little room for manoeuvre, the Huguenots amended their demands to the extent of removing all their requests with one important exception: that of religious freedom for all.

Realising his superiority in military capability at that time, Charles' retort to these revised terms was to offer battle, which the smaller Huguenot forces had no realistic option but to accept. Against such odds, their forces were clearly not substantial enough to achieve a decisive victory, yet their action on the battlefield was brave and resilient enough to deny Charles an outright victory – and thus neither side could claim to be the winner. Huguenot forces had notable successes in other towns across France capturing Orléans, La Rochelle (which became the most important Huguenot town), Auxerre, Vienne, Valence, Montpellier, Nimes, and Montauban.

Ready to do battle for the town of Montrichard, they were called back to take part in the planned siege of Chartres, but this did not materialise beyond a few days as peace negotiations had by then commenced. By the end of this second war, Montmorency lay dead, the royal treasury was even more depleted and the lack of a decisive engagement (which now became a watchfulness by royalist Catholic forces over their enemy) led to the *Peace of Longjumeau,* a so-called 'peace' that was little different to the one agreed to at Amboise at the end of the first war.

Yet as one war ended so another began, and this time it was the turn of the Netherlands against Spain, eventually leading to the separation of the north and south provinces of the Netherlands. The war was to last spasmodically from 1568 to 1648, thus becoming known as the *Eighty Years War*. William of Orange led two failed invasions of the mercenary armies of the Dutch Calvinists in 1568 and 1572.

* * * * * *

The Third War (1568-70)

The 'peace' lasted just five months following a foiled plot hatched by the Cardinal de Lorraine to capture the two prominent Huguenot leaders Condé and Coligny, both of whom had managed to evade capture beforehand and make their way to La Rochelle. And it was now that international events began to impact on the struggle within France.

The Huguenots were deeply affected by the events leading up to and including the revolt of the 'gueux'[30], who were determined to prevent the implementation of the Inquisition in the Netherlands, and who had already felt the full weight of repression under the cruel hand of the Duke of Alba, Philip II of Spain's representative in the Netherlands. Thus, mutually beneficial alliances within each camp were made. For the Catholics: Spain, the Pope and the Duke of Tuscany; for the Huguenots: William of Orange of the Netherlands – fighting for independence from Catholic Spain – and Elizabeth I of England.

On the Catholic side, the Cardinal de Lorraine drew ever closer to Spain whilst keeping an eye on events in England. The Guise family looked to oust Elizabeth and install their niece, the Catholic Mary, Queen of Scots – cousin of Elizabeth and who, as long as Elizabeth remained childless, was next in line to the throne of England. Thus, the resumption of the religious wars in France had now widened to give the struggle for religious supremacy a more international theme.

The Huguenot plan was to fortify the south west of the country as that part of France could reasonably be considered more Protestant than Catholic. This strategy worked well for some time, but then the wheel of fortune turned yet again when at Jarnac, a town just west of Angouleme in the south west of the country, the Huguenot army suffered a double blow with a shattering defeat and the death of the Prince de Condé. Coligny then led his surviving forces to confront a slightly larger Catholic army, commanded by the young Duke of Anjou, on the plain of

Moncontour, also in the perceived Huguenot heartland, and it was here his army was again defeated. Unbowed, Coligny somehow managed to regroup what must have been the shattered remnants of his forces, leading them on a long march across the south of France to achieve a remarkable defeat of a Catholic army along the way and thus prevent them breaking the Protestant hold on the south.

Coligny may have felt all was near to lost, but fortunately for him, the royal treasury had once again become seriously depleted with the costs of maintaining armies in the field over a long period of time and so a third 'peace' was brokered between the warring factions at St Germain, signed by the king on 22 August 1570. It was a more favourable one to the Protestants this time in that it named towns and strongholds where Huguenots could practice their faith unhindered including four strongholds: La Rochelle, Cognac, La Charité-sur-Loire and Montauban, which they were allowed to hold for a period of two years. Confiscated property was to be returned to its former Huguenot owners and, most importantly, there would be some legal equality in France for persons who were of the Protestant faith.

Catherine de Medici, the Queen Mother, followed up the *Peace of St Germain* with determined diplomatic efforts to bring harmony between the leaders of both religious parties. The chief military leader of the Huguenots, Admiral Coligny, was invited by Catherine de Medici to take up a position on the King's Council whilst offering one of her sons (a younger brother of Charles IX, the French king) as a suitor to the unwed Queen Elizabeth of England. Furthermore, after much delicate negotiating with the widowed Protestant Queen of Navarre, Jeanne d'Albret, Catherine de Medici now secured the hand of Jeanne's son Henri of Navarre in marriage to her daughter Marguerite (Margot) thus hoping, perhaps rather over-optimistically, that the union would help to bind the Huguenot and Catholic factions together.

In spite of all Catherine de Medici's efforts, in towns and villages throughout France unity was seriously lacking – in fact, a mutual wariness and barely-concealed hostility were, in some regions, ominously growing as what could possibly have been contained as a manageable fissure of general division now widened into a seemingly unbridgeable chasm, with more new ideals beginning to be adopted by the Protestant leadership. Protestants began to speak of the theory that any prince persecuting their Church should forfeit the right to be obeyed. In 1573, Francois Hottman's *Francogallia* was published in which he wrote of the existence of a mythical Frankish constitution that gave the people the right to elect their king – thus the people could be seen to govern through their frontispiece the elected king – and this document would subsequently further draw together not only those of the Protestant faith, but, arguably, some people brought up in the Catholic faith who were seriously considering the merits of both faiths with a view to possibly changing faith.

Significantly, and probably inevitably, more disquiet between the two factions arose in other areas of life. Protestants were often to be found in the newer, more economically lucrative forms of trade, such as printing. They also possessed a deeply-held belief in ensuring their flocks were literate – for how were they to read the word of God unless they were literate? Nor did the Protestant faith accommodate the 'over 100 feast days' that the Catholic Church celebrated, and this too gave them the edge when it came to business as they could, and did, bring to bear a greater number of productive working days per year.

Many years of war and persecution were resulting in a subtle drawing together of people of the new faith in numerous aspects of their daily lives, not just in religious matters. This grouping together was also true for those of the Catholic faith, who viewed bible studying and the church singing of men and women together as heresy and against God's word. They were acutely aware of the disadvantage in business they were at, seeing their Protestant counterparts continuing to work on feast days when their own businesses did nothing but suffer from lost production.

Business disparity of the above kind was fuelled by ongoing inflation in the cost of staple items such as food, rent and heating. Sharply rising prices continued to inflict severe hardships, and this must have seemed relentless and unstoppable to all who had to endure them.

From the 1560s, many people, whatever their religious beliefs, had struggled to make ends meet and, as is often the case, adversity was breeding deep and sometimes violent distrust, making the path to true peace even more unattainable as Catholics and Protestants inevitably eyed each other antagonistically. Unsurprisingly, there were many in both camps who disapproved of *any* attempts at appeasement or compromise.

- 4 -

The St Bartholomew's Day Massacre and the final Five Wars 1572-88

The spark for another conflict was again a massacre. But, this time, one that would go down in history as the bloodiest and most savage to date. What makes it even more regrettable is that it took place during an event that could have done much to heal wounds, and to point the way to a more peaceful future. It is of course the infamous St Bartholomew's Day Massacre of 24-5 August 1572. Many prominent Huguenots had gathered to witness the marriage of the Huguenot 19-year-old Henri of Navarre to the Catholic Princess Marguerite of France .

On 17 August the marriage took place on a dais outside the Cathedral de Notre Dame, after which Henri escorted his new wife inside and walked her up the nave. Leaving her at the choir to hear Mass, Henri and his retinue then waited outside during the lengthy celebration of Mass[31][xxxi]. Catherine de Medici and her son King Charles IX both appeared outwardly keen at the prospect this marriage held to reconcile both religious parties, and to therefore end the Wars of Religion, but generally many Catholics and Protestants disapproved of the match, including Admiral Coligny and Henri's mother Jeanne of Navarre, although both had felt

---

[xxxi] Robert Knecht, *Hero or Tyrant? Henri III, King of France 1574-89* (Abingdon, 2014) p48.

obliged to accept it as it was assumed the marriage would bring some gains to the Huguenot cause. In reality, the marriage service itself became a means by some Catholics to lure as many prominent Protestant leaders and their followers as possible to Paris.

The festivities celebrating the marriage were planned to continue for days, but the mood in the capital changed to one of outrage when a would-be assassin fired a gun at Gaspard de Coligny on 22 August, following his visit to the king. Coligny's arm was broken and although he suffered severe gunshot wounds he survived the attempt on his life. The Huguenot leaders were angry as many suspected the Guise family of plotting this attempted assassination. They advised Coligny to retire to the safety of a Huguenot enclave, but he refused to leave, fearing it would infer he did not trust the king's ability or intention to protect him. The would-be assassin has never been identified with any certainty[xxxii].

The Huguenots demanded justice from the king for this attempt on Coligny's life. It was a hot summer and tempers matched the heat of the season as Huguenots threatened to riot if justice was not forthcoming. During the night of 23-4 August, King Charles IX, his mother the Dowager Queen Catherine de Medici, and his brother, Henri d'Anjou, were among those who hastily gathered to decide what action needed to be taken. The debate raged for some hours with the royal councillors and Catherine at first advising, then insisting, that the king should give the order to kill Coligny and the Huguenot leaders. Eventually, the king gave in to their demands with the chilling words, *'Well, kill them all so that no man be left to reproach me.'*

Those words were immediately acted upon. In the early hours of Sunday morning 24 August, the Mayor of Paris was ordered to lock and guard the city gates, secure boats and make ready the city

---

[xxxii] Robert Knecht, *Hero or Tyrant? Henri III, King of France 1574-89* (2014) p49.

militia. Shortly after these orders were issued, soldiers arrived and knocked loudly on the door of Coligny's lodgings; they killed the guards that opened the door before hastily seeking Coligny's bedroom. They dragged the sleep-dazed Coligny from his bed, stabbed him several times then threw his body out of the window onto the ground below. Accounts of what had taken place rapidly spread including an alleged report that the Duc de Guise had mocked Coligny's body by kicking him in the face while at the same time stating that this had been the king's will.

Believing that the king approved, at a given signal of the bells ringing out, the local Catholic population including the militia began to slaughter anyone not of their faith. The militia played a key role by encouraging the Catholic population to wear white crosses[32] on their hats or arms as well as ensuring that every Catholic household displayed a lighted torch in the window – thus making Huguenots a much easier target, being unaware of this command.

By morning it became apparent that the events of the night before were but a prelude to carnage that can only be likened to opening a Pandora's box. The terrified King Charles IX was for a time powerless to stop the slaughter that was now clearly out of control: his alarmed authorities tried in vain to halt the massacre as over the next three days and nights the butchering continued with rivers of blood running down the streets of Paris as men, women and children were dragged out of their homes and slaughtered. Many who escaped the carnage were traumatised for a very long time by the scenes they had witnessed. Even those who resided in the Louvre were not immune with 40 of Henri de Navarre's 'gentlemen' (close aides and compatriots) being put to death.

Henri de Navarre – as yet an unknown leader – and his cousin Henri, Prince de Condé (son of the late Louis, Prince de Condé) were dragged before the king and threatened with death if they did not convert to the Catholic faith. They agreed to become Catholics although for the next four years Henri de Navarre was held prisoner at court and lived in constant fear of his life. Condé, after a while, managed to escape and sought shelter in Germany, whilst Switzerland allowed Andelot, Coligny's younger brother, to live there in exile.

The massacre spread to the provinces during the next few months with areas of vocal Protestant minorities being the main targets. Amongst the numerous towns beleaguered in this overflow of the St Bartholomew's Day Massacre was Orléans, where, during the nights of 26 and 27 August, another massacre of Huguenots was ruthlessly undertaken, with bands of Catholics roaming the streets, indiscriminately murdering, and exulting in their vile acts as they progressed[xxxiii]. The events of those violent and bloody days in August came to collectively be known as the *St. Bartholomew's Day Massacre,* during which an entire generation of Huguenot leaders was mercilessly extinguished[33].

As a result of the massacre and its wider aftermath, the Protestant Church of France began to decrease during the following months as large numbers of Protestants, despairing of the situation and terrified at the escalating violence, foreswore their faith; but not all was lost as many others developed a deep and abiding distrust in their king, leading to an upsurge in written political resistance with works such as *The Defense of Liberty against Tyrants*[34]. Thus, the Huguenot 'state within a state', although diminished in size, became hardened, much as a blacksmith's hammering of steel on the anvil will harden the metal thus strengthening it, and their congregations rapidly sought to establish a chain of command. They collected their own tithes, provided local government to the people – including social welfare within their communities – and most importantly they maintained their own armies in each area, thus achieving their own autonomy within the wider context of the nation. There was now very little fighting in terms of military confrontations, and for a few months

---

[xxxiii] Mack P. Holt, *The French Wars of Religion 1562-1629*, 2nd edition (Cambridge, 2005) p94.

at least it seemed that Catholicism, with its superior royal and social influences, had gained the upper hand.

* * * * * *

The Fourth War (1572-3)

In November 1572, on what must have seemed an unstoppable wave of Catholic successes, the king declared war on the city of La Rochelle (deemed the capital of the Protestant strongholds) as the people refused entry to the royal governor; and neither would they pay taxes to the king following the St Bartholomew's Day massacre.

In February 1573, the king's army, led by Henri d'Anjou, laid siege to the city, with the unfortunate Henri de Navarre in tow as a hostage. La Rochelle, however, possessed formidable defences, and the indomitable Protestant citizens held out[35]. Being a port with an almost impregnable harbour they had access to supplies from the sea at the start of the siege. La Rochelle's other significant natural defence was its landward isolation as access to the town was across marshland.

At first, the commanders of the royal army were confident that they could take the city after no more than a short siege, but the determined citizens were well organised, resulting in the city being fully provisioned and garrisoned, and much strengthening of the defences had been undertaken. It may not have known it at the time, but the royal army faced a daunting adversary. The king's commanders ordered forts to be built on either side of the port entrance; they also stationed a heavily equipped vessel in the middle of the bay thus cutting off all help to the city. The siege dragged on with many casualties on both sides; four major assaults on the defences were repelled even though the last of these saw a breach in the walls of the bastion. The courageous defenders refused to give an inch, and brave women poured boiling tar and threw stones and rubble at the attackers.

The casualties and fatalities mounted, with many royal commanders perishing in the attacks. By May, after just three months' siege, the royal treasury was once again feeling the strain of financing an army and additionally the siege had effectively reached a stalemate, and thus peace terms were offered to the Rochellese, whereby the Huguenots of just three areas – La Rochelle, Nimes and Montauban – were promised freedom to practise their religion.

After valiantly defending the city for six and a half months to have only gained this much, the *Treaty of La Rochelle* left Protestants feeling angry at the unfairness of the terms, but they decided to buy time with this treaty to regroup and retaliate when, or perhaps if, they were ever in a stronger position to do so.

* * * * * *

The Fifth War (1576)

Charles IX died in 1574, apparently tormented with guilt over his part in the St Bartholomew's Day Massacre. His brother, Henri, Duc d'Anjou (also King of Poland) now ascended the throne as Henri III of France. The people recalled that in the past he had been a strong guiding hand, but their hopes that he would bring peace to their troubled land were to be painfully dashed on the rock of seemingly intractable religious discord.

Yet, neither were the Huguenot leaders idle during this period. Condé gained support from the German princes, in particular Jan Casimir, in the form of troops and money to finance a new war. Meanwhile, Henri de Montmorency, together with the Seigneur de Damville, the Governor of Languedoc, raised another sizeable army to march to the Huguenots' aid. Montmorency, although Catholic, ruled the largely Protestant region of France from which the family took its name; but was nonetheless related to senior Huguenot leaders – the Coligny brothers[36].

In 1576 the joyous news that Henri de Navarre had escaped from the French court and was heading for his native Navarre reached the elated leadership. As Henri de Navarre rode towards his homeland, the inspiration he gave to an embattled Protestant people must have helped in his efforts to gather an army in readiness for the fight that would surely come. A further stroke of luck for the Protestants arose when no less a figure than the king's younger brother, the Duc d'Alençon, last of the line of Valois, declared for the anti-royalists. He was portrayed by his followers as a more fitting king than his brother and one who would rule wisely and justly over all his people. Naturally, it was claimed he would cut taxes. This was a worrying turn of events for Catherine de Medici, the king's mother, knew that the last thing needed in France at that time was yet more division.

In the spring of 1576, financed by England, Jan Casmir led 20,000 troops over the border into France and eventually met up in near to Paris with the Huguenot armies that had been gathered together. The king and his councillors, faced with such a large retaliatory force, had no other option but to negotiate. The *Edict of Beaulieu,* known as the *Peace of Monsieur*[37], was signed in May (a popular month for these treaties) and this time the terms were very favourable towards the Protestants, including the requested 'chambres mi-parties'[38]. These new courts were linked with the Parlements of Grenoble, Bordeaux, Rouen and Toulouse, with another court in Paris. The Paris Chambre de L'Edit[39] remained operational until it was formally dissolved in 1669[xxxiv]. In fact, the Huguenot leaders, in separate agreements drafted at the same time, were granted significant settlements: Henri de Navarre was confirmed Governor of Guyenne; Henri de Condé was awarded the Governorship of Picardy, and Hercule, Duc d'Alençon, became the Duc d'Anjou, with a long list of other titles besides.

The Crown also had to agree to pay the bills of Jan Casimir's troops. The Paris Parlement subsequently refused to accept these humiliating terms resulting in a few of the towns that had been

---

[xxxiv] Diane C. Margolf, *Religion and Royal Justice in early modern France - The Paris Chambre de L'Edit 1598-1665.* (Kirksville, Missouri, 2004) p x.

designated by the treaty to be henceforward Huguenot resisting the invading troops when they arrived. Furthermore, the Estates General, meeting at Blois in the autumn of 1576, also did not deliver the longed-for progress that the Huguenot leadership had presumed. More often than not, the forthcoming elections would only be advertised at the Catholic Church service for Mass and therefore the only elected persons, intentionally, were Catholics – thus the chambres mi-parties failed to become the equal representation of both Catholic and Protestant faiths as had been promised.

* * * * * *

The Sixth War (1577)

The Estates General[40] finally assembled in 1576, an event that the Huguenots had been demanding for quite some time; however, rather ironically, when it was convened there were practically no Protestant delegates in attendance, no doubt due to the biased advertising of venues. This imbalance of Catholic versus Protestant representatives led to the Estates General, such as it was, trying to deliver the long-held Catholic concept of one religion within the French kingdom. Henri III thus felt strong enough to call for new taxes and revenues to fund this ideal, yet many members of the Estates General saw no reason for further expenditure; besides, they were all too well aware that the cost of the wars of religion were increasing the national debt beyond a sustainable point; in other words: France was now living beyond its means.

A further important event this same year was the inception of the Catholic League by Henri, Duc de Guise. To mitigate this possible threat to his overall authority, King Henri III placed himself at the head of the League and a royalist army was assembled with a remit to take back some of the Protestant towns along the Loire Valley. In May 1577, the Protestant stronghold of

La Charité fell to the Catholic League. This victory in isolation was not enough to win the overall struggle though, as the main Protestant forces were scattered across the south of France, thus enabling the *Peace of Bergerac* to be signed in July. This agreement was similar to the earlier peace declaration of 1576 other than placing greater restrictions on places of worship for Huguenots; it was not popular with either side and inevitably could not last for long.

* * * * * *

The Seventh War (1580)
Otherwise known as the 'Lovers War', this was a brief resumption of hostilities. Henri de Navarre's appropriation of the city of Cahors was soon followed by the *Treaty of Nerac,* then the *Peace of Fleix,* re-establishing the terms of the earlier *Peace of Bergerac,* effectively returning to the Huguenots important concessions in the freedom to practice their religion, with a designated town in each district being yielded to them, but simultaneously forbidding them to practice their religion elsewhere. They were allowed to keep nine strongholds as well as a degree of representation in four provincial assemblies.

* * * * * *

The Eighth War (1584-9)
Following the peace agreement, Henri de Navarre wisely decided to consolidate his position and wait for the wheel of fortune to turn yet again, which it soon did, starting with the death in 1584 of the Duc d'Anjou, youngest brother of Henri III, who, like his brother, was childless; whereby the heir presumptive to the throne of France was suddenly none other than the Protestant Henri de Navarre[41]. The constitution of France still held to the principle that the Catholic religion of the

king and country were identical: one faith, one law, one king, and now the very real possibility of a Protestant accession was viewed with great alarm.

Pope Sixus V, upon hearing the news, immediately issued an edict which excommunicated Henri de Navarre and his Protestant cousin, Henri Prince de Condé, as he judged them both to be heretics and hence unfit to be included in the French line of succession. Yet, not all Catholics appreciated the Pope's interference in France's internal affairs, whereas other Catholics interpreted the Pope's actions as giving approval to certain members of the Catholic faith who might seek to take possession of the French throne. So it was, that Henri, Duc de Guise, nicknamed 'Le Balafré' ('Scarface', from an earlier battle scar) who was a military hero as well as being descendant of the House of Guise's earlier heroes, quickly grasped the opportunity to place himself as a potential 'heir' with a miraculously discovered pedigree revealing no less an historical figure than Charlemagne as an ancestor.

Henri III tried to persuade his brother-in-law, Henri de Navarre, to convert to Catholicism to allow for a peaceful transition from one monarch to the next, but the latter felt bound to remain a loyal Protestant or risk losing his core base of supporters.

The charming and enigmatic Henri, Duc de Guise, resolved to reinstate the Catholic League as a means of opposing a 'heretic' acceding to the French throne. The *Treaty of Joinville* was signed between the Catholic League and Philip II of Spain in December 1584 whereby Spain agreed to subsidise the League in an attempt to undermine the French government. Spain continued to pay vast amounts to the League for the next decade.

The Duc de Guise's powerful relations held vast tracts of land, both on the borders of France and within it heartland, including the Duc de Mayenne (Burgundy), the Duc d'Aumale (Picardy), the Duc d'Elbouef (Normandy), the Duc de Mercoeur (Brittany) and the Duc de Lorraine. As well as this aristocratic powerbase, there was an increasingly ardent middle class, particularly in Paris, governed as it was by the League's Committee of Sixteen.[42]

Henri III's strategy was to attempt to reinstate himself at the head of the League. He had after all been the effective head of the League ten years earlier. In his attempt to regain overall control, he was forced to sign the *Treaty of Nemours* on 7 July 1585, which rescinded all previous edicts of pacification, and banned the practice of the Protestant religion throughout France. Furthermore, it excluded Protestants from holding royal office and ordered everyone of the Protestant faith within garrison towns to either return to Catholicism or face being exiled. Finally, it excluded Protestant Henri de Navarre from the French succession. And thus began one of the longest and most blood-stained periods in the history of France as the armies of the three Henris (King Henri III, Henri de Navarre and Henri, Duc de Guise) engaged in an all-out civil war that became alternatively known as the *War of the Three Henris*.

At this time, the Catholic League controlled most of the north and east of France whereas the Huguenots mainly held sway over the south and west. Henri de Navarre and the Prince de Condé again sought aid from Queen Elizabeth and the Protestant German princes. As a result, an army of German mercenaries donated by Jan Casimir of the Palatinate again entered France. The Duc de Guise, upon hearing of this, took command of the League army whilst Henri III sent his army led by the Duc de Joyeuse to prevent the German mercenaries and the Duc de Navarre's army from once again joining forces. The first conflict of this war was Navarre's stunning victory at the Battle of Coutras where he routed Henri III's army and killed the Duc de Joyeuse. However, the Huguenot triumph was short-lived as Guise's army overwhelmed the German mercenaries and sent them home.

In the meantime, the population of Paris was being swayed by the fiery rhetoric of League preachers; the Committee of Sixteen enflamed the Catholic population's discontent with Henri III and his inability to destroy the Protestants and their faith. In the eyes of Parisians, such moderation surely implied weakness. In May 1588, a popular uprising took place with the erecting of barricades on the streets of Paris (the first of many of this form of demonstration in the centuries to follow). Alarmed at the militant mood of the populace, Henri III was forced to flee his capital city thus leaving the Committee of Sixteen in complete control and they lost no time in welcoming the Duc de Guise into the city.

The League called for a meeting of the Estates General, and this was convened at Blois in the autumn of 1588. The League suggested that the heir to the French throne should be the Cardinal de Bourbon, uncle of Henri de Navarre. As an old man, if he had acceded to the throne he would have become no more than a puppet for the Guise faction. Yet there was an even greater fear amongst Protestants that Henri III would be forced to abdicate by the Estates General and proclaim Henri, Duc de Guise, King of France.

Henri III sent an invitation to Henri, Duc de Guise, for a private meeting in the king's apartments on Christmas Eve 1588. The seemingly unsuspecting Duc de Guise appeared unaware that it was a trap, and the rows of archers standing sentinel on the route to the king's suite surprisingly did not arouse his suspicion, nor did the 40 gentlemen waiting in the anteroom to the king's chamber ring any alarm bells, but as the Duc de Guise entered, the doors behind him were slammed shut and bolted from the inside – there was no escape. He fought his assassins valiantly, but was hacked to pieces, his body burnt, his bones dissolved, and the ashes scattered to the four winds thus leaving no trace and no shrine for pilgrims to congregate. This fate was shared by his brother the Cardinal de Guise, leaving the Duc de Mayenne the sole member of the House of Guise to lead the League.

The pace of events now accelerated. The League's printing presses began producing malicious revolutionary pamphlets. The Sorbonne University openly declared that the deposition of Henri

III was both imperative and crucial, and that any citizen would be ethically obliged to kill the king, thus openly encouraging the crime of regicide.

Faced with a hostile League army, Henri III took the previously impossible step of joining forces with Henri de Navarre and swiftly the combined kings' armies set off to recapture Paris. However, history still would not give victory to Henri III. Whilst the armies encamped at St Cloud, a monk named Jacques Clement requested an audience with Henri III, who, unsuspectingly, granted his request, and whose generosity was rewarded with a knife thrust into his spleen by the assassin. The wound did not at first appear life threatening, but as infection set in it became clear his days were numbered. As he lay dying in the Chateau de St Cloud in early August 1589, he sent for Henri de Navarre and named him his successor to the throne.

The inconceivable had happened – a Protestant had become King of France – but he would have to pay a high price to retain his crown.

- 5 -

The Wars of the League 1589-98

Some of the followers of the late King Henri III transferred their loyalty to his chosen successor and distant relative[43], **Henri de Navarre** – now proclaimed Henri IV, King of France – but significantly far from all. His hold on the French crown was tenuous, to say the least, at this point in time. The Catholic League was behind many coups in major cities across the Kingdom of France as large numbers of citizens, most of whom were moderate in their feelings towards religious freedoms, found themselves suddenly confronted with rough justice meted out in the form of hangings.

Faced with a Spanish-financed Catholic League army led by Mayenne, Henri de Navarre knew he had to successfully do battle in the north if he wanted to secure his position. On 21 September 1589, the two armies met at Arques[44] a few miles southeast of Dieppe. The battle resulted in a serious defeat for Mayenne and for the League. Henri de Navarre continued the momentum of success as he rode through Normandy taking many towns, culminating in a spectacular victory at Ivry on the south-eastern outskirts of Paris in March 1590. Shortly after this battle, the League's alternative candidate to the French crown – the elderly Cardinal de Bourbon[45], who had been taken prisoner by the late Henri III in 1588 – died, thus further diminishing the League's stance.

The Story of the Huguenots – a Unique Legacy

Henri now turned his thoughts and his army's direction to the capital Paris and throughout the spring and summer of 1590 his forces lay siege to the city; however – conscious that the people within were now technically also his subjects – he chose a compassionate tactic by permitting the women and children to leave the city. This show of benevolence shocked King Philip II of Spain into issuing orders to his most feared and most able commander, the Duke of Palma, to immediately set out with his army with instructions to supply those within the city, although no pitched battle took place between the two sides[xxxv].

In 1593, the Estates General met in Paris to choose their own candidate for the throne of France; they were determined it would be one of the 'old' faith. Philip II of Spain recommended his daughter, the Spanish Infanta Isabella, as her mother Elisabeth de Valois had been sister to Henri III. He went on to suggest that the Infanta should be married to a suitable French nobleman such as the Duc de Guise. Parlement, mindful of the Salic Law of Succession, hastily passed a new law forbidding any foreigner inheriting the crown. Alarmed and realising he could lose his right to the throne of France, on 23 July of that year following a five-hour discussion with the Archbishop of Bourges, Henri de Navarre decided upon the drastic course of converting to Catholicism when he reportedly uttered the now famous words in the church of St Denis '*Paris vaut une masse*'[46].

* * * * * *

Henri de Navarre was crowned Henri IV in the cathedral of Chartres instead of the traditional venue of Reims Cathedral as the latter was still under the League's control.

The coronation of Henri IV in February 1594 did not mean an end to hostilities as both Protestants and Catholics were suspicious

---

[xxxv] Robert Watson, *The History of the reign of Philip II, King of Spain. 7th edition* (London, 1839) p467.

- 50 -

of Henri's sudden conversion to the Catholic faith, even though he had removed the League's chief objection to his succession. On the other hand, he found to his frustration that some previously ardent supporters were now withdrawing their loyalty following his conversion. In the spring, Henri entered Paris without firing a single shot; as he did so, the Spanish garrison marched out of the city, but Henri knew he would still need to apply a lot of diplomatic guile in order to reconcile the two sides. He achieved this by spending large sums of money buying support from many nobles in the form of pensions. Besides this, he gave a great deal of money to towns, again in exchange for their support. Henri joked that the loyalty of the king's 'bonnes villes' (good towns) was 'vendu, pas rendu' ('sold, not made') yet he was well aware that purchasing loyalty was far cheaper than having to finance another war.

Philip of Spain's forces continued to fight on with those League lords who refused to accept Henri IV as their rightful king. Doullens and Calais were amongst others towns captured by this Catholic union during 1595-6.

Henri lay siege to La Fere (a Spanish settlement within French territory) while Catholic forces attacked and took Amiens. Finally, in 1598, Philip II – faced with mounting financial problems at home – signed a treaty (the *Treaty of Vervins*) with France, ceding all the captured towns. Four months after this treaty was signed, Philip II was dead, and so was his goal to stem the tide of 'heresy' – all seven of the Spanish Netherlands provinces had gained independence and were now Protestant. Of the remaining rebellious League leaders, Henri, Duc de Guise, surrendered in 1595, followed by Mayenne in 1596 and lastly Mercoeur two years later[xxxvi].

As many must have hoped – but few would have dared believe possible – the long Wars of Religion were finally at an end. But

---

[xxxvi] Noel Currer-Briggs & Royston Gambier, *Huguenot Ancestry* (Chichester, 1985) p26.

The Story of the Huguenots – a Unique Legacy

now Henri faced a different challenge: to keep the hard-won peace it was still necessary, indeed paramount, to reassure those of the Huguenot faith that the apparent favour he had shown towards Protestantism's historic enemy was not an indication of preference[xxxvii].

Mindful of the Huguenots' perception of events, in April 1598, three weeks before the *Treaty of Vervins* was signed, Henri IV issued the *Edict of Nantes* stating that Catholicism would be recognised as the State Church, and that the Catholic religion would be reinstated in Navarre, especially its capital Bearn – for so long a separate Protestant kingdom. Importantly, it also gave rights to Huguenots to practice their own religion throughout France with the exception of a few cities such as Rheims, Soissons, Dijon and Sens[xxxviii].

To understand Henri's attempts to reconcile to both sides after 30 years of turmoil and bloodshed, we must be mindful of the fact that the *Edict of Nantes* was not a single document, but one that was made up of four separate documents and the entire contents of the edict (see appendix 1) would appear to be a triumphant piece of diplomacy. The reason for this was so that certain 'sensitive' elements, in particular those allowing Huguenots to fortify towns already under their control, and awarding the Calvinist Church substantial funds, may well have resulted in Parlement refusing to pass the edict into French law[47], had such elements formed part of it. To circumvent such probable obstacles, the granting of such rights was instead contained in one of the additional documents collectively known as 'brevets' – these were secret articles that did not require Parlement's approval as they were classed as Royal Writs, which would be, significantly, legally binding only for the duration of the king's life – after which it would be necessary for future kings, if they so wished, to reissue them.

[xxxvii] Noel Currer-Briggs & Royston Gambier, *Huguenot Ancestry* (Chichester, 1985) p26.
[xxxviii] Ibid. p26.

Collectively, therefore, the edict and its brevets conferred on Huguenots full and equal civil rights, enabling them to hold public office and to retain certain strongholds. Furthermore, it permitted their children to attend schools and universities, and even provided for Huguenot children born beyond French borders but of French parentage to return to France where they would be accepted as true French citizens. This edict thus brought peace to an exhausted France, which by this time was at the very edge of the abyss. At long last the Huguenots had a guaranteed agreement rather than mere armistices[48]. Ironically, they were now being given most of what Catherine de Medici had wanted to offer them almost 40 years before, but which fanaticism and hatred on both sides had prevented.

It was now over 60 years since Huguenots had first been persecuted for their faith. The *Edict of Nantes* permitted freedom of conscience to all as well as granting full civil rights. To ensure equal treatment, all disputes resulting from this particular edict were from then on to be considered in a fair and unbiased manner in the Chambre de L'Edit, and to ensure an even-handed approach the chambre was to be from then on populated equally by both Catholics and Protestants.

Often, but not always, the cases heard in this court were 'appeals' to previous judgments covering a wide range of complaints: blasphemy, illicit marriage, contested inheritances, murders and theft, to name but a few[xxxix]. The edict had given the country a legality for peaceful co-existence between the two faiths, but in the eyes of many in 17th century France it posed a threat. Large numbers of Catholics still strongly disapproved of the Huguenots, while the Huguenots themselves tried to demonstrate loyalty to the monarchy and their country in order to prove themselves good citizens. The Chambre de L'Edit itself was meant to be an impartial forum for interpreting and defining the laws, but

---

[xxxix] Diane C. Margolf, *Religion and Royal Justice in early modern France - The Paris Chambre de L'Edit 1598-1665.* (Kirksville, Missouri, 2004) pxi.

as the Huguenots were usually the minority group, impartiality did not always prevail, and one-sided judgements could all too easily sow discord rather than harmony[xl].

Thus, the *Edict of Nantes* legally appeared to bring about a cessation of the Wars of Religion until its eventual revocation in 1685. Although Henri IV only lived a further 12 years, during this time he restored peace and order to France and was instrumental in returning prosperity to the country, ably assisted by his trusted minister Sully, who by 1598 had sole charge of the country's finances[49].

Henri's experiences during the wars shaped his personality and he knew that success could only be brought about by resourcefulness in encouraging both sides to take an active role in the rebuilding of the country's financial standing. He knew he owed much to the merchant classes and crown officials who had stood by him and he looked to them to help rebuild the economy, turning a huge national debt into an 18-million livres surplus. He promoted new forms of trade including the production of high-class cloth, glassware and tapestries – luxury items that had formerly been imported from countries such as Italy and Holland. He encouraged the construction of new roads and canals thus aiding commerce. Although he was a converted Catholic, he was gifted with being able to reassure his Protestant subjects that he was unbiased towards them through permitting certain privileges whilst at the same time remaining on good terms with the Catholics – for example, through protecting the monasteries and encouraging recruitment into the Catholic clergy. In other words, his even-handed approach gave the country the means to go forward as one nation, if not one faith.

Henri IV successfully applied to Pope Clement VIII to annul his marriage to Marguerite de Valois before taking Marie de Medici – Princess of Tuscany – as his second wife in October

---

[xl] Diane C. Margolf, *Religion and Royal Justice in early modern France- The Paris Chambre de L'Edit 1598-1665.* (Kirksville, Missouri, 2004) p xii.

The Story of the Huguenots – a Unique Legacy

1600. There was great rejoicing the following year when on 27 September 1601 their first child, the future Louis XIII, was born.

Henri's success in reversing the country's ruinous state and his ability to work with those whose aims were parallel to his own made him a highly effectual leader of the French nation. Ironically, he died a victim of the fanaticism he had tried so hard to eradicate. A man considerably ahead of his time, he once said: *'Those who follow their consciences are of my religion and I am of the religion of those who are brave and good.'*

During his lifetime, he was frequently misunderstood, but his tragic and untimely end came on 14 May 1610 when he was mortally wounded by a dagger thrust into him by a fanatical Catholic – François Ravaillac – as he travelled by coach to the Louvre in Paris. It appears that the coach stopped as it met a cart coming the other way whereupon Ravaillac seized his chance and plunged the dagger into Henri. This came on the eve of a planned invasion of the Lower Rhineland over the disputed succession of Julius Cleves.

Henri IV's assassination brought home to many Frenchmen what a great man he had been as the country now sunk into instability for the next 14 years, seeing an ugly revival of the persecution of Huguenots and forcing their subsequent emigration[xli]. In later years Henri IV became recognised by many, including notables such as Voltaire, as the personification of the finest of France and his greatest achievement was the Edict of Nantes.

* * * * * *

The *Edict of Nantes* lasted, mostly intact, for almost a century despite the efforts of Henri's son, Louis XIII, to gradually erode some of the hard-won concessions contained within the edict's

---

[xli] Noel Currer-Briggs & Royston Gambier, *Huguenot Ancestry* (Chichester, 1985) p29.

The Story of the Huguenots – a Unique Legacy

'brevets'. The prelude to the next human tragedy in the history of the Huguenots unfolded further as Louis XIV (himself a grandson of Henri IV) was in time also persuaded by his Catholic advisors to continue the erosion of rights granted by his grandfather until the *Edict of Nantes* had become no more than an almost worthless scrap of paper. And so, when Louis was 'notified' of the almost total conversion of his Huguenot subjects, he felt the time had come to officially revoke the *Edict of Nantes* in full through another decree. This notorious revocation put the two religions on a collision course yet again, but this time it would seem there was no future whatsoever for the Huguenot faith in France, and that Catholicism would triumph in 1685 when the Revocation became law. (see Appendix 2).

- 6 -

From the Edict of Nantes to the Succession of Louis XIV

From the inception of the Edict of Nantes, life for those people of France who professed the Protestant[50] (Huguenot) faith must have been one of overwhelming relief and gratitude that at last they could practice their religion without fear of persecution. Royal officials had worked hard in areas across France to ensure that people who professed a belief in either faith had every opportunity to live peacefully side by side, thus helping to ensure that the edict's provisions were adhered to. For a time, this was the case. Indeed, the spirit of co-operation resulting from the unstinting efforts of the royal officials often led to many Catholics assisting their Huguenot neighbours during later, harsher decades when there were clashes between the Huguenots and Cardinal Richelieu. Therefore, although Catholics and Huguenots had fought each other during the Wars of Religion it would be wrong to assume that all communities were irrevocably divided by faith during the 17th century, or, because of ongoing divisions, that people of either faiths could not co-exist peacefully, despite the wars leaving much destruction and death in their wake.

Discord could in some cases be accommodated peacefully. The village of Bruniqel just outside Toulouse was graced with two chateaux both owned by the same family: the more historic was

The Story of the Huguenots – a Unique Legacy

owned by the Catholic branch, the other - the 'jeaux chateau' – was refuted to have been built by the Protestant branch between 1485-1510, and for three centuries they opposed each other until eventually the owner of the old chateau purchased the newer chateau from its Huguenot owners, and thus, it would appear that harmony was finally restored. There is also evidence that accord within many communities did in fact begin to emerge not long after the Edict of Nantes became law. During this period, both faiths were able to put past grievances to one side and amicably work together not only in the trades they plied, but in the joint fulfilment of civic responsibilities; even religious barriers were lowered to the extent of inter-faith marriages taking place. The ordinary people of either faith exhibited a practical approach and greater tolerance towards their fellow neighbours on a daily basis.

However, there were still barriers within community life which both the French government and the Catholic Church encouraged – one example of such a barrier was the distinct division of cemeteries. Neither Huguenots nor Catholics disagreed with some form of burial separation from one another; after all, Huguenots would, on the whole, prefer their deceased to lie in a last resting place not shared with those of a 'superstitious' faith, and Catholics would not wish their dearly departed loved ones to share a burial ground with those who were not of the 'true' faith. Thus, a gradual evolvement of cemetery partitioning or, where this was not practical, cemeteries dedicated to a single faith, became commonplace over time[xlii].

Whilst this idea seemed perfectly acceptable to Huguenots, there was marked resistance from Catholics, who, perhaps understandably, felt that some restriction needed to be applied, such as only agreeing to the handover of a cemetery to Huguenots if the cemetery was no older than the Huguenot religion. In some areas, the delicate division of a community's cemetery was not

---

[xlii] Keith P. Luria, *Sacred Boundaries: Religious Co-existence and Conflict in Early-Modern France.* (Washington, DC, 2005) p105.

The Story of the Huguenots – a Unique Legacy

without problems as the Pope had declared anyone not of the Catholic faith a heretic, and therefore Catholics believed that burial in the same cemetery as a Huguenot would be deemed a profanity[xliii].

As an example of this, in 1643 in Poitou, the Court of the Grands Jours began its two-year deliberation on the vexed question of shared or divided cemeteries in 69 parishes within the province[xliv]. Those that evaded the courts were in later years subjected to lawsuits. Huguenots were often forced to search out alternative burial grounds and had to bear the additional cost of reburial, as well as face hefty fines, but in reality the courts were hard-pressed to enforce this division in many cases because often families were a mix of both religions[xlv] and if they were joined in life they would naturally argue they should not be separated in death.

Huguenots had to apply to royal officials for a new Huguenot cemetery, but as time marched by, these officials became less amenable towards Huguenots, and often permission was only granted for a cemetery on land that was some distance from the community it would serve so as to deliberately ensure difficulties for mourners. As the decades passed following the inception of the Edict of Nantes, Catholic authorities toiled determinedly towards a goal of complete separation in life and death from those not of the Catholic faith.

* * * * * *

When Louis XIII came to the throne he was just nine years of age and therefore a minor. His mother, Marie de Medici, assumed the reins of government as Queen Regent – unfortunately, although she shared the name Medici with a family predecessor, she did not

---

[xliii] Keith P. Luria, Sacred Boundaries: Religious Co-existence and Conflict in Early-Modern France. (Washington, DC, 2005) p110.
[xliv] Ibid. p139.
[xlv] Ibid. p142.

display the intelligence of Catherine de Medici, or her ability to compromise. One of her first acts was to reverse the foreign policy of her late husband Henri IV and contract a marriage for her son with Anne of Austria, daughter of Philip III of Spain. This news horrified the Huguenots, who were unable to forget the pain and anguish inflicted upon them by Catholic Spain, nor were they able to dismiss, without alarm, the Queen Regent's leaning towards the Jesuit priests for advice as well as squandering the country's coffers on pensions amongst the Catholic nobility. Her late husband, Henri IV, had in the early part of his reign bestowed pensions on various members of the nobility in order to 'foster' old-fashioned values of loyalty, but his strategy had at that time been very effective in binding the nobility regardless of faith to the crown[xlvi].

By 1612, religious war seemed once again inevitable. The Duc de Sully's son-in-law, Benjamin, Duc de Rohan, was a prominent figure in Huguenot circles. He spoke out vehemently against the Queen Regent's Spanish and pro-Catholic policies at an assembly held at Saumur and threatened rebellion on behalf of Huguenots.

In 1617, the refusal of the Estates of Bearn, the French area of the independent kingdom of Navarre, to accept the royal proclamation to integrate the province of Bearn into the kingdom of France brought the issue to the forefront. The Huguenot Assembly of La Rochelle met and issued a statement declaring that Bearn's cause was the cause of all Protestants of France.

At the time that Henri IV had converted to the Catholic faith to become king, one of the conditions of the Pope's acceptance of his conversion was that Henri had to repeal the anti-Catholic laws in force in Bearn and restore Catholic Church lands or give the Catholic Church the equivalent property from the Crown. However, Henri's tragic, untimely assassination had prevented this pledge being fulfilled.

[xlvi] Mark Greengrass, *France in the Age of King Henri IV: The Struggle for Stability.* 2nd Edition (New York, 1995) p226.

In June of that year, his son, Louis XIII, angered by the refusal of the Estates of Bearn to accept the royal proclamation of integration, declared that all ecclesiastical property in Bearn was to be restored to the Catholic Church and compensation be given to those who were dispossessed. In May 1619, the Protestant Reformed Church (Huguenot Church) issued an annulment of the Decree of Restitution in support of the Bearnais. The king travelled to Pau and oversaw the restitution of the Church of St Martin's to the Catholic clergy. Attitudes were hardening – in November, the General Assembly met in the foremost Huguenot stronghold of La Rochelle, and declared the following month that they would support the Bearnais (without asking for Royal permission, as should have been requested, showing the level of anger at recent events in Bearn). In this atmosphere of rising passions, across France Huguenots began to organise, equip and gather into an army – the unmistakable scent of a resumption of war hung in the air.

Louis XIII now commenced a bloody campaign against his rebellious Huguenot subjects. One battle took place on 10-11 June 1622 at Nègrepelisse, a little town a few miles to the east of the predominantly Huguenot town of Montauban in the district of Quercy. Louis XIII took the decision to make an example of the citizens of this small town as he wrongly suspected that the townspeople had, during the winter, mistreated the royal garrison that had been stationed there. The king's orders to his soldiers were to *'treat the Huguenots as they had treated others'*.

These orders were mercilessly carried out by the soldiers – far exceeding any brutality they could surely have presumed had been meted out to the royal garrison only a few months earlier. They set about rounding up and putting to death all able-bodied men to prevent them joining the mustering Huguenot forces, whilst most of the women were in varying degrees physically abused. Many terrified women with little infants tried to flee by swimming to the far side of the river only to find royalists troops waiting for them –

The Story of the Huguenots – a Unique Legacy

the women's cries of mercy fell on deaf ears. Within a very short period of time the streets were so choked full of corpses it would have been difficult to traverse from end to end.

The next day, from within the Citadel, the few remaining Huguenots, made their way to the centre of the town to surrender to the royalist troops – for which they were consequently hanged[xlvii].

The massacre at Nègrepelisse marked the end of this stage of the rebellion but not the end of the war. The Huguenots valiantly prepared to make a last stand at Montpellier under the leadership of de Rohan. Yet, the government, shocked by the action of de Rohan and seemingly desperate to avoid any further escalation of hostilities, immediately offered concessions including recognising the Duc de Rohan as official 'Protector' of the Huguenots, as well as renewing the *Edict of Nantes,* but simultaneously and significantly reducing the number of secure places for Huguenots to freely live and worship – from 150 to 70. This was not the end of the rebellion as the government must have expected and indeed had ardently hoped for, but merely a pause in the bloodshed. However, when hostilities were resumed the king had a new weapon – Richelieu[xlviii].

Cardinal Richelieu had risen to prominence during the reign of Louis XIII who, recognising the cleric's useful talents, had campaigned for his promotion to the status of cardinal, and by 1624 he had risen to the powerfully influential position of France's Chief Minister. As is so often the case with those who achieve eminence he was widely disliked during his own lifetime. Even the king was known to have resented his dependency upon his minister although he could not deny Richelieu's statesmanlike abilities.

[xlvii] Jack A Clarke, *Huguenot Warrior: The Life and Times of Henri de Rohan.* (Dordrecht, Netherlands) p101.

[xlviii] David J Sturdy, *Richelieu and Mazarin: A Study in Statesmanship (*London, 2003) (kindle).

Richelieu was keen to promote France as a great nation on the European stage. He was a Catholic who detested those of the Protestant faith, but he was prepared to accept them if they demonstrated loyalty to France and thus helped promote France's interests internationally. The problem was that Huguenots, resenting the discrimination directed towards them, naturally did not show the requisite loyalty to France, and their open displays of disloyalty were something that Richelieu would not tolerate. An example of this had already occurred in Bearn whose majority of citizens were Huguenots who had refused to apply the *Edict of Nantes* as they were obliged, i.e. allowing the Catholic minority freedom to practice their religion.

At the time of Richelieu's promotion to chief minister in 1624, the Huguenots were in control of eight areas in the south of France as well as having a commander-in-chief in the French army. They had within these areas created provincial assemblies and even a general assembly, thus creating the international perception of France to be a royal state housing some sort of a republic. Rather than an apparently united and internationally respected country at the centre of European politics, France must have been perceived as, and indeed was, a fractured and divided nation. For ten years, Richelieu and Louis XIII vigorously campaigned for the demolition of mediaeval castles in France as they were often used by Huguenots for refuge.

With the onset of the *Thirty Years War*[51], the Huguenots took the opportunity to expand their holdings; thus in 1625 they appealed to the English – their Protestant brothers – to aid them in seizing the islands of Ré and Oleron. English forces landed and attempted to take the forts on each island, but disunity within the Huguenot and English camps, coupled with fearfulness of retaliation by the French crown, meant the gain was short-lived. Both these islands were of significant strategic importance as they were natural defences to the sea entrance of La Rochelle. Predictably, the Huguenot military action was viewed as treachery

The Story of the Huguenots – a Unique Legacy

by Richelieu, who sent a royal army to take disciplinary measures against them.

Louis ordered a fort to be built opposite the defences of La Rochelle to spy upon the Huguenot capital but England, by now a powerful Protestant nation, successfully persuaded the two warring factions to negotiate, and the resulting *Treaty of La Rochelle* was signed by Richelieu and the Huguenot leaders in 1626. Richelieu had gravely considered the implications of English intervention, possibly feeling compelled to comply. This truce, far from resolving matters, gave time to the Huguenots to regroup and build up their forces.

By 1627, they were ready to rise again and, as if proving Richelieu's suspicions correct, they were openly assisted by the English, who were by now watching events across the channel with increasing interest and concern for their Protestant brethren. Charles I, under pressure from Catholic circles who desired a counter-reformation in England, sent troops to try to quell such fierce anti-Catholic ire and determination amongst his subjects to support their fellow Protestants[xlix].

English forces in the meantime landed on the Isle de Ré, but, having failed to capture its citadel, withdrew ignominiously[l]. A second expeditionary fleet under the command of the Earl of Lindsay was dispatched, which in spite of sailing to within sight of La Rochelle offered no help to their fellow Protestants in the beleaguered city, and instead sailed back to England[52]. These provocative events left Richelieu with little choice but to retaliate. The plan was firstly to drive out the English, then to cut off La Rochelle from all sources and means of supply in order to starve the population. As part of his strategy he commanded that a huge 'mole'[53] should be erected across La Rochelle's harbour, which would make it impossible for supplies to reach the town from the

---

[xlix] Simon Sharma, *A History of Britain: 1603-1776* (London, 2001) p69.
[l] Sir Winston Churchill, *A History of the English-Speaking peoples: Vol 2; The New World* (London, 1974) p142.

The Story of the Huguenots – a Unique Legacy

sea. He deployed the royal army around the landward sides of La Rochelle, then settled down to wait until the inhabitants were starved into submission. The siege lasted 14 months. As the siege wore on, the brave citizens of La Rochelle found the scarcity of food caused food prices to soar; worse was to come as they were slowly reduced to eating horse meat and dog flesh. By the end of the siege, those surviving were pitifully reduced to eating scraps of leather boiled in water with vinegar.

On 1 November 1628, Richelieu suggested that King Louis XIII should lead the French army into La Rochelle; Richelieu rode by the king's side into the starving city, then proceeded to the Church of St Margaret to celebrate Mass in thanksgiving for his victory.

Before the siege, the city's population had stood at 25,000. By the time of its defeat only 5,000 citizens survived, many too severely malnourished to resist any more. Richelieu had insisted that the surrender was to be unconditional, but he allowed the starved, defeated population to leave without further punishment, thus showing, some might say, a small degree of magnanimity as the victor.

* * * * * *

Richelieu now turned his attention to the Huguenot strongholds in the southern regions of France. In May 1629, after a siege of 15 days, the city of Privas was captured by the forces of Louis XIII. Privas had been one of the chain of Huguenot strongholds across the south of France, mainly in the Languedoc region from Nimes and Uzes in the east to Castres and Montauban in the west[li], and was considered strategically important as it was midway in the series of strongholds; thus, the overall line of communication would become harder to maintain if this stronghold was taken

---

[li] Christopher Duffy, *Siege Warfare: The Fortress of the early modern world 1494-1660* (London, 1996) p121.

from the Huguenots. Following its capture, between 500-600 Huguenot fighters surrendered, but a few of these attempted to blow themselves up together with the royal troops; when this failed it led to a massacre with the city being destroyed in the ensuing looting and burning. One young girl who escaped the carnage was to become part of Richelieu's household, and later became known as 'La Fortunée de Privas'. Shortly afterwards, the town of Alès was captured, and with this serious breach in the Huguenot chain of fortifications the remaining Huguenot-held towns and cities in the south capitulated within a short space of time.

On 21 August 1629, the second-most important Huguenot city of Montauban surrendered to Richelieu. This had been the last place of Huguenot resistance. After its surrender, Richelieu gave orders for its fortress to be razed to the ground.

Just a few weeks later, on 27 September, the *Peace of Alès* was signed. This gave Huguenots a guarantee that they could practise their religion with judicial protection, but in return they were expected to agree that their major strongholds and political assembles were to be dismantled, and that the cost of the demolition of these defences was to be met by the Huguenot townspeople – much to their dismay[lii].

The surrender of the Montauban fortress effectively ended the campaign in Languedoc. The *Peace of Alès,* whilst it confirmed some of the rights contained in the *Edict of Nantes,* also commanded the Huguenot military wing to be disbanded as well as ordering the destruction of Huguenot fortresses. The treaty went on to confirm that Catholicism was to be restored to areas where it had existed in the period between the *Edict of Nantes* and the *Peace of Alès*. Unsurprisingly, the political rights of the Huguenots ceased to exist, and the government's financial support of Protestant clergy was withdrawn. The defeat at La Rochelle, the

---

[lii] Diane C. Margolf, *Religion and Royal Justice in early modern France- The Paris Chambre de L'Edit 1598-1665.* (Kirksville, Missouri, 2004) p212.

The Story of the Huguenots – a Unique Legacy

loss of the entire Languedoc fortress system and the subsequent treaty were a stern warning to any other areas that might consider rebelling against the French Crown[liii].

Yet fortune's wheel turned yet again in December 1642 when Cardinal Richelieu died followed, just five months later, by the death of Louis XIII. The remaining rights of Huguenots were later confirmed by a royal declaration issued in the name of Louis XIII's successor, the infant Louis XIV, in 1643.

[liii] A. D. Lublinskaya, translated by Brian Peara, *French Absolutism: The Crucial Phase 1620-1629* (Cambridge, 2008) p210.

- 7 -

The Fronde to the Revocation 1648-85

During the minority of Louis XIV, a series of civil wars within France erupted, known as *The Fronde*[54]. These wars were a challenge firstly to the policies begun under Cardinal **Richelieu**; then, **from** 1643 they developed into growing resistance to the 'foreigners' in power – **specifically** the Austrian Queen Regent, Anne, and her chief minister, Mazarin, from Italy.

Cardinal Mazarin was undoubtedly the power behind the throne and it was his extravagant habits that soon began to empty the full state coffers he had inherited from Cardinal Richelieu, who had for some time been amassing great wealth for wars to extend France's status and power. New taxation was requested to refill the country's **coffers, but** in the spring of 1648 the **Parlement** of Paris fought against this proposal, sparking the start of the first of two '**frondes**'. **Parlement** did not want to return to the old ideal of the State being dependent on them and defied **the royal authorities.** Additionally, **Parlement** was keen to curb the power of the monarchy by constitutional reform to permit **Parlement** a voice in government policy making. Between 30 June and 12 July, a list of 27 Articles was drawn up by an assembly of courts; amongst the changes asked for **were the** abolition of the intendants[55], an end to arbitrary **imprisonment,** and reductions in taxation.

The second phase of the Fronde, known as the *Fronde of the Princes,* which took place from January 1650 to September 1653, was a tortuous web of intrigue and counter-intrigue as personal ambitions on both sides swiftly overtook the moral stance of reform.

The war was fought across many of the provinces; even Paris was affected as barricades were yet again erected in the streets; however eventually it was the royalists who won this struggle and the failure of the people to curb the autocratic power of the Crown was not to be challenged again for another 150 years.

Following the conclusion of the Fronde, Mazarin turned his attention to fulfilling Richelieu's unfinished plans of reducing the power of both branches of the Hapsburg empire (Austria and Spain); however, although success here placed France in the premier position within Europe it also dealt a blow to two major Catholic European nations, and, rather self-damagingly, paved the way for the rise of Protestantism across Europe.

At the height of his power, Mazarin died following a short illness, but on his death-bed he recommended specific ministers whom he strongly believed Louis XIV should employ to advise him. Following the death of Mazarin, Colbert emerged as chief minister and, as far as he could prudently be, was a friend to the Huguenots – an able, honest man who took on the reins of an almost bankrupt nation, reforming the country's finances so that once more France's financial position was healthy. Colbert observantly recognised the honest industriousness of the Huguenots whose toil could do much to augment France's wealth. He granted a variety of privileges, patents and honours to protect their industries. When Colbert asked of a merchant what he thought the best means were of encouraging commerce, the man's reply was '*Laissez faire et laissez passer*' – the literal translation of which is: 'Let us alone, and let our goods pass'. Sadly, this advice was not followed[liv].

[liv] Samuel Smiles, *The Huguenots Their Settlements, Churches and Industries in England and Ireland (1889)* (London) pp.138-9.

At this stage, having 'reigned' for 18 years, Louis XIV decided *he* would now begin to rule his realm, explaining bluntly to his ministers – men such as Francois Le Tellier, the Marquis de Louvois and Colbert – that they would simply be ministers who would be charged with carrying out the king's orders. The king's will would be absolute, henceforth, in all matters of government – and Louis' own words summed up his attitude perfectly: *'The State, it is I'.*

Louis was indeed an able man and one who took his responsibilities seriously; he liked hard work and never spent less than eight hours each day on affairs of state throughout his lengthy reign. His Achilles' heel was a love of pleasure. He would spend hours with his confessor, who would often impose penances some of which would in effect order the king to rid the country of Huguenots. Once the king had exonerated himself through the given penance, he would immediately return to his licentious and extravagant way of life. He felt guilty at his inability to truly repent, but as a staunch Catholic, he was persuaded that his sins could be expiated by the extermination of the Protestant faith, which, in his carefully nurtured view, enfeebled France by division – the nation could surely no longer be a two-faith nation. His minister, Louvois, wrote accordingly to the governors of the provinces – *'His majesty will not suffer any person in his kingdom but those who are of **his religion** '*[lv].

Huguenots were again excluded from public office, as they had been before the *Edict of Nantes*. In some areas, the ability to carry out one's trade was linked to one's religious conviction. An example of this was the complaint made by the Corporation of Launderesses, who stated that as they had been founded by St Louis himself, they could not admit heretics. Their complaint was upheld by a decree passed on 21 August 1665.

Louis XIV now appointed 'Commissioners' (one Catholic and one Protestant) and sent each pair into the countryside to hear all

---

[lv] Samuel Smiles, The Huguenots Their Settlements, Churches and Industries in England and Ireland (1889) (London) p143.

complaints and seek a solution to all quarrels arising between the two religious communities, but this was not carried out, unsurprisingly, in an even-handed manner; in fact, in practically all cases the verdict was given in favour of Catholics. The Commissioners' brief went even further, giving them instructions to examine the title deeds of Huguenot churches, but unfortunately in many cases the deeds could not be produced – having been either mislaid in the passage of time or destroyed during the religious wars – and for every church unable to locate its deeds the inevitable decision to suppress was ordered. It is not possible to give an accurate number of how many of these churches were razed to the ground or the number of Huguenot schools closed, nor how many Huguenot charitable establishments and their chattels were seized and passed over to Catholic institutions, but, as an example, it is believed that by 1682, of the 815 Huguenot temples across France, 570 had suffered such a fate.

During the early part of December 1682, *The London Gazette* published an article stating that:

> *Following the Council of State in Paris passing an Order forbidding the practicing of the Protestant religion, the King's Lieutenant in Languedoc, the Duc de Nouailles, had overseen the Decree issued by the Parlement of Toulouse to demolish the Protestant temple at Montpellier*[56].

To the great anguish and bitter resentment of the Huguenots they were even made to smash to pieces the furnishings themselves and take the splintered remains to their cemetery.

The next phase of the erosion of Huguenot rights was the *ordonnance* (decree) against 'Relapsed Heretics', a denouncement resulting in lifelong banishment. If a person asked for the priest's blessing at a mixed marriage or had been overheard saying that he/she should like to enter the Church of Rome or had recanted the Protestant faith or shown even a slight preference towards the Church of Rome, then this decree would apply. However, should that person return to the Protestant faith, they would be arrested and taken before a tribunal. A further *ordonnance* gave powers for a priest and a local magistrate to visit every sick person to ask the question: *'do you wish to die in the Roman faith?'*

However, the visit would frequently involve outrageous scenes of the dying being tortured with stern exhortations directed towards them to abjure their Protestantism before it was too late, return to the true Catholic faith and pray to the Virgin Mary.

Children from the age of 14 years were considered old enough to renounce the Protestant faith. Once a child converted to Catholicism the parents were duty bound by the ordonnances to pay maintenance for their children from then on to live under a Catholic roof. Protestant religious services were infiltrated with spies intently listening to every word the pastor uttered and eagerly reporting any hint of criticism towards the Virgin Mary or indeed any saint of the Catholic Church; if reported, the pastor was swiftly accused of blasphemy.

From the beginning of the 17th century and lasting into the mid-18th, Protestant children were often abducted from their homes and placed with Catholic families, so they could be raised and educated in the Catholic faith. In one heart-breaking case from the town of Albenc in the Auvergne region of south-eastern France, Madelaine Bergerand nearly lost contact with her three daughters. Around Christmas of 1674, Bergerand appealed to the consistory for assistance. She told how, following her husband's death, she had given the care of her children to her late husband's parents (Samuel and Susanne) so she could go to work in Lyon as a servant to provide for her children. Not long after she had left for Lyon, news was given to her that Samuel had abjured the Reformed faith and moved to another city to work.

Before leaving Albenc, he had placed the children in the hands of a Catholic woman so that they would not *'follow the perversion of the religion'* once professed by their grandfather. The consistory was convinced that great pressure had been placed on the three girls to abjure their faith, and they worked tirelessly to get them restored to their mother. An intense three-month legal battle followed between the guardians of the girls and the Huguenot consistory before the courts, in an extreme rarity, decided in favour of their non-Catholic mother[lvi]. The entry in the consistory records about the case and the verdict are telling:

Now this happy success was enough to know that it is to God alone who we should give the glory of this great consolation to his church and to this poor mother, who has put the innocence of these small children under her protection, blessed our care, and guided the sovereign powers against the annexation of the young children (inférieures), in order to remove them from the abyss where the powers (ces dernières) wanted to plunge them.

Another example of how restrictions were imposed on those of the Protestant faith was the prescribed inequality of the legal system: if a petitioner had a questionable lawsuit, rather than lose the case, the petitioner need only state that he was petitioning against a heretic in order for judgement to be awarded in the supplicant's favour. Protestants were being gradually excluded from all Crown offices or municipal posts; they were forbidden to practice law or medicine or any of the generally held liberal professions. The singing of Protestant psalms was banned in their workshops or at the door of their houses and should a Catholic procession pass by their temple doors as they conducted a service they would be obliged to interrupt their worship until all Catholics had gone by.

Thus, the rights of the Huguenots as enshrined in the *Edict of Nantes* were gradually diminished during Louis XIV's reign not

---

[lvi] Dr, Ezra Lincoln Plank, *Creating Perfect Families: French Reformed Churches and family formation, 1559-1685* (Iowa, 2013) pp.242-3.

The death of a loved one was made even more heartbreaking with the ruling that Protestant dead could only be buried at either dawn or dusk, and that no more than ten mourners were allowed to accompany the bier. Furthermore, the joyous occasion of a wedding was deliberately marred with the number of guests being limited to just 12.

only through the destruction of their Protestant temples and bibles and record books, but also through their schools being forcibly closed, and the prevention of those of the Protestant faith from obtaining employment in most crafts, and from entering a Trade Guild.

The death of a loved one was made even more heartbreaking with the ruling that Protestant dead could only be buried at either dawn or dusk, and that no more than ten mourners were allowed to accompany the bier. Furthermore, the joyous occasion of a wedding was deliberately marred with the number of guests being limited to just 12.

Earlier, in 1665, the fervour of priests had been blatantly exposed when they urged an increased intensity of restrictions against Huguenots: '*to cause the formidable monster of heresy to expire completely*[lvii].

By 1681 Huguenots' everyday lives became more and more constrained as the deliberately cruel tactics of the dragoons[57] began to terrorise them. Most of them must surely by now have become fearful of the future, perhaps beginning to seriously consider the option of fleeing their homeland rather than exist under such harsh and unjust conditions. A further shock to the ordinary Huguenot came with the news of several prominent Huguenots, including many nobles of the Court, deciding to reject their Protestantism.

Some efforts were made to somehow fuse the two churches, but these were doomed to failure as any reform of the Catholic Church may have had the appearance of offering an olive branch to the Protestants, and therefore was doomed to failure. Thus, further ordonnances were passed including the banning of any Huguenot from printing religious books without express permission from a Roman Catholic magistrate.

[lvii] Wylie, James Aiken, *The History of Protestantism Vol 1,* (Virginia, USA, 2002) p1769.

The Story of the Huguenots – a Unique Legacy

The next tactic employed was the establishment of a fund in 1676 aptly named Caisse des conversions[lviii] solely for the purpose of purchasing consciences, in other words, to buy back Protestants into the Catholic faith; in particular, if pastors were to be encouraged to return to the Catholic faith a loss of their livelihood might persuade them to abjure their Protestantism. Revenues of vacant bishoprics and abbeys as well as benefices that had been until then Crown revenue were, on the orders of the king, diverted to the fund; therefore, many of these posts were deliberately kept empty for years to provide a steady income[lix].

Curiously, the man chosen to preside over the fund was Paul Pellisson, born a Protestant, but who had in later life converted to Catholicism. The fund's head office was in Paris with various branches around the country; each office was staffed with clerks who would daily produce lists of 'articles purchased', i.e. the souls who had converted to Catholicism for a sum of money. The amount paid varied from area to area with greater remuneration being given to the more eminent or to those with a large family, who would thus bring a multiple conversion to the list. Naturally, the system was open to abuse, with some 'conversions' being recorded more than once. Nonetheless, the king was delighted.

Attention was finally drawn to the king's minsters that value for money was not being achieved through the fund, so, during the early 1680s, harsher tactics were implemented with greater powers being given to the 'dragoons'[58]. These troops of soldiers were specifically tasked with brutally 'persuading' Huguenots to recant their faith, and they went about their task with fanatical sadism. It must be noted that often an army is made up of many men from sometimes different regions of a country and beyond, whose lives

---

[lviii] F. L. Carsten, *The New Cambridge Modern History, Vol 5, The Ascendancy of France 1648-88* (Cambridge, 1961) p140.
[lix] Ibid. p140.

The Story of the Huguenots – a Unique Legacy

are consequently no longer lived within the constraints of their home town or family life; thus, their adjusted life values can become unsympathetic to others, making them more immune to the suffering of others, as they dispassionately set about their tasks – it becomes just a job to them.

In September 1678[59], just a few years before tougher measures were introduced, a poor Protestant bookseller's wife living in Niort, western France, reported there had been 1,200 dragoons in the town during the winter; two of these soldiers had been billeted with her family, demanding that she provide them with at least four meals a day. Terrified of possible reprisals if she refused, she complied and would, she said, 'have given them a fifth meal each day if they had asked for it'[lx]. Others confirmed that if a family was unable to fund the cost of feeding their billeted dragoons, then the soldiers would sell the homeowners' furniture and other possessions, often at a fraction of their worth.

Louvois, the Secretary of State for War, authorised Marillac, the Intendant of Poitou, to billet a regiment of dragoons on Huguenot families in Poitou during March 1681. Later that same year Marillac adopted another tactic – 'selective taxation'[60]. Taille rolls (registers of those living within an area) were prepared, with details of inhabitants listed in one of three columns and taxed accordingly – existing Catholics: partial exemption; new Catholics (those converted from the Protestant faith): wholly exempt; Huguenots remaining true to their beliefs: 100 per cent liability. Naturally the 'old' Catholics resented the full exemption status given to those 'newly converted', perhaps becoming suspicious of their motives.

The dragoons travelled to former Huguenot strongholds across France such as Bearn, the Languedoc, Dauphiné, Poitou, Bergerac and Montauban and thereon to towns such as Castres, Nimes and

---

[lx] Geoffrey Treasure, *The Huguenots* (London, 2014) p343.

The Story of the Huguenots – a Unique Legacy

Montpellier, carrying out their particular brand of 'conversion' as repeatedly and often as forcibly as possible. Frequently, when local people heard that a dragonnade visit was about to occur in the district, Huguenots would convert to Catholicism rather than face the heartless bullying tactics of these troops. One such outrageous incident involved troops deployed near the town of Bearn. They had initially been sent there to observe troops of the Spanish Army, but once a truce was agreed between Spain and France, Louvois thought to set them another task – Huguenot conversion. The troops diligently rounded up several hundred Huguenots from the surrounding districts and forced them into the local church; the doors were closed, and the terrified people were forced to kneel at sword-point as the Bishop of Lescar forcibly gave them absolution[lxi].

By the end of the year, Marillac was able to report 38,000 conversions, but his apparent success was viewed with some scepticism, and Louis XIV, having enquired into this matter, did not like the answers he was given – enforced conversion through acts of atrocity such as robbery and rape; physically dragging people to the altar to be doused with holy water; elderly people being tossed in blankets; boiling water being poured down the throats of Huguenots, and hot irons being applied to the soles of their feet. What deeply alarmed the king was the fact that he had *not* ordered these actions.

A family which suffered persecution by the dragoons at first-hand were the Migaults. Jean Migault was a successful schoolmaster who lived in Mougon, western France; he was liked and respected by most of the community. He later wrote a journal of his own personal experiences of the persecution meted out to his family so that future generations would be able to read what had transpired during these years. On 22 August 1681 as Jean and his wife Elizabeth were leaving the Protestant temple where Jean was

---

[lxi] Samuel Smiles, *The Huguenots Their Settlements, Churches and Industries in England and Ireland (1889)* (London) p152.

- 77 -

The Story of the Huguenots – a Unique Legacy

a reader and secretary, they were confronted by a troop of dragoons[lxii], who followed them home whereupon the quartermaster demanded: 'Change your religion and adopt Catholicism.' Having refused, they were visited by the troop commander, who asked: 'What will you pay me to limit the number of troops I will be billeting in your home?'

Horrified, they explained they had little cash. The commander thoroughly inspected their house and then left; minutes later two soldiers arrived with billeting orders, and, marching arrogantly into the Migault house, they demanded a hearty meal.

The family fled their home, taking shelter in nearby woods with the assistance of a sympathetic Catholic priest, who aided them in their flight. The priest was not the only help the Migaults received from members of the Catholic faith; two sisters, old friends and neighbours, hid Jean and managed to sneak Madame Migault from under the noses of the soldiers guarding her.

The Migaults joined no less than 21 other Protestant families from the neighbourhood who had also fled their homes following the inception of the dragonnade. They were free, they had not denied their faith, but the cost had been very high with the loss of their homes and contents. The soldiers contemptuously looted and sold their possessions for a mere pittance even though some items were quite valuable.

Where were the Migaults and the others to go? They could not live indefinitely in the woods as many had young children. The Migaults had 12 surviving children with ages ranging from 17 years to only a few days old. Once the dragoons left the area, they tried to return to their homes, but the troops unfortunately reappeared and this time when the families fled, their homes were utterly destroyed, leaving uninhabitable ruins.

Madame Migault died in 1683; within two years of their mother's death three of the couple's sons had managed to secretly

---

[lxii] Geoffrey Treasure, *The Huguenots* (London, 2014) p344

leave France: two fled over-land to Germany and the Netherlands, whilst a third took ship to Holland, and a fourth son abandoned his apprenticeship and left to seek his fortune in the New World. In January 1688 following two years of living a fugitive existence in which he suffered great hardship, Monsieur Migault eventually took the decision that he and the rest of the family must also flee their homeland rather than face the continuing brutality and theft imposed upon them for refusing to renounce their faith[lxiii]. Escape abroad was not without its own dangers, however, as it was unlawful for Huguenots to leave the country. Penalties imposed upon those emigrating abroad were severe with the head of the household being sentenced to the galleys for life, and a fine of 3,000 livres for anyone assisting a Huguenot to escape. Interestingly, this same ordonnance governing all contracts for the sale of property by those of the 'reformed faith' was within one year of the date of their emigration declared null and void, which led to many formerly Protestant estates being seized and sold indiscriminately[61].

The Migaults' first attempt to leave France was on a cold dark night. Jean had successfully negotiated for the family's safe passage on a ship leaving La Rochelle for England. He left for La Rochelle with one horse in whose panniers two of the Migault children were ensconced, while a third was seated on the horse's back, with the rest of the family walking alongside. Heavy rain had turned the roads into deeply rutted, sticky, sodden paths which, nevertheless, were still far too dangerous to travel along. To avoid detection, they picked their way slowly across meadows now transformed into swamps, often sinking deep into the mud as they desperately struggled onwards towards the beach where they were to embark. As the beach came into sight they could see fellow refugees quietly waiting for the hoped-for salvation that the ship would offer if things went well.[lxiv]

[lxiii] Geoffrey Treasure, *The Huguenots* (London, 2014) p344.
[lxiv] Ibid, p360

The Story of the Huguenots – a Unique Legacy

Over 50 people were taken out in groups by longboat to the English-owned ship anchored offshore that night, but the Migaults were too large a family unit to be taken as one group. As the sky lightened and a new day dawned, two patrolling guard boats were sighted between the beach and the rescue ship, forcing those still waiting to turn in flight back towards La Rochelle, hurrying as fast as they could, retracing their steps, panic-stricken, along the rain-sodden paths of their earlier route; these poor souls must have been fearful of being arrested at any moment.

The Migaults were among those lucky enough to regain the safety of their lodgings. Terrifying as the experience of that night had been, it did not deter them and within three months they were ready to make another attempt[lxv]. The weather was more favourable to them, the roads drier and full of travellers journeying to religious destinations for the Easter festivities; thus, the family were able to blend into the general mêlée that day. On 19 April after a mercifully uneventful journey, they departed from La Rochelle, arriving at the port of Brill in Holland 19 days later.

News of the Huguenots' plight had been spreading across the borders of France to other countries for some years thanks to the efforts of people such as Pierre Jurieu, exiled in 1681, whose writings had alerted the people of England and Holland. Gradually, this trickle of information became a torrent as increased awareness of the cruelty meted out to the Huguenots lit fires of anger and rage in other 'Protestant' nations against such hideous persecution.

[lxv] Samuel Smiles, The Huguenots Their Settlements, Churches and Industries in England and Ireland (1889) (London) p361.

- 8 -

Post-Revocation: Persecution and Punishment

By early 1685, news had reached court that most of the king's subjects were now of the Catholic faith. Louis XIV was delighted to hear that his kingdom was at last a Catholic nation; on 18 October 1685, he signed the *Edict of Fontainebleau (see Appendix 2)* thus finally revoking in full the *Edict of Nantes*. Louis had been carefully tutored from an early age by his mother, Anne of Austria, with the deliberate objective of forming in his mind a very constricted and idealised outlook on religion, consequently rendering him incapable of understanding, or wishing to tolerate, the Reformation that was sweeping many parts of the known world. His mistress, Madame de Maintenon, continued his discreet indoctrination and made a pact with the Jesuits. Accordingly, she would persuade Louis to revoke the *Edict of Nantes* in return for their approval of her marriage to Louis, which is believed to have taken place the very next day after the *Edict of Fontainebleau* was signed. However, in doing so, Louis' actions would have far-reaching consequences.

The Pope, hearing of this new edict, was elated, and Rome resonated to the joyful sounds of *Te Deums* and processions wending their way from shrine to shrine across the city. In France, medals were struck to 'celebrate' the eradication of Protestantism in the land.

The Story of the Huguenots – a Unique Legacy

Of the 12 Articles contained in the *Edict of Fontainebleau,* Article XII appeared to allow members of the Huguenot church 'freedom of conscience' – if not freedom of worship, but in practice this was a fatal misnomer as many Huguenots were jailed for continuing to refuse to repudiate their faith. Article IX specified that anyone of the reformed faith who had already fled and who did not return within four months of the date of the new edict would forfeit their properties and goods if they remained Protestant[62]. Article X now forbade members of the Huguenot Church from emigrating; this ban was unheard of in European law at that time and effectively meant Huguenots would be forced to reject their faith as they would not be permitted to leave their homeland if they remained Protestant. The edict also set out guidelines for sentencing those who tried to emigrate – men would be sent to the galleys for life and women would face life imprisonment. The same harsh, uncompromising treatment applied to Huguenots who were found to have taken part in illegal gatherings at 'church of the desert' meetings[63]; and for possession of firearms or gunpowder, and for concealing the whereabouts of a pastor[64].

The only persons professing the Protestant faith who were banished were the pastors; they were given just 15 days to place themselves outside French borders with the penalty, if captured after that time, of the galleys for life. Neither were the poor pastors allowed to take any belongings with them – not even their children, some of whom were unweaned infants whose mothers were faced with the heart-breaking choice of following their husbands into exile or of remaining to wean their babies before handing them over to be brought up by a Catholic[lxvi]. It should be noted, though, that not all the Catholic clergy approved of the harsh treatment meted out to the Huguenots, nor did all the Catholic clergy carry out the orders of Louis XIV.

[lxvi] Samuel Smiles, *The Huguenots Their Settlements, Churches and Industries in England and Ireland (1889)* (London) pp.160/1.

Those who were sentenced to the galleys were not all young or strong. David de Caumont, Baron of Montbelon, and Antoine Astruc were both 70 years old. For some, the sight of a fellow human being forced to endure the punishment of the galleys simply because they wished to remain true to their faith brought about a life changing decision. An example of this is Jean Bion, a chaplain on board a galley, who was so deeply affected by the sight of such abject misery and suffering that he sought conversion *to the Protestant faith* at a time of such overwhelming Catholic strength, eventually escaping France and becoming pastor of a French church in Chelsea. He wrote an emotional description of life on board a galley ship, which gives clarity to the suffering that so many Huguenots were forced to endure:

> *...each oar had five men behind it, and in addition the end of the oar was held by a Turk, as he proved to be stronger than the Christians. Each galley had a crew of five hundred men, three hundred of whom were under sentence of penal servitude. The men wore two shirts of coarse canvas, a red serge tunic, and a red cap, to cover their head, which was shaven to indicate their subjection. Each prisoner was attached with chains and beaten if he slacked.*

He also told of how in 1703, in excess of 60 men fell ill off the coast of Italy and how inhumanely they were treated by being herded into a room at the prow of the boat, just three feet high with only one hole – a mere two feet square – for ventilation[lxvii].

Galleys were used as floating prisons; in fact, almost 550 galley rowers were said to have endured this punishment for up to 30 years of their lives. In 1748, galleys were superseded by

---

[lxvii] Museum of London, The, *The Quiet Conquest: The Huguenots, 1685-1985* (London, 1985) p46.

'convict' prisons in naval ports such as Marseille, which listed 34 as being based there. Life as a galley rower was hard indeed; they were kept tied to their bench 24 hours a day on the open deck of the galley. There were 260 rowers per galley divided equally into two gangs at the sides of the boat, each had a 12-metre oar and would be expected to keep to a pace of 20 to 25 strokes per minute. They would serve at sea for two or three months at a time, with the rest of their sentence spent in port where they would be hired temporarily by port craftsmen. Nearly half of all Huguenot galley slaves died in the Royal Hospital for Convicts in Marseille and nearly three-quarters of these deaths were within three years of sentencing.

A further account of galley life can be found in the memoirs of the Huguenot Jean Marteihle, which give a rare eyewitness account of galley life. He had been born in Bergerac in 1684 into a prosperous Huguenot family:

In 1700 when the Duc de la Force was given permission to 'convert' the local Huguenots: 22 dragoons were forcibly billeted with the Bergerac family; Jean's father was imprisoned, and his mother tortured into signing a renunciation of her faith. Jean and a companion attempted to escape to Holland but were captured at the French frontier near Marienbourg and imprisoned in Tournay. Having been condemned to the galleys, the young men were held for several months in Lille. In January 1702, they were advised by the sympathetic prison governor to avoid the arduous march to Marseille by joining the last of the bands of convicts heading for Dunkirk where six galleys of the Atlantic fleet were based. They were given a wagon and spared the worst deprivations of the journey but on arrival, they were assigned to the galleys: Marteihle served first on board Heureuse, then later on the flagship La Palme.

Marteihle did not in fact escape the horrors of the chain-gang for, after several years in the Atlantic fleet, following the surrender of Dunkirk to the English in 1712, he and 22 fellow Huguenots were compelled to transfer to the galleys in Marseille, obliged to undress and stand naked for two hours while their clothes were searched, ostensibly for hidden files. Afterwards came blows when the victims were too stiff to move, and they were dragged back to their places by the chain attached to their necks.

On the same day that the *Edict of Fontainebleau* became law, moves were already in place to destroy the last of the Protestant temples that still stood across France. The great temple at Charenton near Paris had been large enough to accommodate 14,000 people – it took five days to raze this magnificent edifice to the ground. This wanton destruction was repeated at other towns across France including Montauban where the Catholic cathedral of Notre Dame was erected in 1739 as a reminder to any remaining Protestants that only one faith would be tolerated; today it towers over the town as a reminder of past intolerance.

As Huguenots across France stood and inwardly wept at the destruction of their temples, there was no time to grieve at the injustice as they needed to attend to the urgent business of somehow rebuilding their 'Church' – but this time it would have to be underground in order to keep the faith alive; inevitably, this had the tragic effect of consequently weakening the link between those who had fled abroad and their home Church[lxviii].

Post-Revocation, the dragoons were still at work across France terrorising the desperate Huguenots. The Luberon area of southern France was targeted by the Grignan province dragonnades, which successfully 'converted' those of the Protestant faith in the villages of Lacoste, Merindol, Lourmarin, Joucas and Cabrieres.

[lxviii] Church of England Council for Christian Unity, *Called to Witness and Service*: The Reuilly Commons Statement, with Essays on Christ, Eucharist and Ministry, (1999) p56.

Women who refused to abjure their faith were not sent to the galleys but instead their 'punishment' would be incarceration. Amongst the Durand family archives can be found entries relating to the family. Francois Guillaume had been born in Montpellier in the Languedoc region[lxix]. Francois became a ministre de la religion pretendue réformée when he was 20 years old before becoming a rector of the church at Genoulliac, north of Montpellier. In 1680, he married Anne Brueyx de Fontcouverte, their marriage being blessed the following year with the birth of a son, Daniel Francois. Within a few months of the birth of her son, Anne Durand was arrested by Jesuits. Anne was to share the same fate as many other Protestant wives by being incarcerated in a nunnery for the rest of her life[lxx].

However, the activities of the dragonnades were not limited to the south of France alone: across swathes of Normandy, Brie and Champagne, in and around Chartres, Rouen and Dieppe, Caen, Meaux and Nantes the dragoons arrival brought fear and violence. Le Havre surrendered before the dragoons' arrival, such was the sheer terror that an impending visit aroused in those of the Protestant faith. During their four-day terrorisation of Rouen, the ill-disciplined, unruly soldiers forced the head of each Huguenot household to recant their faith.

When evidence of further atrocities perpetrated during the dragonnades was eventually brought to Louis XIV's attention, he was so repulsed by its vile actions that he gave orders for brutalities to cease; however, far from obeying the king's orders, all future acts of violence were carefully hidden from the king by his deceiving ministers.

Some families were so traumatised by such brutality – such as Jean Mallandain, his wife Marthe and their two young sons, who lived in the area near Goderville – that they attempted to flee on foot towards the coast, but on 14 January 1686 they were captured

---

[lxix] The Durand Archives.
[lxx] Ibid.

in Doullens, Picardy and imprisoned until their forced deportation to England over two years later.[65] Ten days after their arrest, Jean and Marthe were transferred from Doullens to a chateau at Dieppe, but their children were not listed on the transfer order, no doubt they were fostered by local Catholic families. Marthe was to remain at the chateau, but Jean was transferred to Aumale, 75kms north-east of Rouen.

The Huguenot, Jean Perigal, also imprisoned at Aumale, wrote an account of his imprisonment:

In the prison at Dieppe, I met other prisoners who had been arrested for their religion like me, but within a few days we were told it was the will of the King for us to be sent to the dungeons of the chateau of Aumale. We were taken there in a cart of men, women and girls; some of whom were put in the rooms of the chateau and others in the cellars. The cellars were make of brick, all equally deprived of light, where we were fed only with bread and water. One of our brothers, named Jean Malandain, a strong and robust man, was led to an underground cellar which was more than one hundred steps underground[66]. When we were reunited, Jean was so happy. Our presence was a reinforcement to his body and spirit, and he greatly rejoiced in our company. We could speak easily from one dungeon to the other; as three of them were very close to each other, only having a door separating us. When we made devotions, one amongst the three of us would say a prayer that the others could hear; this was a great consolation. That we did not expect to be long in these dungeons meant little – we did not think of leaving, although we could have done so extremely easily by forsaking our faith.[lxxi].

In the face of such ruthless persecution, countless Huguenots could see no alternative but flight; yet, with numerous troops and

---

[lxxi] The Mallandain Archives.

gendarmes constantly patrolling all exit routes, and inducements being offered to those who would betray those trying to escape, it became more and more hazardous to pursue this choice. Post-Revocation, anyone betraying a Huguenot runaway would be rewarded with half their goods. In May 1686, a further edict issued by Louis XIV declared that any escapee and any person found to be aiding their escape would be condemned to death.

Just when it appeared that life for Huguenots had become untenable in France, Louis XIV, in an about face, took the decision in February 1688 that the remaining Protestants who had stubbornly and courageously refused to renounce their beliefs should be deported. Accordingly, he wrote to Monsieur Freydeau de Brous, the superintendent of Rouen:

'Having estimates in connection with making leave the small number of my subjects who have persisted to now in their obstinacy not to abjure the Protestant religion, I write you this letter to tell you to withdraw from the chateaux and prisons of your Department, those Protestants that they contain, to take them to Dieppe, and there embark them in a vessel which shall carry them out of my state.'

Jean Mallandain was taken back to the chateau at Dieppe on 27 March 1688 where he was reunited with his wife Marthe. One month later they were deported. Jean and Marthe had been listed as 'confesseurs'. The deportation order stated:

Noms des confesseurs qui par les orders du Roi Louis XIV furent amenez de diverses prisons au chateau de Dieppe en Mars et Avril 1688 et embarquez par le meme ordre le 27 Avril, pour etre transportez en Angleterre – Goderville: Jean Malandain, Marthe Baudouin sa femme[67].

Jean was 43 years of age and his wife 30 at the time of their deportation. A further 92 prisoners were expelled with them but among the passenger list there is no trace of their two small sons when they boarded the 40-ton sailing ship. The voyage took 20 hours, but they were blessed with a calm sea crossing, eventually landing at Dover. They then travelled on foot across Kent to Gravesend, and from there, boarding a sailing boat that took them up the Thames to London, arriving on 1 May[lxxii].

[lxxii] The Mallandain Archives.

- 9 -

Decisions and Harsh Realities

With each new repressive measure sanctioned, so the numbers of Huguenots choosing to flee their homeland steadily rose. Where were they to go, and what route would they take to a new land? It is worth considering the routes available to them at that time. Numerous families from northern France made England their preferred destination given the narrow channel of water that separated the two nations, or the Netherlands if they preferred a land pass, while others from perhaps Brittany chose to flee to the Channel Islands. Other points of exit, for example, for those living in or near Metz or Neufchatel was across the land border into Germany; from Lyon and surrounding areas they journeyed to Switzerland; from Grenoble, the shortest route was to Turin which was for a while the favoured choice of those from Nice until Louis XIV gave orders to block this route. Countless families and individuals chose one of the major ports of La Rochelle, Bordeaux or Nantes to escape to English ports such as Falmouth, Dover or Southampton. Often boats would be crammed with people anxiously waiting to depart their homeland and fearful of being discovered on board by the authorities at the last minute[68].

Once across the border, whether over land or sea, they did not necessarily stay in the area, but somehow in time found the strength to travel onward to seek a new life. Having arrived in a

The Story of the Huguenots – a Unique Legacy

more tolerant country, the persecution had at last hopefully ended, but families fleeing their French homeland had faced a difficult and often dangerous journey, travelling mainly at night to avoid detection by the authorities, and although there are stories of some Catholics, sympathetic to the Huguenots' plight, assisting them in hiding or escaping, many groups or individual Protestants were betrayed to the authorities by zealous Catholics. Similarly, in mainly Protestant countries such as England, Catholics might either be aided or their whereabouts made known to the authorities, depending upon how compassionate others were to their fellow beings, whatever their religion.

In January 1686, an ordonnance came into force which lowered the age to just five years old[69] at which any Huguenot children should be placed under the supervision of Catholic parents or a similarly suitable person as directed by the local judge.

Anne and Francois Guillaume Durand's five-year-old son was one of the children forcibly removed from his family. In later life, he wrote to the Marquis de la Fare, a relative living in Montpellier, telling him how he had been abducted as a young boy through the orders of Louis XIV and raised without contact with any of his family members; not even his grandfather dared approach him. According to family legend, Francois Guillaume fell to his knees pledging himself and his successors to God. He announced that each future generation would supply a minister to the Protestant Church if he and his wife and son could be aided in escaping to start life anew in another country.

Records show that the pledge was honoured by the Durand family for the next three hundred years with just 3 exceptions: his son Daniel Francois was educated, and then seemingly forced into the legal profession, by the Jesuits, and during the 19th century Col. Anthony Durand's sons died in infancy, and as a consequence the last generation of the family died childless [lxxiii].

[lxxiii] The Durand Archives.

The Story of the Huguenots – a Unique Legacy

Many further affirmations followed the *Edict of Fontainebleau* giving rise to diverse problems such as the civil status of Huguenots. The records of births, marriages and deaths had always been within the local religious leader's remit; however, the local Huguenot pastor had ceased to exist in France following the *Peace of Alès*[70]. Without the religious ministers of the Protestant faith, how could these social events be recorded for all those who had not returned to the Catholic faith? The solution to this impasse was for the king to grant permission for deaths to be recorded with the secular authorities from 1695. Yet, incredibly, it was often the case that new 'converts' to Catholicism would, with their dying breath, refuse the Catholic rite of extreme unction, asking instead to be allowed to die in the Protestant faith. To thwart anyone choosing to die in this way, King Louis decreed that any man who refused extreme unction and survived would be sentenced to the galleys; any woman doing so would be imprisoned[71]. If they died before this sentence could be carried out, their corpse was to be dragged around the streets on a hurdle. It is an interesting insight into the character of Louis that, during the following year, he requested that his officers show leniency in enforcing such an act on a corpse.

In December 1698, a further declaration had been issued that ordered tight supervision of the new converts, who now found their religious practices being keenly observed on an almost daily basis[lxxiv], for example their attendance at mass, and also in marriages – which were to be celebrated only in Catholic churches. Furthermore, baptisms of Huguenot children into the Catholic faith were to take place within 24 hours of birth. There was even an obligation for a Huguenot to provide a certificate confirming his or her Catholic conformity should they need legal aid or to obtain a legal or medical degree; the certificate had to be signed by a Catholic priest to ensure the document's integrity as it was

---

[lxxiv] Derek H. Davis (Ed.) and Elena Miroshnikova (Ed.), *The Routledge International Handbook of Religious Education,* (London, 2013) p115.

assumed the bearer could not be wholly trusted to have honestly converted.

An example of this concerns Anthony Lauzy, who had been born a Huguenot, but who, aged 27, chose to abjure his faith in order to receive a Certificate of Abjuration. He, as others too would have been, was required to swear upon the Book of the Gospel and declare the Oath:

I Promise, Vow and Swear, and most constantly Profess, by God's Assistance, to keep entirely and inviolably unto Death, this self-same Catholik and Apostolik Faith, out of which no Person can be saved.

The oath was preceded by a catechism in which the person concerned had to acknowledge the seven sacraments, transubstantiation, the existence of Purgatory, the veneration of the Saints, and images of Christ, the Blessed Virgin and the Saints, and furthermore that *'the power of indulgence was left to the Church by Christ Jesus, and the use thereof is very beneficial to Christians'*. Finally, the adjuror would have to swear true and sole obedience in religious matters to the Pope of Rome[lxxv].

The king concluded that Huguenot children might be more malleable; therefore, the declaration also provided schools for Huguenot children in which they would be taught the Catholic faith through forced indoctrination[lxxvi].

Despite the false hopes promised through Article X of the *Edict of Fontainebleau,* many families fled rather than suffer reprisals and further repression; this has been true for many races and faiths throughout history, but it is true to state that the governments and peoples of Protestant nations including England felt immense sympathy towards their French 'cousins' because of the bond of

---

[lxxv] Museum of London, The, *The Quiet Conquest: The Huguenots, 1685-1985* (London, 1985) p40.
[lxxvi] Derek H. Davis (Ed.) and Elena Miroshnikova (Ed.), *The Routledge International Handbook of Religious Education,* (London, 2013) p115.

common religion in an era when politics and religion were inextricably bound together.

* * * * * *

The flight of so many Huguenots from the home of their birth was to have serious and far reaching consequences for their native homeland. Not only was the French economy to suffer profoundly from the loss of so many skilled and industrious citizens[72] – many of whom were master craftsmen and women in, for example, lace making, silk weaving and clock manufacture – but these same displaced people, now living in nations not always friendly towards France, would soon be teaching these skills to the indigenous men and women of their newly adopted countries. Some Huguenots would go on to enlist in their adoptive country's armies and would be called upon to fight against their former homeland.

David Garrick had quoted the words of Louis De Rouvroy, second Duc de Saint-Simon, who was only ten years old at the time of the Revocation, when he later made this evocative and far-sighted comment:

> *...the Revocation of the Edict of Nantes, this awful act that depopulated a quarter of the Kingdom, ruined its commerce and sent our factories abroad to make their countries flourish and prosper at our expense and helped them build new cities[lxxvii].*

Yet another blow to any hopes of retaining Huguenot skills in France was dealt in 1699 when a reinforcement of the ban on Huguenot emigration became enshrined in law[73], sharpening the pain of those Protestants remaining, who were now without churches, schools or pastors – a truly distressing scenario as religion was *the* major part of their daily lives – as much a natural

---

[lxxvii] Catherine Rawlinson and Isabelle Janvrin, *The French in London: from William the Conqueror to Charles de Gaulle* (London, 2016) p66.

function as breathing. At this point France was still populated with whole communities courageously still adhering to Protestantism who were, through being forced to renounce their faith, left with a communal sense of leading a dangerous double life: trying to outwardly appear a true and devout Catholic whilst secretly, and with great fear of being exposed at any time, pursuing their own Protestant faith.

There seemed no alternative but flight for many in the years leading up to, and for a while after, the Revocation but not all families escaping the escalating oppression were able to choose their final destination when they departed their homeland – their more immediate concern was their escape – and the many and diverse methods of concealment such as children in panniers or under bales of straw on carts. Often families would be forced to split up into smaller groups to minimise the risk of a large group being detected with the burden of guilt at not knowing if all of their loved ones had reached safety nor where their final destination would be.

* * * * * *

The unrelenting tyranny in the southeast region of the Cévennes had by now built up like a pus-filled abscess about to burst, spilling a prurient mass of violent indignation that was to be nothing less than the start of open rebellion, beginning with the assassination of Father du Chayla on 14 July 1702.

Father du Chayla was the Missions Inspector for the Haute-Cévennes area, and this particular mission was simply – by one means or another – to convert as many Huguenots as possible, and by brute force if necessary. His fanaticism earned him the undying hatred of all Protestants in the area. Du Chayla had set up his headquarters at the Pont-de-Montvert overlooking the Tarn, the cellars of the property being used to imprison captured Huguenots. That July, a powder keg was metaphorically lit which led to an

The Story of the Huguenots – a Unique Legacy

event similar to the massacres during the Albigensian Crusades of 1209-29[lxxviii].

A band of 60 men had gathered at sunset before sweeping into Pont-de-Montvert soon after darkness had fallen, releasing all the Huguenot prisoners, setting fire to the house and murdering the hated du Chayla[lxxix]. For over two years, guerrilla warfare existed in the region to the extent that it would require two field marshals and approximately 18,000-25,000 troops to supress the valiant band of young men and women who had collectively become known as the Camisards[74]. They had been raised in self-sufficiency, and thus were able to live off the land with a staple diet of not much more than roots and berries sourced locally. The groups were fluid in their tactics – sometimes a leader would command no more than 50 people, but swift regrouping could lead to a force of at least 100. The frustrated Catholics compared the Camisards' method of reprisals and rapid regrouping to the speed of starlings on the wing. And in retaliation for their temples being burnt to the ground, some 200 Catholic churches were treated in similar fashion by the Camisards.

During this period, the Huguenot Church was kept alive only in secret, with the faithful meeting – just as they had been forced to in earlier decades – in remote woodlands and almost inaccessible valleys, caves and cellars. Pastors would often return to administer to their flocks at considerable risk; in the absence of a pastor, a nominated individual would act as a 'field pastor' to oversee the flock's spiritual needs. These brave field pastors came from many different walks of life, but nonetheless still ran the very considerable risk of capture and death[lxxx]. Their tools of religion were cleverly concealed: the tiny Bible a woman could hide in her

---

[lxxviii] Minet, Susan, *Notes on the War of the Cevennes.* The Huguenot Society 43, Vol XVI issue 3 (1939-40) p292.
[lxxix] Ibid, p292.
[lxxx] Ibid, p291.

The Story of the Huguenots – a Unique Legacy

wig; pulpits that could be disguised as barrels, and the communion cup cleverly masquerading as a candlestick.

This was the beginning of the 'churches of the desert', which met secretly and at extreme personal risk – all worshippers knew that if they were found to be practicing the Huguenot faith there was no mercy and if anyone was found to be a pastor who had perhaps returned to administer to his flock, then (until 1762) the death sentence would be carried out. Despite the considerable risks for both pastors and their flocks these churches of the desert continued undercover until the French Revolution[75].

In 1703, no one who had, or was aiding or protecting the Camisards was shown any mercy, and entire villages were obliterated as the order was given that if just one Catholic solider or priest was killed by Huguenots, then the *entire non-Catholic* community was to pay the price of death or imprisonment. Gibbets were erected across Languedoc, as was the stake, and the smell of flesh either burning or rotting must surely have floated across the air as these ghastly implements were kept fully occupied by those punishing anyone thought to be remotely connected to, or even sympathising with, the Huguenots. With sickening cruelty, the flames of uncompromising barbaric intolerance from an earlier century were visited once again upon this area.

On 1 April, intelligence was given to Marshal Montrevil, commander of the royal troops, that approximately 300 persons had gathered to worship in a mill near to Nismes. He set out immediately with his forces and upon arrival commanded the doors be flung open and the worshippers slaughtered. Because the massacre proceeded too slowly for the marshal, he then ordered the mill to be set alight – those remaining were burnt alive[lxxxi]. Soon after this, Marshal Catinat ordered the burning of some 400 villages in this area.

[lxxxi] Samuel Smiles, *The Huguenots Their Settlements, Churches and Industries in England and Ireland (1889)* (London) pp.235/6.

- 97 -

The Story of the Huguenots – a Unique Legacy

This was the beginning of the end for the Camisards. They fought on bravely, but it was impossible for them to hold out against the might of the royal forces ranged against them

The most well-known leaders of the Camisards were Roland Laporte, who was killed in August 1704, and Jean Cavalier, who negotiated their surrender later that same year. The reports left by Mazel and Marion[76] of the extent and imbalance of atrocities committed – 31 Catholic parishes in the Haute Cévennes being devastated by the Camisards compared to 600 Protestant settlements laid waste by troops led by Montreval – provide enough of an insight into the devastation and suffering wreaked during this time for us to understand the inequality of this terrible struggle[lxxxii].

[lxxxii] Minet, Susan, *Notes on the War of the Cevennes.* The Huguenot Society 43, Vol XVI issue 3 (1939-40) p297.

1. The Flight of the Protestants from France

2. Map of France and its borders in the 16th century

3. (left): Martin Luther

4. (right): John Calvin

5. The tomb of Odet Coligny; Canterbury Cathedral

6. Montauban, south-west France, at one time the second-most important Huguenot stronghold

7. Le Château d'Arques-la-Bataille (renamed in honour of the wars of religion) Arques-la-Bataille, Normandy

8. La Rochelle harbour entrance

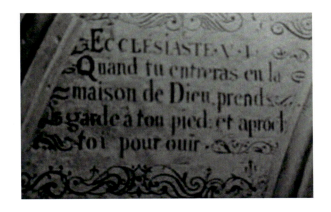

9. The Black Prince's Chantry, the Huguenot Chapel, Canterbury, with verse in French from the Bible

10. The Constance Tower, Aigues Mortes, southwest France

11. Portrait of Guillaume Guion

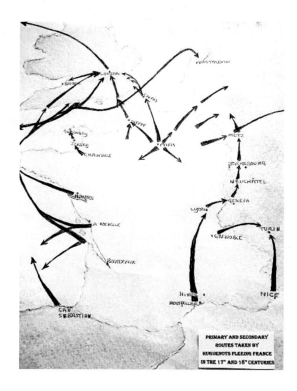

12. Map detailing various routes the Huguenots would have taken when departing France in the 17th and 18th centuries, based on information from various sources

Part Two

The Exodus and the Way Forward

With all hope of acceptance for what they stood for gone within French society, and with their numbers being depleted at an alarming rate, Protestantism in France appeared fragile and had all but expired at the hands of cruel despots actively, in many cases, seeking to enhance their own positions at Court and in government. Then, as in many other countries before and since, it was all too easily possible for a powerful minority of influential careerist intriguers to sway royal opinion, and thereby enable the issuing of orders through which so much subjugation was carried out by men, often little better than mercenaries, who were all too willing to perpetrate the violence and terror that were the essence of actions such as the dragonnades.

It was time to start again for any Huguenot still resisting either forced conversion to Catholicism, or to suffer the agony of pretended conversion whilst worshipping as a Protestant in secret – and at much risk. Weary eyes must have now turned more and more to a land somewhere that would accept them for who they were and what they believed in, and in this faint but dearly held hope, many exhausted Huguenots were to leave their homeland forever, not even their children or grandchildren ever returning, and for this, France as an economic entity was to suffer a serious loss.

- 10 -

Time to Start Again

In the aftermath of the Revocation, approximately 50,000 men, women and children secretly fled their homes to start a new life in England, and a further 10,000 emigrated to Ireland, where their religious beliefs would be tolerated. Yet, the exodus had started even before the religious wars had begun; a significant emigration had begun in 1562 when the number of people – particularly those living in the southern and western areas of France – openly declaring their Protestant faith had peaked, and the high numbers making such declarations continued until a few years after the *Edict of Fontainebleau* of 1685 had revoked the relative freedoms contained in the *Edict of Nantes*.

With the flow of refugees increasing relative to the instigation of increasingly harsh measures in the years before and immediately after the Revocation, it appears that very few Huguenots 'chose' to leave their home country; rather, they felt 'obliged' to flee in order to avoid such treatment. Whilst those leaving did not always seek a new life in countries near to their land of birth, a large proportion did choose to settle in close proximity to France; the Netherlands was attractive due to the rise in Calvinism leading to the establishment of the Dutch Reformed Church in 1571, while England also offered safe haven and asylum, and up to half of the estimated diaspora coming to these shores ultimately settled, predominantly, in what are now the Inner and Greater London areas.

London possessed a staunchly anti-Catholic community and this, coupled with the stories circulating of the terrible outrages perpetrated against the Huguenots, meant these foreigners were in the majority given a warm welcome upon arrival with just a few locals voicing their resentment at these foreign artisans now settling in their districts and being able, through their greater skills, to gain continuous employment. However, some groups of English tradesmen presented petitions to Parliament to seek assistance as their own ability to produce and sell similar items was suffering due to the foreigners.

These Protestant 'foreigners' who sought refuge here – Flemings[77], Walloons[78] and French Huguenots – tended to naturally gravitate to areas where either their friends or members of their family had previously settled, or where their particular trade was already well established. For example, at Mortlake and Fulham in south-west London, they began the manufacture of Arras[79]. Maidstone in Kent saw the Flemings introduce thread and lace-making as early as 1567, and in Devon the now famous Honiton lace owes its origins to a group of Flemish refugees who settled there and began producing lace work of a quality not seen before in England. It was rapidly becoming the case that across the land, Protestants fleeing from persecution in Catholic France settled in, and helped bring prosperity to, the towns they lived and worked in.

Those who sought to leave their homeland by ship's passage would have boarded a wide-ranging size and type of vessels. They came in high summer as well as mid-winter in boats of all sizes; so desperate were they to flee the persecution of their homeland, they surely did not fully consider the risks they had to take on the open seas – rather, they must have felt overwhelming gratitude and relief for having reached a safe haven and would have given thanks to God for having enabled them to reach safety. The local townspeople of these ports did all they could to assist the refugees, taking them into their homes and sustaining them as much as they were able to, but as the years passed and the persecutions in France grew ever harsher, so the numbers of refugees increased to a point where the local people were overwhelmed and had to seek additional assistance from the government.

By this point in time, from all parts of France, Huguenot families were planning their exodus from their homeland to seek a new life. As an example, included in this chapter are four families: two from northern, and two from southern, areas of France, who eventually made their homes in England, and whose descendants still live in this country.

On a moonless night in 1683[80] yet another boat left the northern French port of Dieppe with a cargo of desperate but hopeful Huguenot refugees, bound for the shores of England. The boat was a smallish vessel, and amongst the passengers were Jacques Ouvry, who along with others had fled their home town of Luneray in Normandy to seek a new, unfettered life in England[lxxxiii]. They had felt they had little choice but to leave because they were by then without their place of worship as the order for the destruction of the little temple, Thé de Béze, had been signed on 17 May 1681[lxxxiv].

During the long crossing[81] the Huguenot refugees no doubt consoled themselves that they would be able to make a fresh start in England. Jacques Ouvry was able to set up home in Canterbury for a year before travelling through Kent and then on to Blackfriars in London, finally settling in the established Huguenot community of Spitalfields[lxxxv]. It is recorded that Jacques' house at 29 Fournier Street was insured with the Hand

---

[lxxxiii] The Ouvry Archives.
[lxxxiv] Pierre Lheureux, *Les Protestants de Luneray et leur Église en pays de Caux*, (Luneray, 1937) p22.
[lxxxv] The Ouvry Archives.

The Story of the Huguenots – a Unique Legacy

in Hand insurance company for £300, and that he also owned the house next door. Eventually, his son Jean became the owner of another house in Fournier Street – number 20. Jacques had married for the second time in 1699 to Marie Govis whose family had originated in Lintot, northern France, and they had six children. Jacques died in 1748.

Jean (John) Ouvry, Jacques' son, was admitted as a freeman of the Weavers Company on 28 November 1738. There is evidence that Anna Maria Garthwaite sold three designs to a Mr Ouvry – presumably John Ouvry from the dates of the sales. The designs were for warped patterned silks commonly known as 'tobines'. John was married twice, first to Mary Beauvar, who bore him two daughters – Mary (1732) and Magdalen (1735) – and then a son Peter whose birth in 1741 she survived by only four days. After the death of Mary, John married for the second time – and became the father of seven more children. Peter Ouvry, the eldest son of John Ouvry, was apprenticed to his father in 1755 and inherited the business when his father died in 1774.

The Ouvrys, like many other French Huguenots through the generations remained close to the area where their family and friends also lived and worked. The first to leave the area was Peter Ouvry, who married Francisca Garnault, an heiress whose family lived at Bulls Cross, Enfield[lxxxvi].

Pierre Agombar took the decision to leave his home in Brancourt le Grand, Picardy, a few years after the Revocation, and his name can be found in the 1701 consistory records of the French Church; eventually, he settled in Stepney, east London, where he was married to his first wife, Mary Wishau, in 1699 at St Dunstan's Church. He was a weaver by trade and was admitted to the Worshipful Company of Weavers as a foreign master on 27 May 1723. Following the death of Mary, he was married for the second time at St Dunstan's, on 11 January 1709, his bride

---

[lxxxvi] Museum of London, The, *The Quiet Conquest: The Huguenots, 1685-1985* (London, 1985) p298.

- 103 -

Madeleine Pieron, also a Huguenot, having been born in Amiens. Peter (as he became known) was the father of three sons all of whom were apprenticed as weavers[lxxxvii].

In the south-west of France, the Portal family (mentioned later in Chapters 26 and 28) had lived at the family Chateau de la Portalerie near Bordeaux, but the recent visitations of the dragoons brought them to the decision to leave. They left their home – father, mother and five children – to set off for the family estate in the Cévennes, but they were followed and overtaken by the dragoons, who killed both parents and one child before razing the house they had been sheltering in to the ground. The four remaining children, now orphaned, hid in an oven until the dragoons finally left. Then the three boys and one girl set off on the long and dangerous journey to the coast[lxxxviii].

When they reached Montauban, one of the children, Pierre, fainted with hunger and was taken in by a kindly baker. The other three – Henry, William and Mary – reluctantly left their little brother and pressed on towards the port of Bordeaux. They were given passage on a merchant ship and hidden, as was often the case, in barrels[lxxxix]. They were possibly some of the last children to be safely concealed in barrels on ships before the order to fumigate all holds prior to leaving port was instigated[82].

The final, and very detailed, family story in this chapter comes from the south of France. The town of Montpellier[83] had always been home to 16-year old Guillaume Guion, but increasingly hostile treatment caused young Guillaume to take the decision to flee. The following are extracts of Guillaume's own very detailed account, translated by his descendant David Guyon (Guion),[xc] which gives a wonderfully graphic version of the dangers and

---

[lxxxvii] The Agombar Archives.
[lxxxviii] G. Elmore Reaman, *The Trail of the Huguenots in Europe, the United States, South Africa and Canada* (London, 1964) pp.76-7.
[lxxxix] Ibid pp.76-7.
[xc] The Guion Archives.

The Story of the Huguenots – a Unique Legacy

uncertainties faced at that time by many Protestants seeking to leave their homeland:

My father had recently died, leaving me in the guardianship of my elder brother, Jacques Antoine. Our eldest brother, Jean Guion, had emigrated because of the cruel persecution of the Protestants by Louis XIV; he had entered the service of the King of England, and been disinherited by my father as a result, leaving myself and Jacques as equal beneficiaries of his estate. When Jean learned of our father's death, he wrote to me from London urging me to join him. I had already contemplated escaping, several of my comrades had drawn up a plan to leave France and I had promised to join them. All our family houses and apartments were rented out, apart from one, on the second floor which my brother had kept for the two of us and our many belongings. As my brother was in charge of all the keys, it was impossible for me to take anything without his knowledge.

An opportunity arose when some of our rents needed collecting. Some of our tenancies were close to Nimes, my brother told me he was going there to collect the rents and suggested I collected some of the rent due to us in Montpellier.

As he had hidden all of the keys which locked up our best things, I quickly sent for our locksmith to force the lock, telling him that I had lost the key. This he did, and showed me other hiding places into the bargain, which he also opened. In one cabinet, I had found a silver salver, a bowl, some spoons and some forks, a large and very beautiful emerald surrounded by six diamonds, and a similar ruby. I sold the silver because, luckily for me, the director of the Mint had issued a proclamation that those who possessed old domestic silver could bring it to the mint and receive the value of it in cash. Moreover, the Director knew me; he

The Story of the Huguenots – a Unique Legacy

was a new convert: that was the name given to those who had recently embraced Papism.

I visited a merchant named M. Perier, my neighbour, whose son had told him that I had received a letter from my eldest brother in England. He also knew its contents, and that I had decided to leave France with 6 or 7 other young men that I knew well.

This charitable soul, who had my best interests at heart, took me to one side one day to speak to me privately; he was delighted to hear of my plan and wanted to help me in any way he could. He organised my journey as far as Lyon; I was to travel in the company of a new recruit, sponsored by M. Perier, who was joining his regiment 'La Cornet Blanche'. He also advised me to get together all the money I could and to deposit with him as much as possible from the rents I had collected in Montpellier and from the proceeds of the sale. I succeeded so well, that after deducting enough for my day to day expenses, I handed over 120 Louis d'Or[84] to M. Perier. He advised me to hold on to 10 Louis d'Or to get me as far as Geneva. I then packed myself some clothes from our apartment.

With the arrival of the Recruit, M. Perier sent me word, and I rushed around to each of my associates to tell them to get ready to take advantage of this opportunity; but the only one actually ready to leave was Jacques Carquet, second son of the doctor. His mother told me to bring my things to her house so that she could pack them with his, in a large trunk; this at considerable expense, she sent ahead by carrier to Lyon. We then learned that there was a Sedan chair returning to Nimes with one empty seat; the other was occupied by a Judge. Madam Carquet reserved the empty seat and paid for it herself. We let the recruit go ahead and left ourselves the next morning. We set out happily, as we had been joined by three or four other young men all headed for Lyon on foot.

The Story of the Huguenots – a Unique Legacy

We took it in turns to ride in the Sedan chair and arrived in Nimes that evening. The next day we continued to St. Florin, where we were able to hire two donkeys, so we separated from our recruit and his military companions and made our way to Lyon and collected our trunk from the Customs House.

Being young and inexperienced, we did not feel confident enough to travel unaccompanied to Geneva, so we waited for a favourable opportunity to present itself. Eventually, after a 15-day delay, we left Lyon. We had been advised to travel to Geneva with the carrier, as this would make crossing the border easier. We could not at first find his cart but at the end of the second day, we met the host of the Logis De La Poste at a place called Sardon, who knew of the carrier and we joined up with the carrier in the morning for our journey to Geneva.

That evening we arrived at La Chapelle where we encountered a group of merchants also on their way to Geneva, we made our introductions and joined them in waiting for supper. One of their number got up and came over to talk to me, asking who I was and where I was going. I replied, "To Geneva."

"And who are those?" he asked.

"My comrades," I replied.

"Do you have passports?"

"No," I replied.

"Then how are you going to get past the Fort De L'Ecluse on the border where they check everything in minute detail?"

"With the carrier," I replied. "They assured us that it would be alright at Lyon, and even our groom has undertaken to get us to Geneva without fail."

He shrugged his shoulders, "I'm afraid you have been tricked."

The Story of the Huguenots – a Unique Legacy

After several more exchanges, he told me that we were all in great danger. The landlord of this inn regularly betrays travellers who want to escape from France illegally, so he can claim the reward offered by the King and rob the poor fugitives of everything they have on them and in their 'baggage'.

Having left me to re-join his party and spoke to them, they all rose to the occasion being concerned by our plight; the first thing to ensure was that we were safe from the landlord, then it was decided that when we got to the Fort De L'Ecluse, where they check people who are travelling with the carrier two by two, that each of my companions would team up with a merchant so when the officer examined the merchant's passport, he might not ask for ours. In any event we were to say that we were apprentice merchants and travelling at the request of our masters.

The next morning, we all left together and picked our way down the steep descent; at the bottom, there was a very deep ravine with a bridge across it. We climbed the Credeau, the hill on which the Fort De L'Ecluse is situated. Before we got there my new friend took me to one side, and told me that he had just done a deal with the carrier's valet: it was agreed that if I was questioned by the governor of the fort, I was to say that I was his master's nephew and that he was taking me to Geneva. Having toiled up the hill, we finally arrived outside the castle walls and hailed the guard then waited as the drawbridge was lowered for two horsemen at a time to go in. My protector asked two merchants ahead of us to go first; he and I would follow. The two merchants ahead of us were sent on their way, the drawbridge was lowered once more, and we went in. The Major asked him where he was going and if he had a passport; my friend replied that he was going to Geneva

- 108 -

and handed over his passport. The Major examined it and handed it back. He then turned to me and asked for mine.

"I don't have one," I replied.

"What!" he said, "you come here without a passport. Where are you going?"

"To Geneva," I told him. "I'm going there on my Master's business."

"Who is your Master?"

"M. Longueville," I answered (he was the merchant in Lyon recommended by M. Perier).

The Major continued by asking, "Do you have a letter of authority from your Master?"

"No," I said.

"Have you any accounts?"

"No," I replied.

"How is it that you call yourself a merchant, but you present yourself here without a passport, without a letter of authority, nor any other form of identification; nobody is allowed past here without proper identification," he retorted angrily.

I replied, "If you don't let me through, then I'll have to return to my Master in Lyon."

The carrier's valet stepped forward and told the Major that I was the nephew of his master and due to receive my orders in Geneva. The Major then allowed me through. My protector and I went down to the banks of the Rhone, to await the rest of the party to take the ferry across to Savoy.

We had hardly dismounted when we saw coming, instead of our friends, the Major escorted by a sergeant and six musketeers; he called out to me:

"In the name of the King, you are under arrest; follow me back to the fort."

I had hardly dismounted when he ordered the sergeant to search me. He found two letters from Madame Carquet; he

The Story of the Huguenots – a Unique Legacy

also found in my wallet, my beautiful emerald and the ruby, which he handed over to the Major, who examined it carefully:

"This is a beautiful emerald!"

"I am at your service," I replied. He returned my jewels and gave orders to the sergeant. The sergeant took me to a small dungeon with a low vaulted ceiling cut into the rock; dripping water had turned the straw mattress into a dung heap, smelly, damp, and compacted with age. The old woollen coverlet was worn and torn. Above, there was a tiny window through which rats scurried all night long, running all over me, I covered my head and face, and continually moved my legs.

The next morning, the door of my cell opened, the sergeant came in and ordered me to follow him. He led me to a room where the Governor questioned me at length. Eventually he said that I was a guide, and the letters from Madam Carquet proved it. After two more days of solitary confinement, the Major advised me to go straight home to Montpellier and assured me that if I was arrested a second time, I would be condemned to serve in the galleys. I thanked him most humbly and promised to do as he asked. At that, he replied that I was free, and so were my companions. I went out onto the daylight and found my two friends waiting for me on the parade ground. At last we left the fort to retrace our steps. As the news spread as far as Lyon of the three young men arrested at the Fort De L'Ecluse, everyone we met along our route stopped us and asked if we were they. We confirmed we were and that we would be going back in a few days' time with good passports; so we arrived back in Lyon full of good spirits... [xci]

[xci] The Guion Archives.

The next attempt to escape France was successful as the young men met and travelled with a Genevan master jeweller. A further extract from the detailed notes written by Guillaume describes the final stage of the journey across the border – this time they had to wade across the river at its narrowest point to avoid the official frontier:

...Our route followed the twists and turns of the river and from a viewpoint we could clearly see the Fort De L'Ecluse on the other bank. The only thing separating me from it was the river, which at this point was quite narrow, and could be jumped by a man. When we were level with the fort, my nerve failed me, and I was paralysed with fear. I turned my face away towards the bluff on our side so that nobody in the garrison would recognise me. Once that awful place was out of sight, I told M. Heime how frightened I was. He began to laugh and made fun of me saying: "We are now in Savoy, where the French have absolutely no power."

We finally arrived at the village of Waches and a place of safety at last. After supper, I asked our host to hire us horses for the journey to Geneva. The following morning, the landlord was there to see us off:

"Better to go around by the mill to avoid the guard post," he told the groom. At that I pricked up my ears: "What was that about a guard post? Last night you assured me that there were no more check points."

"Don't worry, they are there simply to collect tolls on the main road," he reassured me. We mounted, and our groom walked ahead, along the banks of the Rhone. When we were near the mill, the guard appeared in the road; our groom stopped me and asked to get up behind. The guards approached with their arms at the ready; he told me to gallop through them, which we did, as the soldiers shouted at us to stop. We kept going, and they ran after us, but we were faster, and they were soon lost to view. Soon after, the

groom asked me to stop so that he could dismount and go ahead on foot once more. Sometime later, we could make out the spires of Geneva in the distance and M. Heime cried out:

"M. Guion, look at our beautiful steeples!"

"I am very pleased to see them, and I do hope we don't come across any more guards," I replied.

"There's only one," he said, teasing me. That made me shudder with fear: so much so, that our groom touched my arm to reassure me that it wasn't a check point, only a toll booth for the bridge; the Duke of Savoy had built a bridge over the river Arve and we had to cross it to get into the town. Finally, we had arrived [xcii].

Although at last safe from Catholic persecution, all four of these families, like many others, had been forced to leave other family members behind in France.

[xcii] The Guion Archives.

- 11 -

Protestant England's Welcome

In England itself, serious questioning of the Catholic Church and its teachings had already begun long before Henry VIII's break with Rome, and as each century unfolded so the voices raised in doubt became louder and spread out to a wider world.

Since the latter part of the reign of Henry VIII, Protestants had arrived on English shores and indeed during the reign of his son Edward VI they were encouraged by the monarchy to leave their homeland and seek asylum here, free from religious persecution. As the numbers of these Huguenot refugees were small at first, they would meet in small groups in one of their own homes for worship. Eventually, as their numbers grew, they requested the king's consent to set up their own churches.

Edward VI was the first sovereign to be both crowned king and Supreme Head of the Church of England. He was a devout Protestant like his uncle, Edward, 1st Duke of Somerset, and Thomas Cranmer, Archbishop of Canterbury, both of whom felt a strong empathy with Calvin's teachings. Four years before Edward's reign was cut short by his early death at the age of 15 years and nine months, the Act of Uniformity was passed on 15 January 1549, which abolished the Catholic Mass in England and coincided with the publication of Cranmer's beautiful *Book of Common Prayer*.

Edward's death, however, resulted in the accession of his staunchly Catholic, half-sister Mary, and this now caused many Protestants to flee England rather than be forced to abjure their faith. Bishop Edmund Bonner, newly restored as Bishop of London by Queen Mary, having been released from Marshalsea Prison[xciii], had spoken out against the royal autonomy being exercised over the Church during Edward VI's reign – hence the loss of his bishopric – but now the price demanded of him for his restoration was nothing less than whole-hearted persecution of the Protestants in England. He was chastised by Mary's Privy Council for his apparent reluctance to increase the pace and intensity of the weeding out of Protestants in London; however, eventually bowing to the considerable pressure placed upon him, he began to take a harsher stance towards non-Catholics, resulting in his overseeing of the burning of those who would not recant their beliefs.

Fortunately for Protestantism in England, Mary's reign was a brief one, and following her death in 1558, Henry's younger daughter was crowned Queen Elizabeth I; like her late half-brother Edward, she had been raised in the Protestant faith, and consequently many of those who had fled abroad during Mary's reign, including Sir Francis Walsingham, now returned. At the time of Elizabeth's accession, although the Protestant faith was again increasing the size of its flock, Protestantism was still in a minority in the country as a whole, and furthermore, Elizabeth had made dangerous enemies of both France and Spain when she offered free asylum to French Huguenots in England.

Bonner, who had worked so fanatically to eradicate Protestantism, was to lose his bishopric for the last time during the reign of Elizabeth when he rejected her claimed right of supremacy over the Church of England, and was sent to

---

[xciii] John Stowe, *A Survey of London: written in the year 1598* (Stroud, reprinted 1997) p433.

Marshalsea Prison, where he died on 5 September 1569[xciv]. In east London, a road and one of the gated entrances to Victoria Park on the borders of Bethnal Green and Hackney is named for him as the park was partially created from land once owned by the bishop.

The St Bartholomew's Day Massacre of 1572 had naturally had a profound effect on the sympathies of the English people towards French Protestants; news of this monstrous mob violence ensured a compassionate welcome to those who had somehow escaped such atrocities to search for a new life and the simple right to freedom of worship. The Protestant Church in England felt immense sympathy for their fellow Protestants in France; to demonstrate that they stood shoulder to shoulder with their French comrades, and by 1590 special prayers had been composed in addition to the *Book of Common Prayer*. One of these new prayers touchingly reads:

> *We thy humble servants, most heartily beseech thee through the merits of Jesus Christ, our Saviour, to protect and strengthen thy Servants our brethren in France, that are now ready to fight for the glory of thy name.*

And, indeed, it *had* come to a fight. Protestants in England were having to prepare the defence of their beliefs and to withstand the onslaught of Catholic aggression from Europe. For a moment, it seemed as though England might succumb: Philip II of Spain had decided to take action against heretical England not only following the execution of the Catholic Mary Queen of Scots in 1587, but also because many of his subjects from the Spanish Netherlands[85] had also sought refuge on England's shores. In 1588 came the mighty armada of 130 fully equipped ships that in addition carried large numbers of priests ready to convert heretics as soon as they landed, but it was

---

[xciv] John Stowe, *A Survey of London: written in the year 1598* (Stroud, reprinted 1997) p433.

never to be – appalling weather at exactly the wrong time for Phillip came to Protestant England's aid, scattering the fleet on which he and many Catholics must have pinned their fervent hopes.

Persecution of the Protestant peoples of the Catholic kingdoms of Spain and France had left these beleaguered inhabitants with little choice than to secretly depart from their homeland, leaving most, perhaps all, of their possessions behind, and they were mercilessly harried in Flanders and throughout France right up to the borders, and wherever possible were prevented from making good their escape. The French king went as far as issuing a formal ultimatum to Elizabeth demanding that his fugitive subjects should be banished from England and returned to France; when this was ignored, the Pope was asked to intervene, which he did by denouncing the refugees as 'drunkards' – but this time they were ably defended by the Bishop of Salisbury, John Jewell, as being fine, upstanding, hard-working characters who had been forced to leave all their goods and possessions behind not for base reasons but for the cherished freedom to practice their religion. Tellingly, Jewell went further and questioned the Pope's judgement in sheltering so many unsavoury characters such as 6,000 usurers and 20,000 courtesans within the walls of the Vatican[xcv].

Interestingly – and understandably, considering the draconian measures applied on an almost daily basis towards French Protestants on the direct orders of the French monarchy – Calvinists began to revile the concept of Republicanism. John Calvin, however, regardless of the democratic element of his *Ecclesiastical Ordinances,* was not averse to the monarchic system per se, and mindful of the support given to French Protestants by the monarchy in England, he wrote to Elizabeth to reassure her that he was a supporter of the monarchical principle, and he also

---

[xcv] Samuel Smiles, *The Huguenots Their Settlements, Churches and Industries in England and Ireland (1889)* (London) p75.

forbade the distribution in Geneva of John Knox's theories regarding republicanism[xcvi].

Elizabeth's Secretary of State, William Cecil – a steadfast Protestant – had continually encouraged European Protestants to settle here given their reputation for hard work and sobriety. Accordingly, the main criteria for acceptance in England was to be of the Protestant faith[86] as well as being accomplished in various trades that would benefit the English economy, particularly if those skills could subsequently be taught to the local population. To avoid antagonising the indigenous population, small groups of refugees were settled in many different areas of the country, thus diluting the impact on locals as much as possible – a methodology of 'dispersal' that has resonance in modern times too.

As the only way refugees could arrive from Europe was by boat, landing at the nearest coastal towns from where they had embarked in France and elsewhere, it was inevitably the southern and to a lesser extent the eastern shores of England which saw many initially trying to settle in or near to these ports. Boats carrying Flemings often docked at Deal, Harwich, Great Yarmouth and Dover. This last port was also a favourite of French Huguenots. Over a period of time, there were four distinct arrivals of refugees into this port. During Elizabeth I's reign, there was an influx of Dutch; the second wave were French refugees during the reign of James I; the third were Walloons, who founded their Church in 1646, and lastly, the fourth and largest group seeking asylum were a further influx of French Huguenots in the years leading up to and for a few years after the Revocation of 1685[87].

It should be noted that until early in 1558, Calais was in fact part of England; thus, it would have been far easier once you had gained entry to Calais to simply take ship for England itself. Henry VII of England, mindful of security, had earlier proclaimed a

---

[xcvi] Desert, Dennis, *The Stranger Communities and the Established Church*. The Huguenot Society, Vol XXVII (2003) p2.

foreigner could not take up an office in Calais unless they could show they had 'continued in English for three descents'[xcvii].

As mentioned previously, in 1562, the Protestants of Calais were alleged to have planned a betrayal of Calais[88] to England; failure had resulted in swift retribution and their expulsion from the town although some succeeded in avoiding detection and thus remained. As this attempt occurred during the seemingly relentless religious wars in France, no doubt many chose to embark for Dover[xcviii] and some settlements such as Southampton thrived. Sandwich, as did Rye, who took in large numbers of both Walloons and Huguenots until the town was overwhelmed with the arrivals[89].

At that time Canterbury had countless vacant properties as the fortunes of the city had declined since the destruction of Thomas à Becket's tomb and the consequent loss of revenue from pilgrims. These early Walloon and Huguenot refugees retained contact with their homelands, even travelling back and forth for business purposes. After all, many of these early refugees had held onto the hope that they would one day be allowed to return to their homeland to live and worship freely, and in so doing take with them full details of their forebears – but these hopes were cruelly dashed by the Revocation in 1685.

Although the most important condition for being accepted into the country was to be of the Protestant faith, the Privy Council felt that these newcomers should be relocated a little inland in the interests of national security. Thus, Canterbury was selected as an admirable place for them to settle although this too had the usual caveat: that the newcomers being relocated were to already be of a certain standing in society, such as fine cloth weavers.

During Elizabeth I's reign, over 100 Huguenot families were noted as arriving and settling in Canterbury, but following the

---

[xcvii] Overend, G.H., FSA, *Strangers at Dover 1 1558-1644.* The Huguenot Society Proceedings, Vol XI (1889) pp.93-4.
[xcviii] Ibid, p97.

Revocation, larger groups were recorded arriving in Canterbury, some for just a short period of time, but others such as the Lefevres [90] choosing to make it their permanent home. At one point over 2,000 looms were in production in the city, operated by Huguenot silk weavers, giving an immense boost to the local economy. These 'strangers', as they were styled, were from 1575 allowed to use the Chapel of St Alphege for their worship[xcix] yet, within a year, so successful had the settlement of Huguenots become that the congregation had already outgrown this little church, and they were granted permission to use the western crypt of Canterbury Cathedral itself.

With the eventual demise of large scale weaving in Canterbury the inevitable closure of the last weaving shop came in 1837 or thereabouts[c]. There is one last 'thread' to the history of weaving in Canterbury though, which occurred around 1897 when Miss C F Phillpotts and Miss K Holmes established a weaving school on the second floor of 39 High Street, where women and girls from the poorer classes were offered a place to gain skills necessary for employment and, who knows, among these 'students' there may well have been some of Huguenot descent. The venture proved such a success that the school moved in 1899 to the building next to the King's Bridge. Today, the school is no longer in existence, but the name of the building ensures the memory of it lingers on – *The Weavers*.

Large numbers of the earlier Walloon and later Huguenot refugees were weavers, but with one important difference: the Walloons were primarily weavers of fine woollen cloth known as worsted, whereas the Huguenots were highly skilled silk weavers; in fact, they were so accomplished they were responsible for providing these shores with some of the finest silk weavers ever to bless this country. Post-Revocation, the refugees arriving could no

---

[xcix] John Boyle, *Portrait of Canterbury* (London, 1974) p100.
[c] A. J. Garnier, Revd., *The Crypt of Canterbury – the French Huguenot Church* (Canterbury, 1965.) p10.

longer anticipate a return to their homeland and these later arrivals did not therefore stay long in Canterbury.

As these strangers lived separately to the rest of the community in Canterbury, inevitably disagreements amongst themselves erupted over time – some disputes were related to trade while others were connected to the practice of their religion. Gradually, the hostility generated by these quarrels led to many leaving Canterbury to travel to perhaps the greater prospects offered by London, and so it came to be that a very sizable population of refugees chose to settle there to live and work[ci].

[ci] Michael H Peters, *Eglise Protestant Français de Cantorbery* (Mickle Print) p6.

- 12 -

Assimilation, Integration and Discord during the Tudor and Stuart Eras

As the capital city of England, and for the bustling commercial port that it was, London must have been a place of immense contrasts to migratory waves of foreign settlers, as indeed it would have been to indigenous arrivals from other parts of the kingdom. Those seeking a new life in England had been grateful to empathisers of their situation, one such friend having been Sir Francis Walsingham, Secretary to Her Majesty Queen Elizabeth, who passed away on 6 April 1590 at his London home in Seething Lane – to the immense grief of the Huguenot strangers to whom he had always been such a firm and steadfast friend[cii]. He had been a staunch Protestant himself and his great understanding and sympathy towards his fellow Protestants had arguably contributed to royal policy that was so conducive to encouraging influxes of all these people escaping persecution.

But not all the indigenous population welcomed the strangers, and trading restrictions were eventually placed upon them; for example, they were not permitted to keep 'open shop' but to work

---

[cii] *The Dutch Church* Registers, Austin Friars, London 1571-1874. pxxvi.

The Story of the Huguenots – a Unique Legacy

behind shuttered windows to prevent the public gazing upon their wares[ciii].

Yet London must have seemed almost overwhelming in its sheer scale, its unrelenting pace of noisy commercial activity and its already overcrowded streets and dwellings, all of which would have surely impacted on the refugees: far from all Huguenots had been town dwellers; in fact, more often than not they had been born and raised in rural villages and hamlets[91], and so for those who chose to travel inland and make their home in London, this was yet another challenge to be faced and overcome.

With close living and unsanitary conditions common at that time, the constant threat of disease was certainly no respecter of religion, and in 1593 plague yet again paid a visit to the land. London records provide us with a figure of at least 1,700 fatalities in just one week. As is often the case, a reason for such an ill omen had to be established, and, of course, vengeance taken. Accordingly, on 1 May, citizens attacked the homes of Huguenot strangers, and the following verses were fastened to the walls of Austin Friars:

> *You strangers that inhabit in this land!*
> *Note this same writing, do it understand;*
> *Conceive it well, for safety of your lives,*
> *Your goods, your children and your dearest wives*

By order of the Privy Council, the Lord Mayor and Aldermen issued orders for special constables to be sworn in from among merchants and tradesmen to restore order, and by the end of the disturbances a number of apprentices and tradesmen had been convicted of rioting, and were punished by being placed in the stocks, and whipped[civ].

[ciii] Scouloudi, Irene, (ed.), *Huguenots in Britain and their French Background 1500-1800* (London 1987) p49.
[civ] *The Dutch Church Registers, Austin Friars, London* 1571-1874. pxxvi.

- 122 -

Towards the end of the reign of Queen Elizabeth 1, the population of the City of London and its contemporaneous suburbs[92], together with Westminster, Lambeth and Stepney, was estimated to be 250,000 [see table 1]. During the course of the next century, that figure would grow rapidly to approximately 600,000[cv]. London's population was now ten times the size of any other town or city in England; it was constantly being rejuvenated with new blood, attracting many people from other towns, cities and hamlets throughout the land as well as from overseas, particularly France. Like a magnet it drew those wishing to make or increase their fortunes: from the wealthy to the poorer, but aspiring, classes; from those seeking apprenticeships to commercially ambitious merchants. These new arrivals helped maintain and grow the capital's population despite the high death rate in that era, due to recurring outbreaks of plague and other contagions – these mass, indiscriminate killers were all too frequently stalking the streets.

London was still a recognisably medieval city, and was to remain so until the Great Fire of 1666[cvi] swept away much of its medieval structure including famous landmarks such as old St. Paul's. London had been primarily built from wood and as the population grew, its housing became ever more closely packed. After the Great Fire, stringent building regulations belatedly became law, but at least now the city was to be rebuilt in non-combustible materials such as stone and bricks[93]. Consequently, however, many sought to move outside of the city as both accommodation and business premises were becoming less costly to build and maintain beyond the city walls as, significantly, the new building criteria did not extend there.

In 1593, an Act of Parliament had made it illegal to enclose common or waste land within three miles of the City. During the

---

[cv] Plummer, Alfred, *The London Weavers Company1600-1700*, (London, 2015) p3.
[cvi] Ibid, p3.

years 1605-15, the City Corporation, with the king's blessing, commenced laying paths and trees in the area known as Moorfields for the enjoyment of London's citizens. Many French Protestants arriving there would have experienced these public open spaces. A great number of weavers are recorded in the Weavers Company records as living and working in the liberties and suburbs of London, such as Norton Folgate, Bishopsgate, Shoreditch, Aldgate, Southwark and Whitechapel[cvii].

In both the Elizabethan and Jacobean eras, London was a noisy, almost haphazard, jumble of buildings ranging from great palaces to the meanest hovel, and virtually side by side with these dwellings were many diverse business premises, public buildings, churches and, remarkably, many gardens with their great variety of flora and fauna. It seemed as if every inch of the City of London had by now been put to some type of use in one way or another. Thus, to any newcomer it must have appeared overcrowded, odorous and chaotic. Indeed, Dr William Harvey,[94] a resident of London during the reign of James I, commented on the *'filth and offal scattered about and the sulphurous coal smoke whereby the air is at all times rendered heavy, but more so in the autumn'*[cviii].

Much of the area outside of the City of London was festooned with a wide variety of uncoordinated structures: houses, cottages, sheds and workshops – slowly the march of development was stretching out towards the nearest villages: to the north-east, Bethnal Green and Shoreditch; to the east, Mile End, and to the south, Bermondsey and Lambeth. The traveller, as he journeyed towards the great city itself, would pass through a labyrinth of yards, courts, alleys and lanes, most of which were unpaved. Often, and only loosely joined up by these narrow passages, the buildings themselves would contain many nefarious characters.

[cvii] Plummer, Alfred, *The London Weavers Company1600-1700*, (London, 2015) p7.
[cviii] Ibid. p3.

The Story of the Huguenots – a Unique Legacy

However, not all of what were fast becoming the 'suburbs' of London contained criminal elements; for example, Southwark was mainly home to 'upstanding' citizens, who were often master craftsmen: weavers, felt makers, tanners, carpenters, coppersmiths – to name but a few, with usually each family living above their business premises[cix].

Those Huguenots who had escaped from the land they had called 'home' during the time of Richelieu's chancellorship found a warm welcome in England, given not just by Elizabeth I but also James I and later his son Charles I. James had given this pledge as assurance to the French Church in London on 21 May 1603: *'If anyone should dare to molest you, and you address yourselves to me, I will give you justice[cx].'*

* * * * * *

Early in the 1600s, James I, conscious of the importance of mulberry trees in silk production, and keen to aid the refugee silk weavers and the associated artisans, wrote letters to all his lord lieutenants suggesting they might like to buy and plant mulberry saplings – *'at the rate of three farthings[95] a plant, or at six shillings the hundred'* – as a nationalistic gesture. He suggested that the less well-off might like to purchase a packet of mulberry seeds. A four-acre mulberry plantation was created in the gardens of Buckingham Palace on the orders of James I and his queen, Anne of Denmark, who, following her husband's enthusiastic lead, founded her own mulberry plantations at Greenwich Palace and at the royal palace at Oatlands in Weybridge, Surrey. James I's enthusiasm for the project led to the importation of approximately 100,000 mulberry saplings.

[cix] Plummer, Alfred, *The London Weavers Company 1600-1700*, (London, 2015) p4.
[cx] Gwynn, Grace L., MA, *The Huguenot Settlements in London, Special Number of Le Lien (Eglise Protestante Française de Londres) p2.*

But enthusiasm overtook caution as the saplings planted were all black mulberries (*morus niga*) grown mainly for their fruit, not their leaves – it is the leaves of the white mulberry (*morus alba*) that are the essential food for silk worms, a valuable lesson that had previously been learnt by both the French and the Italians; in fact, Henri IV of France ordered the planting of white mulberries in the gardens of the Tuileries in Paris specifically to aid silk production. In 1609, William Stallenge's book *Instructions for the Increasing of Mulberry Trees* clearly stated that both black and white mulberry leaves can be given as food to silk worms but that the black varieties tend to result in a coarser, weaker silk thread.

Efforts to produce home-grown silk were to continue into the reign of Charles II, but the failure of this project was really due to the British climate – whereas black mulberries will tolerate a colder, wetter climate, white mulberries require a much warmer one. And as the country was experiencing a mini ice-age in this period, the chances of white mulberries flourishing were very slim indeed. Today, there are more than 100 sites in and around London that are still home to Mulberry trees planted in the early 17th century; some sites are home to several trees while others nurture just one. A few of the sights are famous, such as the Tower of London, the Middle Temple and Syon Park, whilst there are lesser-known but nonetheless remarkable sites in Bethnal Green and Spitalfields.

* * * * * *

Richelieu had helped conclude the marriage negotiations between Louis XIII's sister Henrietta Maria and the Prince of Wales – the future Charles 1 of England – which took place in June 1625. This was, for France, an important political marriage designed to prevent a similar union with France's current enemy Spain. The devots[96] were in favour of this marriage as they hoped it would encourage a more lenient attitude by the English government towards their Catholic brethren in Protestant England, but it would eventually lead to refugee misgivings and fear during the reign of Charles I.

Richelieu had been pleased with James I's private undertaking that he would not enforce laws against Catholics; nor would Catholics be prevented from celebrating Mass in the privacy of their own homes. There was a significant clause in the marriage contract confirming that Henrietta Maria would remain a Catholic, that she would be allowed her own chapel and priests to officiate at all religious services, and that any children of the marriage would be raised in the Catholic faith until they reached the age of 12. The Queen's faith, however, did not make her popular amongst her English subjects, who, Catholic or Puritan, came to despise the king's own high Anglican faith[cxi].

Charles I was not universally a popular king, and neither was his inept favourite Buckingham. In 1626, Charles refused Parliament's request for Buckingham's impeachment in exchange for their approval of allocating much needed funds to pay for war against Spain. Instead, Charles, following discussions with his Council, demanded that forced loans be paid, with the careful but nonetheless veiled threat that Parliament might not be called again if the loan was not forthcoming. Mindful of his subject's wariness of Catholicism, Charles sent his wife's Catholic attendants back to France much to the anger of her father Louis XIII, who was at that time preparing to attack the Huguenot fortress of La Rochelle.

The citizens of La Rochelle sent an urgent appeal for aid from England, and Charles, wary of keeping a balanced view as head of the Anglican Church, duly responded – with disastrous results.

* * * * * *

[cxi] Victor L. Tapié, *France de Louis XIII Et de Richelieu* translated by D Mc N Lockie (Cambridge, 1984) p147.

In 1642, the English Civil War had pitted Royalists against Roundheads, and saw the Puritans (Roundheads) triumph over the Royalists (Catholics) by the end of the war in 1646.

Oliver Cromwell became head of the Commonwealth, and Protector of England just four years after the abolition of the monarchy following the execution of Charles I on 30 January 1649. He did not try to force any changes on the Huguenots, allowing them to continue as before. Earlier in his career he had promoted religious freedom, but during the first year of his Protectorate he instigated penal laws against Catholics in England, Scotland and Ireland, including confiscating large tracts of land owned by Catholics.

With the demise of the Commonwealth, an invitation was issued in 1660 to Charles, eldest son of the executed Charles I, to reclaim the throne, and it was Charles II who sought England's return to prominence in European commerce by encouraging certain foreign skilled artisans, such as silk weavers, to set up their trades and settle in England. It had been noted that previous settlers from France had made a substantial contribution to the English economy, so it was hoped this success could be repeated. This was the period just after both the Great Plague and then the Great Fire of London, and thus the king was keenly supported by the Committee of Trade, which felt the industrious Huguenots would play a significant role in rebuilding the City of London as well as increasing industry and trade.

In the 17th century, a weaver would be expected to work, on average, a 12 to 14-hour day in order to provide for himself and his family. He would often produce an extensive variety of products in wool, linen and, of course, silk. The general term 'wool' covered a wide-range of items, such as rug-making, felt production – often used for hats (although felt is not actually woven) – and fustian, a cheap cloth that could be plain-dyed, corded, striped, chequered and tufted, which would be hard wearing, serviceable and usually favoured for everyday wear by those employed in workshops or warehouses. 'Linen' weavers were producing towelling and ticking, which is a much closer weave, for feather pillows.

Both these trades would gradually be eclipsed by the increased demand for silk. The silk weavers often specialised in certain products known as narrow weaving: ribbons, girdles, garterings, braids, cords and laces, while others specialised in broad weaving producing top quality material for dresses, waistcoats and other garments. Even those broad weavers can be sub-divided into categories, such was the level of specialisation: some would be employed to produce the black, heavy-dyed silk known as 'London Silk', and others to weave light, delicate fabrics such as cobweb lawns, taffetas and pure-silk damask[cxii].

Before 1579, the Sumptuary Laws[97] had forbidden any man below the degree of a knight's eldest son to wear a velvet jerkin, doublet or hose, or to use satin, damask, taffeta or grosgrain for cloaks, coats, gowns or other 'uppermost' garments. Furthermore, women below the rank of a knight's wife were forbidden to wear velvet, silk embroidery or 'nethersocks of silk'[98]. But times and circumstances were changing, and these laws were moderated after 1580 due to the increasing affluence of the minor gentry and major merchants. As time passed, humble persons began to imitate their class-superiors, which further gave rise to an increased demand for the finer materials. The desire to own silk items that were not necessarily pure silk was increasing – there were various degrees of silk materials, such as half silks and slight silks (silk yarn was used as the 'warp' thread, with either cotton, linen or worsted used as the 'weft' thread). The fabric produced would be more affordable to the 'middling' classes as it was not pure silk and proved very popular with which to make garments such as men's waistcoats, women's petticoats, and many items of children's

---

[cxii] Plummer, Alfred, *The London Weavers Company1600-1700*, (London, 2015) p9.

clothing as well as a wide range of soft furnishings for the home[cxiii].

Weaving was such an important trade that the Weavers Company set out proper manufacturing procedures for silk weaving. The following is a description taken from the Company's records:

A Merchant silk-man may deliver silk (yarn) or other stuff unto any Master Weaver that is a freeman, or other which is admitted a Master by the Bailiffs, Wardens and assistants of the Weavers Company. And the silk or other stuff ought to be delivered by weight, and being wrought or fashioned, the owner may receive the same again by weight, and pay the weaver for the workmanship or fashioning thereof, either by the pound or by the dozen, as both parties can agree, allowing sufficient waste upon every pound.[cxiv]

Alternatively, the merchant or silk-man might sell the raw material to the weaver at a certain price and buy back the woven fabric at a price high enough to recompense the weaver for his work.

French fashion was a greatly desired commodity in England, which prior to the Revocation had been extensively imported from France. Once the French Protestants arrived in this country though, they lost no time in setting up their workshops and manufacturing the items they had once produced in France. Thus, the money formerly paid out on imports from France was now expended on home-grown French fashion. It was noted that: '*The English have now so great an esteem for the workmanship of the French refugees, that hardly anything vends without a Gallic name.*'

[cxiii] Plummer, Alfred, The London Weavers Company1600-1700, (London, 2015) p10.
[cxiv] Ibid, pp.10-11.

The Story of the Huguenots – a Unique Legacy

There had been a wide variety of manufactured fashion items that had once been made in France and sold to England. One example of these were buttons, and in 1698 a Sumptuary Law was passed stipulating exhaustive regulations relating to the manufacture of these items[cxv].

William of Orange's fondness for Huguenots caused a dip in their popularity, however, as many of his subjects – the broad, indigenous population – felt the Huguenots were being favoured over them. Daniel Defoe wrote: *'We blame the King, that he relies too much on strangers, Germans, Huguenots and Dutch'*.

Indeed, when a bill for the naturalization of aliens was suggested in 1694, an unhappy member of the House of Commons, John Knight from Bristol, stated: *'Let us first kick the Bill out of the House, then the foreigners out of the kingdom[cxvi].'*

Perhaps some of the Huguenots who had settled in Bristol had offended him. Yet there were many more individuals in the country who did welcome the strangers, and who admired their expertise in the various skilled trades they excelled in to the advantage not only of themselves but of their adopted nation too.

One of those trades was calico printing[99], which the Huguenots[cxvii] carried out from premises near Richmond, south-west London, with another factory being opened initially in Bromley, now part of south-east London, before production was later moved to Lancashire. For a time, the embargo on the importation of printed goods from India was to the Huguenots' favour, but during the reign of Queen Anne a tax was imposed on

---

[cxv] William Cunningham, *The Growth of English Industry and Commerce in Modern Times.* (New York, 1968) p515.
[cxvi] M. Glozier (Ed.) and D. Onnekink (Ed), *War, Religion and Service: Huguenot Soldiering 1685-1713* (Abingdon, 2007) p67
[cxvii] William Cunningham, *The Growth of English Industry and Commerce in Modern Times.* (New York, 1968) p517.

domestically-printed goods, thus making the importation of printed material from overseas far more attractive.

The weaving industry had frowned upon the increased demand for printed calico materials, seeing this as a serious competitive threat that was detrimental to their own trade. Of all the vehement assaults on the wearers of calico, Daniel Defoe left an account of one such attack in Colchester, Essex: *'The rioters appear to have mobbed and insulted the women who wore these fabrics even throwing aqua fortis over their clothes and into their carriages.'*

But it was no wonder as the cost of calico was approximately one eighth of the cost of similarly made woollen garments. In 1720, Parliament, sympathetic to the weavers' plight, passed an Act banning the use of calicos, printed or plain[cxviii].

By 1711, London – always a city of contrasts – had rapidly developed into a great port through which goods and materials flowed into and out of much of the rest of the country. And now there were luxury items made by the highly skilled silk weavers from France, living in their newly-built homes in Soho and Spitalfields.

With many of these skilled trades formerly plied in France now being undertaken in London and elsewhere, the result was not only one of strengthening the English economy, but was furthermore one of amalgamating these talented people into English society, such that they were almost imperceptibly transforming from French to English citizens – even to the point of participating in the process of voting, and thus beginning to influence the composition of the House of Commons.

Many voted for the Whigs[100], believers in toleration, in order to help retain the freedom to continue practicing their Calvinist form of Protestant worship[cxix].

[cxviii] William Cunningham, *The Growth of English Industry and Commerce in Modern Times.* (New York, 1968) p517.
[cxix] G. M. Trevelyan, *English Social History: A survey of six centuries – Chaucer to Queen Victoria* (Cambridge, 1973) p332.

The Story of the Huguenots – a Unique Legacy

Although the Archbishop of Canterbury and the Bishop of London were assigned to look after them, this proved to be a mixed blessing as pressure was brought to bear on the foreign churches in both England and Scotland to conform to the Anglican Church; many Protestant refugees, however, quite naturally wished to retain their own simple Calvinist form of worship.

- 13 -

England's Huguenot Churches

In 1550 the French Protestant Church was established by Edward VI when he issued a royal charter to set up a foreign Protestant church in London, otherwise known as the Temple of Jesus at Austin Friars[101]. Johannes á Lasco, a well-respected Protestant Polish refugee and reformer, was the first to be chosen for the position of superintendent of this strangers' church, now a site of worship for Italian, French and Dutch refugees. The Archbishop of Canterbury, Thomas Cranmer, busily reorganising the Church in the Reformed faith, applauded the continental reformers' aid of his mission. He even wrote his own invitations to Johannes á Lasco and to Martin Bucer, the passionate invitation to the latter stating: *'Those who are unable amid the raging storm, to launch out into the deep must take refuge in harbour*[cxx].*'*

The decree issued by the Privy Council allowed this new Church full legal non-conformity and the right to hold worship according to the biblical and apostolic custom. Two Flemish and two French pastors took turns to conduct the services in their mother tongue. In 1550, another building in London was licenced for the French refugees – St Anthony's Hospital in Threadneedle Street[102] – which was to become the principal Huguenot place of

---

[cxx] A. J. Garnier, Revd, *The Crypt of Canterbury – the French Huguenot Church* (Canterbury, 1965.) p4.

worship with a constantly expanding flock as more and more refugees arrived seeking to join the congregation. Edward VI arranged for the use of certain church buildings to be henceforth exclusively designated as places of worship for Huguenots. The earliest of these churches were not just in London, but in areas such as: Kent (Canterbury and Maidstone); Norfolk (King's Lynn and Great Yarmouth); Somerset (Glastonbury) and Hampshire (Southampton). The successful establishment of these churches were added to by further churches being built soon after in Avon (Bristol); Devon (Plymouth) and Gloucestershire (Stonehouse). The widening dispersion of Huguenot populations in England followed with more churches in Essex (Thorpe-Le-Stoken and Halstead), and concentrations can also be found, unsurprisingly, nearer to France in the Kentish ports of Sandwich, Rye, Winchelsea and Dover. When Elizabeth I visited Sandwich in 1573, records show that the children gave an exhibition of spinning, which was 'well liked' by her majesty and her entourage[cxxi].

A good example of one such place is the under-croft, or crypt, in Canterbury Cathedral, one sizable portion of which was dedicated and endowed as a chapel by the Black Prince, and it is here today that the regular services of the Huguenots continue. Amongst the mediaeval bosses can be found various Calvinist verses on the walls with a scroll listing the names of the more eminent refugees who had first arrived in Canterbury.

Pre-Reformation, the cathedral had been dedicated to the Catholic faith and as such contained many costly relics and shrines all of which were swept away on the orders of Henry VIII, leaving a large, dimly-lit vaulted space ideally suited to the Huguenot purpose of worship, and just at the time when they needed a larger space for their growing congregation. Additionally, they requested permission to carry out their trades in this more than adequate

---

[cxxi] A. J. Garnier, Revd, *The Crypt of Canterbury – the French Huguenot Church* (Canterbury, 1965.) p8.

space, and thus it was here they set up their weaving looms and a school in which to teach their children[cxxii].

The first colloque[103] was held in London on 19 May 1581[cxxiii]. The Dutch and French Churches of England held their first synod on 16th March 1603, followed by a further four synods, the last one being held in 1647[cxxiv].

Due to the growing size of the congregations, in 1640 a subsidiary congregation of the French Church at Threadneedle Street was founded, and in 1661 they were given consent to use the Savoy Chapel of London, but crucially there was a condition attached to the agreement – they would have to agree to a French translation of the Anglican Liturgy. This caveat was to mark the start of the stranger Churches beginning to divide into 'conformist' and 'non-conformist'. Over time, a settlement was agreed upon whereby in some towns and cities both conformist and non-conformist Churches could co-exist peacefully.

By the time of the revocation of the *Edict of Nantes*, the already reasonably sized French Huguenot population in London could worship in churches such as that in the Chapel of St Anthony in Threadneedle Street established during the reign of Edward VI[104]. This has remained the premier French church in London although it is now sited in Soho. Johannes à Lasco had drawn up the first set of guidelines for the Dutch and French Churches to adhere to, entitled, '*All the Form and Manner of the ecclesiastical ministry in the Foreigners' Church set up in London*'. This set of instructions became the guiding principle of all the foreign Churches of that time in this country. Johannes á Lasco had become the superintendent for both the Churches, with ministers appointed to each one. In fact, the French Church in

---

[cxxii] Samuel Smiles, *The Huguenots Their Settlements, Churches and Industries in England and Ireland (1889)* (London) pp.127/8.
[cxxiii] John Southerden Burn, *The History of the French, Walloon, Dutch and Other Foreign Protestant Churches* (London, 1846) p29.
[cxxiv] Christopher Joby, *The Dutch Language in Britain 1550-1702, a Social History of the use of Dutch in early modern Britain.* (Leiden, Netherlands, 2015) p97.

The Story of the Huguenots – a Unique Legacy

London was considered to be of such great importance to Calvinists that a request to John Calvin in 1561 to supply a pastor to the French Church resulted in him sending one of his most prominent men – Nicolas des Gallars[cxxv].

It appears that there was some dialogue and mutual respect between the French and Dutch Churches at this time. One of the elders of the Dutch Church, John Utenhove, wrote to John Calvin about the charter Edward VI had given to the two Churches:

> *'We are permitted to exercise church discipline in accordance with God's Word...... The Bishop of London and the other Bishops and the Archbishops of the realm, the Mayor, The Sheriffs and Aldermen of London, are enjoined and strictly commanded not in any way to interfere with our churches, but leave us to act and organise matters in our own way.'*

The first Huguenot church had originally been the Church of St Anthony's Hospital, Threadneedle Street, the French Huguenots were able to obtain a 21-year lease on this building (which dated back to the 13th century), and which thereafter became known as the Threadneedle Street Church. Cruelly, disaster struck in 1666 when the church was destroyed in the Great Fire of London, but, undaunted, the Huguenots set to work to rebuild their church.

The Huguenots' commitment, self-discipline and good citizenship must surely have impressed many, king and pauper alike, for in 1687, James II signed a charter for the building of another French church, this time in Spitalfields. The charter states that:

> *In regard to the Church situated in Threadneedle Streete where they meet cannot contayne the multitude of People*

[cxxv] David C. A. Agnew, Revd, *Protestant Exiles from France, chiefly in the reign of Louis XIV* (Edinburgh, 1886) p28.

which cometh thither…. they may have another place to assemble part of their people therein to serve God after their usuall manner.

The first choice for the site of this new church was Long Hedge Field, and following demolition of the almshouses that existed there, a temple – an annex to the Threadneedle Street Church[105] – was built between Black Eagle Street and Grey Eagle Street, which opened in 1688[cxxvi].

The main source of information relating to French refugees of the time is located in the various Huguenot church registers. There were eleven Huguenot congregations recorded as being active from the middle of the 17th century to the beginning of the 19th century in Spitalfields, Shoreditch, Petticoat Lane and Wapping. Within the pages of the registers for the church known as 'La Patente' can be found an insight into numerous migrations within the vicinity of Brown's Lane, near to present-day Spitalfields market. These registers give details of the French people who lived and worked in the area and give a clear indication that large numbers of them worked as silk weavers or in trades connected to silk weaving.

The Huguenots were a close-knit community as demonstrated by extracts from various records, such as the entry I discovered for the birth of Susanne Malandin, where one of my own ancestors stood sponsor (witness) at her birth.

Vol 22-23 Registers of Threadneedle Street Baptemes p.50
Malandin, Susanne, fille de Jean et Marie sa femme.
*Tem. **Moyise Ouvry** et Sussane de Heule.*
Née le 25 Decembre 1718.

One of the Malandin family descendants has confirmed that Jean's brother Pierre named one of his sons Moyse:

[cxxvi] Museum of London, The, *The Quiet Conquest: The Huguenots, 1685-1985* (London, 1985) p64.

Mallandain, Moyse, fils de Pierre et Marie Anne Hardy sa
*femme. Tem. **Moyse Ouvry**, Marie Mallandain.*
Ne le 30 Septembre. Oct 13, 1723.

I think these two events amply demonstrate the shared intimacy within the Huguenot community[106].

Eventually, in 1841, the congregation of Threadneedle Street moved to the Church of St Martin's Le Grand which served the Huguenot congregation until it was demolished in 1888 to make way for the new General Post Office. A blue plaque marks the site today. The congregation then took up temporary accommodation at the Athenaeum Hall in Tottenham Court Road in a chapel behind Soho Square until their new church was built in Soho Square itself. The church, which took two years to build, was designed by Aston Webb and built by Vauxhall-based Higgs and Hill, responsible for the construction of many well-known buildings in London. It is today the sole survivor of the French churches in London and is still in use by the Huguenot community[cxxvii]. The Queen, to this day, still has to give the monarch's approval of the appointment of a pastor to the French Church.

There were other churches too within Spitalfields that, although they are still architecturally part of the area, have now metamorphosed to accommodate other functions. Amongst the more famous of these buildings is Hanbury Hall, originally built in 1719 as a Huguenot chapel; by 1740 it had been taken over by 'La Patente[107]' which had first opened in Berwick Street, and which is now the church hall for Christ Church Spitalfields.

Built in 1766 on the site of a small chapel at the edge of Henry VIII's artillery ground, L'Eglise de L'Artillerie is now a popular synagogue, in fact it is the oldest Ashkenazi synagogue in London,

---

[cxxvii] Museum of London, The, *The Quiet Conquest: The Huguenots, 1685-1985* (London, 1985) p60.

known as the Sandy's Row Synagogue. It was in use as a Huguenot church until 1786 when it merged with the Dutch Walloon Church. For the next 50 years it was rented to other Protestant groups until the 1840s and the arrival of the Dutch Ashkenazi Jews, who also wanted to settle in Spitalfields to seek a better life.

By the 1690s, the increasing numbers of Huguenots taking flight from persecution in France was clearly leading to a need for an increased number of French churches to accommodate them, and at one point a total of 31 French churches had been built in London, with significant concentrations in the centre or west side of the capital: Marylebone (1656); Somerset House (1653); Castle Street, Leicester Square (1672); and the Savoy in the Strand (1675), and even more so to the east, where the majority of French refugees gravitated to in order to be with fellow artisans and other skilled tradespeople. They worshipped at L'Eglise de St. Jean, Swan Fields, Shoreditch (1687) and, in the highly popular Spitalfields area: L'Eglise de Crispin Street (1693); La Nouvelle Patente, Crispin Street (1689); L'Eglise de Perle Street (1697); Petticoat Lane Chapel (1694); L'Eglise de Bell Lane (1700) and L'Eglise de Wheler Street (1703), and most importantly, La Neuve Eglise (1743). Further afield, the French Church at Wapping (1700) and L'Eglise de Swan Fields, Slaughter Street, Shoreditch (1721) also drew sizeable congregations.

These churches all kept very detailed registers of their congregations including births, deaths and marriages for it was still hoped by some that it might, at some point, be possible for their children to return to their homeland and if they did it would be important for them to be in possession of the full details of their forebears[cxxviii].

As each persecuted refugee left their country of birth, they would take a 'gift' from their home church in order to show their new church that they were entitled to attend communion wherever

---

[cxxviii] Turner, Winifred, BA Lond., *The Archives and Library of the French Protestant Church, Soho Square, formerly Threadneedle Street.* The Huguenot Society Proceedings XIV (4) 1932-3, p558.

they settled. This gift, or token, was usually made from base metal or wood and were known as a méreaux; it was deliberately small so that it could be easily concealed about their person. Importantly, it was an introduction to their new church to prove that they were true Calvinists[108], and therefore a good method of preventing Catholics or spies from entering the country under false pretext. When a prospective new member of the church arrived, they would be expected to give their Témoignage[109] – their 'true intention'. Furthermore, it would be anticipated that a member of the congregation would stand guarantor, having had contact with the newcomer's former church.

Today, the registers of the Livre des Témoignage of the Threadneedle Street Church still faithfully record new members' details, this being the main church for the London Huguenots of those times.

In order to become part of the congregation, all prospective new members had to fully vindicate their true intention as evidence of their genuine Protestant beliefs, and the wording – *'Témoignage, avec attestation'* or *'Témoignage par ecrit'* – would be written next to their names in the register to confirm they were true followers of the Huguenot faith[cxxix].

In its simplest form, the Témoignage was a certificate given to worshippers by their local church as proof that they were indeed genuinely Protestant, and it offered some degree of security to the congregation against the infiltration of spies and informers. During periods of increased migration, however, certification was not always given due to the sheer scale and speed of so many arrivals. In these instances, other methods of gaining acceptance in a new church were applied. The most basic form of acknowledgment was to use the words: *'gallérien, sorti des gallères'* [110] or just the word *'confesseur'* – these words usually sufficing for those who had suffered for their faith.

[cxxix] Noel Currer-Briggs & Royston Gambier, *Huguenot Ancestry* (Chichester, 1985) p42.

Other refugees who also had not had time to obtain their Certificate de Témoignage before departure may have been fortunate enough to already have family living and worshipping in the area they chose to travel to, which meant that a family member would stand guarantor for the new arrival. However, when there was no one to vouchsafe a refugee, enquiries would have to be made to ensure, as far as possible, that they were genuine. In a rare few cases the guarantor would actually be the Catholic Church itself, which provided the necessary evidence with the words '*a fait abjuration de la religion Romaine et a été admis member de cette église*'[111].

As the years went by, the numbers seeking admission tailed off, and so the frequency of the need for témoignage declined, and the recording of new arrivals would simply state: '*par son témoignage même*' or an even briefer wording, '*lui même*', meaning 'he himself'.

The admission of persons to a Huguenot church in England did not only apply to those seeking refuge because témoignage was also required for all applicants' children. A young person between the ages of 13 to 24 years would be admitted as a 'confirmed'[112] member of the church, which usually took place at certain times of the year. At 'Confirmation', a parent or a close relative of a child would step forward to introduce them before the child made their own responses to their church.

In May 1682, the Témoignage registers of London recorded the arrival of the wife of Louis Gaucheron – Elizabeth from Dangeau, Orléanais – who is mentioned in the records again in July when she was given a pair of shoes (Louis had arrived the previous year). In 1685 Louis' father, Charles, and his second wife, Marguerite, together with Louis' younger brother Pierre and his wife and two young sons, left their homes in France to seek a new life in London [cxxx].

[cxxx] The Gaucheron Archives.

Samuel Pepys regularly attended the French church in Threadneedle Street. His wife was from a Huguenot family and no doubt this influenced his choice of where to worship. He recorded in his diary one such service he attended in November 1662, and how he also heard a sermon in French at the French Episcopal Church, Savoy[113], recalling that the minister preached with his hat off – a sign of conformity with the Church of England. There were, over the years, frequent attempts to persuade non-conformists such as the Calvinists to conform to the Church of England, and although a number of French churches did in time comply, their services were still performed in the French language.

The most important feature of a Huguenot church was, and still is, the pulpit – the central focus of the congregation from which the pastor[114] delivers the sermon, the main focus of Huguenot worship. Not all the Huguenot churches chose to conform, such as the L'Eglise de Leicester Fields (today known as the Orange Street Chapel) which, with the passing of time, suffered an inevitable dwindling of its congregation as, naturally, the later generations did not share the same haunting passion for their chapel as their forebears had; nor did they have the collective memories of persecution and '*camarade*' that those earlier generations had been bound by. This chapel over time became Anglicised, but in the end, this was not enough to preserve it as a Huguenot chapel, and, with what must have been great reluctance and sorrow, it was forced to close its doors in 1787[115].

The French Church of the Savoy became the favoured place for Protestant worshippers settling in and around the centre and west of London[cxxxi].

Further afield, St Peter's in Sandwich, Kent, and the Southampton church of St Julian were given under licence from the king to the French refugees[116].

[cxxxi] Gwynn, Grace L., MA, *The Huguenot Settlements in London, Special Number of Le Lien (Eglise Protestante Française de Londres)*, p5.

Elizabeth I had tried to maintain a balance between the moderates and the puritanical reformers, but the Puritans gradually gained ground during the reign of James I, a significant example of which was the formation of a group in the City of London to purchase Church tithes and livings, enabling them to position like-minded Puritans in many Church of England parishes. For most of the strangers, the main difference between their own churches and the official Protestant Church of England was that the Church's hierarchy included bishops, although some of the wealthier families, keen to integrate into English society, appeared to have been happy to accept this. Yet, not everyone was pleased with this migration from their own churches as this now led to a fall in income from collections which the poorer members of the Huguenot Church often heavily relied upon[cxxxii].

Upon the accession of Charles I, the charter granted by Edward VI was renewed, allowing Huguenots and other refugees to continue as before, but the danger to their continued wellbeing coming from Archbishop Laud and the Catholic French Queen Henrietta Maria, neither of whom shared the same liberal attitude, led many refugees to the worry that the intention now was to reintroduce Catholicism as the main religion of the land – yet this may not have been Laud's true objective.

The appointment of William Laud as Archbishop of Canterbury in 1633 also did much to alarm those who followed the doctrines of Calvinism due to Laud voicing his argument that a consistory of laymen was unnatural in the affairs of the Church, and that the Church's own duly appointed bishops should lead the way forward. The year before his appointment as Archbishop he had prepared and delivered a damning report to the Privy Council relating to the foreign churches in the realm. He seems to have determined upon a course of action whereby he would eventually force the complete integration of all Calvinists. He was determined

---

[cxxxii] Desert, Dennis, *The Stranger Communities and the Established Church.* The Huguenot Society, Vol XXVII (2003), p2.

to force their compliance in the use of the Anglican liturgy (although he did permit them to continue their services in French).

Always happy to promote his viewpoint of the refugees, Laud bitterly disliked their congregations, once telling the king that they were:

> *...great nurseries of nonconformity, had no use for bishops, and harboured many spies and informers, and that their insistence that the pulpit was of greater importance than the communion and particularly wearing their hats in church offended the native English.*

Laud was eventually impeached for high treason in May 1641 by the Long Parliament[117] and sent to the Tower of London. Amongst the charges laid against him was his apparent attempt at causing a rift between the Church of England and other reformed Churches. Jean Bulteel, a French minister of Canterbury, noted that Laud's impeachment was greeted with jubilation by the reformed Churches, and that *'it is as merry as lambs when the wolf is shut up'*.[cxxxiii]

Although the Huguenots were through these events exculpated from Laud's grand plan, they did start to integrate by the third or fourth generation of their settlement, and because of this some would have quietly transferred their place of worship to an Anglican church as part of this process. However, one major factor that led to a swifter demise of the French Church was the 1753 Marriage Act. Until then, marriage could and did take place anywhere the couple chose for their nuptials, the only stipulation being that they were conducted before an ordained clergyman of the Church, but this had led to marriages often being conducted in secret without parental consent – several were later discovered to have been bigamous. Some weddings were even conducted at the Fleet Prison.

[cxxxiii] The Huguenot Society of Great Britain and Northern Ireland, Quarto Series, vol LIV (1979), p51.

The Marriage Act of 1753 made it illegal for couples to wed unless the ceremony was conducted by a vicar in a parish church or chapel of the Church of England, and parental consent had to be given if couples were under the age of 21. If a minister was found to have married a person below the age of consent, the maximum penalty that could be imposed was 14 years' transportation. The only faiths exempt from this law were Jews and Quakers; all other faiths – including non-conformists and Catholics – had to be married in an Anglican church with a member of the Anglican Church conducting the service, this being the only record of a marriage that was legally acceptable. This limitation of where non-conformist or Catholic couples could marry caused immense distress to their communities until an amendment was inserted into the 1836 Marriage Act[118] that from then on allowed couples of these faiths to marry in their own churches with their own ministers conducting the service.

Huguenots in the centre and west of the capital were by then able to worship at two of the more established French churches, either as strict Calvinists (Threadneedle Street in the City – as non-conformists), or they could follow the Anglican form of worship translated into French (at the Savoy church in London's West End – as conformists). Around these two churches two distinct French Protestant communities began to flourish. By the mid-1700s there were nine French Protestant churches in the East End, including the aforementioned La Neuve Eglise in Fournier Street[119], with 12 more French churches in the West End, most of which offered a meticulous Calvinist form of worship. All were administered through strictly laid-down guidelines known as *Le Discipline Ecclesiastique des Eglises Réformée de France*. Ministers were permanent, paid members of the Church unlike others whose positions were unpaid. The duties of ministers, elders and deacons are all carefully detailed in *Le Discipline*: to preach the word of God; instruct, admonish,

The Story of the Huguenots – a Unique Legacy

exhort and censure their flock; to administer the sacrament, and to oversee the governance of the Church, and the morality of the congregation.

They also dealt with correspondence to and from other churches and were called upon, when applicable, to send deputations to the civil authorities. Among other duties they were required to oversee appointments of paid employees, maintain church buildings and ensure that sacraments were administered in a satisfactory and proper manner[cxxxiv].

Apart from these shared duties, elders were expected to distribute méreaux for the monthly communion, and to collect contributions for the upkeep of the church.

Poor relief was the remit of deacons. From these details, it is possible to see that the French churches were well ordered and efficiently run.

There was one other church that later generations of Huguenots chose as their place of worship – Christ Church in Spitalfields, and although it was not built primarily as a Huguenot church, it nevertheless still has an ongoing regular connection with one Huguenot family – the Rondeaus.

The Rondeau family can trace their history back to 1556 and the birth of Jean Rondeau at Wasigny in the Ardennes region of France[cxxxv]. The family first came to Spitalfields in 1681: this was Elizabeth, daughter of Isaac Rondeau, and her husband Job Jacob and their children. They were followed in 1685 by Elizabeth's brother Jean, who for several years lived in Brick Lane, moving in 1723 to a house he had built at 4 Wilkes Street, Spitalfields[120]. On 18 November 1694, Jean had married Jeanne Martha Challon at the Threadneedle Street Church; the marriage entry records that Jean had been a 'native of Paris'. On 31 July 1728, Jean was elected along with the town clerk and solicitor to attend Parliament

---

[cxxxiv] The Huguenot Society of Great Britain and Northern Ireland, Quarto Series, vol LIV (1979), p51
[cxxxv] The Rondeau Archives.

The church had been one of 50 planned new churches to replace those lost in the Great Fire of 1666. It was in 1729 that the new parish of Spitalfields was formed, having previously been part of the parish of Stepney. Nearly 50 years had passed since the Revocation had driven so many Huguenots to seek a new life in Spitalfields; with the inexorable march of time the older generation had passed away, and it was their children who now worshipped in this new church, including some of the Ouvry family; indeed, there is a plaque to the memory of James Ouvry and his wife Ann, who died in 1759 and 1767 respectively.

as delegates acting on behalf of the newly-built church to ensure that Christ Church Spitalfields was endowed and consecrated.

Jean Rondeau's son, John (Jean), one of 12 children born in Brick Lane, became a master weaver, and took an active part in Christ Church over the years undertaking various roles culminating on 22 December 1761 with his appointment by a majority of 103 votes as sexton of the church, a position he held until the day he died 29 years later on 27 October 1790. He had married a widow, Margaret Roberts, in 1749 in a Fleet wedding ceremony[121]. They were blessed with three children, Margaret, John and James. John and Margaret left the house in Wilkes Street in 1773 and moved to Booth Street.

Jean's great, great, great, great, great grandson, Stanley Rondeau, continues the family's many years of active involvement with Christ Church to this day[cxxxvi]. A plaque in memory of Jean Rondeau as the first sexton of the church, and of his wife Margaret, is today on view in Christ Church.

[cxxxvi] The Rondeau Archives.

- 14 -

England: Aid & Legal Status

With public sympathy running high in London amidst genuine concerns for the welfare of these desperately impoverished, ragged refugees, the managing by the Crown of any apparent government ambiguity over the question of religion was made more difficult simply because it could easily be viewed as a sign of falseness to, and betrayal of, the Protestant Church.

The Anglican Church of England, keen to support their fellow Protestants, and Anglican bishops across the country became significant benefactors to Huguenot worshippers once the French Church itself became unable to offer financial support due to what must have seemed an unrelenting, ever-increasing influx of French Protestant refugees. Between 1681-94, a total of £90,174[122] was collected by the Anglican Church of England to aid their fellow Protestants[cxxxvii]. Before this major influx of refugees in 1681, collections to financially assist the Huguenot refugees had been garnered throughout England, and in the following year Scotland also made a collection. From the year 1628 these became a regular occurrence throughout the kingdom[123].

When Charles I acceded to the throne in 1625, he gave orders for all officers of the Crown to: '...*permit strangers, members of*

[cxxxvii] Albion: *The Proceedings of Conference of British Studies at its Regional and National Meetings: Vol 8 No 3, 1976, p221.*

the foreign churches and their children, peaceably to enjoy all the privileges and immunities which had been formerly granted to them'.

By 1681 England was welcoming Huguenots from all walks of life, both the great and the humble, but especially those in professions, and these included merchants, doctors, schoolmasters, ministers, artisans, mariners and shipwrights. Accompanying the men, there were of course women and children who were, virtually without exception, all in need of urgent assistance upon arrival.

Charles II and his brother, the future James II, were faced with the unenviable problem of how they were to show not only their own but also their government's support for the Huguenots without damaging their relationship with their cousin Louis XIV, who had provided them with support when they had been in exile.

Charles II as head of the Anglican Church felt compelled to add the Huguenots to the Civil List, not least due to the debate then raging over the Exclusion Bill[124] in the hope that questions relating to his successor might be deflected. Importantly, by being added, the Huguenot community was now able to directly and legally seek financial assistance from the government[cxxxviii].

Charles issued, in 1681, the first of four national (royal) Briefs to give charitable assistance to French Protestants because, even before the *Edict of Nantes* was revoked, the growing numbers of Huguenots seeking refuge here was sufficient to be debated and acted upon in the interests of England; indeed, a review of the Témoignage records from the Threadneedle Street Church[125] show that the greatest influx of refugees from France would appear to be in that same year, following the inception of the notorious dragonnades in March. The first brief requested that a two-year fund-raising campaign should be instigated nationwide. This

---

[cxxxviii] Caroline Shaw, *Britannia's Embrace: Modern Humanitarianism and the Imperial Origins of Refugee Relief* (Oxford, 2015) p19.

The Story of the Huguenots – a Unique Legacy

appears to have been an overwhelming success with the considerable sum (for that time) of £14,268.18s.0d[126] being raised. Within the records kept at the Guildhall Library, the largest single collection of 1681 was that made by St Dunstan's in the East, which donated £90, followed by the Spitalfields community which contributed £28[cxxxix].

During the latter part of 1681, the first of the Gaucheron family had arrived in England, the records for immigration showing that 30-year-old Louis travelled from his home town of Châteaudun, Beauce, Eure-et-Loir. He was just one of many refugees who would have to rely on charity: indeed, the records of the Threadneedle Street Church state that 19 grants were paid out to him totalling £5.12s.6d. On 10 January 1682, Louis was paid ten shillings in order to be able to travel to Ipswich, where in 1681 the Royal Lustring Company had been established by Royal Charter[127]. Ipswich had gained a reputation for the manufacture of sailcloth, but French linen (methernix) was believed to be a superior cloth for sails. The Company of Elders and Deacons of the Threadneedle Street Church gave funds for a linen manufacturing company to be established in Ipswich that same year, and it may well have been at this company that Louis Gaucheron began his working life in this country[cxl].

In April 1686, an Order in Council sanctioned a public collection to help relieve the newly arrived silk weavers. As so many had fled with practically nothing, they must indeed have been grateful for the Royal Bounty, administered by a lay French Committee comprising the foremost Huguenot immigrants within the community. They were given responsibility to distribute £16,000[128] per annum amongst the poorest refugees and their dependants.

[cxxxix] Beeman, George R. I., *The Huguenot Society, Notes on the City of London Records dealing with the French Protestant Refugees, Vol VII* (1) *(1901-02)*, *pp.109-110.*
[cxl] The Gaucheron Archives.

Amongst the beneficiaries was Jean Mallandain; records show that he was in receipt of funds totalling £7 in 1705, with a further sum of £8 being awarded in 1707 to Jean and Marthe[cxli]. The records further confirm that he was both a 'confesseur' and a farmer, and that Jean and his wife were resident in Spitalfields. A second committee consisting of ecclesiastics led by the Archbishop of Canterbury, the Bishop of London and the Lord Chancellor was created for distressed pastors and their churches to apply to for assistance, this committee being given an annual sum of £1,718[129] to dispense from the public treasury.

The French Committee's first report, dated December 1687 and published in 1688, states that 13,050 French refugees were now settled in London, with the greatest number being in the Spitalfields area.

Although funds had been made available to those in need from various collections as well as from the Royal Bounty, William III clearly felt the need to comment on the financial distress still suffered by so many, and he conveyed his concern to Parliament on 23 November 1695 in a statement:

Compassion obliges me to mention the miserable circumstances of the French Protestants who suffer for their religion. I most earnestly recommend to you to provide a supply of money suitable to these occasions.

In response to the king's impassioned plea, Parliament passed legislation to permit William to borrow £515,000 for the cost of civil government and the royal household, with a caveat that £15,000 of this sum had to be assigned to the relief of distressed Huguenots, and, significantly, that this sum was to be provided annually – surely indicative of the government's serious intentions of helping the French Huguenots.

The French Committee was in charge of the distribution of funds, and a perusal of their records is enough to show how well-

---

[cxli] The Mallandain Archives.

ordered and thought-out the entire process was, right down to the document that all supplicants were required to sign, or append their mark: a pre-printed statement acknowledging not only the sum they were to be in receipt of, but also the exact date of receipt as well as for what reason the aid was being granted. Not all supplicants were individuals requiring aid, however; there were also many individuals in need of medication, the French Committee would require doctors to submit details of the medication prescribed together with the costs and the patients' details. The doctor would only be reimbursed once he had certified and signed the claim. Details of the treatment given to inmates of the Pest House[130] were likewise properly documented in order for reimbursement to be made by the French Committee[cxlii].

The first grant known as the Royal Bounty was paid out of the Privy Purse in 1686 after which annual grants were made in half-yearly instalments through to the reign of George III, assisting many poor Huguenot refugees and their families to survive.

In 1932 in the basement of the French Hospital in Victoria Park, documents were discovered that provide detailed information of the French Committee in its administering of six major and two minor funds for the distribution of relief from 1686-1876 including the first brief of James II on 5 March 1686; the second brief on 31 January 1688, and the Royal Bounty of William and Mary 1689-94[cxliii]. There were also two smaller private funds donated in 1690-1 and 1695[131].

Not all of the donations were of valid coinage; at that time, the silver coinage in circulation had become devalued partly through being clipped (that is to say the edge of the coin was gradually reduced so that the clipped silver taken from the coin could be sold). Within the Guildhall records are a number of entries relating

---

[cxlii] Albion: *The Proceedings of Conference of British Studies at its Regional and National Meetings: Vol 8 No 3, 1976, p225.*
[cxliii] The Huguenot Society of Great Britain and Northern Ireland, Quarto Series, vol LI (1974), p1.

to 'bad money', and a glance at the following extract[cxliv] shows to what extent illegal coinage had been 'gifted'. This extract uses the pre-decimal characters of pounds, shillings and pence, the latter being indicated by the letter 'd'.

Received £ s d	Bad £ s d	Good £ s d
3. 4. 3³/₄	1. 19. 0	1. 5. 3³/₄
3. 4. 2	2. 2. 3	1. 1. 9
13. 0. 0	10. 0. 0	3. 0. 0
16.14.11	10. 9.11	6. 5. 0
18.15. 0	16. 5. 0	2. 10 .0
20. 0. 8	20. 0. 8	0. 0. 0

Within this 'bad' money no doubt there would have been some foreign currency, as records show Dutch and Spanish coins being found within the collections.

Since 1660, Louis XIV had been steadily removing any remaining hard-won liberties still held by those of the Protestant faith. The last legal meeting place of Huguenot deputies (the Synod of Loudun) had been closed. Across Europe, the deliberate use of increasing violence to enforce further, and harsher, anti-Protestant measures in France, was viewed with mounting horror and dismay. Amongst those who watched with unease these events unfold across the Channel was Charles II, who, in spite of his family connections with the French royal family[132], felt compelled to issue a strong protest to Louis XIV:

I conjure you in the name of the great Henri[133], whose precious blood circulates in both our veins, to respect the Protestants whom he looked upon as his children. If, as is reported, you wish to compel them to renounce their

---

[cxliv] Beeman, George R. I., *The Huguenot Society, Notes on the City of London Records dealing with the French Protestant Refugees, Vol VII* (1) *(1901-02), p110.*

religion under pain of banishment from your Kingdom, I offer them asylum in that of England.

Charles tried to introduce a general Act of Naturalisation for the refugees, but this was at first defeated by the House of Commons. The outlook for the strangers in England was not totally grim, however. An Order was signed at Hampton Court on 28 July 1681 that formally gave them free importation of goods, and letters of denization as well as assistance to help them move from place to place to seek work. The King's Order was reported in the *London Gazette* in September of that year; as follows:

This day was published an Order of His Majesty in Council, dated 28 July at Hampton Court; Wherein His Majesty is pleased to declare, that he holds himself obliged in Honour and Conscience, to Comfort and Support all such afflicted Protestants, who by reason of the Rigours and Severities which are used towards them upon the account of their Religion, shall be forced to quit their Native Country, and shall desire to shelter themselves under His Majesties Royal Protection, for the preservation and free exercise of their Religion; and in order to hereunto, His Majesty was pleased further to Declare, That he will Grant unto every such distressed Protestant, who shall come hither for refuge, and reside here, His Letters of Denization under the Great Seal, without charge whatsoever; and likewise such further privileges and immunities as are consistent with the Laws, for the Liberty and free exercise of their Trades and Handicrafts; and that His Majesty will likewise recommend to his Parliament at their next Meeting to pass an Act for the General Naturalisation, of all such Protestants as shall come over as aforesaid; and for the further enlarging their Liberties and Franchises granted to them by His Majesty, as reasonably may be necessary for them. And for their encouragement, His Majesties own Natural

The Story of the Huguenots – a Unique Legacy

born subjects; and that they shall have all the Privileges and Immunities that generally His Majesties Native Subjects have, for the introduction of their Children into Schools and Colleges. And his Majesty was likewise pleased to Order, that all His Majesties Officers, both Civil and Military, do give kind Reception to all such Protestants as shall arrive within any of His Majesties Ports in this Kingdom and furnish them with free Passports, and to give them all assistance and furtherance in their Journeys to the places to which they shall desire to go. And the Right Honourable the Lords Commissioners of His Majesties Treasury are to give orders to the Commissioners of His Majesties Customs, to suffer the said Protestants to pass free with their Goods and household stuff whether of a greater or a smaller value, together with their Tools and Instruments belonging to their Crafts or Trades and generally all what belongs to them, that may be Imported according to the Laws now in force, without exacting anything from them. And for the further Relief and Encouragement of the said necessitous Protestants His Majesty hath been pleased to give Order for a general Brief through His Kingdom of England, Dominion of Wales, and Town of Berwick for Collecting the Charity of all well-disposed persons, for the relief of the said Protestants, who may stand in need thereof. And to that end, that when any such come over, being Strangers, they may know where to Address themselves to fitting persons, to lay their Requests before his Majesty, His Majesty was Graciously pleased to appoint the most Reverend Father in God, His Grace the Lord Archbishop of Canterbury and the Right Reverend Father in God, the Lord Bishop of London, or either of them to receive all the said Requests and Petitions, and to present the same to His Majesty to the end of such Order may be given therein as necessary[cxlv].

[cxlv] The London Gazette – 8 October 1763. The Burney Collection: British Library.

The Story of the Huguenots – a Unique Legacy

During the reign of William III and Queen Mary substantial sums were given from the Civil List for the aid of Protestant refugees. There were also other charities involved in supplying financial help to the needy French Protestants, and amongst these noteworthy organisations was the Society of Saintonge and Angoumois, founded to assist aged and unemployed refugees, and to pay apprenticeship premiums for children of Huguenot descent. Parliament also awarded grants throughout the 18th century, which were unfortunately steadily reduced in size as the century wore on.

In 1793, the first Aliens Act came into law, which made it mandatory for those arriving in the United Kingdom after January 1793 to provide their name, rank, occupation and address to the local Justice of the Peace. From 1798, any 'housekeeper' who took in a lodger who could be described as an alien was required to provide personal details of the alien to the overseer of the parish, who in turn was required to send copies that were eventually filed with the Aliens Office[134]. Until 1873, citizenship could be acquired by one of two methods: Denization – conferred by letter patent, the cheaper option for refugees seeking to make this their permanent home (although this did have some limitations); or Naturalisation – granted by Act of Parliament after five years' residence (the advantage to this option being that it granted the same rights as a natural-born citizen, subject to taking the Oaths of Allegiance and Supremacy).

- 15 -

To Aid One's Fellow Man

Of the relatively more affluent Huguenot families, many showed compassion through their financial support of their less fortunate countrymen and women, one shining example being their foundation and continued support of the French Hospital.

In October 1681 the City of London Court of Common Council offered *'a large and commodious house near Bunhill Fields'*[135] to accommodate the sick and infirm of the Huguenot community. A treasurer of the hospital, Paul Dufour, had used the considerable inheritance left to him by his wife in 1734 to set up a trust, which over time paid out to those in need in Soho and Spitalfields, as well as providing funds to the hospital in order that it could offer relief to those awaiting admission; he also provided £15,400 in annuities to the trust, consequently enabling a series of grants to be paid out to those in need via the French Committee (Westminster) and La Maison de Charité (Spitalfields and Soho)[cxlvi].

It was during the winter of 1689-90 that La Maison de Charité de Spitalfields had been founded, becoming more frequently known as 'La Soupe' owing to this being the staple diet of the supplicants. Silk weavers were particularly susceptible to the

---

[cxlvi] The Huguenot Society of Great Britain and Northern Ireland, Quarto Series, vol LII (1977), p1

frequent swings and roundabouts of commercial trade, such as interruptions to raw silk importation, fashion demands and smuggling, and many families, tragically finding themselves in dire financial straits, were grateful to the assistance that La Maison de Charité was able to provide. Beneficiaries included many who were living in Bethnal Green, for example, journeyman[136] weavers who had fallen into poverty.

The records of La Maison de Charité de Spitalfields are contained in Le Grand Livre[137], which shows a doubling of its financial expenditure during the winter months of 1738-40 as applications for aid, mainly portions of basic foodstuffs, increased. Within this period a 'portion' comprised $^1/_2$ lb of dry bread, 4oz of bread in the soup and $^1/_2$ lb of meat. Portions were handed out three times a week to supplicants. Within the pages of Le Grand Livre in April 1741, a memo reveals to us the details of its outlay – in that month it had given out 1,061 portions at a cost of 1s 6d[138]. Based on April's figures, and in order to fulfil the requirements of those in need for a year, it was estimated that La Charité would need to spend in the region of £1,000 in the forthcoming year as they could expect to be petitioned to provide 12,732 portions. The winter preceding these entries had been extremely harsh with continuous frost for no less than nine weeks from Christmas to the end of February – during this time no doubt many poor souls would surely have perished[cxlvii].

To illustrate the often-ongoing hardships that were endured, I have included just two cases from the records:

Mallandain: *Marie-Anne, wife of Louis aged 50 and her child, living in Bethnal Green by the Old Hampshire Hog – two portions per week.*

Ouvry: *Sarah, wife of Jean, living in Anchor Street aged 30, and her two children – three portions per week.*

[cxlvii] Marmoy, Charles F. A., La Soupe: La Maison de Charité de Spitalfields, The Huguenot Society, vol XXIII (3), 1979, p145

The increased cost of providing nourishment to those in need, together with the rising costs of distribution, led to a rethink of policy, and ultimately La Charité was forced by such relentlessly increasing demands on its finances to change its policy. It would now become a 'bread only' charity, its final distribution of soup being made on 21 September following payment to the butcher, William Barrow, for the meat provided during the previous three months as detailed on the final invoice. From this time onwards, La Charité became known as 'La Maison de Charité du Pain'[cxlviii].

Yet not all the entries are grim reading, and on a more uplifting note some of the case closures were actually the result of the subsequently improving circumstances of the supplicant. A useful map of the City of London and Westminster based on Le Grand Livre gives an indication of the areas of greatest poverty.

The French Hospital received the not insubstantial sum of £500 from the will of Jacques de Gastigny in 1708 for the specific purpose of extending and improving the Pest House into a hospice for distressed French Protestants and their descendants, with a further bequest of £500 stipulating that the interest from this second sum was to be used for the provision of bed linen, clothes and other necessities for the inmates[cxlix139]. As the City of London was reluctant to sell land next to the Pest House, it was decided to seek out another site; therefore, some land, known as the 'golden acre', was leased in March 1716 from the Ironmongers Company for 990 years at an annual premium of £400 together with a peppercorn rent. Construction of the new hospital to house the elderly, poor or sick commenced the same year. In 1717, a petition was presented to George I, requesting that the hospital be granted a Royal Charter of Incorporation. The charter, dated 24 July 1718,

---

[cxlviii] Marmoy, Charles F. A., La Soupe: La Maison de Charité de Spitalfields, The Huguenot Society, vol XXIII (3), 1979, p145.
[cxlix] The Huguenot Society of Great Britain and Northern Ireland, Quarto Series, vol LVI (1983), p8.

was entitled *The Governor and Directors of the Hospital for Poor French Protestants and their descendants residing in Great Britain.* The first governor of the hospital that became known as *La Providence* was Lord Galway (son of the 1st Marquis de Ruvigny) who had distinguished himself at the Battle of Aughrim in 1691, and who had, for a short while, been appointed Commander-in-Chief in Ireland before being granted estates in Ireland.

The hospital officially opened its doors in November 1718; by the year 1760 it was caring for 234 poor Huguenots[cl]. It was from the outset a source of pride amongst the Huguenots of London, who bestowed upon it gifts and legacies. It was originally built to house 80 inmates who were 'the poorest sort of their nation' according to the charter, but the success of La Providence led to the building being extended through the addition of two new wings in 1730.

Records of the Duval family show that the founder of its second English branch, Jean-Pierre Duval was a diamond merchant who had established his business with his two brothers in premises in Hackney, east London. Jean-Pierre took an interest in the often-tragic fate of Huguenot refugees in the capital. His son, Louis-Jean-Francois, jeweller to the English Court, following his father's benevolent footsteps, also provided material and moral support to the hospital destined for the French poor and their descendants. In 1777, the generous Genevan jeweller, the same Louis-Jean-Francois, became a governor of the French Hospital.

13 members of his family succeeded him in this. Even today the family tradition of serving the French Protestant Hospital continues through various Duval family members including Peter Duval the current Deputy Governor and his son Alexander Edward who joined the Board of Governors in 2000[cli].

[cl] The Huguenot Society of Great Britain and Northern Ireland, Quarto Series, vol LVI (1983), p7.
[cli] The Duval Archives

The Story of the Huguenots – a Unique Legacy

Demand for its invaluable services must have placed too great a strain on its financial position, however, because, by the end of the Napoleonic Wars, the hospital was in financial difficulties, forcing a reduction of inmate numbers to 30 by 1815.

George Lefevre of the well-known Lefevre family in Canterbury is mentioned in the records of La Providence. George presented a printed petition dated 23 April 1904 stating that he, George of Shephardswell, near Dover, could trace his ancestors on his paternal side back to when they had fled persecution during the reign of Louis XIV, and that the first family member was secretly brought across in a wicker cradle. The record goes on to state that George had once been a senior partner in a large merchant and manufacturing business in Canterbury, but that unfortunate circumstances had caused the demise of his trade.

George Lefevre had also been a member of the Consistory of the French Church in the crypt of Canterbury Cathedral for 25 years. He was petitioning for outdoor relief[140] due to the failure of his health, his trade and now his old age. In fact, George did become an inmate on 5 November 1904.

And, also within the hospital records can be found an entry for Mallandain – David Mallandain's daughter, Elizabeth. Her admission application confirms her father being from the province of Picardy, and that he was a 'refugee pour Cause de Religion' (a normal description for a Huguenot who had suffered direct persecution from the French authorities). Elizabeth, aged 66, was admitted on 12 September 1804; described as weak and unable to care for herself, she remained a patient there until her death later that same year[clii].

Many churches supported inmates of the French Hospital over the years, including L'Eglise Londres, which maintained a number of its 'infirm' members, as did L'Eglise de Wheeler, which paid two shillings per annum towards a pension for Charlotte

---

[clii] The Mallandain Archives.

Gaucheron until her death in 1725[cliii], and, further afield, L'Eglise de Southampton, which paid a pension for Alexandre Arabin during his stay at the French Hospital.

La Providence moved to a new site in June 1865 following its purchase in 1862 of three acres of land in Victoria Park, Bethnal Green; however, this was sadly not to be its final site. Damage sustained during World War Two, and the threat of a compulsory purchase order, caused the directors to move the hospital once more – this time to Horsham in Sussex, where it remained until 1960[cliv]. The hospital's final move was to Rochester, Kent where it still flourishes, not as a hospital for impoverished Huguenot refugees but as sheltered accommodation for those of proven Huguenot descent[clv].

Over the years, a number of churches and societies financially sponsored inmates of La Providence, and an examination of the records of L'Eglise de Londres shows that it 'maintained a number of infirm members', whereas L'Eglise de Savoy only assisted, at any one time, between three to six inmates until 1729. The churches not only assisted the living – records reveal payments for burial, as is noted in the records of L'Eglise de Wandsworth, which lists the pension and funeral expenses for Marie Tibault, on 17 December 1728.

It was not only financial donations that were gifted; Dr Samuel Byles, medical officer at the French Hospital for 30 years, wrote the words to *Huguenot Refugee*, a four-part song that was often sung at French Hospital court dinners. (See Appendix 4)[clvi]. La Providence was fortunate to receive many gifts over the years, including 63 bottles of champagne sent in 1787 by Princess Lamballe, the best friend of Marie Antoinette.

[cliii] The Gaucheron Archives.
[cliv] Museum of London, The, *The Quiet Conquest: The Huguenots, 1685-1985* (London, 1985) p81.
[clv] The Huguenot Society of Great Britain and Northern Ireland, Quarto Series, vol LVI (1983), p10.
[clvi] Museum of London, The, *The Quiet Conquest: The Huguenots, 1685-1985* (London, 1985) p518.

It is said that adversity can bring people together and this was certainly true of the Huguenot refugees. Class barriers did not exist between them in England. The Marquis de Ruvigny opened his house and his purse to those refugees from France who were unable to financially support themselves. Others who had sufficient funds to set up in business would where possible employ their fellow refugees, providing opportunities for regular employment to as many of them as they could, fuelled no doubt by the fact that refugees arriving here with no means of supporting themselves or their families were unable to claim the Poor Relief available to those born in this country.

The story of people such as James Morisse of Dieppe is, however, a very different one in terms of his 'escaping' from France. During the wars between England and France, he had been captured by the English and was held prisoner in Plymouth.

James had been born of Protestant parents and raised in the Protestant faith even though the tyranny in France at that time made it necessary for him, like others, to practice their faith in secret. Some of his relatives had already made their home in England, and James desired nothing more than to be able to live and work here with them – and above all to openly worship God without fear of persecution[clvii].

Friends of James tried to aid him in obtaining his liberty as the following wording demonstrates:

> *We de Certeffie that beside the Testimony of many refugees in this town that knew the family of James Morisse of Dieppe of the Province of Normandy in France, we have been to this prison and examined him upon the ground of the Religion, we found him to be protestant earnestly willing to stay in England for Ever. He was taken in a merchant man Called the Eagle belonging to Nantes, coming from St. Domingo. He is nineteen years old.*

[clvii] Fairbrother, E.H., (Miss), *A French Protestant Prisoner of War.* The Huguenot Society, Vol X No2 (1912) p309.

In testimony, whereof we put our hands. Made in Plimouth the 29 January 1702/3.

James De Joux, minister,
Francis Delacombe,
Aures Delacombe.[clviii]

Once again, the theme of their abiding faith is very much a recurring one in the struggle of the Huguenots for their very survival.

[clviii] Fairbrother, E.H., (Miss), *A French Protestant Prisoner of War.* The Huguenot Society, Vol X No2 (1912) pp.309/10.

- 16 -

London Settlements

Wherever Huguenot refugees finally settled, that area swiftly and inevitably took on a distinctly French air. Spitalfields was of course not the only part of London to become home to Huguenots, but it was definitely the most populous of all their London settlements. A metaphorical 'stroll' around Huguenot London in this chapter will give an insight into other parts of the capital they chose to live and work in.

Greenwich

Many officers, as well as the lower ranks of William III's army, found their fellow countrymen had chosen to reside in Greenwich, no doubt to be close to the elderly Marquis de Ruvigny, who had already taken up residence there. The marquis had for many years held a trusted position in the French government and had on several occasions represented France at the English court as an envoy. He seemed to have a perfect life, but after the revocation, he was prevented from holding public office in France because of his Protestant beliefs.

Finding life much changed since the Revocation, the marquis took the decision to leave France and settled in Greenwich, where he came to be much admired and respected amongst his fellow refugees. In 1686, he oversaw the founding of the French church at

Greenwich, but until this Huguenot chapel was completed the congregation was permitted to hold their services at the local St Alphege Church. It was the writer and diarist John Evelyn, who, on 24 April 1687, wrote:

At Greenwich, at the conclusion of the church service, there was a French sermon preach'd after the use of the English liturgy translated into French, to a congregation of about 100 French refugees, of whom Monsieur Ruvigny was the chiefe and had obtain'd the use of the church after the parish service was ended.

Greenwich was to become a significant Huguenot settlement after the Revocation, but like all the other areas where Huguenots chose to live and work it gradually assimilated the 'foreigners' into the English way of life. Today, its Huguenot community is remembered by the altar railings in St Alphege Church which are believed to have been designed by Tijou.

Wandsworth

Not far away, Huguenot influence was having a significant influence in Wandsworth. The earliest recorded Huguenot refugee in Wandsworth was Nicholas Tonnet, who, according to his memorial in All Saints Church, lived there from about 1631. The Huguenots of Wandsworth did not set up their own church until around 1682 when they wrote to Bishop Compton, a well-known guardian of the refugees, to petition that:

...they find it difficult and expensive to get to the French church of the Savoy (Westminster) for worship, most of them can only speak French: would the Bishop therefore please licence a minister, M. Brevet and a lecturer or reader Jacques Taumur.

21 signatories were appended to the document. That same year, £20 was granted to fit out a place of worship for the French

The Story of the Huguenots – a Unique Legacy

Protestants. The 'French Chapel', as it became known, was once thought to have been a Presbyterian chapel, but would now be rented by the Huguenot congregation. It had been situated in a small alley just off Wandsworth High Street. The congregation was 'conformist'; in other words, it used for its worship a translation of the official English prayer book rather than a Calvinist one, but they followed the Calvinist rules of creating a consistory, much to the annoyance of the Bishop of Winchester whose diocese included Wandsworth, and who, in 1683, ordered them that:

> *henceforth there be no consistory but that they yearly should choose two Churchwardens and they should call a vestry consisting of the heads of the families worshipping there[clix].*

The French chapel flourished, and its congregation grew in numbers following the movement of many Huguenots from the centre of London to the more pleasant and healthier neighbourhood of Wandsworth; however, by the mid-18th century there was the inevitable gradual decline of regular attendees due to the integration and anglicisation of subsequent generations.

Wandsworth's Town Hall proudly displays the borough coat of arms which reflects the Huguenot presence; part of this armorial device displays drops of water on a golden background, symbolising the tears of the Huguenot refugees.

In 1687, a Huguenot burial ground was opened, which later became known as Mount Nod – perhaps a euphemism for the last resting place of all those who would now sleep for eternity. Today this cemetery is sandwiched between two busy roads and lies virtually forgotten; the once-grand, but now neglected gravestones can be viewed only through gates that are firmly padlocked. It is tragic that these forsaken headstones and family tombs are all that

---

[clix] R. A. Shaw and R. D. Gwynn and P. Thomas, *Huguenots in Wandsworth* (Wandsworth, 1985) p13.

mark the final resting place of many French families, presenting as they do such a sad epitaph to the once vibrant Huguenot community that did so much good here.

A memorial was erected in 1911 in the grounds of the cemetery to commemorate the Huguenots of Wandsworth. Over a century later, Wandsworth council has undertaken a restoration of this cemetery which was closed to all further burials in 1854.

A large proportion of the Huguenots who settled in Wandsworth came from areas in and around Dieppe and Rouen, but Protestant Dutchmen escaping persecution also chose to settle here as it was favourable to their particular trades too – amongst these were those manufacturers of metal goods, such as frying pans, skillets, kettles and brass plates. They settled near to Frying Pan Creek, one of the small streams that feeds into the Wandle delta, an ideal place for the manufacture of these products. Huguenot silk dyers and hat makers also appreciated the Wandle river and its tributaries.

One of the more prominent silk weavers of the area was Nicholas Garrett, who owned a mill in Somerstown[141]; he became a very wealthy man and left the enormous sum of £1,000 of East India Company stock (subsequently valued at £1,760) to the Weavers Company upon his death in 1726[142]. Notably, this sum was specified for the building and endowment of six almshouses for the benefit of the poor weavers of Spitalfields[clx].

Calico printing was another successful trade in the area, but in 1696 a petition was submitted to the House of Lords protesting against a proposed Bill that would, if passed, ban the wearing of printed and dyed calico throughout the United Kingdom.

Among the 39 signatories was Peter Mauvillain, who was liked and greatly respected within the calico printing trade, and

---

[clx] R. A. Shaw and R. D. Gwynn and P. Thomas, *Huguenots in Wandsworth* (Wandsworth, 1985) p12.

who had already established his printing works in Mitcham[143] as well as Wandsworth. At the height of production, he was employing approximately 200 people on these sites. The scale of this enterprise and a deeper look at the cutting-edge techniques during that era ably demonstrate an entrepreneurialism beyond all others at that time. Some of the lands he rented are now part of the Morden Hall Park estate. He was buried in St Lawrence's churchyard, Morden, as were his brother Stephen and son Peter[clxi].

A group of refugee felters and hat makers, who had fled from Caudebec in Normandy, also chose to settle in this area bringing with them the secrets of 'felting' hair from rabbits and beavers; indeed, their skill was such that their hats were highly prized across Europe. Hats have long been, until relatively recently, a much sought-after item of clothing for men and women, and for many years even children would not be expected to be seen in public without a hat.

The quality of the river water was ideal for their manufacturing processes – a significant factor for good quality dying and bleaching. Furthermore, the fast flow of the Wandle largely prevented ice forming during the winter months, thus preventing any major loss in production.

One refugee at the forefront of this developing trade was silk dyer Peter Dubuison who had perfected a method of fixing a red dye known as *Wandsworth Scarlet[144]*. It was also favoured by the East India Company for its soldiers' uniforms[clxii].

Amongst other trades that flourished in the area at this time were fishing, market-gardening[145], printing, leather-making, shoe-making and flour-milling.

[clxi] E N Montague, *Ravensbury Mitcham Histories* (The Ravensbury Print Works, 2008) pp.63-5.
[clxii] R. A. Shaw and R. D. Gwynn and P. Thomas, *Huguenots in Wandsworth* (Wandsworth, 1985) p11.

Soho

Soho was an area west of the city of London which attracted a high number of French Protestants; indeed, it was an area favoured almost as much as Spitalfields. This area, as well as Clerkenwell and the City itself, was favoured by clockmakers and those whose trades were connected to the *art of time,* such as 'escapement maker', 'engine turner', 'fusee cutter', 'springer', 'secret springer', 'finisher', and 'joint finisher'; in fact, often the occupants of whole streets were engaged in a trade connected to clock making.

It was also an area greatly favoured by silver and goldsmiths; the workshops of Paul Crespin, Nicholas Sprimont and Paul de Lamerie were all, at one time, within the boundaries of Soho.

Unlike Spitalfields, which had often been a safe haven for non-conformity, Soho had no such history; indeed, until the reign of Charles II in 1660 the area that was to become the parish of St Anne, Soho, was mainly green open spaces with paths criss-crossing the surrounding fields, contrasting with the intensive urbanisation seen in the area today. But change was coming as additional housing was required to meet the needs of an increasing population, fuelled in part by the steep rise of the French Protestant influx.

After visiting the house in Soho of a shopkeeper and his family in 1725, a 'German gentleman' wrote a description of his experience:

Once on a Sabbath Day I was requested to dine with a shopkeeper in this Parish: the man's income I believe might amount to about seventy pounds per annum, and his family consisted of one wife and a daughter of about eighteen, they were extraordinary economists, brewed their own beer, washed at home, made a joint hold out two days and a shift[146] three days; let three parts of their house ready furnished, and kept paying one quarter's Rent under another[clxiii].

[clxiii] Sheppard, Francis W., *The Huguenots in Spitalfields and Soho.* The Huguenot Society, Vol XXI (1968) p359.

Not all the land in Soho could be used for building due to there being a designated area of waste ground where there had once stood a Pest House and burial ground for the thousands who had perished in the Great Plague of 1665, and which was apparently still unused in the early 19th century. In 1720, John Strype, vicar of Leyton (at that time in Essex) describes one street in the neighbourhood, Berwick Street, as being *'a pretty handsome street, with new built houses and inhabited by the French, where they have a church*[147]*'*. In the mid-18th century, William Maitland observed that: '*Many parts of this parish so greatly abound with French that it is an easy matter for a stranger to imagine himself in France'*.

Following the French Revolution, there was yet a further influx of refugees, but this time it was notable that they were mainly Catholics – with, ironically, a sizeable proportion of priests amongst their numbers. However, this time the main reason for fleeing was not religious, but rather to escape the brutal upheavals, both social and political, of that period.

Clerkenwell

Unlike other areas of London where Huguenots chose to settle, there does not exist a great deal of written records about Clerkenwell, but within its narrow streets and alleyways could be found workshops full of flammable goods – indeed, fire was an ever-present danger. Perhaps because a significant number of their ancestors had been forced to leave their goods and money behind in France, Huguenot craftsmen were especially conscious of insuring themselves against this risk. Sun Insurance fire policy registers[148] reveal craftsmen with French names in many streets. Indeed, a search through the insurance policy records reveals some of the Huguenots who lived and worked in Clerkenwell, such as: Arthur Houle living in Exmouth Market (known then as Brayne's Row), a silver chaser whose work included delicate engraving on

The Story of the Huguenots – a Unique Legacy

watchcases; John Anthony Deschamps of Howards Place, Bowling Green Lane, an engine turner by profession; Lewis Furneaux, who lived in Rosoman Street, a watchmaker, and, further along the same street another watchmaker, Robert Chassereau[149]. The insurance records also give us an insight into the many diverse trades these Huguenot tradesmen were carrying out[150].

Finsbury

Not all areas of London retain obvious monuments or buildings to indicate the past presence of Huguenots – sometimes the evidence is hidden within records, yet a simple search can often unearth some surprising results. For example, to the north and east of Clerkenwell lies Finsbury, and this too became a place for Huguenots to live and work in. Peter Mallandain had been born at 29 Dunk Street, Mile End, and was baptised at St Dunstan's, Stepney, on 28 October 1798. He married Elizabeth Hodges on 17 June 1821 at St George's Church in Hanover Square, Mayfair. Peter was an inkstand maker and appears in numerous trade directories within the Finsbury area of that time. By 1823, Peter and Elizabeth were living at 12 Banner Street, off Bunhill Row, and an entry in the records of the Sun Insurance office shows that he had insured the contents of their brick and timber home, including wearing apparel, printed books, plate and glass stock and utensils for the sum of £100. The family moved in 1825 to nearby James Street, but a further entry in the Sun Insurance records shows the family continuing to insure their worldly goods with them. Mallandain & Co. was, furthermore, one of the 14,000 exhibitors at the Great Exhibition of 1851, proudly displaying three different types of table inkstands in the North Gallery[clxiv].

[clxiv] The Mallandain Archives.

Chelsea

The Treaty of Utrecht between France and England was signed in 1713 bringing to an end the War of the Spanish Succession. Not all welcomed the cessation of hostilities, the weavers were alarmed by news of a proposed treaty between the United Kingdom and France, so much so that later the same year they presented a petition to parliament stating that the government had, through various Acts of Parliament, so successfully stimulated the growth of the silk industry that it was now deemed 20 times greater than it had been in the year 1664. The petition also went on to point out that the black silk for hoods and scarves that had been manufactured in the United Kingdom for the last 25 years had grown in annual value to over £300,000 in the previous few years, and that these materials that had hitherto earned income exclusively for France prior to the refugees settling here was now generating significant value at home. Indeed, the industry was now so valuable that in 1718 John Appletree, a Worcestershire businessman, visualised the idea of the United Kingdom commencing silk farming, thus removing any reliance at all on imports from Italy of raw silk.

He was granted a patent and established the Raw Silk Company. He then set about raising funds by offering the chance to the public to financially contribute to this venture. He paid £200 for a 61-year lease for Chelsea Park from William Sloane as the site had been suggested as an excellent place to grow mulberry trees. Within a short time 2,000 trees were planted and a large heated house was built to nurture the silk worms; in 1723 satin was, for the first time, created from the raw silk produced by English silk worms. But this success was extremely short-lived as the company was soon in financial trouble, possibly following the recent changes to the import tax on raw silk. The trees and the house were sold off just one year later.

* * * * * *

Huguenots populated areas further afield well beyond the boundaries of London: from the north of England to the south and east to west there are to be found any number of small settlements, various aspects of which can be found in later chapters of this book.

- 17 -

Spitalfields and Silk Weaving

Spitalfields took its name from the Hospital and Priory of St Mary's, founded in 1197. 'Spital' was a common medieval word used to describe a hospital. It had remained a largely rural area until after the Great Fire of London, when development of the area was granted to ease overcrowding in the City of London.

The origins of silk-weaving in Spitalfields can be traced back to before the 1680s, but as ever greater numbers of Huguenot silk weavers sought refuge in the area, so the silk industry grew rapidly.

Spitalfields at that time covered a wider area than it does today and included large sections of present-day Bethnal Green, Shoreditch, Whitechapel and Mile End New Town. Between 1685 and 1700, an estimated 25,000 Huguenot refugees settled here. The area took on a distinctive gallic appearance as houses sprang up that displayed more French than English architecture – the builders tailoring their construction to their clients' requirements.

By the late 17th century, the need had arisen to provide housing for the lower orders of the silk weaving trade, and it was in nearby Brick Lane and the surrounding area that developments sprang up with rows of neat, small houses built on a limited budget to cater only for people's most basic needs. By the middle of the 18th century, the parish had been completely built over. Once a pleasant country retreat attracting the gentry, by the 1750s Bethnal Green had become saturated with hordes of the unwelcome poor in search of work and shelter[clxv].

From the 1720s, the area of Spitalfields itself had begun to be developed through the construction of elegant houses for wealthy master weavers, such as those that still grace Fournier Street and Elder Street. Today, a walk down Fournier Street (formerly Church Street) reveals some of the uniquely original architectural touches applied to these houses; for example, the wooden panelling of the shutters that open out onto the street. Should you be able to step inside, you would view the original ornate woodwork that survives still in just a few properties. Sadly, with the passage of time, much of the beautiful and intricate carving that once graced the interiors has now gone, although fortunately a small number of examples do still exist in privately owned properties in the area. Some of these houses are famous more for their previous occupants rather than their architecture. One such house, no.14, was built in 1726, but leased to silk weavers, who were eventually commissioned to weave the silk for Queen Victoria's coronation gown[clxvi151].

As Spitalfields was outside the City of London, it was not subject to the strict controls applied by the City Guilds, and an earlier settlement had already been established by those Huguenots who had discovered the added bonus that the cost of living here was much lower than any other part of London; thus Huguenot weavers soon began setting up their looms in their own homes[clxvii].

Their Calvinist belief in the virtue of hard work, self-discipline and thrift had the direct effect of bringing a degree of sobriety to the East End of London; indeed, the editor of *Stow's Survey of London* paid tribute to the character and industriousness of these refugees:

[clxv] John Marriot, *Beyond the Tower: A History of East London* (London, 2012) p59.
[clxvi] John Costella, *Walk with me Charles Dickens* (Bloomington, 2014) pX.
[clxvii] The Mallandain Archives.

Here they have found quiet and security and settled themselves in their several trades and occupations; weavers especially. Whereby God's blessing surely is not only brought upon the Parish by receiving poor strangers, but also a great advantage hath accrued to the whole nation by the rich manufactures of weaving silks and stuffs and camlets, which art they brought along with them. And this benefit also to the neighbourhood, that these strangers may serve for patterns of thrift, honesty, industry and sobriety as well[clxviii].

The silk industry was one which not only brought great wealth to the country but also to some of the individuals whose skills and enterprise surpassed all others. Those who chose to establish their homes and their looms in Spitalfields began producing large quantities of lustrings[152] and velvets as well as mixed fibres (silk and wool). Lustrings was a newly discovered and imported innovation from Lyon that enabled lustre to be given to silk taffeta, which had become very popular within English society – it was known as silk lustring or English taffeta. The secret had been brought over from Lyon by the refugee Mongeorge, thus reducing considerably the importation of such material – to the remarkable extent that Spitalfields went on to gain the lion's share of this lucrative market to the detriment of Lyon.

In 1681, a Royal Charter incorporating the Royal Lustring Company was granted; one of their first undertakings was to lobby Parliament for an Act banning the importation of foreign lustring and alamodes[153] on the grounds that the high quality material being produced in Spitalfields rendered importation no longer necessary. This, and a further charter granted in 1698, increased the powers of the company by giving them:

[clxviii] **The Mallandain Archives.**

the sole right of the making, dressing, and lustrating plain and black alamodes, renforcez[154] and lustrings in England and Wales for 14 years.

However, before this charter expired, public tastes had changed, and new textiles became fashionable; unfortunately, the Lustring Company was forced to close following the loss of all its financial assets.

* * * * * *

Weavers would naturally want to ensure the family business continued through successive generations; two options were available to the family – either to teach their children the trade, or alternatively they could arrange for them to be 'apprenticed' to another master weaver to learn the knowledge and skills necessary to produce the high-quality cloth so desirous of their discerning clientele[155]. The Dupen family arrived from France and settled in Bethnal Green, remaining there for several generations. In 1688, John Dupen was indentured as an apprenticed weaver for seven years; his indenture certificate still survives within the Dupen family records, and a photo of this rare original document has been included in this book.

An indenture was a legally binding document, and a translation of John Dupen's indenture is as follows:

This Indenture, Witnesseth, that John Dupon[156], son of John Dupon of St. Dunstan Stepney in _____ doth put himself Apprentice to John Nipping, Citizen and WEAVER of London, to learn his Art and with him (after the manner of Apprentice) to serve from the day of the date hereof, unto the full end and term of Seven years, from thence next following to be fully complete and ended. During which term the said Apprentice, his said Master faithfully shall serve, his Secrets keep, his lawful Commandments everywhere gladly do. He shall do no damage to his said Master, nor see to be done of others, but that he to his power shall let or forthwith give warning to his said Master of the same. He shall not waste the [resources] of his said Master nor lend them unlawfully to any. He shall not commit Fornication, nor contract Matrimony within the said term. He shall not play at Cards, Dice, Tables or any other unlawful Games whereby his said Master may have any loss. With his own goods or others, during the said term, without License of his said Master he shall neither buy nor sell. He shall not haunt Taverns or Playhouses, nor absent himself from his said master's service day or night unlawfully: But in all things as a faithful Apprentice, he shall behave himself towards his said Master and all his, during the said term. And the said Master to his said Apprentice in the same Art which he useth, by the best means that he can, shall teach and instruct or cause to be taught and instructed finding unto his said Apprentice meat, drink, apparel, lodging, and all other necessaries according to the custom of the City of London, during the said term. And for the true performance of all and even the said Covenants and agreements, either of the said Parties bindeth himself unto the other by these presents.

In Witness whereof, the Parties above named to these Indentures Interchangeably have put their Hands and Seals, the eighth day of May Anno Dom 1688 and in the fourth year of the reign of our Sovereign Lord King JAMES the Second over England.

Witnesses: John Nipping,
Charles Burroughs [clxix].

[clxix] The Dupen Archives.

The government had throughout shown a keen desire for the French refugees to teach the natives their skills, and so they also passed on their knowledge to the indigenous population with such aptitude that soon locals were able to equal and, in some cases, excel their teachers. French towns – Tours and Lyon in particular – lost highly skilled artisans to Spitalfields, and it was from these areas that three French refugees, Lauson, Mariscot and Monceaux – who stood head and shoulders above all other weavers both for their skill with the loom and the art of teaching – had travelled[clxx].

Throughout most of this period the Spitalfields weaver continued to thrive, but, alarmingly, imports continued to increase due to the natives' partiality for French materials and fashions[157].

London's silk industry was not only populated by weavers, and in and around the predominantly 'silk' district of Spitalfields there could also be found any number of associated trades necessary for the silk weaver to draw on in order to produce his finished high-quality material.

By 1721, the manufacture of silk in this country had increased to an annual value of £700,000, and the government passed an Act to encourage this industry still further. This Act provided for the exporter to reclaim part of the export duties paid based upon the import duties levied on the raw materials. Life did not always run smoothly for the silk weaver and his workers. The imposition of high import duties on French silks consequently led to widespread smuggling of silk from France[158]. The Weavers Company expended a great deal of time and effort in trying to bring the smugglers to justice, but this met with only limited success.

As membership began to decline, the Weavers Company decided to embark on a policy of admitting 'qualified' persons to the 'freedom' at 50 per cent of the usual fee: in 1761, the Court of Assistants took the decision that for the forthcoming year any qualified person wishing to become a freeman[159] but whose

---

[clxx] Samuel Smiles, *The Huguenots Their Settlements, Churches and Industries in England and Ireland (1889)* (London) p269.

The Story of the Huguenots – a Unique Legacy

financial circumstances made this impossible would be permitted to pay only half the fee normally due. Non-members of all ages and ranges of experience applied. This policy was instigated to deter those of low income from either forming their own companies or possibly even rioting in protest, as well as encouraging new membership of the Guild. One of the resulting applications for this reduced fee was listed for Lewis Gasquel, a French Protestant refugee weaver from Nimes. Lewis had fled his homeland in May 1752, arriving in Lausanne, Switzerland. He then travelled to Holland before finally settling in Ireland, where he took the oath and made the declaration approved by William III to encourage French Protestants to settle in Ireland[clxxi].

In 1763, further stringent efforts were made to curb smuggling, but the official enquiry ordered by the Committee of the Privy Council noted that smuggling, in spite of measures put in place to curb it, had instead increased, and was directly impacting on the livelihoods of weavers, which in turn gave rise to further riots erupting in Spitalfields.

The weavers' and journeymen's ongoing desire to protect the prevailing level of wages began to force their employers, whose main aim was after all to drive up both profits and productivity, towards the emerging new technology-based practices to achieve these goals. The breakup of the joint venture of weavers and their masters soon gave rise to acrimonious 'disagreements' especially on the topic of wages, leading to the famous 'Spitalfields Acts' of 1773, 1792 and 1811. The Act of 1773 gave the aldermen of London and the magistrates of Middlesex the powers to set the wages of weavers and journeymen during the quarter sessions, and penalties were imposed both on the master and any journeyman or weaver who flouted these pay scales. The 1792 Act included some legal rights for weavers working on, amongst other materials, mixed silk, and the Act of 1811 extended rights to female workers,

---

[clxxi] Alfred Plummer, *The London Weavers Company 1600-1700* (Abingdon, 1972) p318.

- 182 -

who had been overlooked in the earlier Acts. Such legislation was meant to give justice, but it eventually led to the demise of the silk trade in Spitalfields. Many masters decided to move out of the Spitalfields area into other areas of silk manufacturing such as Norwich, Manchester, Paisley or Glasgow, where they could pay cheaper wages by being outside the county of Middlesex – the only area legally covered by the Spitalfields Acts until they were finally repealed in 1824.

The journeymen weavers had other formidable supporters during their many years of struggle: there had been the Levellers[160] from the time of the English Civil War; the populist John Wilkes during the 1760s, and then the Chartist[161] movement in the 1830s. In fact, radicals such as Leveller leader John Lilburne campaigned tirelessly on behalf of the common working man, including silk weavers; despite imprisonment and brutal torture at the hands of the royalist government, he was successful in arousing immense sympathy for them amongst other groups in English society.

In 1816, following the Napoleonic Wars, a deep recession was felt by many, but especially by the impoverished weavers. A public meeting was held on 26 November at the Mansion House in London to discuss some possible relief for the weavers, and it was noted that a significant proportion of them – some two thirds – were without employment or any other means of support:

> *some had even deserted their houses in despair unable to endure the sight of their starving families, and many pined under languishing diseases brought on by the want of food and clothing.*[clxxii]

With the repeal of the Spitalfields Acts in 1824 came destitution for the weavers and their families as the silk industry of the area dwindled. By 1831, there were still 50,000 people living in Spitalfields and the areas close by who were reliant on the demand for silk production to earn a living, yet an estimated

---

[clxxii] The Spitalfields Silk weavers: London's Luddites, p16 [PDF]

30,000 during the 1830s were unemployed for often lengthy periods due to the relentless march of the Industrial Revolution.

One business empire that can be said to have emanated in Spitalfields, hence its inclusion in this chapter, was founded by George Courtauld. Son of Samuel Courtauld, himself a Huguenot silversmith, George was born in 1761, and served a seven-year apprenticeship with Peter Merzeau before setting up his own business as a throwster in Spitalfields. Eventually, in 1785, George emigrated to America, where he met and married Ruth Minton. Yet he was to return to England in 1794, going into partnership with his cousin Peter Taylor at a mill in Pebmarsh, Essex – and thus the company known as George Courtauld & Co began its successful journey into the rapidly developing world of commerce and capitalism. They expanded this business through the acquisition of a further mill at Bocking, Essex, and by 1810, George had begun another business of his own – a silk mill at Braintree, Essex. Courtauld developed a silk spindle for use in his mill, patenting his invention in 1814. Samuel employed mainly children from the age of ten to work at his mills, firstly local children, then as his business grew he started to employ children from further afield, mainly girls from workhouses in London. George Courtauld fervently believed he was also training the girls for adulthood, and in a letter written in 1813 claimed that his mill would provide a nursery of respectable young women fit for any of the humbler walks of life.

Sadly, not all was as bright and cosy as this picture paints. Complaints of girls being beaten by the woman supervisor in the end led to George's own daughters being given supervisory responsibility for the girls, and to their credit they devised a system that was fair and correct enough to reflect each girl's work and character. Although the girls were banned from talking while they worked, they were nonetheless encouraged to sing hymns.

In 1818, George returned to America, having handed over the business to his son Samuel who, with his partner Peter Taylor,

The Story of the Huguenots – a Unique Legacy

built further mills at Halstead and Bocking. Within seven years, Samuel had installed steam power at Bocking Mill, and power looms at Halstead. By 1850, Courtauld's three mills employed over 2,000 people. Samuel died in 1881, but the company continued its run of success through sheer diligence and hard work. In 1900, the company acquired the British rights to the viscose process for making *synthetic* silk; then in 1916, it started the production of sulphuric acid and carbon disulphide at a factory in Trafford Park, Lancashire. By 1936, the company was often advertised as the leading manufacturer of men's and women's hosiery, with Courtauld's rayon being described as the best in the world.

Just nine years before, George Courtauld had formed a partnership with his cousin; mechanisation had begun to make inroads into the handloom weaver's livelihood when the first power loom had been invented by Edmund Cartwright in 1785, and although his machine was cumbersome to operate, in time the advent of such an efficient mechanised loom led to the demise of hand-loom weaving[clxxiii].

* * * * * *

In a Poor Law Report dated 1837, Dr James Kay[162] described the methods and conditions of a weaver and his family:

> *A weaver has generally two looms, one for his wife and another for himself, and as his family increases the children are set to work at six or seven years of age to quill silk; at nine or ten years to pick silk; and at the age of twelve or thirteen (according to the size of the child) he is put to the loom to weave. A child very soon learns to weave a plain silk fabric, so as to become proficient in that branch; a*

[clxxiii] Arthur Birnie, MA, *The March of History: The Early Nineteenth Century to the Present Day (retrospect 1760-1832)* (Edinburgh) p12.

weaver has thus not unfrequently four looms on which members of his own family are employed. The houses occupied by the weavers are constructed for the special convenience of their trade, having in the upper stories wide, lattice-like windows which run across almost the whole frontage of the house. These 'lights' are absolutely necessary in order to throw a strong light on every part of the looms, which are usually placed directly under them. Many of the roofs present a strange appearance, having ingenious bird-traps of various kinds and large birdcages, the weavers having long been famed for their skill in snaring song-birds. They used largely to supply the home market with linnets, goldfinches, chaffinches, greenfinches, and other song birds which they caught by trained 'call birds' and other devices in the fields of north and east London.

Some of these wide, high, multi-paned top-floor windows can still be seen in older buildings in and around Spitalfields today.

Although the skilled weaver did put his children to work to support the family business very early in their lives, and while he was often relatively well-paid, the weaver could, however, be periodically reduced to poverty; partly this was caused by economic depressions in the cloth trade, one of the earliest recorded being that of 1620-40: '*On the occurrence of a commercial crisis the loss of work occurs first among the least skilful operatives, who are discharged from work*[clxxiv]'.

This and other issues could lead to further outbreaks of rebelliousness that was sometimes aimed at their bosses and betters, and sometimes at migrant workers, who were seen as lowering wages and taking work away from 'natives'.

[clxxiv] G. Dodd, Charles Knight (ed.), *London*, (Knight, London, 1842) p396.

A sizable deputation of several hundred starving Spitalfields weavers assembled at Mansion House in March 1837 to present a petition which stated:

TO THE RIGHT HONOURABLE THE LORD MAYOR
May it please your lordship – The humble petition of the Operative Broad Silk Weavers of Spitalfields and its vicinity most respectfully showeth that your petitioners are in a state of the greatest destitution and misery from the want of employment, thousands being at the present moment in a state bordering upon pauperism, without any hope of relief, unless the recommendations of her most gracious Majesty can be carried into effect.
We therefore humbly pray your lordship to take our deplorable case into your serious consideration and adopt such measures as your lordship may in your wisdom think prudent, to relieve the distress that the operative broad silk weavers of Spitalfields are now labouring under.

As a direct consequence, meetings were held to discuss the petition and what best means could be applied to speedily alleviate the poor weavers. A fund was set up and the queen herself sent an interim donation of £100 to the Lord Mayor of London – other donations swiftly followed, and a committee was appointed to oversee and distribute the relief money. Many of the committee members had visited the poor weavers and were distressed to learn that these people's needs had been so great that they had been forced to sell their few possessions on an almost daily basis, including furniture and even clothes, merely to survive. Not only was this due to the exceptionally low wage rates prevailing at the time but there was also a serious drop in trade, and many weavers never again plied their trade, instead seeking work in other spheres – if possible[clxxv].

[clxxv] The Rondeau Archives.

In 1839, a Royal Commission compiled a report on *'The Condition of the Hand Loom Weavers'* as by then their long-term means of earning a living was being seriously undermined by the invention of the mechanised Jacquard looms[163]. The commissioners in part based their report on their visit to William Bresson's house in Orange Street. William was a velvet weaver and loom broker, and to supplement his income he rented out looms in his house to journeyman weavers. The report states that William's house was a small one containing but three small rooms, with a fourth barely large enough for six looms. It goes on to say that the two families who occupied the house had to pay the exorbitant rent of £16 with an extra charge of £2.5s[164] per annum for the small strip of flower garden in the front. The commissioners also noted:

> *...there is no cess pool nor sewer to carry off the soil from the privy, and close to the house runs a stagnant ditch filled with abominable black filth for which there is no drain[clxxvi].*

Charles Dickens visited Spitalfields in 1851 with his close friend and sub-editor William Willis. The silk weaving trade was waning by this time, but Dickens was fascinated by, in his words: *'the ramshackle wooden constructions upon tops of homes, formerly weavers' workshops, used for breeding pigeons'.*

Yet, the first thing he noticed when he arrived in the area was the number of unemployed, pallid-faced silk weavers silently and dejectedly seated on doorsteps fronting houses that were now decaying and dirty from neglect. Clearly their fortunes had continued downwards with the unstoppable march of mechanisation. Previously the area had been home to between 14-17,000 weavers, notably all of them silk weavers, whereas by the time of Dickens' arrival, the number had dwindled to just ten[165]. However, Dickens noted with glad

---

[clxxvi] Cruickshank, Dan, Spitalfields: The History of a Nation in a handful of Streets (London, 2017) p327

The Story of the Huguenots – a Unique Legacy

surprise the unusual architecture: '*It is as if the Huguenots had brought their streets along with them from France and dropped them down here[clxxvii]*'.

* * * * * *

The weavers were reliant on designers to produce patterns for them to weave. Within the Spitalfields area were two famous designers. Anna Maria Garthwaite was not of Huguenot descent, but worked closely with the Huguenots in the area. Anna moved into one of these houses on the corner of Princelet Street and Wilkes Street with her sister (who, as mentioned in an earlier chapter, was a neighbour of the Rondeau family). Anna Maria had been born and raised in Grantham, Lincolnshire, where she trained as a watercolour artist, but soon after arrival in London she began creating designs for silk textiles. Her designs were of such outstanding quality that the local silk weavers were purchasing these as soon as they became available; a photograph of one of her designs, bought by John Rondeau in 1741, is included in this book [clxxviii]. She created over 1,000 design patterns during her career, unrivalled by any other designer. One of her designs, woven by a highly skilled Spitalfields Huguenot silk weaver, was made into a sumptuous gown that can still be viewed in the Museum of London. It was worn only once by Ann Fanshawe on the occasion of her father's appointment as Lord Mayor of London in 1752 – especially important to the family as her mother had died 12 years earlier, and Ann therefore took her mother's place as Lady Mayoress.

The second designer was James Leman of Huguenot descent, and who became apprenticed in 1702 to his father, Peter, a wealthy master weaver. The family lived in Steward Street, Spitalfields. James displayed a remarkable flair as a designer and creator of

---

[clxxvii] John Costella, *Walk with me Charles Dickens* (Bloomington, 2014) pp.290-1.
[clxxviii] The Rondeau Archives.

patterned dress fabrics. His talent was such that he become renowned as the indisputable specialist in both fields throughout the kingdom. Within the Victoria and Albert Museum in London are fine examples of his initial designs, some of which date back to 1706; a few are touchingly inscribed with the words: *'for my father, Peter Leman, by me, James Leman'*.

James was appointed Foreign Master to the Weavers Company in 1711, and he took an active part in the Weavers Company until his death in 1745.

One of his designs is believed to have been used to produce the canopy for the coronation of George II, and it is preserved amongst the Victoria and Albert's historic textiles collection.

- 18 -

Huguenot European Emigration

For various reasons, countless Huguenots who left France did not always settle in the first country they sought refuge in. A great number were encouraged to seek their new life further afield, and this book would certainly be incomplete without a mention of those who travelled onwards to their eventual, final settlements. As the extent of the Huguenot diaspora is vast and far-flung, and the list of countries many and varied, I have divided these entries into continents.

EUROPE
The Channel Islands
Being in such close proximity to France, these islands were a natural refuge for those seeking to escape from persecution. The first migration of Huguenots took place in 1548, but Henri II's edicts quickly increased the flow of refugees to these tiny islands, where Protestantism swiftly and firmly took root except for the turbulent hiatus of a few very uncertain years following the death of the Protestant Edward VI, and the accession of his staunchly Catholic half-sister Mary. With Mary's death barely five years later enabling their half-sister Elizabeth to become Queen of England, the tide of migration once more resumed.

The Story of the Huguenots – a Unique Legacy

Although many refugees travelled onwards to other countries, the seeds of Calvinist Protestantism were to grow quickly here, so much so that a synod in 1576 on Guernsey chose to approve the Calvinist form of worship. Jersey, Sark and Alderney also adopted the Huguenot faith, but it seems that the extremely strict adherence to the doctrines of the faith were to prove too much for some, fuelling consequent emigration to England or America[clxxix].

Daniel Francois Durand, the son of Francois Guillaume Durand and his wife Anne (whom we previously learnt about when they were being punished for their faith) had been educated by the Jesuits. He studied at the Bar and by the age of 20 had graduated from Montpellier University. In 1702, 22-year-old Daniel joined the French army, his commission, ironically, being signed by Louis XIV. Three years later, the Durand family made good their escape to Holland. Daniel's passport states:

...we Councillor of State, Administrator of the Province of Languedoc etc. certify that Sr. Daniel Francois Durand, Advocate, his wife and one child have left Montpellier to go to Lyon.

Daniel and his family eventually arrived in Holland one year later, where he was finally reunited with his father[clxxx].

1715 saw the birth of Daniel's son, Francois Guillaume Issaie, in Nijmegen. He was the first to fulfil the pledge his grandfather had made, when at the age of 23 he was accepted as a candidate into the Dutch Church; just over five years later, he was appointed to the Walloon Church in Canterbury, then in 1751 he was nominated by Sir John Ligonier, Lieutenant Governor of Guernsey, to the parish of St Sampson in the Vale, and was

---

[clxxix] G. Elmore Reaman, *The Trail of the Huguenots in Europe, the United States, South Africa and Canada* (London, 1964) p101.
[clxxx] The Durand Archives.

- 192 -

The Story of the Huguenots – a Unique Legacy

ordained deacon and priest on 1 September 1751, thus beginning the family's long association with Guernsey[clxxxi].

Ireland

Queen Elizabeth I had been the first to encourage settlement of the skilled Huguenots into Ireland, but this was not totally successful, no doubt due in part to the crown's inability to control the warring factions in Ireland[166], whereas James I achieved greater success when refugee merchants were encouraged to settle in Waterford and Dublin. But it was during the reign of Charles I that the linen making industry was established at Waterford, when, by the king's invitation, French and Flemish workers had been encouraged to emigrate to Ireland. The Earl of Stafford, in order to give the new industry a good start, put a great deal of his own wealth into this enterprise[clxxxii]. Other settlements during this time were at Clonmel, Carrick-On-Suir and Chapelizod, but by the 1670s they had significantly declined[clxxxiii]. A second wave of Huguenots arrived following increased pressure and cruelty during Louis XIV's reign. By 1684, it was estimated that 430 Huguenots were living and working in Dublin, but this number sharply increased to approximately 600 following the Revocation – only to fall again as both French and Irish Protestants hastily fled to England during the Jacobite Rebellion of 1745[clxxxiv].

The most important Huguenot influx took place following the accession of William and Mary, whereupon Huguenots of a broad range of diverse trades as well as the military and those of the nobility were encouraged to settle in Ireland.

William of Orange brought the Crommelin family from Holland when he came to England in 1688, doing all he could to

---

[clxxxi] The Durand Archives.

[clxxxii] G. Elmore Reaman, *The Trail of the Huguenots in Europe, the United States, South Africa and Canada* (London, 1964) p95.

[clxxxiii] Raymond Hylton, *Ireland's Huguenots and Their Refuge, 1662-1745* (Sussex, 2005) p25.

[clxxxiv] Ibid, p35.

- 193 -

The Story of the Huguenots – a Unique Legacy

encourage them to settle in Ireland to establish the linen industry there.

Portarlington became home to large numbers of military personnel once they were pensioned off following William's military victory in Ireland. William was put under immense pressure by Parliament to considerably reduce his military costs, yet he was greatly indebted to large numbers of Huguenots, and therefore felt an obligation to those who had demonstrated such loyalty, something that many would do again in the future. A further dilemma facing him were the rumours that the deposed Catholic Stuarts were planning an invasion in the vicinity of Cork on the south coast of Ireland, hoping to raise an army and march on Dublin. But to do this, the Stuarts and their followers would have to travel through the Irish Midlands, which would almost certainly mean passing close to the town of Portarlington. The Viscount of Galway at that time – Henry Ruvigny – was a prominent Huguenot leader and keen to settle retired Huguenot officers in and around the town, and thus a useful military pocket of Protestant resistance would be in the direct path of the Stuart advance. One such retired Huguenot officer was Guillaume Guion, who, as soon as he had been discharged from his regiment, had been given a passport and testimonials as well as free passage to Ireland and, upon arrival in Portarlington, given a pension[clxxxv].

At the time of his arrival in 1697, he would have found the area undergoing an immense expansion – the sounds of building work all around must have filled the air as both French and Irish Protestant builders toiled to meet the demand for extra housing. Guillaume settled into his new life, and he was granted naturalisation on 24 March 1699. Less than a year later, he married Elizabeth Cadroy with whom he had several children. Guillaume's position in the town was heightened when he was elected an Elder

---

[clxxxv] The Guion Archives.

of the Church on 7 May 1702 at just 32 years of age; an entry in the baptismal registers dated 31 October records the baptism of his daughter, Catherine Elizabeth Guion, the register being signed by none other than Isaac Dumont de Bostaquet[clxxxvi].

Portarlington had been confiscated from its Catholic owner by William of Orange following the 'Glorious Revolution' of 1688 and bestowed on Henry Ruvigny, one of his Huguenot commanders. Ruvigny soon began encouraging veterans and their families to settle in the town and its environs, with the offer of a pension for as long as they remained there, and they were also expected to form a local territorial army in case of trouble. The first settlers began arriving after the signing in 1691 of the *Treaty of Limerick*[167], but many more followed after the *Peace of Ryswick* in 1697 concluded the *War of the League of Augsburg*, after which Ruvigny was given a mandate and funds to help settle veterans in and around the town.

The area of Portarlington had been chosen for strategic reasons as it was suspected that the French might well try to stir up rebellion by firstly landing an army at Cork or Waterford and secondly a convenient point for the two armies to converge upon looked to be Portarlington.

Not all welcomed the new wave of Huguenot 'foreigners', the Church of Ireland openly disapproving of the non-conformist worship they practiced, which in turn caused some of the settlers to conform to the Anglican Church doctrines. The apprehension and unease felt by the conformists towards the non-conformists remained, although both sides appeared to learn to at least tolerate one another.

Not all of the veterans viewed Portarlington as a permanent place to settle, and many of those who were financially secure chose to move on to other places as and when the opportunity arose, such as the more affluent city of Dublin, but those who were more financially vulnerable – perhaps dependent solely on their

---

[clxxxvi] The Guion Archives.

The Story of the Huguenots – a Unique Legacy

pension to survive – seemed forced to remain there. Frequently, the pensions were paid late as politicians tried to reduce the burden on the exchequer of so many recipients, whilst Ruvigny and his staff did battle on the side of the pensioners. An example of a veteran who relied solely on his army pension, and who was to suffer the most, was Guillaume Guion – unable to leave as he was without an alternative means of financial support. He had raised a family and, by the time he died in Portarlington in 1740, at least two of his children still lived in the town[clxxxvii]. The Huguenot church the Guion family would have worshipped at continued to use the French language for its services until the early 1800s[168].

The church was to be repaired and eventually rebuilt in the 1850s following its noted bad condition; its past had certainly seen better days, and these included the time when, in 1715, it had been presented with two handsome gifts by Caroline, Princess of Wales: a bell for its tower, and the other (the more famous) a silver plate adorned with the inscription '*a l' église conformist á Portarlington[clxxxviii]* '.

The passage of time also saw several boarding and finishing schools[169] created in the later 18th and early 19th centuries to cater for those who wished their children to be taught not only the French language but French culture too as well as more mainstream subjects. If you should visit Portarlington today, you will find quite a few families there that can trace their ancestry back to Huguenot descendants[clxxxix].

Scotland

A number of schools and universities readily accepted Huguenots as their students. They were particularly welcomed by Sir Patrick Drummond, the Conservator of Scottish trade in 1625, who

---

[clxxxvii] The Guion Archives.
[clxxxviii] Powell, John S., *The French Church Portarlington: after the French*. The Huguenot Society, Vol XXVII No 4 (2001) p574.
[clxxxix] The Guion Archives.

The Story of the Huguenots – a Unique Legacy

encouraged them to settle at Campvere. But a new life in Scotland was not always going to be as smooth as it would initially seem. The immigrants wanted their own pastors to travel to Scotland and set up new churches. There were no strong objections from the Scottish Presbyterian (Protestant) Church. Presbyterianism – was very similar in many ways to Calvinism[cxc] – so in time the need for French pastors lessened as the Huguenots were able to blend in with the Presbyterians, and in fact they went on to play a key role in organising the future structure of the Scottish Presbyterian Church[cxci].

A range of industries were begun in Scotland following the arrival of the Huguenots; examples of those being plied by them was Deschamps, who, having settled in Scotland in the 1650s, began a practice of gathering rags in the streets for paper making; another, Daniel Marot, was the first to bring delftware to the attention of the Scottish housewife – again, he had been trained in France and Flanders before escaping persecution.

Although a French Church was set up for the refugees, most of the Church's records would appear to have perished. However, all is not lost as records and letters of the Board of Trustees, which had been formed in 1727 for the Improvement of Manufactures and Fisheries, were uncovered by John Mason, who later wrote a detailed account of the weavers of Picardy based on these records. He described how, in 1730, refugees such as Francis Bochard and Claude Paulin set up the manufacture of cambric in Edinburgh, where they began spinning and weaving and teaching the locals the skills for growing and preparing flax for weaving into linen. It is believed that the city councillors of Edinburgh, keen to encourage such highly skilled and industrious people, donated to them five acres of land for their enterprise[170 cxcii].

[cxc] Norman Davies, *Europe: A History* (London, 1997) p494.

[cxci] G. Elmore Reaman, *The Trail of the Huguenots in Europe, the United States, South Africa and Canada* (London, 1964) p89.

[cxcii] Springall, Anthony, *A Huguenot Community in Scotland: The Weavers of Picardy*. The Huguenot Society, Vol XXVII (1998) p97.

The arrival of a number of these Huguenots in Scotland took place a few decades after the revocation of the *Edict of Nantes* due to a revival of Protestantism in the area of Picardy, north-east France; this was due to Huguenots having either 'voluntarily' converted or been forced to convert to Catholicism. But, a few years later in 1690, a Calvinist preacher by the name of Givry chose to take the enormous risk of returning to Picardy, where he preached to an audience outside Templeux. His passionate sermon was to have a profound effect as 500 of the attendees immediately chose to abjure the Catholic faith despite the serious consequences of being labelled a lapsed Catholic; some at that point chose to leave their homeland to start again as Protestants elsewhere. Of those who stayed, they and their descendants became, and remained, one of the largest Protestant congregations in Picardy right up to the second half of the 19th century[cxciii].

On 14 May 1724, Louis XV hardened his attitude towards Huguenots by issuing sterner penalties against them including barring children of Protestant parents from inheriting, and by declaring such children illegitimate. This penalty was targeted particularly at Protestants living in rural locations where the family farm had for centuries past been handed down from father to son. It was the final blow for Francis (Francois) Bouchard and Claude Paulin, who took the decision to leave France via Tournai arriving in London in October 1724.

The Board of Trustees for Fisheries and Manufactures was established in Scotland three years after Bouchard and Paulin arrived in London; it had been primarily formed to boost economic development, and suggestions were put forward to offer skilled cambric workers and their families financial assistance if they would relocate to Scotland. Each family that accepted the offer was also to be given a house containing a kitchen, a subterranean

---

[cxciii] Springall, Anthony, A Huguenot Community in Scotland: The Weavers of Picardy. The Huguenot Society, Vol XXVII (1998) p98.

vault, a bedroom, a place for storing yarn, and a garden the size of one third of a Scottish acre[171].

Wood to construct four looms per family was also provided, and raw materials were available at discounted rates; settlers were given local tax exemption with the right to buy, sell and trade without resorting to the use of a middleman[cxciv].

Each master who accepted this generous offer had to agree to take on one new apprentice every five years for the purpose of teaching him every aspect of the trade.

Not all the Huguenot recruits were skilled weavers. Others who were targeted as being necessary to the success of the settlement included undertaker Nicholas Dassauville whose craftsmanship would be useful for the construction of vital equipment such as the looms; indeed, many of the weavers were recruited by Dassauville, who had been offered a contract by the Board of Trade to draft in skilled workers and their families. One man was even enlisted to come to Edinburgh with his family specifically to manufacture brushes and combs – necessary for the manufacturing processes of cambric and linen.

To the disappointment of the Board, Nicholas Dassauville would not be one of the first to arrive to oversee the planning and construction of the site, but he did travel over with the second party via Rotterdam and London[172].

Everyone was given temporary accommodation and living expenses whilst their homes and the factory were constructed.

Initially, it was the women of the families who contributed the most significant success in Scotland as they undertook a three-month tour of Glasgow to teach others the French method of weaving, and were so successful that two of the women, Anne Dassauville and her married daughter Anne Fleming, were given

---

[cxciv] Springall, Anthony, *A Huguenot Community in Scotland: The Weavers of Picardy*. The Huguenot Society, Vol XXVII (1998) pp.97-9.

The Story of the Huguenots – a Unique Legacy

permanent employment as 'spinning mistresses' with a salary of £15 per annum[173] at a spinning school in Paisley[cxcv].

The Board did all it could to ensure the success of the enterprise in every way possible, but sadly it was fraught with many production and marketing difficulties that included numerous complaints, ultimately leading to Huguenot families leaving Scotland for London. By 1800, the former Huguenot homes in 'Picardy Edinburgh' were so badly decayed they had to be demolished[cxcvi].

Germany

The *Thirty Years War* (1618-48) had left parts of Prussia in a ruinous state – many towns and cities were razed to the ground, and it needed the stimulus of hardworking Huguenots to help rejuvenate the country. The *Peace of Westphalia* stipulated that equality would from then on be given to Lutherans, Reformed (i.e. Calvinists) and Catholics, but this did not bring the desired tolerance and harmony overnight. Although Lutherans and Calvinists were both branches of Protestantism, a number of Lutheran states viewed Calvinists with suspicion (the Hohenzollern rulers of Prussia were to convert to Calvinism from Lutheranism in the early 17th century), fearful of their Protestant 'brothers' intent. Other parts of Prussia[174], whose rulers were genuinely sympathetic, became a welcoming haven.

The Elector of Prussia, Friedrich Wilhelm, was a Calvinist; indeed, his wife was a great-granddaughter of Coligny, and he did much to encourage Huguenots to travel to, and set up home in, Prussia, particularly in Brandenburg – an area that was unique as it tolerated both Calvinism and Lutheranism[cxcvii]. This area had been severely damaged during the *Thirty Years War;* its soil was barren, its industries laid waste. He enthusiastically welcomed the

---

[cxcv] Springall, Anthony, *A Huguenot Community in Scotland: The Weavers of Picardy.* The Huguenot Society, Vol XXVII (1998) p102.
[cxcvi] Ibid, p105.
[cxcvii] Norman Davies, *Europe: A History* (London, 1997) p494.

The Story of the Huguenots – a Unique Legacy

Huguenots, seeing their numerous and diverse skills as extremely fortuitous in the necessary task of rejuvenating his lands, and cities such as Schwabach (Brandenburg-Ansbach) and Erlangen (Brandenburg-Bayreuth) were soon populated with Huguenots.

Other states with like-minded, sympathetic rulers keen to encourage the Huguenots also extended an offer of welcome, among them the Hessian principalities of Hessen-Cassel with its university city of Cassel, where Denis Papin had, like many of his Huguenot colleagues, gained employment. The Landgrave Friedrich II (nephew to Friedrich Wilhelm, the Great Elector) had great empathy with the Huguenots, stating: *'I would rather sell my silverware than deny these poor people asylum.'* A man of his word, he duly set up a colony at Friedrichsdorf in 1687, which, incidentally, the grateful refugees named in his honour.

Some of the first Huguenots to settle in Friedrichsdorf were from the Privat, Rossignol, Foucar, Dippel and Agombar families. Although a member of the Agombar family had previously chosen to leave Picardy in France to seek a new life in London, Solomon Agombar and his wife Marie decided to leave France a few years after the Revocation, choosing to travel to Prussia to make their home in Friedrichsdorf. The descendants of Solomon and Marie Agombar continued to live in the vicinity of Friedrichsdorf for several generations until the last male Agombar died in 1940[cxcviii].

Further south, many principalities did not wholeheartedly embrace the reality of these new Huguenot settlers; ironically, Württemberg – where Luther, in nailing his theses to the cathedral door, had unknowingly initiated the 'Reformation' – showed dogged resistance to any settlement before eventually bowing to the inevitable[cxcix]. An example of the high-level keenness to embrace and welcome Huguenots was the *Edict of Potsdam* in 1685, which states:

[cxcviii] The Agombar Archives.
[cxcix] Privat, E.C., *The Huguenots in Germany*. The Huguenot Society, Vol. XXI No2 (1966) p115.

- 201 -

The Story of the Huguenots – a Unique Legacy

All rights, privileges and other benefits…accrue not only to those who arrive hereafter in Our Lands, but also to those who escaped from France before publication of this Edict and took refuge in these Our Lands, before previous religious persecutions; but those who are devoted to the Roman Catholic faith have in no way to presume to like favour.

We propose to set up Commissions in each and every one of Our Lands and Provinces to which the said Frenchmen may apply both on their arrival and afterward, and receive from them counsel and assistance; whereby We most graciously and earnestly enjoin all Our Governors, Governments, and other Servants and Commanders in towns and in the country, in all Our Provinces, through this public Edict and also through special orders, to take Our said French Evangelical-Reformed co-religionists, all and sundry, as many of them as shall come to Our country, under their special care and protection, to maintain and keep them expressly in all the Privileges hereby graciously conceded them, and in no wise to suffer that the least harm, injustice, or vexation be done them, but rather that they be shown all help, friendship, and good treatment. We have signed this Edict for record with Our own hand and have had Our Seal of Grace imprinted on it.

Given at Potsdam, October 29, 1685
Friedrich Wilhelm
Elector

This document[cc] not only granted asylum to Huguenots, but furthermore gave every possible assistance for them to travel to cities such as Hamburg and Frankfurt-am-Main, and onwards to many other towns and cities, including the major centres of

---

[cc] C. A. Macartney, *The Hapsburg and Hohenzollern Dynasties in the 17th and 18th Centuries* (New York, 1970) p274.

Brandenburg, Magdeburg and Berlin, and the Hanseatic League port of Königsberg in the easternmost part of Prussia. The edict also stated that their property would be free of taxation for 12 years, and that houses would be built for them; importantly, the edict granted them freedom to worship according to their Calvinist beliefs as well as the liberty to build their own churches and elect their own ministers.

Financial aid was provided by the authorities to assist those arriving in the various German principalities. One example of the aid given can be seen in the records of Frankfurt-am-Main where, between 1665 and 1705, 50,000 florins were spent in assisting 97,816 Huguenot refugees passing through the town from France[cci].

The most welcomed were those with industrial and agricultural skills, in addition to those with a commission in the army. Berlin and Magdeburg gained much from the Huguenots and became centres of industry, but the area that could lay claim to the greatest success was undoubtedly Friedrichsdorf.

The early Huguenots who came to the town travelled from more than one area of France – the majority had left their homes in northern France from regions such as Picardy, Ile de France and Champagne, but a few had travelled much further – from provinces in the south, such as Dauphiné, Provence and Languedoc. Because of this assortment of originating areas, they inevitably brought their own region's dialect, which in many families remained their spoken language for several generations – perhaps not in its purest form, but still French nonetheless[ccii]. Much as in London, there had been Huguenot families who for generations still spoke amongst themselves only in French. Berlin could lay claim to almost 25 per cent of its population being

---

[cci] Privat, E.C., *The Huguenots in Germany*. The Huguenot Society, Vol. XXI No2 (1966) p116.
[ccii] G. Elmore Reaman, *The Trail of the Huguenots in Europe, the United States, South Africa and Canada* (London, 1964) p105.

Huguenot by the early 1700s, an astonishing statistic, and the beautiful Huguenot Cathedral in Berlin – Französischer Dom – was originally built based on the design of the temple of Charenton. Partially destroyed during the Second World War, Französischer Dom was rebuilt in 1977-81, and is today still a place of worship. Part of the church now houses a Huguenot museum.

The German Huguenot Society was founded on 29 September 1890. The driving force behind this was the minister of the reformed congregation in Magdeburg, Doctor Henri Tollin.

Denmark

Although a colony of Huguenots had already settled at Fredericia in the eastern part of the Jutland peninsula, this area did not become home to Huguenots until 1719-20. King Frederic IV encouraged the settlement not for religious reasons but economic ones. The king wanted to create a tobacco plantation so that Denmark could become self-sufficient in producing enough leaves to satisfy its home market, but this venture proved to be a failure. One reason was that the colony was very small – even as late as 1850, its maximum numbers peaked at no more than 500.

To give some indication of the continued migration of the Huguenots, one of the families who settled there were the Duponts[175]. Philipp Dupont was believed to have been born during the siege of La Rochelle in 1628 to Maria Sedan and Nicolas Dupont. Philipp did not long remain in France, instead travelling with his parents to Germany where he became a forpagter[176]. He married Jeanne Massey in 1650 and his first child Philippe Dupont – was born in Mannheim, Pfalz in 1652. By the time that Philippe's son, Matthieu, died in 1743, he had moved to Fredericia. Several generations later, descendants of the Duponts are now living in England[cciii].

[cciii] The Dupont Archives.

The colonists who settled in Fredericia soon set about structuring their society with a school and a temple of the 'reformed' faith, appointing their first pastor in 1722. The cost of constructing their temple was raised from other Huguenot communities in Denmark, Holland, Belgium (Wallonia)[177] and Germany.

The Netherlands

Holland and the Netherlands, being the nearest countries to northern France, drew large numbers of Huguenots to their lands primarily across the land border, but in both of these countries not all the refugees made the first place they landed their permanent home, as we have seen with the Durand and the Migault families.

The Franco-Dutch War had begun in 1672, and Louis XIV, having been keen to take control of the Netherlands, signed a secret treaty with England before invading. When the sizable French army led by Condé and Turenne swept through Flanders in 1762, they rapidly took three of the seven Dutch provinces. But William of Orange's hatred of France fired his determination to prevent further towns and cities falling beneath the French heel. As the French army neared Amsterdam, its citizens naturally became fearful of the consequences of their city's likely capture. De Witt[178] advised submission, but William scorned his advice and instead proposed resistance, declaring that he would rather die in the last ditch than see the ruin of his country. His countrymen applauded his stance and he now ordered the dykes to be breached to flood a large area around Amsterdam. With England subsequently making peace with the Netherlands, and the path of the French army being either blocked or hampered by stiffening resistance, the Dutch now went on the offensive and had pushed French forces out of all three provinces by 1673.

These events, together with Louis XIV's annexation of the principality of Orange in south-east France (from where the House of Orange originated) had not made Louis popular with his Dutch neighbours. News had quickly spread of his inflicting on the principality's Protestant inhabitants the same cruelty that had been meted out to his own French Protestant subjects, and the Dutch people now resolutely welcomed the Huguenot refugees with open arms. For example, in Amsterdam, Huguenots were granted full citizenship, the right to exercise any trade or profession, and freedom from city taxes for three years.

In Holland, they were exempt from taxes for 12 years, whilst in Friesland the inhabitants were delighted to receive any Huguenot refugee who chose to make their home and living there. Unusually, many of these particular refugees were people of some relative affluence, who had been able to smuggle a great deal of their wealth across the border as it was one of the easiest borders to cross – some of this affluence was later put to good use overseas by William of Orange when he 'invaded' England[cciv]. One very important factor inherent in Huguenot immigration was the considerable number of excellent sailors hailing from coastal areas such as Guyenne, Saintonge and La Rochelle; the armed forces were also well represented in this military exodus, which was to have significant historical consequences for Holland and England in 1688.

Switzerland

As this tiny state was already mainly Protestant and had been the birthplace of Calvinism, it was natural that a number of Huguenots should choose to try to start a new life in Switzerland, which naturally welcomed and indeed sympathised with fellow Protestants seeking freedom from persecution.

From the Duval family records, we are able to gain an insight into the plight of some of those undertaking this venture:

[cciv] G. Elmore Reaman, *The Trail of the Huguenots in Europe, the United States, South Africa and Canada* (London, 1964) p106.

The Story of the Huguenots – a Unique Legacy

Towards the end of the year 1554, the first of the Duval family left their home town of Rouen in northern France, Etienne Duval, an apothecary by trade, travelled with a group of refugees, probably merchants towards the border, their chosen destination was Geneva. Once they crossed the Col de la Faucille they would have their first sighting of the Genevan region laid out before them. Finally, the little troupe reached the city of Geneva and safety passed through the Cornavin Gate[179]. When leaving Rouen Etienne Duval had, although in distress at the need for flight, apparently been quite privileged compared to other Huguenot refugees as he was allowed to take some of his possessions, an exceptional favour of which his uncle, a member of the archbishop's entourage, was probably not aware, although it appears that he contributed to his expulsion, he did at least take with him the sign of his trade – a magnificent Green Monkey (in wood or ironwork) holding a golden apple in his hand [ccv].

Even before 1685, the Swiss had held out the hand of friendship to the early Huguenots who arrived there, but immediately after the Revocation, no less than 8,000 arrivals were recorded. And these refugees would repay the kindness of those that gave them sanctuary not only through their considerable commercial acumen but also through their knowledge and expertise in disciplines that were very much required by the growing towns and cities of the time. Apothecaries, the ancestors of modern general practitioners, were always held in high esteem due to their ability to produce the famous 'Theriaque' and 'Geneva Powders[180],' which were highly prized abroad.[ccvi]

For many, Geneva was the goal – the city where Calvin had set out on his course of reforming religion. In less than half a

---

[ccv] The Duval Archives.
[ccvi] Ibid.

century, Geneva had undergone an immense change, first shaking off the rule of the Duke of Savoy, then wholeheartedly embracing the reformed religion, thus eroding Catholic dominance to finally result in the city's acceptance of Protestant administration rather than civil power. This was not an easy transition, but it did ensure an empathy with those fleeing from France. Ironically, its importance lay in the blossoming of ideas conveyed from France by those of the reformed faith unable to fulfil their ideas in their country of birth. Geneva, although welcoming, was in many cases a staging post as many of the refugees had already decided to travel onto Basle, Zurich, Berne and Lausanne.

Destitution was the unavoidable lot of large numbers of the refugees; thus, to aid these poor unfortunates, the Protestant cantons set up a fund to provide travel expenses for those wishing to journey onwards[ccvii].

Hungary

Protestantism spread east across Europe throughout the 16th century, although it was as early as the 1520s that Martin Luther and his doctrines first became known to the Hungarians. The town of Debrecen (the second largest city in Hungary at that time after Budapest) was to take an important role in the growth of the reformed faith and was designated the title of 'Calvinist Rome' as it was, and still is, home to the Great Reformed Church, which remains the most well-known building in the town, and the largest Protestant church in Hungary. The foremost teacher of Calvin's theology, Albert Szenci Molnár, had studied in Heidelberg and visited Geneva. He learned the Genevan psalms, becoming able to sing these in Latin as well as in German, and he personally translated them into Hungarian. He edited the Hungarian Psalter, and worked hard to promote Calvinist ideals and principles within

---

[ccvii] Samuel Smiles, *The Huguenots Their Settlements, Churches and Industries in England and Ireland (1889)* (London) p181.

The Story of the Huguenots – a Unique Legacy

the country. In 1624, Molnár translated John Calvin's most important work, *The Institutes*, a work viewed by one Hungarian pastor thus: *'after the sacred books of the apostles this one is the best'*.

Many Hungarian students visited or chose to continue their studies in the Netherlands and England; during their visits to the latter they learned more about the Puritan movement, which followed the teachings of Calvin. From the 16th century, there gradually developed a system of governance within the Hungarian Reformed Church for congregations to be administered by the local councils and pastors. Puritans wanted to divide the church governance so that elders could be elected by the congregation, which did in fact became compulsory in 1791.

An interesting example of how extensively some Huguenots were making themselves new lives in countries outside France comes in the form of an English Huguenot of clearly French descent – Richard Debaufre Guyon, who was born in Bath, but who served for six years in the Hapsburg Imperial Army, resigning his commission in 1840. For eight years, he lived the quiet life of a country gentleman in Hungary with his Hungarian-born wife Mária Splényi, but this tranquillity was shattered in 1848 by the conflict that became known as the Hungarian War of Liberation. Richard Guyon duly became a major in the National Guard, swiftly gaining the reputation of a brave and able commander. After the victory of the Hapsburg and Russian armies, he was forced to flee the country, resettling in Turkey. He could of course have returned to Britain as he was a British citizen, but instead he chose to join the Ottoman army, assuming the name Kurshid Pasha[181], yet he was able to retain his Christian beliefs as he was a highly respected member of the army[ccviii].

[ccviii] The Guion Archives.

Russia

This huge country, which strides both the European and Asian continents, was at the time of the Revocation ruled by Tsar Peter the Great, who openly encouraged Huguenot immigration. He wanted – indeed, needed – their expertise, but it was noted that only a small number of families appeared to have accepted the Tsar's invitation[ccix]. A large proportion of those who did arrive emigrated from Germany in the 1700s, some being soldiers, and some being artisans, and the settlement in St Petersburg over time became large enough for the establishment of a Huguenot church.

The Duval family records again reveal the experiences of some of the more successful descendants of earlier Huguenot refugees.

Louis-David Duval, was the founder of the branch of the family that settled in Russia. He began his career in London before leaving for Russia in 1745, and settled in St Petersburg in 1754, where he dealt successfully in precious stones. The Empress Catherine named him Court Jeweller, which helped in the development of his soon flourishing business. He employed several Genevans, notably Francois Sequin the miniaturist, and Jean Ador, a specialist in the making of gold tobacco boxes ornamented with magnificent paintings in enamel, several of which were executed by Nicholas Soret and the two brothers Claude and Pierre-Etienne Theremin.

On the death of Louis-David Duval in 1788, the eldest of his sons, Jacob-David, took over the management of the jewellery business while taking care of the education of his two younger brothers. In the confusion caused to the

---

[ccix] M. Glozier (Ed.) and D. Onnekink (Ed), *War, Religion and Service: Huguenot Soldiering 1685-1713* (Abingdon, 2007) p229.

business by the Continental Blockade and the fall of the rouble, and in the middle of the ensuing bankruptcies, he put the family's great jewellery business back on its feet and, by perseverance, succeeded in making the ministers and courtiers, with Potemkin at their head, pay the greater part of their debts. In this he was helped by the protection given him by the Empress Marie Feodorovna, who, after the death of Louis-David Duval, spoke several times of her happy memories of him, and in her will specially recommended the Duval family to her sons – the Czar Nicholas and the Grand-Dukes Constantine and Michael[ccx].

One of the greatest artisans was born in St Petersburg on 18 May 1846. His name – Peter Carl Fabergé. His father was Gustav, and his mother the Danish-born Charlotte Jungstedt.

Gustav Fabergé's paternal ancestors were Huguenots. The family originated from La Bouteille, Picardy. They fled from France after the Revocation, settling first in Germany near Berlin. In 1800, they moved to Pernau (today Pärnu) in the Baltic province of Livonia, at that time part of Russia. A jeweller by trade, Gustav set up his business in St Petersburg. Peter took over the family business, by now known as the House of Fabergé, when his father retired in 1860. Peter worked hard to expand his knowledge through, in part, a grand tour of Europe to better study some of the finest goldsmiths' work in Germany, France and England. He returned to St Petersburg, and married Augusta Julia Jacobs in 1872. During the next ten years, he worked alongside his father's trusted worker Hiskias Pendin from whom he gained a great deal of valuable knowledge. In 1882, Pendin died, and so Peter took on the sole management of the company. His younger brother became his assistant, designing some of the finest pieces of jewellery of the era.

[ccx] The Duval Archives

Together, the brothers triumphed at the Pan-Russian Exhibition held in Moscow in 1882. Peter was awarded a gold medal for one of his beautifully crafted objects. This exhibition, and in particular one of the exhibits, a replica of a 4th century BC gold bangle from the Scythian treasures in the Hermitage, now attracted the attention of no less a figure than Tsar Alexander himself.

In 1885, Fabergé was appointed jeweller and goldsmith to the Russian Imperial Court. The elaborate, fanciful eggs that he created for members of the court, as well as the less expensive eggs that were crafted for the general market, remain Fabergé's best-known creations. In all, 50 unique eggs were produced for the imperial family, and each included an element of surprise, a tradition that began with the first egg, known as the *Hen Egg*, which Alexander III commissioned as a gift for his wife, Empress Maria Fyodorovna. This first egg was an extravagant extension of the tradition of exchanging decorated eggs to celebrate the Russian Orthodox Easter. Its unadorned white enamel shell housed a yellow-gold yolk, which opened to reveal a golden hen nesting in a bed of suede edged with stippled gold, intended to evoke the straw of a hen's nest. The hen, in turn, opened to reveal the final surprise – a miniature version of the Russian imperial crown crafted in diamonds and rubies, holding a small ruby pendant egg.

In 1900, Fabergé participated in the Paris Exposition Universelle; he was awarded a gold medal and the Cross of the Legion of Honour, bringing him to the attention of a worldwide audience. By 1905, he had opened workshops in Moscow, Kiev and London, employing over 500 people. Yet, the Kiev studio closed after just five years, and the London workshop after another five years. With the onset of the Russian Revolution of 1917, and the deposition of the Romanovs, Fabergé's remaining studios were seized by the revolutionary government, which handed them over to a committee of employees, only to be finally closed a year later. Fabergé fled to Switzerland, where he died in 1920.

Such was the scale and urgency of Huguenot emigration, however, that it was not confined solely to the European continent. To appreciate the impact it was to have on far away countries and regions, and to understand its lasting effects on world history, we must look further afield – indeed, much further.

- 19 -

To Explore the Furthest Reaches

Beyond Europe, the prospect of safety and freedom of other continents was beckoning, encouraging many Huguenots to risk everything to travel so far away across the world in what could be a valiant attempt to try to start a new life. To Africa and Australia, across the Atlantic Ocean to the New World, the often-hazardous journeys were made.

AFRICA
South Africa
Jan van Riebeeck and his family had emigrated to South Africa from Texel in the Netherlands on 24 December 1651 as passengers on one of three boats bound for South Africa; eventually land was sighted on 5 April 1562, and within the week work had begun on a supply station. Jan van Riebeeck had signed a contract with the Dutch East India Company, formed in 1602 by the Dutch Republic (present-day Netherlands), to build the supply station for the company's ships as they passed by on their way eastwards. That first winter was indeed very harsh, and a number of his companions died due to dwindling food supplies and intemperate weather.

Van Riebeeck was given strict instructions not to colonise the region, but to build a station and to erect a flagpole for signalling to ships and to the smaller vessels that would escort them into the bay. But a few months after his arrival a naval war broke out between England and the Dutch Republic (July 1652 - April 1654) hastening the need to complete a fortification. The fort became the first European settlement in the area and the founding of the Cape of Good Hope was attributed to van Riebeeck.

The Dutch East India Company had taken the decision to encourage Huguenots to emigrate to South Africa, particularly if they were from a farming background as they valued and needed the skills of smallholders, including sheep and crop farmers. The immigrants were required to take the Oath of Allegiance to the company and in exchange were offered free passage on condition that they stayed for at least five years; they could take on as much land as they could reasonably work. They were provided with an advance so that they could purchase the necessary tools and seed, which, as part of the deal, they would not have to make repayments on until the first harvest. They could be released from the agreement only if the company chose to do so and on condition that they paid their passage home. The six-week long journey was hazardous for a variety of reasons: storms, pirates and, above all, illness – particularly scurvy. The Dutch East India Company also encouraged the Huguenot migration to South Africa because they held the same strong religious beliefs. Upon arrival, they were given a warm welcome by the governor Jan van Riebeeck, and his French-born wife, Maria de la Quitterie.

The Huguenots settled into life in South Africa mainly in an area approximately 60 kilometres north-east of the Cape and the Berg Valley, which later became known as Franschhoek (Dutch for 'French corner'). Amongst the arrivals was Francois Villion, who together with others such as du Plessis, Roubaix de la Fontaine, de Chavannes, de Villiers, du Pré, Le Roux and Rousseau chose to settle on the furthest tip of this continent. Some of these names are amongst those listed who subsequently became governors of the Dutch colony.

However, as the soil was more conducive to vines they started to turn their attention to vine planting, cultivation and wine production. In 1693 when John Ovington visited the Cape, he noted:

Their vineyards have been established over an area of more than seventy-five English miles, yet they still have their eyes on large pieces of virgin soil before them. In this district they farm with livestock, plant maize, establish vineyards and improve everything conscientiously for the greatest benefit .... Their vineyards, which they have multiplied to a large variety of cultivars, can now also provide the passing ships...

It had taken the Huguenot settlers the best part of three years to clear the land for cultivation. Goodwill and friendship helped them achieve this, but gradually they began to grasp that they had not fully understood the full terms and conditions of their future in South Africa, nor the role they were expected to play within its society. The Dutch East India Company expected them to merge into the local community and become 'good Dutch farmers' whereas the Huguenots had believed they would be able to continue to maintain their own French way of life and, in particular, their own French language.

Until their French pastor Pierre Simon departed, they had been able to retain their French identity, but once he had left, they were no longer allowed to have their own French-speaking pastors or primary school teachers, leading to the disappearance of the French language within two generations[ccxi]. Despite this, Huguenot settlers did make a success of their lives in South Africa and they became affluent farmers during the 18th century. Indeed, their settlement still thrives today with well-known, world-class wines being produced from their vineyards. The lasting concession they

---

[ccxi] Noel Currer-Briggs & Royston Gambier, *Huguenot Ancestry* (Chichester, 1985) p71.

had to make was in accepting their slowly diminishing French way of life and language, leading to their children being taught the Dutch language, and agreeing to their church services being held alternate weeks in Dutch, then French[ccxii].

One particular story, which is a fine example of the tenacity of the refugees who emigrated to South Africa, is that of the Jouberts from La Motte d'Aigues in Provence. Pierre Joubert had hidden a bible inside a loaf of bread[182] when he fled Provence. He was the first French owner of any land in South Africa, and had settled on the first piece of land allocated to him in October 1694, which became known as *La Motte* in the Franschhoek district of the Berg Valley, where from 1709 until 1741 he farmed cattle on the previously uncultivated soil.

In 1688, the ship *Berg China*[183] arrived in Table Bay (see table 3). Among the refugees on board were Paul Roux, Jacques Malan and the brothers Jean and Pierre Jourdan. Two years before this in June 1686, Francois Du Toit had arrived in Table Bay aboard the *Vrijheijt*. His grandson, Gabriël Du Toit, had become *La Motte's* second French owner, when he purchased *La Motte* in 1751 at the age of just 22 years. Gabriël's wife was expecting the first of 14 children, and all they owned apart from *La Motte* was a firearm and a horse. As an enterprising Frenchman, he laboured hard to turn his land into a workable farm and vineyard including the construction of the manor house itself.

By 1753, the young Gabriël owned ten cattle, had planted 4,000 vines and sown eight bags of wheat according to surviving records. Through the years, the number of cattle, vineyards – and, it must be noted, slaves – substantially increased. By 1782, 25,000 vines had been planted, and he was at this point able to establish a cellar on the farm. A watermill at *La Motte* bears the date 1721, but more likely it was built by Du Toit between 1751 and 1793.

[ccxii] Noel Currer-Briggs & Royston Gambier, *Huguenot Ancestry* (Chichester, 1985) p71.

Du Toit's death in 1793 led to *La Motte* being subdivided, but two of his sons, Gerhardus Johannes (10th child) and Roelof (13th child), subsequently bought the land.

Gerhardus Johannes was the first owner to have been born on the farm. He bought a section from his father's estate, then four years later sold it to his brother Roelof. In 1812, Roelof ended the family ownership of 62 years when he sold *La Motte* to a Hollander.

Since 1694, *La Motte* has had 19 owners, nine of whom were of French origin – Retief, Roux, Cilliers and others following on from Joubert and Du Toit.

Today, many South African families can trace their roots back to the early Huguenots, just a few of whom are: de Klerk (Le Clercq), Visagie (Visage), du Plessis, TerBlanche, Franck, Fourie, Marais, Theron and Jordaan (Jurdan). One of the most popular names is du Preez (Des Pres). Numerous French-sounding farm names are still in existence in the western Cape. Wine is still a valuable source of income to South Africa, which in this respect is entirely indebted to the diligence and hard work of the early Huguenot refugees, many of whom had been former owners of vineyards in France. At Franschhoek, a memorial to commemorate the arrival of the Huguenots in South Africa was unveiled on 7 April 1948.

AUSTRALASIA

Australia

Although Australia has a well-known history of receiving convicts, the story of how they were transported there is not so well documented. Australia had not been a refuge for Huguenots in earlier centuries, but their descendants began to arrive in the 19th century. Most convicts were kept below deck for much of the long arduous journey undertaken in ships reliant solely on prevailing wind direction and speed. Locked up in unhygienic, dark, restricted and often wet holds that were perfect breeding grounds

The Story of the Huguenots – a Unique Legacy

for any number of ailments, these transportees suffered an appallingly high proportion of fatalities, with the deaths of up to a quarter of one ship's convicts testifying to these horrendous conditions. Not all the convicts were Huguenots, but one Huguenot survivor was a watchmaker by the name of Abraham Buzeau.

Amongst those pioneering families hoping to make their home in this uncertain land called Australia were a plentiful number of Huguenots paying their own passage. Sometimes, though, a family would seek assistance to join a family member who had been transported. One such instance was Mary Ammonet[184] whose husband, Samuel Gilbert, had been sentenced for being in possession of forged bank notes, and was duly transported in 1816; having survived the inhumane conditions of the journey, he did in fact eventually prosper to become a baker in the town of Parramatta.

Not all Huguenots had to pay – often, those from rural areas were given financial assistance as their already proven skills and therefore worth were needed for very essential agricultural purposes[ccxiii], and nor did all the Huguenots travel from England; the ship *La Rochelle* made several trips from Hamburg to Queensland, and while some voyages were relatively well organised, inevitably, not all were. One particular voyage led to outbreaks of dysentery and typhus that preceded the deaths of almost one-sixth of the passengers. An enquiry was held whose findings attributed these tragic deaths to overcrowding with inadequate clothing and medical supplies as well as poor ventilation and a lack of proper food and water[ccxiv].

There are a number of famous Australian men and women who are descendants of Huguenots. This book would not be complete without a mention of a few of these illustrious Huguenot sons and daughters:

[ccxiii]Nash, Robert (ed.), *The Hidden Thread: Huguenot Families in Australia,* p30.
[ccxiv]Ibid, p31.

Marie Beuzeville Byles (1900-79) was a descendant of two Huguenot families. She became the first female solicitor in New South Wales, and was also a prominent conservationist, being one of the initiators of Bouddi National Park. Marie was one of the first Australians to show an interest in Buddhism. The Beuzeville family had come originally from Normandy.

Charles Chauvel (1897-1959) whose family had fled to England in 1685 from Blois in the Loire Valley. Charles was a great Australian film producer and director; his best-known films include *Jedda* and *40,000 Horsemen*.

Freda Du Faur (1882-1935) became Australia's first female mountaineer, being the first woman to climb Mt Cook, the highest peak in New Zealand. Her ancestors, the Du Faur family, were originally from Gascony.

Charles Joseph La Trobe (1801-75) is more than likely the most well-known Huguenot descendant in Australian history. He was the first Lieutenant-Governor of Victoria, guiding it through its very difficult early years. His diligence and single-minded dedication to government affairs left a lasting legacy. His family originated from Languedoc in the south of France.

THE NEW WORLD
America
Several Huguenot settlements were founded in America[185], South Carolina being one of the earliest of these, later becoming known as 'The Home of the Huguenot'. Created in 1562 by Jean de Ribault at Port Royal, it fragmented when their leader was called back to assist in the Wars of Religion.

A further attempt at Huguenot colonisation was made in 1564 by Rene Laudonniere; it was named 'Le Carolina' on the banks of the St John's River[186]. Sadly, this too floundered, with the final death knell being inflicted by the Spanish, who took the town and mercilessly put the inhabitants to death. Yet a further attempt was made at colonising Port Royal in 1670, and this time it

The Story of the Huguenots – a Unique Legacy

prospered[ccxv]. At first, it was populated by English and Dutch, but Charles II encouraged French refugees to start a new life there too, and so in 1679 they settled in the area that was to become known as Charlestown. One of the refugees was the Reverend Elias Prioleau, who had left the town of Pons in western France to seek a new life, and was to become the first pastor of the original Huguenot church in Charlestown. The Huguenots' prime concern was to maintain their French Church and thus although they were loyal to the English crown, they refused to follow the rites of the Anglican Church. As time passed, however, the French community became assimilated into the majority English-speaking population.

We have seen that many Huguenots chose to travel onwards some years after their departure from France; quite a few that had first settled in Amsterdam subsequently decided to make a new life in America, with many finally settling in the Dutch colony of New Netherland[187]. Their pastor, Pierre Daillé, founded the first temple in New York in 1686, but the Huguenots' official congregation had already been founded in 1628 in L'Eglise Français á la Nouvelle-Amsterdam, today known as L'Eglise du Saint-Esprit, and which continues to conduct its services in French, as well as offering the hand of friendship to all those from across the world.

Ninety miles north of New York is the town of New Paltz[188]. This area is one of the oldest continuously inhabited settlements in what is now the United States. The Huguenot settlers had originally come from an area that is now part of modern day southern Belgium, and began making their home on the banks of the Wallkill River in 1678. There are still a number of original buildings in New Paltz, the oldest of which is known as Jean Hasbrouck's house[189]. Jean's son, Jacob, built the Dutch-style house in 1721.

Following the Revocation of 1685, large numbers of French Huguenots soon swelled the population in the New World to such

---

[ccxv] G. Elmore Reaman, *The Trail of the Huguenots in Europe, the United States, South Africa and Canada* (London, 1964) p111.

an extent that three more congregations were founded at Orange, St John's and Jamestown. North Carolina also had a settlement, established in 1707 on the Trent River. Its founder, Philippe de Richelbourg, was a minister, and later joined the colony on the Santee River, South Carolina, where he continued to live and preach until his death in 1718.

Many Huguenots put down roots in what was to become New England, having sailed from ports in the Netherlands and the Channel Islands. Some of these families settled in Salem, but as the numbers of Huguenot refugees seeking a new life grew, so permission was given for them to journey further afield to places such as Massachusetts and Boston[ccxvi]

Gabriel Benson from La Rochelle helped found a settlement west of Boston named New Oxford, which for a while bourgeoned until 1694 when it was attacked by Indian tribes, who unfortunately returned to the town in 1696; this last attack was the ultimate demise of New Oxford although a revival was attempted in 1699 only to meet the same fate. The Indians became incensed by some of the Jesuit population and attacked the settlement, killing many of the settlers.

In 1686, a group of Huguenot families from La Rochelle, Saintonge and Poitou – but by then living in London – agreed a contract with the Atherton Company to buy the land at Narragansett (Rhode Island) so that they, with their families, could start a new life there. But, tragically, after five full years of hard work and toil, they were to discover they had been deceived and did not, after all, own the land, forcing them to leave for other parts of America[ccxvii]. But, even at this relatively early stage of European emigration, there were already countless other settlements across this vast New World, such as Manakin on the James River near Richmond, Virginia, which became such an

---

[ccxvi] G. Elmore Reaman, *The Trail of the Huguenots in Europe, the United States, South Africa and Canada* (London, 1964) p113.
[ccxvii] Ibid p115.

The Story of the Huguenots – a Unique Legacy

important settlement that its crossing over the river was named *The Huguenot Memorial Bridge*, and there is also a Huguenot High School.

Undeniably, the Huguenots made their mark on American history – two of the original signatories of the peace treaty giving independence to the emerging 'United States' were of Huguenot descent – John Jay and Henry Laurens. One refugee, Isaac Bethlo from Picardie, gave his name to the island on which stands the Statue of Liberty. It remained Bethlo Island until 1956.

The American Huguenot Society was founded in 1883. The rector of the French church in New York, Alfred V. Wittmeyer, had spearheaded the establishment of this society.

Canada

A few attempts were made to colonise this country[190] by Huguenots, the first settler being Pierre Chauvin, a nobleman from Dieppe, who travelled to St Laurent to set up the first trading post in 1599-1600. He had planned to return to France and offer a new beginning to any Huguenots who wanted to start a new life in a new country, but on his death his plans lay largely unfulfilled. In 1603, Pierre Dugua de Mons, originally from Royon in northern France, was given permission by Henri IV to travel to Canada and set up a trading post to deal in furs; he also granted Dugua the Lieutenant Governorship of what was then known to the French as Acadia[191]. In 1607, Dugua lost those exclusive trading rights, and shortly afterwards the colony was abandoned. Then, in 1608, a new expedition set out to explore and hopefully discover a new land. It was led by Champlain and it was he who discovered Quebec, founding the first permanent French settlement in North America.

The Catholic Church, encouraged by Richelieu, was continuing relentlessly to try to persuade Huguenots to renounce their faith – Richelieu went to great lengths, even setting up a completely Catholic company, *One Hundred Associates*, otherwise known as

The Story of the Huguenots – a Unique Legacy

the New France Company, to encourage Catholics to emigrate to Canada. Although Huguenots were allowed to take passage there, their numbers were extremely limited as a matter of deliberate policy aiming to prevent or at least restrict the setting up of temples for those of the Huguenot faith.

Richelieu did, however, unwittingly achieve one of his finest successes through his encouragement of French overseas expansion. A perusal of the Articles of Association he had drawn up for the *One Hundred Associates* reveals it to be an extremely forward-thinking document, particularly in the stance taken on how to treat natives of overseas territories, and the descendants of the French people that were to settle in these new lands, and does not differentiate between Catholics and Huguenots:

The descendants of the French who colonise these countries, together with the savages who will be brought to a knowledge of the Faith and make profession of it, shall henceforth be considered native-born Frenchmen, and as such may come to live in France when they wish, and acquire property there, make wills, succeed as heirs and take gifts and legacies in the same way as true nationals and native-born Frenchmen, without being required to take out letters of denization or naturalisation.

Unfortunately for Richelieu, many of the French Huguenots who chose to take up the offer of life in an overseas colony would *never* share the same religious views as he, and thus the future of these colonies would be very different to the one Richelieu had envisaged[ccxviii].

Not all of those who decided to make a new life in Canada travelled directly from France; among those who eventually chose to leave England for the last time to settle in the New World was John Mallandain[192], who had served with the Dutch East India

---

[ccxviii] Noel Currer-Briggs & Royston Gambier, *Huguenot Ancestry* (Chichester, 1985) p57.

The Story of the Huguenots – a Unique Legacy

Company. Two of his children from his second marriage, firstly his son Edward, then in 1861 his daughter Charlotte, took the decision to cross the ocean to Canada where their descendants, to this day, still live and work[ccxix].

SOUTH AMERICA
Brazil

Early in the 16th century, Admiral Gaspard de Coligny[193] encouraged his fellow Huguenots to consider beginning a new life in Brazil, which was at that time known as *France Antarctique*. Coligny suggested to Henri II that an expedition should be undertaken to consider the possibility of expanding trade by establishing a settlement there. Coligny's motives were in part to establish trading links, but he was also mindful of the possibility that fellow Huguenots had a better chance of worshipping freely by being able to live and work in a new land. France had traded with France Antarctique for some years, mainly importing 'Brazil' wood[194].

Coligny did not travel with the expedition, but he did enrol his friend Nicolas Durand de Villegaignon[195] as captain of the fleet. The expedition sailed out of port in 1555 in two ships whose passengers comprised 600 colonists and soldiers. There were a small number of Catholics, but the majority of the colonists were Huguenots from La Rochelle and Geneva. When they arrived in Guanabara Bay, they began to build a settlement on the island of Serigipe, later renamed Villegaignon Island. One of the first buildings they erected on the island was a fort, which they named for Coligny. The settlement flourished and by 1556 Villegaignon wrote letters addressed to Henri II, Coligny and John Calvin requesting another fleet be sent with colonists. Three further ships were fitted out to transport a further 300 settlers under the command of Sieur De Bois le Comte, a nephew of Villegaignon.

[ccxix] The Mallandain Archives.

The local people and the colonists made friends and seemed to live amiably side by side – but not all was harmonious.

Within the confines of Fort Coligny, tensions arose between the Catholic and Huguenot settlers. To calm matters, it was agreed that the settlement should be divided in two: one Catholic and the other Huguenot, but even this did not fully resolve matters, leading to the expulsion in October 1557 of nearly all the Huguenots from the island. In January 1558, the remaining Huguenots sailed back to France, a homeland they knew they could no longer feel safe to practice their faith in, their morale surely now at a critically low point.

- 20 -

Riots, Justice and Retribution

Although the silk weaving trade was a major source of income in this country, various events impacted from time to time on the success of this trade. In March 1697 a fresh wave of riots took place against the importation of cheap foreign silks, during which workers were actually encouraged by masters to take to the streets in protest as the import of silk was not in the interests of either party. Parliament was alarmed at the violence as weavers, acting against those whom they saw as threatening their livelihoods, marched to destroy the silk mills in Lewisham (now in south London) and demolishing the machine looms operating in the mills. Weavers also lay siege to the headquarters of the East India Company's chief of staff, Joshua Childs.

The government was forced to take action as amongst the many lobbying on behalf of the industry were prominent organisations such as the Royal Lustring Company. Several Acts of Parliament were speedily passed during the period up to 1700 to protect the industry.

The skill and innovations brought to Spitalfields by the newly arrived strangers was noted at the time:

Whereby God's blessing surely is not only brought upon the parish by receiving poor strangers, but also a great advantage hath accrued to the whole nation by the rich manufactures of weaving silks and stuffs and camlets, which art they brought along with them. And this benefit also to the neighbourhood, that these strangers may serve for patterns of thrift, honesty, industry, and sobriety as well[ccxx].

There were no set rules that stated the price each piece of finished silk would be worth, nor was there a prescribed length, and thus the price paid to a weaver or other less skilled worker could vary significantly. This gave rise to much uncertainty and social unrest in times of hardship when the rawness of acute hunger would arouse even the mildest to anger; these were the times when those on the verge of starvation would have to witness the injustice of the trappings of wealth being enjoyed by the masters and their families.

Added to these inequalities was the fact that the finished silk was derived from a production line formed of many other workers that included dyers, throwsters, drawer boys[196] and quill winders[197]; a variety of factors could adversely impact on this line, such as illness or a lack of raw materials for processing. When raw silk was not readily available from the usual sources it would be necessary to import from further afield and of course delays in these long-haul orders could and did occur due to man-made or natural events such as war or weather. All these factors led to financial insecurity for those working in silk-weaving businesses – often with dire consequences.

On Tuesday, 13 June 1719, there was a serious disturbance on the streets of the City of London, when a mob of 4,000 angry Spitalfields weavers prowled the streets attacking calico printing works and any women wearing Indian calicoes[198] or linens. The weavers, fearful of the impact on their livelihoods of this new and cheaper fashion, doused the unfortunate wearers of calico

---

[ccxx] Alfred Plummer, *The London Weavers Company 1600-1700* (Abingdon, 1972) reprinted 2006. p146.

The Story of the Huguenots – a Unique Legacy

garments with various liquids including ink. The Lord Mayor of London, alarmed at this disorder, called in the city's militia to restore order. Two rioters were arrested and taken to Marshalsea Prison, but as soon as the armed militia departed, the rioters re-grouped and adopted a new strategy, which was to tear any suspect garment from the backs of the women wearing them. The riot was not quelled until Sunday night after several more arrests. Substantial sentences were handed out to those caught attacking the wearers of calico garments, including, in some of the more serious cases, transportation to the colonies for up to seven years.

In 1720, the weavers took their complaints about the sale of calico to Old Palace Yard[199], Westminster, as well as resuming attacks on wearers of the hated calico. In the following year, the second Calico Act became enshrined in law as a result of these disturbances[200]. The Act included penalties for anyone found wearing calico and for quite a while after its inception, the London Weavers Company even paid informers to bring calico wearers to court. Incidents of calico gowns being despoiled continued until at least 1785, but did over time become less frequent.

But now the struggling weavers were faced with yet another threat to their ability to earn a living. The influx of Irish weavers was soon to cause great distress and hardship as they were prepared to accept far lower wages than the established Huguenot silk weavers. Whilst the Huguenots had the advantage of a far superior quality of work, it seems that not everyone wanted to pay for such flawless material.

Tensions were often high between the local French refugee population and the new Irish refugees, and unsurprisingly tensions turned into violence and rioting: in July 1736, the flashpoint occurred when local Huguenot labourers were employed to build the new church of St Leonards in nearby Shoreditch. Suddenly, the relief they must have felt at having employment and thus the wherewithal to put food on the family table was turned into

The Story of the Huguenots – a Unique Legacy

disbelief and then outrage when they were dismissed and replaced by Irish labourers who were now given employment – at two-thirds of the level of the wages they had previously been paid. Consequently, and with sad inevitability, a crowd of up to 4,000 gathered at two local public houses believed to have been frequented by the Irish labourers, which the angry mob proceeded to ransack. The three days of rioting only ceased when the militia were sent in to restore order to the streets[ccxxi].

Generally, skilled silk weavers had initially been prosperous, but there were periods when circumstances caused a dip in trade, which inevitably affected everyone engaged within the production chain, whether the silk weaver himself or the lesser skilled worker, such as the throwster[201]. For much of the 17th and 18th centuries, the silk weavers of London's East End were periodically engaged in disputes with their employers over wages, working conditions and other issues, but it was increased mechanisation deployed en masse within the industry that was soon to become a major concern – one that would dwarf all others.

The weavers and journeymen won an early victory when they were granted by law the 'right of search' – a power won in particular by journeymen weavers, which allowed them to seek and, where applicable, to destroy weaving work done by 'outsiders' – often those who had not completed a recognised apprenticeship or who were working for less than the specified wage rates.

Silk weavers also used this right to search on several occasions from 1616 to 1675 in order to block the introduction of the engine loom with its multiple shuttles. The weavers and their employers joined forces as the engine loom became widely used whereas restrictions on this new technology might have kept both wages and profits high, it was not long though, before approval of the workers' violence by master weavers began to dissolve as it

---

[ccxxi] Frank McLynn, *Crime and Punishment in Eighteenth Century England*, (London, 2002) p221.

became apparent that profits were being jeopardised by this disruption.

By 1763, it was significant that over 7,000 looms were idle due to the lucrative reclaim on import duties placed upon foreign silk via export duties. Tempers had boiled over in October of that year when thousands of journeymen yet again took to the streets of Spitalfields. On 8 October, *The London Gazette* newspaper gave a detailed report of the riots that had taken place:

...Whereas it has been humbly represented to the king, that there have been several tumults and riots of the Journeyman Silk-Weavers in the parish of St Matthews in Bethnal Green, Christchurch Spitalfields and St Leonards Shoreditch in the County of Middlesex. That, in particular, on Monday and Tuesday 3rd and 4th October instant, several of the said journeyman and a great number of other evil-minded persons masked and disguised and armed with cutlasses and other dangerous weapons assembled at different hours of the day and also in the night-time, about the houses of several journeyman Silk Weavers, who were at work in manufacturing certain silks; and in a most outrageous manner, broke open the said houses, and cut and destroyed the Silk Works in the looms to the value of several hundred Pounds, and also maimed and wounded several of the said Journeymen and threatened the lives of them and their families, and broke and destroyed all their furniture and goods.......

1763 also saw the end of the Seven Years' War between the United Kingdom and France, and this led to a resumption of normal trading relations, but, much to the silk weavers' distress, the increased imports of French silk began to weaken the weavers' ability to earn a living wage, yet again giving rise to running battles between master and weaver.

By January 1764, the weavers were finding life increasingly harsh due to the slump in demand for their skills at the rates they needed to charge in order to support their families. They had earlier petitioned Parliament to request the imposition of double duties upon all foreign silks. Hearing of Parliament's dismissal of their petition, they decided to march to the House of Commons on 10 January – the day set for the re-opening of Parliament following its Christmas recess – to demand a total ban on foreign silks. As members arrived they were confronted with grim-faced weavers determined to make those in power aware of their plight and the extreme hardships endured by their families. This time, Parliament listened to their grievances, and duly passed laws lowering the import duty on raw silk, as well as banning the importation of silk ribbons, stockings and gloves. Dealers in silk were asked to give pledges that they would gradually decrease the number and quantity of the orders they placed with foreign companies, and such measures, together with financial aid being offered to the poorest families, cooled the anger of the weavers, albeit only for a short while.

In 1765, as a direct consequence of the sporadic rioting and the unlawful attacks made on personal property, an Act was passed declaring it illegal to gain entry with malicious intent to despoil or destroy any silk goods in the process of being manufactured in either a shop or house. This Act was to play an important part in an event that took place in 1769, which was to show that no matter how diligent or hardworking a person may be, when hard-pressed they can and will react out of character through sheer desperation. Much as their ancestors had done in France in earlier centuries, the Huguenot descendants fought back.

Two years after the implementation of this Act, wage disputes were again at the forefront when masters, who had reduced piece rates, found disgruntled weavers had cut silk from their looms. A case went before the Weavers' Court later that year at which the weavers demanded that the 1762 prices from their 'book'[202] should be applied, and the court found in favour of the weavers because there had been some evidence that masters had reduced wages

The Story of the Huguenots – a Unique Legacy

without prior agreement. During the summer of 1769, however, some of the masters again attempted to force a cut in rates. This time the weavers decided to band together in secret clubs to resist. The clubs, which can be seen as the forerunner of trade unions, were illegal at that time, and were given somewhat rebellious handles such as 'The Bold Defiance', which met at the *Dolphin Tavern*, Cock Lane[203].

To raise funds to fight for a proper rate, it was agreed that they would levy a tax on all loom owners or workers of looms. This was an illegal levy, but nonetheless History shows that desperate people often resort to desperate measures. One master who was 'invited' to pay this levy was Lewis Chauvet, whose factory stood in Crispin Street, Spitalfields. But Chauvet not only refused to contribute – he banned his workers from becoming members of these clubs and from donating to their fighting fund. Prudently, he also paid private guards to watch over his looms, but in September, silk handkerchiefs were cut from his looms in retaliation for his undercutting of prices. Chauvet, not to be intimidated by what he perceived were a few poor weavers, instead decided to fight back and sought out a 'compliant' weaver, Daniel Clarke, who, if paid handsomely, would be willing to testify that two weavers – John Valline (of Huguenot descent) and John Doyle (of Irish descent) – had taken part in the cutting from his looms. Both men, along with others, had been present at earlier meetings held in local public houses to plan such action, but both men strenuously denied the charges[ccxxii].

A stand had been taken by the wealthy owners against the weavers and, in order to enhance this, the Crown decided that the sentence of hanging as prescribed by the Act of 1765 should be passed on both men. Furthermore, after due deliberation, the king took the decision that the sentence should be carried out not at Tyburn (the traditional site of hangings in London) but in Bethnal

---

[ccxxii] Peter Linebaugh, *The London Hanged: Crime and Civil Society in the Eighteenth Century* (London, 2006) p278.

Green itself [ccxxiii] – home to many weavers and an area often classed as part of Spitalfields – thus placing a strong emphasis on the fact that the law would be upheld. On 6 December, the appointed day for the sentence to be carried out, crowds gathered in the streets along the route from Newgate to Bethnal Green to witness the final journey of John Valline and John Doyle. The two men were transported in an open cart. The portable gallows followed them in a second cart.

Today, outside the *Salmon and Ball* public house is a busy crossroads, and it was on this site nearly two and a half centuries ago that the gallows were erected while the crowd angrily threw abuse together with various brickbats at the unfortunate workmen. To the final breath of their being, John Valline and John Doyle protested their innocence, but the sentence was hurriedly carried out, apparently due to the ugly mood of the crowd. For 50 minutes after their lives had ended, they were left hanging before being cut down and their bodies handed over to their friends and families.

However, rough justice was meted out later that day to Lewis Chauvet when fellow weavers, angry at the execution, took to the streets and amongst the damage they wreaked was the destruction of his house. Although others were accused later of being co-conspirators with John Valline and John Doyle, the Crown prudently decided that all further executions would be carried out at the usual venue of Tyburn.

The wheel of fortune, however, continued to turn, and on a cold snowy day in April 1771, Daniel Clarke took a walk in Spitalfields. No doubt he hoped local people had forgotten his testimony against John Valline and John Doyle (and others) but his luck was to run out that day. Someone appears to have recognised him, and called out *'There goes Clarke, that blood-selling rascal!'* – and immediately a hostile crowd gathered to heckle and jeer. For a short time, he was able to affect his escape by seeking refuge in

---

[ccxxiii] Jerry White, *London in the Eighteenth Century: A Great and Monstrous Thing* (London, 2013) p245.

the house of a local resident, Mary Snee. But many had been so enraged at his appearance that enough of them were determined to seek him out and gain retribution for his false evidence. The mob broke into the house, found Daniel then stripped him, and dragged him out into the street by his feet towards the brick fields. Eventually, after numerous duckings into the freezing water of Hare Street Pond, Bethnal Green, where he was pelted with stones by the angry crowd, the mob finally allowed him to climb out alive – barely. Shortly afterwards, he expired, unrepentant of his falsehoods[ccxxiv].

[ccxxiv] Peter Linebaugh, *The London Hanged: Crime and Civil Society in the Eighteenth Century* (London, 2006) p281.

- 21 -

The Glorious Revolution and the Huguenot Regiments

The accession of James II to the thrones of England and Scotland in 1685 was at first welcomed by most, if not by all, of the country. The Whig party had proposed an Exclusion Bill in an effort to prevent his accession due to his decision in 1669[204] to openly convert to Catholicism. Consequently, he did not accept the special liberties granted to the strangers, but he could not revoke these privileges as those same people were proving popular through their honest endeavours to ply an 'essential' trade, demonstrating great skill and an ethic of working hard.

At the start of his reign, he appeared to accept that England was a Protestant nation within the Union established in 1603 when James VI of Scotland had also become James I of England[205]. James II, however, gradually began to try to sway opinion towards a return to Catholicism[ccxxv]. His two daughters from his first marriage had been raised as Protestants, but his second marriage, which had been unfruitful for well over a decade, finally produced the much longed-for son and heir, who would now be raised as a Catholic. But, by the time of the birth of his son, James II had offended many sections of society through his autocratic demands

---

[ccxxv] Simon Sharma, *A History of Britain: 1603-1776* (London, 2001) p310.

including a return to the old faith, and by appointing Catholic officers to the army – in direct contravention of the country's existing laws[ccxxvi].

On 24 May 1688, an Act of Parliament was passed granting freedom of worship to non-conformists; this was one of several measures whereby it was hoped that official toleration would lead to a widespread acceptance of religious beliefs without the fear of suppression.

Amongst those who sympathised and who were keen to offer support to the Huguenots was the Bishop of London, Henry Compton, who was prominent in assisting the collection of aid for the traumatised and often destitute refugees. James II was not, however, in accord with his bishop's crusade, having him removed from his diocese as soon as possible[ccxxvii].

James had offended many with his approval of his cousin Louis XIV's revocation of the *Edict of Nantes,* and it now began to appear that England, which had long been a welcoming haven for French Protestant refugees, would now ignore the suffering of those same people who became, increasingly fearful of the all-too-predictable repercussions if there should be a return to Catholicism, and began to look at alternatives. The king's counsellors, alarmed at the direction of events, secretly drew up an invitation to William of Orange, the husband of Mary, the eldest of James II's Protestant daughters, to contest the throne[206].

The French army before the Revocation comprised a number of Huguenots including Louis de Bourbon, Prince of Condé, but within a few years of the Revocation it was estimated that as many as 18,000-21,000 fighting men and 500-600 officers had fled overseas due to religious intolerance in France[ccxxviii].

[ccxxvi] Sir Winston Churchill, *A History of the English-Speaking peoples: Vol 2; The New World* (London, 1974) p304.

[ccxxvii] Simon Sharma, *A History of Britain: 1603-1776* (London, 2001) p311.

[ccxxviii] Museum of London, The, *The Quiet Conquest: The Huguenots, 1685-1985* (London, 1985) p103.

The army that William of Orange raised in the Netherlands comprised a large percentage of Huguenots. The significance of the inclusion within William's forces of so many Huguenots cannot be overstated as they played a very significant part in the Glorious Revolution of 1688. Amongst these Huguenots was Isaac Dumont de Bostaquet, owner of considerable estates in Yerville, Normandy. He had fled France shortly after the Revocation. At first, he had reluctantly agreed to sign an abjuration of his Protestant faith in order to protect his family from the enforced billeting of large numbers of dragoons in their home, but within a short while, he was bitterly regretting his action. Suffering the agonies of betraying his beliefs, he watched helplessly as old friends and neighbours were also forced to abjure. Eventually, when it became known that every member of his family would be forced to sign the detested document, he felt he was left with little choice other than to flee. He had intended that as many family members as possible who wished to leave France would do so with him, and what had been a small party at the outset gradually grew into a very sizeable group as others joined them, all seeking ship. Upon arrival at the coast they were set upon by the coast guards, who opened fire, scattering several of the party; de Bostaquet was wounded and forced to flee without his family[207].

He eventually arrived in Holland where he was warmly welcomed by William of Orange, who appointed him to the same rank in the Dutch army that he had held in France. De Bostaquet wrote about the persecution and his flight in his memoirs; he also penned a detailed account of the expedition led by William in 1688.

As William planned the expedition to take the throne, more and more French refugee officers volunteered to join his cause. At first, the Dutch fleet, having assembled at Maas, was forced to return to port due to a fierce storm that raged for three days scattering the ships, and with the loss of some of the vessels.

The Story of the Huguenots – a Unique Legacy

Amongst those missing was a ship that had on board at least 60 French officers and volunteers. Eventually, the damage the surviving ships had sustained was repaired, and the fleet set sail for the second time on 19 October. As the fleet progressed, it was noted by those on board that its progress was being observed on either side of the Channel.

The fleet landed at Torbay, south Devon, on 5 November, the anniversary of the gunpowder plot, which, when William was reminded of this, caused him to remark to Burdett: '*What do you think of Predestination now?*'[ccxxix]. Soldiers disembarked, and the army marched along roads that were more akin to tracks and footpaths filled deep with mud created by the autumn rains. At Exeter, they were warmly welcomed, and de Bostaquet was delighted to discover that many of his fellow countrymen had already settled there and had their own church and pastor[ccxxx].

The army was rested for a week before it set off again, marching this time towards London, gathering more and more willing volunteers from among the local gentry. Meanwhile, James II's army slowly retreated as William's drew nearer. Finally, William and his army arrived in the capital and were greeted with great acclaim by the populace as their saviour. Upon hearing of William's tumultuous welcome, James hastily made plans for flight, and the government – rather than repeat the mistake of placing the crown of martyrdom on the head of an overthrown monarch as had been the case with James' father, Charles I – permitted him to quietly leave the kingdom[208]. Meanwhile, the refugees amongst William's army were pleasantly surprised to find that so many of their fellow countrymen and women had also happily settled in various parts of London – notably the areas from Soho in the west to Spitalfields in the east.

[ccxxix] Sir Winston Churchill, *A History of the English-Speaking peoples: Vol 2; The New World* (London, 1974) p315.
[ccxxx] Samuel Smiles, *The Huguenots Their Settlements, Churches and Industries in England and Ireland (1889)* (London) p218.

Although William of Orange had been 'invited' to England, Parliament was unclear as to what course of action it should take as James II was still technically the anointed king. Parliament debated the issue of succession, and agreed:

Whereas the late King James the Second, by the assistance of divers evil counsellors, judges and ministers employed by him, did endeavour to subvert and extirpate the Protestant religion and the laws and liberties of this kingdom[209].

William made it clear, though, that he was not going to be just Consort to his wife Mary – he wanted to jointly rule with her. At first, Parliament was against this proposal, but William's stance on this issue was utterly unequivocal. Many in Parliament, mindful of the real possibility of civil war if this matter was not speedily resolved, conceded to his demand although William was, upon acceptance of the throne, required to sign a Bill of Rights designed to curtail the royal powers.

On 24 May 1689, William endorsed the Act of Toleration, which gave a guarantee of religious toleration to Protestant non-conformists, including French Protestants who had settled in the Kingdom[210]. William's accession to the throne meant the country was once more a Protestant nation where all those professing to this faith would be allowed to do so in peace.

The Bill of Rights Act was enshrined in law in December 1689, stating that:

The Bill firmly established the principles of frequent parliaments, free elections and freedom of speech within Parliament[211]. It also includes no right of taxation without Parliament's agreement, freedom from government interference, the right of petition and just treatment of people by courts.

As soon as William had arrived, the work of uniting the country under his rule began. Scotland was relatively amenable to

The Story of the Huguenots – a Unique Legacy

William, but parts of Ireland were vehemently opposed to a Protestant ruler, particularly the Irish Catholics, who remained staunchly loyal to the former Stuart king. James II had decided to land in Ireland as the first step in retaking his kingdom, the area known then as Tryconnell[212] being especially loyal to him. Additionally, William's old enemy, the king of France, now gave financial backing to James, and in Ireland up to 40,000 Catholic Irish armed themselves in his name within weeks of his landing at Kinsale in March 1689.

It was starting to appear that William would have a difficult task to retain Ireland as part of his kingdom as his forces were neither great in number nor experience. He had disbanded many of his foreign regiments or sent them to Flanders to do battle with Louis XIV's army, which was deliberately offering a distraction in order to assist James. But all was not as dire as it seemed.

As soon as news arrived in London of the odds being stacked so heavily against William in Ireland, four Huguenot regiments were hastily re-formed: three were infantry and one cavalry, which was led by Colonel Schomberg[213], until his death during the Battle of the Boyne in 1690 [ccxxxi].

No sooner had the regiments re-formed than they were sent to Ireland to join the assembled Protestants in the north prior to marching southward to do battle. This came at Carrickfergus, which fell to them within a week, but not without heavy losses. Colonel Schomberg had within his command an old friend of the Marquis de Ruvigny – Isaac Dumont de Bostaquet[214], who retained his former rank of captain

The strict Calvinist William of Orange, Stadtholder of the Netherlands as well as King William III of England, Ireland and Scotland, was concerned about the loyalty of the English army; he now cautiously decided that the troops to be deployed in Ireland should come mainly from the loyal forces that had formed part of

---

[ccxxxi] Samuel Smiles, *The Huguenots Their Settlements, Churches and Industries in England and Ireland (1889)* (London) p221.

The Story of the Huguenots – a Unique Legacy

the invasion that had put him on the throne. Thus, the newly formed regiments were the first totally French Protestant units deployed[ccxxxii], and this trust in them represented a heaven-sent opportunity for Huguenots to prove their loyalty to William and their country of adoption. Each Huguenot infantry regiment was a single battalion of 13 companies, whereas the cavalry regiments were made up of just nine.

To begin with, all did not go well for the expeditionary forces in Ireland partly due to the government's inability to efficiently provide the proper logistical support that would enable supplies for the troops to get through and keep them in operational readiness for combat. This led to the arrest of John Shales, commissary-general of provisions. Schomberg did not escape criticism either. The Huguenots for the most part proved their worth despite losses either in battle or through sickness as the army made its way through Ireland during 1689. Schomberg, having lost large numbers of his soldiers through illness and food, clothing and medical deprivations, decided to follow the example of the opposing Jacobite army that was also reluctant to pursue the fight as the weather deteriorated; thus, both sides retreated to winter quarters.

William followed events in Ireland closely and, mindful of the threat of James Stuart – who was aided with a sizable well-equipped French army by Louis XIV – and acutely aware of the importance of subduing Ireland, took the decision to personally take charge of and lead the campaign the following year rather than simultaneously try to pursue the continental war with Louis. Lessons had been learnt from the logistical and strategic mistakes made during 1689, and so meticulous care was now taken to ensure that proper and regular supplies were always available.

William landed at Carrickfergus in the north of Ireland on 14 June 1690, his army at that time numbering some 36,000 men of

---

[ccxxxii] M. Glozier (Ed.) and D. Onnekink (Ed), *War, Religion and Service: Huguenot Soldiering 1685-1713* (Abingdon, 2007) p97.

English, French, Dutch, Danish and German nationalities. It was without doubt the largest invasion force that had ever set foot in Ireland[215]. He told those assembled that he had '...*come to ensure the people of Ireland would be settled in a lasting peace.*'

Included amongst William's troops was his elite force – the Dutch Blue Guards – who were in fact Dutch Catholics and they were in possession of the papal banner on the day of the battle that would decide the fate of monarchs and nations for years to come. There was also a considerable number of Ulster Protestants[216], whilst James' army contained a number of French regiments, and, moreover, within these were German Protestants. Ironically, in spite of there being Protestant troops within James' forces when they had landed in 1689 and he had set up his parliament in Dublin, he had foolishly confiscated Protestant lands. This led to Protestant fears that they would be faced with persecution, and large numbers fled – taking with them their skills and their capital.

William left Belfast on 22 June, and his well-equipped army marched south towards Dublin. Just 30 miles north of the city is a natural barrier the River Boyne which William and his forces would need to cross. After two days, William and his army had reached Carlingford, and then after a short rest they marched on towards Dundalk, where James had already assembled his army, but by the time William's army had arrived at the town, James and his troops had vacated it. James had made a grave error that was to prove fatal to his ambitions: having learned the size and strength of William's army, he ordered his troops to retreat from what had been a strategically well-chosen place to stand – the key geographical feature that is the pass leading to the Boyne.

This battle for Ireland, known to History as the Battle of the Boyne, was recorded by 50 eyewitnesses; amongst these were three prominent Huguenots, and there is a particularly detailed account within the memoirs of Isaac Dumont de Bostaquet, an extract of which is quoted here:

The advance guard had just arrived when the King decided to approach the river in order to study the enemy camp which was just on the other side – the Boyne cannot be forded there at high tide. The enemy fired at the King from their battery there and a cannonball came so close to him that it carried away part of the sleeve of his coat, tore his shirt and wounded him slightly. This news alarmed the whole army but made us consider Providence and God's goodness and the care He took to preserve our Prince so miraculously[ccxxxiii].

William and his army pitched camp on top of the plateau with its view of the River Boyne below, and they could see that the river was passable in several places. James' army headquarters were stationed at Ramullin, some distance from the riverbank[ccxxxiv]. William ordered a direct assault from the front across the Boyne with his right wing, led by Colonel Meinhard Schomberg, who was instructed to march upriver to the village of Slane to turn the enemy's left flank.

On the other side of the river, James was in the meantime refusing to listen to his advisors, who felt that William would indeed order his troops to cross the river at more than one point – and too late he realised his error – as William's army began to cross the Boyne in several places on 1 July[217].

The details of the death of the Duke of Schomberg during the battle are also taken from de Bostaquet's memoirs:

He had crossed the river where the infantry had crossed higher up than where we had crossed but at the same ford. The Marquis de Ruvigny's younger son, La Caillemotte, was in command of a detachment of the three French

---

[ccxxxiii] Diane W. Ressinger (Ed.), *Memoirs of Isaac Dumont de Bostaquet: A Gentleman of Normandy* (The Huguenot Society Publications, New Series, No. 4, London, 2005) p228.
[ccxxxiv] The Orange Order, *The Battle of the Boyne from the point of view of Europe and Louis XIV*, p3.

The Story of the Huguenots – a Unique Legacy

regiments which was ordered to cross the river to pursue the enemy who had some troops in a small village. There had been dogged resistance there and La Caillemotte was wounded in the thigh. Many other officers were killed or wounded there. One of my relatives, du Busc...took a musket ball in the leg. But the enemy was driven from their position and the French regiments advanced.

The enemy had placed some cavalry behind a hill in order to back up their infantry and as La Melonière marched on them, three of their squadrons fired on our French regiments and overwhelmed them. The Duke had no cavalry with him and ordered a lieutenant (who had been guarding the river bank) to charge. This officer had only 40 men and was unable to hold out against the enemy cavalry. He did his duty, skirmished twice with them and had two horses killed under him. He acted courageously but his troops were no match for the cavalry.

...At first the Duke did not want either to take up arms or to retreat, and the enemy had fallen upon him in great numbers, forcing him to act. His equerry Montargis was marching in front of him and shouted to him to keep to the right. But he went to the left and five or six enemy troopers slipped through the infantry and pursued him, recognising him by his blue riband. They wounded him with several sabre thrusts, which did not kill him as has been thought. The enemy troopers were being fired upon as they passed. When a ball pierced the great man's throat, he fell dead. Thus ended the life of our eighty-year-old hero.[ccxxxv].

With the death of Schomberg, William stepped in to lead his forces without any consideration for his own personal safety; he

---

[ccxxxv] Diane W. Ressinger (Ed.), *Memoirs of Issac Dumont De Bostaquet: A Gentleman of Normandy* (The Huguenot Society Publications, New Series, No 4, London, 2005) p229.

The Story of the Huguenots – a Unique Legacy

could be seen in the thick of the fighting, which continued unabated until 5pm that day when James retreated, leaving William as victor. De Bostaquet describes the events at the end of the battle:

The King ordered us to march towards Drogheda. We found a great many dead, for the enemy had departed in haste, abandoning all their baggage which was looted. We were halted for some time and that evening had orders to go with Colonel d'Onep, a Dane, to take night duty guarding the camp. Count Schomberg pursued the enemy until nightfall and killed many. He was waiting for orders to charge which did not come. He did not yet know of his father's death. We thought that the loss of Schomberg probably accounted for what seemed to be the King's lack of enthusiasm for pursuing the enemy[ccxxxvi].

The Battle of the Boyne was a resounding victory for William of Orange and his army. Two days after the battle he marched his forces into Dublin and into the pages of the history books. But victory came at a price as amongst the dead were a number of his Huguenot comrades including La Caillemotte. Although his wounds did not at first appear to be life threatening, he had asked to be taken from the field to Dublin, where he died a short time later.

Ireland had been won by William and his army, and as their work there was now ended, he proceeded to arrange for his men to be paid for their part in this conquest[218].

[ccxxxvi] Diane W. Ressinger (Ed.), Memoirs of Issac Dumont De Bostaquet: A Gentleman of Normandy (The Huguenot Society Publications, New Series, No 4, London, 2005) p231.

- 22 -

Citizenship, Faith and Loyalty

The year 1708 was a momentous one for the refugees who had settled in the United Kingdom as the Foreign Protestants Naturalisation Act now entered the statute book, giving full citizenship to those Protestant refugees seeking a new life here. So many were eager to acquire 'naturalisation' that to the indigenous population the national identity seemed under threat, and so, under such pressure, the Act was repealed just three years later.

Jean Mallandain was granted the right to citizenship in 1710 after swearing an oath to Queen Anne[ccxxxvii]. The 1708 Act had been instigated as a means of encouraging hard-working Protestants to settle here, as reflected concisely in the wording of the Act:

> ...whereas the increase of people is a means of advancing the wealth and strength of a nation; and whereas many strangers of the Protestant or reformed religion would be induced to transport themselves and their estates into this Kingdom, if they might be made partakers of the advantages and privileges which the natural-born subjects thereof do enjoy.

[ccxxxvii] The Mallandain Archives.

The Act had allowed for the simple process of the taking of the Oath, but this was limited to those of the Protestant faith as it also required the person to take the Sacrament – clearly something non-Protestants would not be prepared to do; this simple legality was a two-way gift as, in return, Huguenots gave their undying loyalty to the British Crown. Later Acts gave the Secretary of State discretionary powers to naturalise a person who wished to live here on the condition that they took the Oath and paid the appropriate fee[ccxxxviii].

The story of the Huguenots so far surely proves their having earned the right to British citizenship – already, we have seen so many examples of their sobriety, virtuousness and steadfastly strong work ethic. Pastors regularly oversaw their flocks' children, ensuring they did not disturb others with their play, and publicans were requested to report any French customers' over-indulgence[ccxxxix]. Their temperance was even held up as an example by the famous artist William Hogarth in his painting *Noon,* which aptly demonstrates the two contrasting stances taken by very different sections of the population: loose morals displayed on the left side clashing visually with the self-discipline and piety of the Huguenots, who are seen on the other side of the painting departing their church in an orderly and sober fashion after morning service.

Anti-Catholic legislation, which had been generally in place since Henry VIII's break with Rome, had in part been mitigated in 1778 by the introduction of the Papist Act that aimed to give wider religious toleration and to absolve Catholics from taking the religious oath when joining the army. Lord George Gordon, a powerful and staunch Protestant, raised a petition against the Act, and marched on Parliament in June 1780 drawing huge crowds as he did so. Then the mood of the people turned angry

---

[ccxxxviii] Laurie Fransman QC, *Fransman's British Nationality Law 3rd edition* (London, 2011) pp.135-6.
[ccxxxix] Jane Cox, *Old East Enders* (Gloucs, 2013) p289.

The Story of the Huguenots – a Unique Legacy

and they began to riot. The army had to be called upon to restore order, and it took a full week to bring peace back to the streets. During this time, however, some 300 rioters had been killed.

It seems that handbills given out during the march urging Protestants not to wear blue cockades in their hat, nor to associate with anyone who did, were also claiming that the wearing of such a cockade was the mark of a troublemaker, and this no doubt enflamed the mood of the marchers. Paradoxically, it did bring some sympathy for Catholics living in England, leading eventually to the Catholic Relief Act passed in 1791, which legalised Catholic worship and allowed for the provision of Catholic schools, and for Catholics to practice law.

In 1745, Huguenot loyalty to the Crown was again put to the test when the Young Pretender, Bonnie Prince Charlie, raised an army with the intention of regaining the throne his father had lost. *The London Gazette* published a list of Spitalfields master-weavers who were prepared to support the call to arms, along with their dependants and servants; out of the 133 masters in the area, no fewer than 80 were of Huguenot origin; next to the owner's name in the newspaper, a bracketed figure gave the number of men from their households who were ready to be enlisted. Amongst the masters' names were those of James Ouvry (19) and John Ouvry (10)[ccxl].

History has shown that the French refugee, whilst having suffered shockingly under religious intolerance and persecution, did arrive in his destination country equipped, indeed blessed, with a number of attributes that would help ensure his survival: the skills to contribute to many diverse occupations (not only those related to weaving); discipline and industriousness – and these refugees came from all walks of life. The French Relief Committee noted in 1687 that of the 13,050 who had arrived in

---

[ccxl] Museum of London, The, *The Quiet Conquest: The Huguenots, 1685-1985* (London, 1985) p98.

London there were: '*140 'quality', 143 minsters, 144 lawyers, physicians, traders and burghers, the rest being artisans and workmen*[ccxli]'.

Although the marriage of female Huguenots to English men would mean that French surnames were inevitably superseded by English names, it was often the later generations of the male line of Huguenot families who chose to 'anglicise' their names – perhaps to show their loyalty to the land they had been born in rather than the one from which their ancestors were derived (thus Blanc, in some instances, became White) – and such a move could also quite naturally have been career-focused in some cases as they may well have encountered discrimination in attempting to gain employment within the businesses of indigenous people. It is also quite possible, with at least some degree of wider religious tolerance being formalised into Acts of Parliament and therefore British law, that Catholic businessmen would be able to operate freely in commerce, and that within this framework, some would have chosen to take an adversarial stance and refuse employment to people of French (and therefore potentially Huguenot) sounding names.

Successive waves of migration have always left their mark on the area they settled in and such a legacy from France has remained down the years in this country, particularly in London, with the result that some streets and, in some cases, entire areas, still retain a clue to their earlier history: Petty France; Tuileries Street (Bethnal Green) and Fournier Street and Huguenot Place (Spitalfields)[219].

[ccxli] Jane Cox, *Old East Enders* (Gloucs, 2013) p287.

- 23 -

French Inheritances

To preserve the family inheritance in France, the difficult decision to 'conform' with the Catholic Church was often the only option that would stand a chance of preventing the family from being disinherited. To defiantly refuse abjuration of faith would result in persecution and punishment if the family remained in France, and to escape, or to attempt to escape, would inevitably also lead to disinheritance, the loss of all material possessions and the forfeiture of the family's right to live as before.

One such family faced with this emotive choice was the Romillys, who held considerable estates near Montpellier; to preserve this legacy for future generations, the family was forced to feign its conformity to the Catholic Church. Secretly, the head of the family continued to worship according to the Protestant faith, but at great personal risk – the catastrophic penalties if discovered were then still very applicable.

Etienne, the only son of the head of the household, had been born a year before the Revocation, but had been raised as a staunch Protestant. In 1701, he decided to travel to Geneva, where a chance encounter with a man by the name of Saurin[220] changed the course of his life. It was at this point that Etienne chose to travel onwards to England where so many of his fellow Huguenots had chosen to make their home, he wrote a letter to his father to

The Story of the Huguenots – a Unique Legacy

acquaint him of his decision soon after his arrival in London – a city where he hoped to earn a living and be able to make a life for himself [ccxlii].

Within a few years of Etienne's arrival, he had married Judith de Monsaillier, and set up a business as a wax bleacher. His father remained in France, sending his son financial aid from time to time until his death, shortly after which a distant Catholic relative took possession of the family estate, and the money which had been such an aid to Etienne and his family suddenly ceased.

Etienne now faced serious financial difficulty that tragically led to bankruptcy; he was greatly troubled by his misfortune, eventually leading to ill-health and an early death. His wife and eight children were left almost penniless. His youngest son, Peter, was in time apprenticed to Lafosse, a London jeweller and fellow refugee; he worked hard and on completion of his apprenticeship decided to travel to Paris to seek work as a journeyman. In due course, he travelled south to Montpellier to see the lost family estates. He returned to London and married Margaret Garnault (another Huguenot family descendant) and set up his own business. The family lived frugally on the income from the business, then Fate – in the form of a substantial inheritance from a member of his wife's family (M de la Haize) – provided the opportunity for his son Samuel to be articled as a clerk in Chancery Lane.

Samuel had been born on 1 March 1757, the second son of Peter and Margaret [221], but by the time of his birth his mother was an invalid, so the care of her son was left to a female relative. He remained a clerk in Chancery Lane for some years until he was admitted to the membership of Gray's Inn in 1778, and it was during this time he discovered an interest in politics, which, through his regular attendance of hearing debates in the House of Commons, steadily grew. He was called to the bar on 2 June 1783,

---

[ccxlii] Samuel Smiles, *The Huguenots Their Settlements, Churches and Industries in England and Ireland (1889)* (London) p327.

- 252 -

and became a famous law reformer of his era, who during his term of office as Solicitor General (1806-7), campaigned passionately for lessening the harshness of capital punishment for the more minor offences of those that were listed at that time. He was also a staunch opponent of the slave trade.

In June 1780 whilst at Gray's Inn, he had witnessed the Gordon Riots. He had assiduously worked hard to improve his earlier sparse education, and although his career path was at first a slow meander he took silk[222] in 1802, then in 1806, he was knighted and took his seat as Member of Parliament for Queenborough. His family's lost inheritance in previous generations was now being rebuilt by its gifted descendant on this side of the Channel through his rise to prominence and knighthood.

A further example of how a Huguenot family's inheritance could be put in jeopardy or indeed lost can be demonstrated through the records of the Gascherie/Gashry and Chesneau families. The Gascherie and Gashery families became related on 10 December 1696 when Suzanne Gascherie was wed to Francois Gashry at St Mary Magdalen, Old Fish Street, London. The couple were blessed over the years by the arrival of 12 children. Their eldest child, Susanne Gashry (Gascherie), eventually returned to the area of France from where her family had originated – La Rochelle, and she died there in 1762. Madeleine Gashry took legal action upon the death of her sister Susanne, on behalf of their mother Suzanne, widow of Francois Gashry, to try to reclaim the lands and monies inherited by the Catholic Bonneau family, who were distant relatives.

During November 1762, Madeleine had instructed agents in La Rochelle to act on her mother's behalf as the family were at the time living in Amsterdam and The Hague. Below is an extract of a letter sent by the firm of Noordingh and Domus of La Rochelle, dated 25 December 1762:

We pray you to give our compliments to the vende and to tell him that Mrs Gashry has not made a Will at all and as

The Story of the Huguenots – a Unique Legacy

she is regarded as born English the Estate is seized lacking heirs to reclaim it following the laws and treaties between the two Crowns in like case. Proofs are necessary establishing her birth and her connection with the relations who present themselves to inherit and they send their Power of Attorney all correct and legalized by the Ambassador in France as well as the other documents. There is an income but that is reputed a difficult matter. We will render in this affair every service that is asked of us.

PS it is necessary to point out to Messrs Vernede & Co that when I am questioned as to the name of Mr Gashry it will be necessary to add "known in France under the name of Gascherie[223].

The case continued to become more and more involved as a forest of documentation was required to prove family relationships, including copies of baptisms, marriages and burial register entries together with copies of wills and marriage contracts. Most importantly, documentation relating to the ownership of the land in dispute was also required – all this to prove that the lands should have been inherited by Suzanne Gascherie upon the death of her daughter rather than the estate being automatically passed to distant French relatives[ccxliii]. A settlement was finally reached after much patient negotiation whereby both parties were able to claim a portion of the estate. However, the *Edict of Toleration* that gave all citizens equal rights was still some years in the future; no doubt the lack of a will signed and dated by Susanne Gashry (Gascherie) would have been a substantial impediment to the Protestant family inheriting from her, but at that time French law still greatly and deliberately favoured Catholics.

[ccxliii] London Metropolitan Archives, *original documents relating to the Gasherie, Gashry and Hanrott families.*

1. A méreau token

2. The French Hospital, Victoria Park, Hackney

3. Jean Dupen's indenture of apprenticeship

4. Residents of the French Hospital

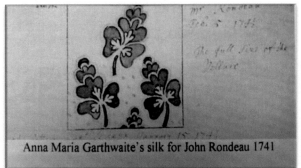

5. Silk design for John Rondeau

6. Huguenot houses of Spitalfields

7. The Bank of England, Threadneedle Street, London

8. One of the bobbins displayed on the outside of a Spitalfields house

9. Intricate carving detail, exterior of a house In Spitalfields

10. Franschhoek, South Africa, one of the many places Huguenots settled in

11. The Bethnal Green mulberry tree – currently under threat

12. An original Jacquard loom

13. Memorial to the Huguenots of Wandsworth

Part Three

Huguenot Enhancement of Life

in the United Kingdom – A Legacy

Although wide swathes of English society welcomed the gifted Huguenot refugees, we have seen occurrences that demonstrate not all of the population greeted these 'foreigners' with open arms. Perhaps due to fears of the changes that might be caused to the existing social order, many people were worried that any resultant modification would bring a loss of identity, or a threatening of livelihoods, by the inroads of so many foreigners so suddenly, and indeed, it was inevitable that the country would begin to change with such a sustained influx of entrepreneurial refugees.

On a more positive note, the country benefitted from these hard-working refugees: they provided fresh skills that the government wished not only to welcome, but also – and with very sound business rationale – wished to encourage to be taught to the native population. Whereas the country had largely been an agricultural society with 'cottage' industry trades peppered amongst its population, by the mid-18th century the outlook had changed rapidly; fresh skills were leading to new innovations and techniques that directly enriched many areas of society, and some of these would go on to fuel what would become known as the Industrial Revolution.

These skills were even more diverse than was at first realised, reaching a zenith during the Georgian period, and are unfolded in the following chapters.

- 24 -

Commerce, Benevolence and The Word

BANKING

It is without questions that the world of banking and commerce as we know it today can be traced back to the Huguenots.

Following on from the military successes in Ireland, the Bank of England was created – primarily to control the enormous debts incurred particularly as a result of the wars between England and France. An Act of Parliament providing for the original subscriptions to the Bank's capital was passed on 25 April 1694[224]. There had been several ideas put forward to set up a national bank before this Act, but the one that gained favour for founding a Bank of England [ccxliv] was that of William Paterson[225]. Many influential people did not readily support the plan, some saying that they did not understand the rationale for it and therefore would not back it, and besides, there would surely be an imminent peace with France, and so there would be no occasion for it. Others said this project came from Holland and therefore they would not hear of it, since there were too many Dutch 'things' already, a common cry often heard when the native population feels itself in a precarious position.

[ccxliv] The Bank of England, *History and Functions*, p6.

It is no exaggeration to state that a significant number of people of Huguenot descent were involved in the founding of the Bank of England, including several merchants who were amongst the most eminent and wealthy Huguenots to settle in England, as well as seven of the original 24 directors. The first governor, Sir John Houblon, subscribed £10,000, and his brothers James and Abraham were also subscribers. The three brothers were sons of a Huguenot refugee, who had set up in business in a house that he had built in Threadneedle Street soon after the Great Fire of London.

In 1689, John Houblon was elected as Alderman of the City of London, and was knighted the same year. He was Master of the Grocers' Company from 1690-1, and also served as Lord Mayor of London from 1695-6 as well as being appointed Governor of the Bank of England and Lord of the Admiralty. In gratitude for his services to the Bank, he was presented with a silver tankard inscribed:

The gift of the Directors of the Bank of England to Sir John Houblon, Governor, Lord Mayor of London, in token of his great ability, industry and strict uprightness at a time of extreme difficulty. 1696.[ccxlv]

Sir John's image could be found on the reverse of the £50 bank note from 20 April 1994 until it was withdrawn from circulation on 30 April 2014. Indeed, another area of banking that can lay claim to Huguenot involvement is the bank note itself.

Furthermore, the Minutes of the first Court of Directors of the Bank of England, taken on 27 July 1694, state the basis upon which depositors should gain access to their money – indeed, the three methods agreed upon at that meeting eventually evolved into the modern-day processes that for many years allowed us to withdraw money from our accounts: bank-notes, passbooks and cheques.

[ccxlv] The Bank of England, *History and Functions*, p7.

The Story of the Huguenots – a Unique Legacy

* * * * * *

COMMERCE

England in the late 17th century was undergoing considerable commercial change, in part undeniably driven by a degree of Huguenot influence, and this included another emerging area where Huguenots were already active – the world of stocks and shares. In 1697, a broker by the name of John Castaing, a Huguenot broker, instigated a twice-weekly list, *Course of the Exchange,* still published today, and now known as the *Stock Exchange Daily Official List*. This list is the third oldest daily newspaper publication.

Stocks and shares had been traded for a while, but the arrival of the Huguenots helped to heighten this activity. Some had managed to liquidate their assets before fleeing France, and were naturally keen to reinvest their liquid assets in England. A famous coffee house, *Johnathan's*, opened in the 1680s, and soon became a meeting place for those trading in stocks and shares, the fluctuating value of which could be due to so many factors, and therefore, then as now, it was paramount that brokers had the most up to date information to help reflect what was (and was not) the correct values. *Johnathan's* coffee house, together with *Garraway's*[226], employed boys to seek out information from vessels docking in the Port of London, arriving back, hot foot, at their employers with news both good and bad. The boys would also source information through a mix of friendship and a little bribery of the servants of wealthy city merchants. Overhearing of conversations also formed part of the boys' overall information, which would then be displayed on a board in the coffee house. Entry to the coffee house was only gained upon payment of one old penny, which entitled the payee to free coffee. John Castaing frequented *Johnathan's,* and it was here that his first list was published giving details of stock, bullion and exchange rates. His lists were greatly depended upon by the numerous traders frequenting the coffee houses[ccxlvi].

Another famous stock-broking company was founded by the Huguenot Philip Cazenove. His family had fled to Geneva in the 1680s, then travelled onwards to England settling in London. Philip Cazenove started working for his brother-in-law, John Menet, in 1819 before going into partnership with him in 1823 as Cazenove & Co.[227] The company continued to grow and by the 1930s had become one of the leading stock-broking firms.

In the 1980s, the company was a major advisor to Margaret Thatcher's government. The last member of the Cazenove family to work in the company was Bernard Cazenove who retired in 2004 just before the company merged with J P Morgan.

* * * * * *

BENEVOLENCE

Friendly Societies in this country were a Huguenot creation. The clubs were formed by workers to provide financial support in times of hardship. These societies had been in existence in France (*Association de secours Mutuels*) and indeed, the first 'benefit' society had originated in Lille as long ago as 1580[ccxlvii]. Among these early clubs were The Friendly Benefit Society, originally named the Society of Parisians (1687), The Norman Society (1703), The Society of Lintot (1708), The Friendly Society (1720), and The Society of Protestant Refugees from High and Low Normandy (1764). These societies paved the way for the later English versions[ccxlviii].

[ccxlvi] Records of the London Stock Exchange: leaflet No 53.

[ccxlvii] Kershen, Anne, *Strangers, Aliens and Asians: Huguenots, Jews and Bangladeshis in Spitalfields 1660-2000* (Oxon, 2005) p113.

[ccxlviii] Waller, William, *Early Huguenot Friendly Societies*. The Huguenot Society, Vol VI (1900) p204.

The Norman Society of Bethnal Green remained in existence for over 150 years, keeping its records and accounts in French until 1800. It finally closed its doors in 1863, probably because as time had passed the reason for its original inception – the relief of French refugees – had long ceased due in part to Huguenots being gradually assimilated into English society. This does not mean that all the French mutual societies died out, however. We should bear in mind that from the ingenuity of those desperate Protestant refugees were born many of today's institutions, such as The Foresters and Odd Fellows[ccxlix]. The early Methodists were aware of these societies and of their members' provision for sickness, old age as well as burial costs, and so had meaningful connections with them[ccl].

Not all societies were presumed non-political; indeed, one friendly society, de Picards a Wallons, whose meetings were held at *The Sign of the Turkish Slave* in Brick Lane, Bethnal Green, openly recorded on 24 August 1799 that it had no political affiliations[ccli], perhaps perceiving this declaration as necessary due to accusations that such societies were politically motivated, a claim that had been uttered more than once during periods of considerable unrest, for example, during the Cutters' Riots.

By 1793, friendly societies were in such abundance that the need for regulation of these organisations was being seen as having become essential, and therefore the requirement now existed for them to be officially encompassed in an Act of Parliament – the George Rose Act.

The Huguenot Friendly Benefit Society, founded in 1687 as the Society of Parisians[228], held its meetings at *The Norfolk Arms*, William Street. Membership was limited to just 61 persons of the

---

[ccxlix] Samuel Smiles, *The Huguenots Their Settlements, Churches and Industries in England and Ireland (1889)* (London) p265.
[ccl] Clive Murray Norris, *The Financing of John Wesley's Methodism c1740-1800* (Oxford, 2017) p51.
[ccli] The London Metropolitan Archives, *The Pensions Archive Trust Research Guide, Huguenot Friendly Benefit Societies, p2.*

Protestant faith aged 18-41 years old and living within three miles of Christ Church, Spitalfields, all of whom were required to pay an entrance fee of 2s 6d, and additionally they would be required to pay 1s each month towards 'The Box'[229] plus a further 4d towards the monthly 'evening's entertainment'. Failure of a member to attend would result in a fine of 2d. However, the benefits of membership were 8s per week 'sick pay' up to a total of 52 weeks – if a member was ill for longer than that, the sick pay would decrease to 4s per week. Members were also entitled to a 'death benefit', but this was to be paid in two portions – £3 upon sight of the body, and the balance of £2 paid once the burial had taken place.

If a member was admitted to the French Hospital, *La Providence*, they were entitled to 6d per week, but were no longer eligible for the death benefit. All the benefits were dependent upon the society's reserve funds – if they should fall below a certain level then the benefits would be adjusted to accommodate the fall in these funds[cclii].

The rules also stated that no member would be permitted to play any game, and if a member spoke contemptuously of another member, or interrupted another officer, or blasphemed against another member, then the culprit could be fined. The ultimate misconduct, according to the rules, was as follows:

> *If there be recognised among us a perjurer, a false witness, a blasphemer or if anyone be ill-disposed towards the Protestant Religion or the Government of the State, or accused of great crimes [crimes énormes], he shall be proceeded against with all the vigour of our laws*[ccliii].

There were other rules designed to maintain a lawful framework within which the society should function, and amongst these is one that relates to the secretary or clerk of the society: he

---

[cclii] Waller, William, *Early Huguenot Friendly Societies.* The Huguenot Society, Vol VI (1900) p204.
[ccliii] Ibid, p205.

must not be appointed from within the membership, but once appointed, must attend every meeting and be paid the sum of 5s per meeting. Later, as the years passed, and membership dwindled, so the fees had to be increased amongst those remaining in order to somehow compensate for the losses in a valiant attempt at continuing the society[ccliv].

By and large, other societies adopted similar rules for the governance of their own society. There was one specifically formed for Dutch Protestants, and the following is a quotation taken from the Dutch Church archives:

January 1699, a contract between the Deacons of the London Dutch Church and a London Dutch Club of working men. The bookkeeper and Treasurer collected the contributions of the members which were handed to the Deacons for a sick fund. Paid out to sick or injured on demand of Bookkeeper and Treasurer after investigation by the Deacons. Should the Club break up, the funds to be given to the poor of the Church but would continue as long as one member was on the books. Rules made could be altered by the Bookkeeper and Treasurer. The members pledged their persons and property for the carrying out of the rules.

The number of societies grew in keeping with their success. As an example, by 1813 at least 3,000 people living in Bethnal Green were members of a Friendly Society[cclv]. Members of these societies likewise paid fees into a fund which would distribute money to the poor and sick, and a member could eventually claim a pension from the society if their circumstances proved it to be necessary.

* * * * * *

[ccliv] Waller, William, *Early Huguenot Friendly Societies.* The Huguenot Society, Vol VI (1900) pp.204-5.

[cclv] John Marriot, *Beyond the Tower: A History of East London* (London, 2012) p76.

The Story of the Huguenots – a Unique Legacy

Clubs for meeting like-minded persons were a concept readily embraced by Huguenots who wished to socialise, and at the same time acquire friendships forged through similar hobbies and interests.

Many of the more studious Huguenot refugees from France chose to pursue an academic career once they settled here, and, accordingly, a variety of clubs were soon formed for the pleasure of all such persons. One of the most famous was the Mathematical Society of Spitalfields (1717). They had first gathered at the *Monmouth Head* tavern, Monmouth Street, on Saturday evenings to test each other with various mathematical puzzles, and a 'fine' of 2d was levied on any member unable to solve the challenging problem put to him, a very real incentive indeed.

The Mathematical Society had been a great success for a considerable period of time, as it encouraged its members to increase their knowledge by attending lectures at the meetings. However, gradually the declining membership, down from 54 in 1839 to just 19 in 1845 led to the Mathematical Society writing to the Royal Astronomical Society, who responded on 10 May of that year:

A meeting of the Council of the Royal Astronomical Society took place yesterday, and I brought forward the suggestions contained in your recent letters to me relating to the venerable Mathematical Society of London, and the Council were unanimous in regretting that this ancient Society of 130 years standing should be on the eve of dissolution and decline. The members of the Council were also, I believe, unanimous that if the nineteen surviving members of the Mathematical Society should in their liberality and public spirit wish to keep the mathematical and astronomical and philosophical portions of their library together, and should kindly and considerately offer to present it to the Royal Astronomical Society, that the

- 263 -

Council of the latter would not only be grateful to them for this act of judicious benevolence, but would be willing to elect all the members of the Mathematical Society members for life of the Royal Astronomical Society.

As mentioned before, walking around Spitalfields or Soho in the mid-18th century would have conveyed a distinctly French ambience – often the conversation swirling around from young and old alike would have been overwhelmingly in French, but a stranger to the area trying to find his way around would not have had his task made easier because the houses were rarely numbered, and the pedestrian would instead be guided to his destination by shop and inn signs, which would often be in French; these included *La Navette* (The Shuttle) in Brick Lane, and *La Cloche* (The Cover) in what is now Princelet Street[cclvi]. Inns and public houses were once meeting places for Huguenots, who had welcomed the chance to meet in these establishments, not only for socialising, but to hear of work, or to do business – simple, early forms of networking.

There is another type of society that can be thankful to Huguenots for its existence, and that is gardening societies, which in fact began life in Spitalfields[cclvii]. The history of one family is inextricably linked to this. On 30 October 1770, the wedding of Ann Gaucheron, granddaughter of Louis (whom we noted earlier as arriving in England in the 1680s), to John Kemp took place at St Dunstan's Church, Stepney. The Kemps were one of the well-established families whose skill and diligence brought about flourishing market gardens in and around east London. John Kemp's garden was situated on the corner of Cock Lane near St Leonard's Church. Market gardens had begun to appear in east London in the early part of the 17th century, particularly in Bethnal

---

[cclvi] Jane Cox, *Old East Enders* (Stroud, 2013) p281.
[cclvii] G. M. Trevelyan, *English Social History: A survey of six centuries – Chaucer to Queen Victoria* (Cambridge, 1973) p247.

The Story of the Huguenots – a Unique Legacy

Green – cheek by jowl to the City of London. These gardens had become extremely popular as a way of substituting the earlier sources of fruit and vegetables, as well as flowers, from the Continent. Often the gardens were subdivided and leased out. The descendants of John Kemp and Ann Gaucheron continued to tend the family market garden until the very end of the 18th century [cclviii].

There were a number of keen gardeners amongst the Huguenot population, many of whom would band together to hold flower shows. Their love of birds is almost legendary – a variety of finches as well as linnets were kept by weavers in cages in their workshops; the sweetness of the birdsong would have lifted the spirits of anyone wearying from their days' labours. They would proudly show their birds to other bird fanciers and look upon other owner's birds with a certain amount of either disdain or envy. They were also keen breeders of spaniels and pigeons [cclix].

* * * * * *

Education seems to certainly have been taken very seriously by the vast majority of Huguenots, as a means of enriching and enlightening young minds, as well as thereafter providing opportunities for all Huguenot children and young people to acquire the essential skills with which they could, one day, ply an honest trade.

By the 1720s, ministers and officials of the Threadneedle Street Church were becoming very concerned at the very apparent rapid increase in the numbers of poor and orphaned children of Huguenot descent in the capital. It was clear that, through a lack of education and familial awareness, they were at acute risk of losing all conscious connections with their Huguenot heritage.

[cclviii] The Gaucheron Archives.

[cclix] Jane Cox, *Old East Enders* (Gloucs, 2013) p290.

The Story of the Huguenots – a Unique Legacy

At a meeting held on 12 October 1718, it was decided by the church elders and ministers that they should found a charity school for these unfortunates. Plans were drawn up, and a school was built at a cost of £100 on the site of *La Cour de l'Hôpital*[230]. The school was large enough to house 100 children – 50 girls and 50 boys. The school opened its doors for the first time on 1 September 1719. All the girls' places were soon filled, but it took a little longer for a full quota of boys to be enrolled. The children were divided into groups according to their ability in reading and spelling rather than the now more commonplace method of age of the child[cclx].

The first staff of the school were Thomas and Anne Brohier and Catherine Isambert. In December 1737, Catherine Savoye, the married daughter of Mme Isambert, was engaged to teach needlework to the girls, a skill greatly valued by prospective employers during that era.

Eventually, Mme Savoye assumed the role of headteacher in the girls' department when her mother retired in 1741. A second school was opened nearby in 1745 next to the recently built *La Neuve Eglise*[231]. In 1765, a meeting of the Threadneedle Street Consistory recorded that the school must move with the times in order to best serve the needs of its pupils and the wider community – teaching could no longer continue wholly in French as a command of the English language would undeniably give the children a better chance of entering into apprenticeships[232][cclxi].

By 1773, however, pupil numbers were dwindling to such an extent that on 31 March the Consistory reluctantly agreed to admit up to 12 children from outside the church membership – the very significant step had been taken that the school would no longer be exclusively for Huguenots and their descendants.

[cclx] Keith Le May, *Charity Schools' provided by the French Protestant institutions in London 1682-1831*, Proceedings of the Huguenot Society, XXVII (1) (1998) p66.
[cclxi] Ibid, p67.

The Story of the Huguenots – a Unique Legacy

Numerous schools were established in London as well as on the outskirts of the capital, including several famous establishments such as the Westminster Protestant School, founded in 1747. The school was paid for by subscription with an appeal for funds launched that aimed to set up and run this school based on a desire to allow French refugees of all classes fair and proper access to education[cclxii]. We have already seen that orphans and children of poor Huguenots were being admitted to the workhouse, or were growing up illiterate for want of an education. The strong desire to correct this situation, together with a belief in education *per se* for those of the Protestant faith led to 100 subscribers being recorded within just a few years of the founding of the school. Subscribers were expected to contribute at least ten shillings annually.

The monies raised enabled the school to feed, clothe and house 30 children (15 boys and 15 girls) as well as to educate them according to the Reformed religion. The Westminster Protestant School became a girls' only school in 1812, remaining so until it closed in the 1920s. But, although the school ceased almost a century ago, the Westminster French Protestant School Foundation is still in existence, and to this day provides financial assistance to educate children of Huguenot descent.

Another well-known school that owes its creation to a Huguenot is Cheam, south-west London, whose founder was David Sanxay. Large numbers of boarding and day schools were launched by various refugees all around the capital for boys and girls in places such as Islington, Chelsea, Greenwich and Marylebone[cclxiii]. The pastor community provided teachers to some of these schools and, in some cases, a pastor would be selected for the dual responsibility of school minister and teacher. One example of this was Jean Bion whose experiences as a chaplain on board a galley ship had had such a profound effect on him, taught in Chelsea.

[cclxii] Museum of London, The, *The Quiet Conquest: The Huguenots, 1685-1985* (London, 1985) p89.
[cclxiii] Ibid, p89.

The Story of the Huguenots – a Unique Legacy

Within the groups of refugees who came to settle here were teachers who were able to find a position close to where they first made their home – in areas such as Canterbury, Southampton and most notably in London – where the church at Threadneedle Street listed no less than eight teachers amongst its flock.

The Huguenot Church had included within its charitable remit the education of its flock, particularly the poor, who were unable to pay for their own education. The oldest record of the Church's intent can be found in the 1682 accounts and consistory minutes, when concerns were raised about locating adequate premises and sufficient schoolmasters to teach children of the poor, including orphans, to read. The first recorded appointment was Jean Vermallet. The Pest House also acquired a teacher, Gabriel Danger, who taught both children and adults. From 1682-4, the teachers were paid from funds raised by the Church, but thereafter, records show that the cost was met from the Briefs[233] of Charles II[cclxiv].

Although the Threadneedle Street Church continued to distribute poor relief from its funds, the French Committee not only helped alleviate poverty, but was also tasked with the duty of maintaining and financing the schools. The Committee set up two sub-committees, one for each of two designated areas – Westminster and Soho were one, and London and Spitalfields the other. At first, the sub-committees appointed just one headmaster, but as the years went by so the numbers of teachers grew in line with the rise in student numbers, and by 1706 each sub-committee employed three teachers until, eventually, a gradual decline in student numbers led to the inevitable reduction of employed teachers[cclxv]. No doubt this foresightedness to educate and ensure

---

[cclxiv] Keith Le May, *Charity Schools' provided by the French Protestant institutions in London 1682-1831,* Proceedings of the Huguenot Society, XXVII (1) (1998) p64.

[cclxv] Ibid, pp.64-5.

- 268 -

The Story of the Huguenots – a Unique Legacy

self-sufficiency among the refugees helped immensely in their assimilation and integration within English society.

Yet not all Huguenots chose a Huguenot school for their child's education. In 1792, John Mallandain petitioned the Blue Coat School for financial aid to educate his eldest son, John; this is an extract of his appeal:

> *To the Right Honourable, Right Worshipful, Governors of Christ Church Hospital, London.*
>
> *The humble Petition of John Mallandain of the Parish of St. Matthews, Bethnal Green, Middlesex, Sugar Refiner, sheweth that your Petitioner had a wife and three children to provide for, and being in low circumstances he finds it difficult to maintain and educate them without assistance. Your petitioner therefore applies for one of his said Children, John Mallandain of age of seven years and upwards, to be received into the benefits of the said hospital.*

Fortunately, the petition was granted, and young John was admitted to the school on 10 May 1792. The school was a charitable establishment that had been founded by Edward VI in 1552. The day after John completed his education he became apprenticed to his father in the Musicians Company[234], but his career path was not to be a melodious one. Instead, within a few years, he had become a cadet in the East India Company having been recommended by William Gather and John Bibb[235]. John Mallandain served in the East India Company for nearly 30 years working his way through the ranks to become Lieutenant Colonel by 1829[cclxvi].

Apart from academia, another type of school founded in the 1680s was a school for riding and fencing. It was established in the area near to Piccadilly by Solomon Foubert, who had a similar profession in Paris until the school there was forced to close, and

---

[cclxvi] The Mallandain Archives.

The Story of the Huguenots – a Unique Legacy

so the Fouberts emigrated to England and set up their school in London. There is even today a passage in the area named after Foubert[cclxvii].

* * * * * *

Important as education was to the Huguenots, the challenge of trying to find good schools to send their children to must have been dwarfed by the difficulties they faced in obtaining decent housing for all the family or individuals in need, and in this respect, those less fortunate were in some cases blessed by the compassion of others more financially able.

In 1757, in Richmond, then part of Surrey, the two unmarried daughters of Sir John Houblon decided they wished to assist those less fortunate, and so they decided to endow a trust with land to build almshouses and, to ensure the financial security of the trust, to donate some properties at Harrow, north London, and Bollinhatch in Essex to provide an income [cclxviii].

The almshouses were to offer a home for nine poor single women. The Houblon daughters lived nearby in Ellerker House with their widowed mother. In her will, Rebecca gave two acres of land in Richmond Field, *'in a shott called Church Shott'*.

The original stipulation for gaining entry was that the supplicant had to be Protestant (this is no longer the case) and someone who lived a virtuous, sober and honest life. A provision of £9 for the inmates was also put aside to furnish each of them with a substantial gown, which had to be of a brown hue, this gift being given to them annually at Easter.

In 1907, Lady Alice Archer Houblon wrote a book detailing the lives of the Houblon family and in it she describes the almshouses:

[cclxvii] Museum of London, The, *The Quiet Conquest: The Huguenots, 1685-1985* (London, 1985) p89.
[cclxviii] Richmond Charities, *Houblon's Almshouses,* (Richmond) p2.

...the road to London passes scarcely fifty yards from the wrought iron gate which leads into the high walled, peaceful sanctuary within where one can imagine oneself in the past and conjure up a vision of the two little old ladies, Mistress Rebecca and Mistress Susanna, tripping across the quadrangle to read a chapter of the Bible to the white-capped inmates of the tiny houses. They would have walked down the green lane on their own land all the way as they owned many acres on Richmond Hill.

The lane is today called Houblon Road and, remarkably, the almshouses externally remain as they were when first built; the interiors have of necessity been modernised over time[cclxix].

* * * * * *

TO SPREAD THE WORD - PRINTING

When Huguenots were barred from printing and selling religious books in France, the countries that witnessed the greatest influx of Huguenots working in these industries were often Holland and England. Citizens of both countries took a keen interest in the printed word, being receptive to new methods of printing that would enable them to expand their knowledge through reading.

One Huguenot refugee, Jacob Christophe Le Blon, invented a new method of colour printing. Although Jacob was born in Frankfurt am Main in 1667, his ancestry was French – his father's family had fled there from France in 1576. Jacob had moved to Amsterdam by the time of his marriage in 1705, and by 1710 he had begun experimenting with red, yellow and blue plates. In 1717, the year following his wife's death, he had decided to move to London, where, shortly after his arrival, he set up a company named The Picture Office. He was fascinated with the idea of producing colour copies of paintings. He applied to George I for a

---

[cclxix] Richmond Charities, *Houblon's Almshouses*, (Richmond) p2.

The Story of the Huguenots – a Unique Legacy

patent for his three-colour printing process that was granted in 1719. Six years later, he privately published a pamphlet entitled *Coloritto* describing the process that he had invented. This is the first recorded published description of trichromatic colour printing.

BOOKBINDING

The family of R. Riviere & Son, bookbinders, had started a new life in England following the Revocation of 1685. The second son of Daniel Valentine Riviere, Robert was apprenticed to booksellers Messrs. Allman when he left school in 1824; within five years, he had set up his own bookshop in Bath, and was taking on a modest number of orders for bookbinding. In 1840, he decided to move premises to London at 28 Queen Street, Lincoln's Inn Fields, before a further move to 196 Piccadilly. Through his quality of workmanship, he gradually built an excellent reputation, which led to many commissions from titled society including the Duke of Devonshire, who contracted him to undertake numerous projects.

Queen Victoria and other members of the Royal Family also commissioned him to bind various books, including the most important commission of his career – the binding of 1,000 copies of the official descriptive and illustrated catalogue of the *Great Exhibition of the Works of Industry of all Nations* in 1851. His other famous work was the restoration and rebinding of the original *Doomsday* book in 1870. He died on 12 April 1882 at his home near Regent's Park[cclxx].

PAPERMAKING

The White Paper Makers Company was formed by 15 men amongst whom were nine Huguenots, who joined forces to set up mills producing high quality white paper. It began in January of

---

[cclxx] Museum of London, The, *The Quiet Conquest: The Huguenots, 1685-1985* (London, 1985) p180.

The Story of the Huguenots – a Unique Legacy

1686 with the granting of a patent for '...*the art of making of all sorts of writing and printing paper, and to imprint our arms upon such paper*[cclxxi]'.

The patent also stated:

> ….. *they had lately brought out of France excellent workmen and already set up several new-invented mills and engines for making thereof, not heretofore used in England*[cclxxii].

Later that same year, James II issued a Charter of Incorporation giving them official and legal status as The Company of White Paper Makers. Of the original 15 men, several had resided in Southampton, but not all had lengthy family histories with the area. Adam de Cardonnel had arrived in England as a refugee from Caen, Normandy, and gained his rights through denizenship in 1641, first working in London as a merchant before acquiring naturalisation status in 1657. Within a few years, he moved to Southampton, where in 1662 he was sworn in as a burgess as well as being appointed Collector of Customs, a post he held for 20 years.

Nicholas Dupin lived in Portsmouth and had been naturalised in 1670, the son of Theodore Dupin of Auion, Somar. Like his fellow refugee de Cardonnel, he too became a burgess. They had taken out a lease on a watermill known as 'Up Mills' at South Stoneham in Hampshire, and by 1696 an inventory had been compiled from which can be derived the scale of the paper-making operation there. Four mills operated on the site, but there were also various other buildings for specific processes related to the manufacture of paper. In the year that the inventory was undertaken, the company mills were producing approximately 4,000 reams of paper. A reasonably-sized workforce would have been necessary to operate the mills and the various outbuildings.

[cclxxi] Thomas, J. H., *Hampshire and the Company of White Paper Makers, p137.*
[cclxxii] Ibid, p139.

Although employee records are incomplete, the local parish register gives an insight into the local population, which appears to be in part made up of refugees of French origin. One example of this is the entry in May 1701 in the parish register of the christening of Anne, daughter of Peter and Esther Jacques, which says: *'belonging to the Paper Mills'*. There are many more entries similar to this one, including some which mention the family being of French origin[cclxxiii]. This is not meant to infer that the only foreigners in South Stoneham were French – indeed, the registers also contain entries referring to christenings of children whose parents were Dutch, as well as English, and the advantage of this particular cultural mix was clearly the compatible range of skills and ideas that could be drawn together from a diverse range of foreigners from whom the locals would learn how to produce very fine quality paper.

The White Paper Making Company from time to time advertised in *The London Gazette* the prevailing rate of sales of their paper at their London head office, but unfortunately over time a gradual erosion of the superiority of the product, as well as the inclusion of some inferior paper within orders – known as 'perversion of stock'– caused a decline in sales until inevitably the company was obliged to sell the mills[cclxxiv].

Henry Portal, had evidently worked hard in England, now taking the decision to set up his own papermaking company. He had learned his trade from a fellow Huguenot, Gerald de Vaux, at one of the mills in South Stoneham. He took out a lease on Bere Mill, Hampshire, in 1710, where he was to employ many Huguenots and their descendants, and this must have enhanced his growing reputation as a fine subject for he was granted naturalisation the following year. He was so successful that in 1719 he was able to lease nearby Laverstoke Mill.

[cclxxiii] Thomas, J. H., *Hampshire and the Company of White Paper Makers,* pp.141-2.
[cclxxiv] Ibid.p145.

The Story of the Huguenots – a Unique Legacy

In 1723, the Governor of the Bank of England let it be known that a protective paper was needed for future bank notes. On 27 November 1724, an important contract was signed between the Bank of England and Henry, which stated that his company guaranteed to produce a higher quality paper for bank notes than the earlier supplier had been able to. The new paper was duly supplied, and circulation of the innovative banknote began in 1724. By 1725, the bank note paper had been refined at Laverstoke Mill to include a watermark, which has become a feature of all United Kingdom banknotes ever since. The improvement of techniques used in the production of paper for banknotes led to such superior quality of this type of paper that Henry Portal's company retained the contract for over 270 years until the company was acquired by De La Rue, who continue to produce the paper banknotes.

* * * * * *

The Fourdrinier family had originated in the Caen area of northern France. Henry Fourdrinier and his family moved to Groningen, Holland, where a son, Paul, was born in 1698[cclxxv]. The family moved to England in the 1720s. Paul had been trained as an engraver, and following the completion of his apprenticeship he had left Holland to begin working in London[cclxxvi].

Henry Fourdrinier, son of Paul[236], did not follow in his father's footsteps, but instead became apprenticed to William Baker, a stationer in Lombard Street. In time, Henry became a member of the Drapers Company. He clearly worked hard, and soon the company he had joined as an apprentice had become a partnership – Baker & Fourdrinier. Baker had leased a warehouse in Sherbourne Lane from the Drapers Company, but by the 1790s

---

[cclxxv] Peter Simpson, *The Forgotten Fourdrinier; The Life, times and work of Paul Fourdrinier* (Bloomington, 2017) [E-Book]
[cclxxvi] Ibid.

Henry had taken over the lease of these premises. Henry and Jemima Fourdrinier were married in the early 1760s, their first son Henry being born on 11 February 1766, who was to have three younger brothers: Charles (1767), John (1770) and Sealy (1774), with a sister Jemima being born in 1772[237]. The younger Henry married Sarah Ann Walker in 1790 and they were blessed in time with four sons: Joseph William (1793); Charles John (1794); George Henry (1795) and Edward Newman (1800).

Henry senior died in 1799 having profitably expanded the business by the purchase in 1790 of the Two Waters Mill at Hemel Hempstead in order to produce paper for sale at the Lombard Street premises[238]. Three of his sons – Henry, Charles and Sealy – continued to run the business after their father's death.

The year 1800 was to be a significant year for the Fourdrinier brothers as they were introduced to Leger Didot by John Gamble, brother-in-law of Nicholas-Louis Robert, a Frenchman from Essonnes, just south of Paris, who had been working for a French papermaking company. Didot had funded some of Nicholas-Louis Robert's experiments with paper making machines in an attempt to manufacture paper by machine rather than the restrictive and time-consuming hand-produced method. It was felt by the Fourdriniers that if a machine could fabricate paper in a fraction of the time it took to hand-make one sheet at a restricted size, then it seemed commercially very reasonable to assume that such a machine would be worth investing in. With this in mind, the Fourdriniers decided to purchase one third of the rights to the patent that John Gamble had taken out in 1801, and two years later they ploughed money into building an engineering works in Bermondsey to manufacture the machines, appointing Bryan Donkin to oversee production. In 1804, the Fourdriniers purchased the lease of the old flour mills at St Neots in Huntingdonshire to experiment further with improving the basic machine design, and the first working machine was constructed here. But the wheels of industry did not run smoothly. Didot, the man who had originally funded the initial prototypes, proved a difficult man to work with, not only because he continually chose to work alone, but also because he patented his designs without discussing them with Donkin – the man given responsibility for design and engineering.

Alarm bells began to ring for Charles Fourdrinier as the ever-mounting costs began to eat into the assets of the business. Charles[239] decided to sell his rights to the patent; Matthew Towgood, a banker who had joined the Fourdrinier businesses in the 1790s, also decided to remove his capital, some £60,000, from the business, and accepted the mill at St Neots in recompense. Henry, however, had received a substantial sum of money from his father-in-law Joseph Walker on Walker's death, and he bravely used this to continue funding production of the machines. This must have seemed an enormous risk to take, given that others were withdrawing investment in the business, but it seems to have paid off: by 1806, his 20 machines were producing approximately 11 per cent of the country's entire paper output.

In 1807, Henry and his youngest brother Sealy patented a new machine capable of producing continuous paper. This invention represented an immense step forward in paper production because, at last, production time would be significantly decreased, as well as simultaneously giving the customer some choice of the overall size. The marketing strategy was to emphasise the reduction in manpower required. Each machine was sold for £150 plus an annual user licence fee of £380; prospective customers were assured they would recoup the outlay in a very short time. In theory, the annual licences as well as the one-off purchase price should have given Henry and Sealy a steady income, but debts began to mount as production slowed, and monies owed for licences remained unpaid. Henry and Sealy spent the considerable sum of £60,000 trying to protect their patents, but they were declared bankrupt in 1812[cclxxvii]. Even the Russian tsar had ordered

---

[cclxxvii] Museum of London, The, *The Quiet Conquest: The Huguenots, 1685-1985* (London, 1985) p180.

The Story of the Huguenots – a Unique Legacy

two machines to be manufactured, and this order alone should have given the Fourdriniers £700 per annum for ten years[240].

Years later, in 1840, Parliament awarded the brothers a £7,000 grant in acknowledgement of their immense contribution to mechanised paper production. The paper trade felt the grant from Parliament was inadequate given the significance of the brothers' invention, and so raised a subscription from its members with which to pay the family an annual income.

In the meantime, Henry had moved to Hanley, Staffordshire, where his son George had established a business at Ivy House Mill manufacturing tissue paper specifically for applying pottery transfers.

Henry died in 1854, aged 89, possibly heartbroken at the failure of his mechanised papermaking business. At the time of his death approximately £51,000 was still owed by those manufacturers who continued to fraudulently use his plans without paying for the necessary legal permission.

Today, the name of Fourdrinier is still maintained through the company Hunt & Fourdrinier, London, but the male line from Henry Fourdrinier died out with the passing away in 1879 of his nephew Henry William. However, a female descendant of Sealy, Dominique Wood, née Guillermoprieto, currently lives in Surrey.

CARTOGRAPHY

A prominent Huguenot, Jean Rocque, for a time lived in Soho. He had begun his career as a surveyor, map-seller and publisher from business premises at the *Canister and Sugarloaf*, Great Windmill Street. As a cartographer, he began by preparing plans of gardens and estates some of which were owned by the Crown; indeed, the first of these maps detailed the layout of Richmond Gardens[241] and was published in 1734. Three years later, he began specialising in maps of London, which were published in 1746[cclxxviii]. The 24

[cclxxviii] Varley, E.H., John Rocque, the Map-maker and his Huguenot associations, Huguenot Society Proceedings Vol XVII (1945-46), p467.

maps he prepared are still known as the most accurate of the period. Rocque's maps are of particular interest to Huguenots as they detail the location of each of the Huguenot churches in London many of which are either no longer French Protestant churches or have been razed to the ground.

He also produced and published two books: *The English Traveller* in 1746 and *The Small British Atlas* containing 54 maps in 1753; there was also a second edition of this atlas in 1762. Apart from London, he also surveyed and produced maps of many counties in England including *City and Suburbs of Bristol* (1750), *County of Salop* (1752), *County of Middlesex* (1754), *County of Berkshire* (1761) and *County of Surrey*, this last being published by his widow Mary Anne Rocque in 1765.

Jean Rocque was held in such high esteem that he was appointed topographer to the Prince of Wales in 1750. He lived in various parts of London as well as Soho, but it was while residing in Charing Cross that disaster struck during the night of 7 November 1751, as recorded in *The General Advertiser*:

> *On Wednesday night between 11 and 12 o'clock, a fire broke out in the house of Mr. Rocque, a draughtsman and printseller, next door to the Rummer tavern Charing Cross, which burn't with great violence, and, in a short time, entirely consumed that house, together with the Rummer, a silversmith's shop, a haberdasher's, and a linen draper, and did considerable damage to others adjoyning ...*

However, Jean Rocque was not one to be bowed by such a terrible event, and on 18 June 1752 he placed the following notice in *The Daily Advertiser*:

> *John Rocque, Chorographer and topographer to their Royal Highnesses the late and present Prince of Wales, being returned from Paris where he had lately been obliged to renew his stock consumed in the Fire at Charing Cross,*

begs leave to acquaint his subscribers to the County of Salop, that the plates of that Survey are again in hand, and in good forwardness, and likewise his subscribers to the Counties of Berks, Oxfordshire, and Buckinghamshire, that the actual survey of them is carrying on with all possible care and with such expedition that he hopes by the ensuing winter to produce something for the general satisfaction, both of the said subscribers, and others who may be disposed to favour him in like manner.

Again, and again, the determination of these industrious people to succeed is ably demonstrated. That same Huguenot spirit which had faced such intolerance and persecution in France was the same spirit that now confronted and, in many cases, triumphed over immense adversity of a different sort in England – one that would have overwhelmed the majority of people to whom Fate had not been kind. It was proof indeed that Huguenots had learnt to be strong during such testing times.

- 25 -

Science and Service

History shows us again and again that although the mention of the word 'Huguenot' will invariably call to people's minds the industry of silk weaving, these resourceful refugees in fact excelled in a wide variety of areas, and amongst other diverse spheres were the worlds of medicine, science and the military.

MEDICINE
The London Hospital in part owes its existence to a Huguenot – a Dr Andrée, whose family had originated in Rheims, and who was one of a group of people who put together the idea for this hospital. Another Huguenot, Colonel Peter Lekeux, became a hospital governor of the London Hospital, and even the windows of the hospital were cleaned by a French window cleaning company[cclxxix].

Women all over the world can be grateful to the Chamberlen family – inventors of obstetrical instruments widely known as the forceps. Down the centuries, childbirth has always been a risky business, and complications such as the baby in the wrong position could endanger either the baby's or the mother's life, or both. The invention of the forceps has undeniably saved many lives and continues to do so to this day, and it is to William

---

[cclxxix] Jane Cox, *Old East Enders* (Gloucs, 2013) p289.

The Story of the Huguenots – a Unique Legacy

Chamberlen and his family that gratitude is merited. They were Huguenots, who in 1569 fled from Paris to England following Catherine de Medici's ban on 'Protestant' physicians.

William's sons[242] became members of the Barber Surgeons Company. As the years passed by, father and both sons all became successful practitioners of obstetrics.

The actual inventor is assumed to be Peter the Elder because although both Peters had trained in obstetrics, it was Peter the Elder who was appointed surgeon to Queen Henrietta Maria (wife of Charles I).

Having invented this life-saving instrument, the Chamberlen family were keen to keep their invention secret. The use of forceps was a closely guarded secret passed down the family for at least 100 years by means of the elaborate concealment of the implement in a gilded box, followed by the blindfolding of the mother, and allowing no one other than a Chamberlen to be in attendance. The original forceps, missing for many years, had been hidden by Peter the Younger's wife, Ann, and were not rediscovered until 1813, when they were found under the floorboards of the attic of their residence in Essex. However, despite all this subterfuge, models of these forceps had begun to appear in the early 18th century[cclxxx]. Hugh Chamberlen was the author of the first proper English textbook on the subject of midwifery in 1673 entitled *The Accomplished Midwife*.

Apothecaries were part of the Worshipful Company of Grocers (today they are one of the 12 senior livery companies of the City of London known as the Great Twelve) who by the mid-16th century were on a par with today's pharmacists, providing various medical mixtures for sale. At this point, a prominent Huguenot by the name of Gideon de Laune took the lead in petitioning for the pharmacists to be separated from the Grocers' Company, requesting they be permitted their own company. Gideon de Laune had reason to be

---

[cclxxx] Prioleau, William, *The Chamberlen Family and the introduction of obstetrical instruments.* The Huguenot Society, Vol XXVII (2002) pp.705-7.

The Story of the Huguenots – a Unique Legacy

optimistic: he had already achieved the lofty position of apothecary to Anne of Denmark, wife of James I, and this appointment assisted him in gaining the king's ear.

Consequently, on 6 December 1617, the Worshipful Company of Apothecaries was incorporated by Royal Charter. Some years later, James I spoke of his decision to grant the petition with these words:

> *I myself did devise that corporation and do allow it, the grocers, who complain of it, are but merchants; the mystery of these apothecaries were belonging to apothecaries, wherein the grocers are unskilful; and therefore, I think it is fitting they should be a corporation themselves.*

Sir Theodore de Mayerne's father had fled hurriedly from Lyon to Mayerne near Geneva following the St Bartholomew's Day Massacre. Theodore was born in Mayerne, but he was listed as living in St Martin's Lane in 1613 and 1614. He was appointed Chief Physician, firstly to James I, then afterwards to Charles I, and became a member of the Royal College of Physicians in 1616, but his lasting fame lies with his case reports as he was one of the first physicians to record all the physical signs of an illness rather than just prescribe remedies. One of Mayerne's formulae is still used as the foundation for the oil used in the monarch's coronation[cclxxxi].

* * * * * *

SCIENCE

In the late 1690s, the word 'science' also embraced mathematics, mechanics, astronomy, botany, chemistry and natural philosophy, and again we see Huguenot involvement in these vital disciplines:

[cclxxxi] Museum of London, The, *The Quiet Conquest: The Huguenots, 1685-1985* (London, 1985) p120.

The Story of the Huguenots – a Unique Legacy

Abraham de Moivre was born in 1667 in Vitry, Champagne. When just 18 years old, Abraham left his home town, and travelled to London, settling in St Martin's Lane. He and his brother Daniel are listed in the records of the Savoy French Church in 1687, the same year that he received denization. He was elected a Fellow of the Royal Society in 1697. De Moivre and Halley were co-founders of the science of life contingencies, the former writing *The Doctrine of Chances: a method of calculating the probability of events in play* published in 1718, which he dedicated to Sir Issac Newton, a close friend of his, who in old age would often refer questioners to De Moivre. He also discovered the equation for calculating the rate of interest on life annuities and life assurances, his book on the subject, *Annuities upon Lives,* being published in 1724. He died in 1754 and was buried in St Martin in the Fields[cclxxxii].

Denis Papin, born in Blois in 1647, the son of Denys and Magdaleine, studied at the University of Angers before receiving his M.D. (Doctor of Medicine) in 1669. His love of mathematics lured him to Paris shortly after graduating, where he began working as an assistant to Christiaan Huygens[243], who, having recognised his potential, encouraged Papin in his experimentation[244].

He left France for England in 1675, where he worked under Robert Boyle, and it was while in his employ that he began to experiment with creating a 'digester'. He was admitted to The Royal Society[245] in 1680; by profession a chemist, he created the prototype pressure cooker[246] with a safety valve, and published an account of this in 1681. The cooker was used for softening or cooking bones by boiling them in a closed container with water under pressure – the valve was critical to prevent the steam pressure building up beyond a point at which it would explode. His other invention was the first steam engine with a piston, which he published an article on in 1690.

[cclxxxii] Museum of London, The, *The Quiet Conquest: The Huguenots, 1685-1985* (London, 1985) p130.

The Story of the Huguenots – a Unique Legacy

In 1687, Papin left England and travelled to Germany to accept the appointment he had been offered as Professor of Mathematics at Marburg University. He was one of a number of Huguenots who had chosen to travel to Germany to advance their careers. He continued to experiment whilst teaching, but found his remuneration a constraint on his life. He was appointed a place at the court of the Landgrave of Hesse in Cassel in 1695 before returning to England in 1707, where he died just a few years later.

James Six's family had settled in Canterbury. They were originally Walloon silk weavers, but with the demise of this trade James Six decided to pursue a different career, and in 1780 he became the inventor of the first thermometer that was able to show the maximum and minimum temperature within the same instrument. He took a series of temperature readings in which he discovered that air temperature usually decreases in height during the day, the reverse occurring at night[247]. He was made a Fellow of the Royal Society in 1792 in recognition of his invention, the design of which has changed little over the past 200 years – the domestic thermometer is still based upon Six's design[cclxxxiii].

John Theophilus Desaguliers designed and installed the first air-conditioning system for the House of Commons in 1723. He had been born on 12 March 1683, at La Rochelle, the son of a French Protestant clergyman, who had left France for England at the time of the Revocation. John was educated at Christ Church, Oxford, where he received a Master of Arts degree in 1719. He later became an assistant, as well as a friend, of Sir Isaac Newton having moved to London, and was admitted to the Royal Society where he was awarded the prestigious Copley medal[248] no less than three times.

His contributions to science consist of a *Treatise on the Construction of Chimneys* translated from the French, and,

---

[cclxxxiii] Museum of London, The, *The Quiet Conquest: The Huguenots, 1685-1985* (London, 1985) p138.

published in 1716, *A System of Experimental Philosophy* of which a second edition was issued in 1719. These were followed by *A Course of Experimental Philosophy* in two volumes published in 1734; and, in 1735, he edited an edition of Gregory's *Elements of Catoptrics and Dioptrics*. He also translated Gravesande's *Mathematical Elements of Natural Philosophy* from its original Latin. Although he took clerical orders, his lasting fame is within science and engineering. He invented the planetarium – a machine able to establish the exact distance between the planets – from theories generated by Newton and Copernicus; others before him had attempted this, but none had previously been able to represent the sun to scale within the solar system[cclxxxiv]. He became the third Grand Master of the Grand Lodge of Freemasons, and did much to improve the standing of Freemasonry. He died in 1742, and was buried at the Savoy Church.

John Dolland, whose family had fled their home in Normandy at the time of the Revocation, originally set up as one of the Spitalfields weavers, but a change of career followed his studies in mathematics, optics and astronomy, all undertaken in his spare time, and which led him to re-invent the achromatic[249] lens in 1758. In recognition of his work, he was awarded the Copley medal by the Royal Society. He also became optician to George III.

John passed on his knowledge to his son Peter, who in 1750 had opened a little optical workshop in Vine Street, Spitalfields. John eventually laid aside his weaving loom to join his son two years later in new premises that proudly displayed a sign of Gold Spectacles and Sea Quadrant in the Strand. Peter was able to improve his father's binary telescope by creating a trinary one, which became extremely popular with astronomers. Peter became renowned as a leader in the optical instrument industry, earning the epithet 'the father of practical optics'.

[cclxxxiv] Audrey Carpenter, *John Theophilus Desaguliers: A Natural Philosopher, Engineer and Freemason in Newtonian England* (London, 2011) p40.

The Story of the Huguenots – a Unique Legacy

In 1851, the Dollands were again presented with an award – a Great Exhibition medal for the excellence of their optical instruments[cclxxxv]. In 1927, they joined forces with Aitchison, a company established in 1889. Today, the name Dolland & Aitchison still graces many high streets up and down the land[250].

* * * * * *

CONSTRUCTION

A little-known fact about Huguenot contributions to this country is the design and building of the first Westminster Bridge.

James Vauloué, a watchmaker by trade, designed the engine used to drive in the piles for the first Westminster Bridge, whilst another Huguenot, Charles Labelye, designed the actual bridge. Charles Labelye, described as a very ingenious watchmaker by an acquaintance, went on to say that, having viewed the model of the planned bridge he felt it to be a superior design. The plan to build a bridge spanning the Thames from Westminster to Lambeth had met for some years with stiff opposition, but eventually an Act was passed to build the bridge, and the funds allocated for the construction.

But, not all went well for Charles Labelye; his engagement had been met with anger amongst many English architects, who were delighted when, whilst still under construction, one of the piers shifted approximately a third of a yard. Pamphleteers rubbed their hands together gleefully; amongst the leaflets ridiculing Labelye was Batty Langley's *Survey of Westminster Bridge,* published in 1748. This bridge had been the first time a construction had been erected by laying the foundations in caissons[251], but the piers were built directly on to the soil, not onto piles, and was most likely the cause of the slippage. Unbowed, Charles Labelye oversaw the

---

[cclxxxv] Museum of London, The, *The Quiet Conquest: The Huguenots, 1685-1985* (London, 1985) p132.

remedial work carried out, and the bridge was finally opened on 18 November 1850.

The Gentlemen's Magazine described it as '*a very great ornament to our metropolis, and will be looked on with pleasure or envy by all foreigners*'.

* * * * * *

ASTRONOMY

Sir Francis Beaufort (1774-1857), an Irish-born Huguenot, trained for five months in astronomy at Dunsink Observatory, Dublin, before joining the Royal Navy for whom he later became the official Hydrographer. He invented the scale for measuring wind speed, named after him, and was knighted in 1829[cclxxxvi].

Several members of the Rambaut family have made contributions to the field of science. The first Rambaut to leave France was Jean Rambaut, who had been born in 1740 at Duras, Lot et Garonne, and who settled in Dublin in 1754[cclxxxvii].

His grandson, William Hautenville Rambaut, was born in 1822, and studied mathematics and physics at Trinity College, Dublin. Through the good auspices of his uncle, Romney Robinson, he was given the position of assistant astronomer at Birr Castle, Co. Offaly. The third Earl of Rosse had only recently built the largest telescope in the world at that time[252]. Trials of the Birr Castle telescope were undertaken in 1845, which showed for the first time the spiral nature of what have become known as 'external galaxies'. William was the first person to draw these based on his observations through the telescope, an example being his drawing of the M51 or 'whirlpool galaxy'.

[cclxxxvi] Rambaut, Philip M., *The Rambaut Family: Astronomy and Astronautics.* The Huguenot Society, Vol XXVII (1998) p113.
[cclxxxvii] Ibid, p110.

One of William's younger brothers, Revd Edmund Rambaut, had a second son, Arthur, born in Waterford in 1859, who also attended the 'family' college of Trinity, Dublin. After a year teaching science at his old school in Armagh, Arthur returned to Trinity College and took up the position of assistant astronomer, which he held for ten years. In 1897, Arthur applied for, and obtained, the position of seventh observer at the Radcliffe Observatory, Oxford. Arthur became a Fellow of the Royal Society in 1900; he died in 1923 and his obituary describes him as *'an astronomer of eminent ability, varied attainments, solid achievements, and great charm of manner'*. Together with his uncle, William Hautenville Rambaut, he is credited with locating and cataloguing nearly 10,000 stars[cclxxxviii].

The Rambaut family connection with science and the stars continues through Arthur's great nephew. Dr Paul Rambaut joined NASA in 1968 just before the launch of *Apollo 7* in October of that year. His primary working objective was to ensure the nutritional aspect of the astronauts, and, amongst many other things, to study the effect that weightlessness can have on the human body, including bone density and muscle weakness in a zero-gravity environment. Paul continued to work at NASA assisting with the joint venture between the Soviet Union and the United States that culminated in the Apollo-Soyuz docking of 1975[cclxxxix].

* * * * * *

MILITARY
The history of this country would have undoubtedly taken a different path without the Huguenots and their prowess on the battlefields of Europe and their courage in this sphere should not be forgotten.

[cclxxxviii] Rambaut, Philip M., *The Rambaut Family: Astronomy and Astronautics.* The Huguenot Society, Vol XXVII (1998) pp.110-16.
[cclxxxix] Ibid, p117.

The Story of the Huguenots – a Unique Legacy

Among the Huguenot refugees who fled to England in 1697 was a young man by the name of Jean Louis de Ligonier. He had been born in Castres, south west France, on 7 November 1680. His father, Louis Ligonier, Sieur of Monteuquet, died in 1693 leaving his widow to bring up the family of seven children of which Jean Louis was the second-eldest son[ccxc]. As a devout Protestant, he chose to leave his homeland and travelled to Ireland to join his uncle, an officer in one of William of Orange's Huguenot regiments[ccxci]. He first saw active service in 1702[253] in the British army during the Duke of Marlborough's campaigns, and it was his immense courage at the storming of Liege that drew him to the duke's attention. The Battle of Blenheim was next, a major battle of the *War of the Spanish Succession* at the end of which he was the sole surviving captain; his courage and ability ensured his rise through the military ranks becoming aide-de-camp to George II in 1729. In 1742 he was sent to Flanders to command a division fighting the War of the Austrian Succession (1740-48) His gallantry at the battle of Dettingen in 1743 was marked by George II awarding Ligonier Knight banneret[254]. By 1746 he had been given command of the British forces in Flanders [ccxcii]. He was well liked and greatly respected, his brilliance leading to his eventual elevation in 1757 to the position of Commander in Chief. He was awarded an earldom in 1766 aged 86 and was recognised as being one of the greatest military leaders of the United Kingdom. He died in his 90th year.

In 1706, a brigade of foot soldiers had been created through the recruitment of Huguenot soldiers pensioned off after the battle for Ireland in order to fight in the War of the Spanish Succession[255]. Mention has already been made of Friedrich, 1st Duke of

---

[ccxc] T. A. Heathcote, *The British Field Marshals: 1736-1997: A Biographical Dictionary* (Barnsley, reprint 2012) e-book.
[ccxci] Ibid e-book.
[ccxcii] Samuel Smiles, *The Huguenots Their Settlements, Churches and Industries in England and Ireland (1889)* (London) p240.

Schomberg; this German count served in the French army from 1651 during which time he discovered French Protestantism, becoming a lifelong convert to the faith. He had been an important and well-respected member of the French military, but his rigid adherence to Protestantism made it necessary for him to retire and leave France. He settled for a time in Brandenburg before travelling onwards to Holland, where he joined William's invasion army along with the Marquis de Ruvigny.

Thus, many Huguenots of all ranks left their homeland, and entered the service of foreign armies. One such refugee who had fled to Geneva[256] in 1689 was Guillaume Guion. Geneva had received an immense number of Huguenot refugees, but the arrival of so many able-bodied men was seen by some as a heaven-sent opportunity not to be missed. The Protestant Regiment was formed from those willing to fight for Louis XIV's enemies – such as William of Orange, who belonged to the League of Augsburg[257] and was himself from Huguenot lineage; his great-grandmother had been a daughter of Admiral Coligny.

Guillaume soon joined up as a young officer. The Duke of Savoy, unsure which side would win, tried to keep both Protestants and Catholics as his friends without openly declaring for either, but found the contemptuous and arrogant attitude of the French king towards him and his subjects increasingly difficult to accept[258]. Consequently, the duke ordered his forces to take the castle of Casteldelfino, and during this skirmish on 8 November 1690, Guillaume was wounded by an arquebus[259]. His left arm was completely shattered, but his wound was attended to and he was given a bed. Soon afterwards, heavy snowfall forced the army to withdraw down the valley, and Guillaume was left behind.

Six days later, he was found by another regiment also in retreat due to the bad weather, but by then his arm was gangrenous. To save his life, his comrades carried him to St Pierre, three miles away, where his arm was amputated on 20

The Story of the Huguenots – a Unique Legacy

November – without anaesthetic. Incredibly, he re-joined his regiment on 1 January 1691, continuing to serve until a stalemate was reached in the spring of 1697[ccxciii]. Peace negotiations began in May of that year; one of those involved in the negotiations was William of Orange, who had, following the Glorious Revolution of 1688, become king of England and Scotland. Any fears of the Huguenots' civil rights being downgraded were for the time being allayed.

William was keen for them to enlist as soldiers, and to this end he established five Huguenot regiments, guaranteeing them pensions when they retired from the army, and encouraging them to settle in England and Ireland.

In Britain, until modern times, a full, regular armed force was not maintained and kept on stand-by. Instead, during times of peace, personnel would be pensioned off[260], but if war clouds returned, the armed forces would be restored to a wartime footing. This was the case until 1792, when Parliament was persuaded to establish barracks for a more permanent standing fighting force. Recruitment was handled in a different manner too with 'Letters of Service' being given to those willing and able to assemble a regiment of up to 1,000 men, and those who fulfilled this assignment were given a commission as Colonel of the Regiment, which entitled them to also choose the officers of his regiment. Often the forming of a regiment would not necessarily be the responsibility of one man, and it was known for such individuals to tempt their friends to assist in this task through being offered a captaincy in exchange for their provision of 100 men.

To demonstrate how this method of raising an army worked, and to show how many Huguenot names were frequently involved, the following is an excerpt from a commission dated September 1768:

[ccxciii] The Guion Archives.

Henry, Earl of Galway, to be Colonel of the Regt of Dragoons to be forthwith raised for Her Majesty's service in Portugal and to be Captain of a Troop in said Regiment.

This Letter of Service led to the re-forming of La Fabreque's French Dragoons under the command of the Earl of Galway[261]. Lieutenant Colonel Charles Janvre de la Bouchetière took over command of the regiment on 24 June 1710, with Louis de Boisragon elevated to the position of lieutenant colonel, and Charles de Goullainière promoted to major[ccxciv].

Until 1854, the expenses incurred for the regiment were paid directly to the colonel by the Crown; from the monies paid, the colonel would pay his officers and troops, including the cost of their uniforms, with any 'surplus' money being considered profit for the colonel. As the colonel was ultimately responsible for all aspects of his regiment at that time, there was a tendency to name the regiment after its colonel. But change was in the air, as by 1857 the cost of regimental clothing was no longer the responsibility of its colonel but issued free from public stores[ccxcv].

Another family whose family history is being charted throughout this book is of course the Duvals. Within the family archives it is noted that three branches of the family travelled to England and Thomas Duval, a captain in the service of His Britannic Majesty, was a member of the first branch of the family.

Thomas was chosen to take the news to India of the victory of Aboukir, where he had distinguished himself on board the 'Zealous'. His commission as captain bears the date of the Battle of the Nile. In bringing the news from

---

[ccxciv] Manchee, E. H., *Huguenot Soldiering and their conditions of service in the English Army*. The Huguenot Society Proceedings, Vol XVI No2 (1938/9) p248.
[ccxcv] Ibid, pp.248-50.

The Story of the Huguenots – a Unique Legacy

Egypt to Bombay, Thomas Duval saved the British government enormous expense. India had had orders to put itself in a state of defence, and now all preparations could cease. In recognition, the East India Company voted Nelson a sum of £1,000. Unhappily, Thomas Duval was lost when his ship went down with all hands during an expedition to Newfoundland in 1805.

Thomas' brother, Francis, also served in the British Navy against Napoleon. He took part in the Battle of Copenhagen on board the 'Desiree', a prize of war. In November 1802, he was on the 'Blenheim' under the orders of Admiral Hood. Later, he sailed to the Antilles, and helped in the capture of the French brig (corvette) 'Le Curieux'. In 1805, he was severely wounded on board the 'Athenienne'. In 1807, he was a frigate lieutenant. In 1808, he captured a Russian brig in the Adriatic. It was while bringing this prize to Malta that he was shipwrecked with 11 of his crew on the coast of Apulia (Puglia, southern Italy) where he was made a prisoner of the French. After rather more than a year in captivity, he got permission to go to Geneva to his cousin, who had returned from Russia, but he was suspected of helping his compatriots, and the French Residents in Geneva sent him off to captivity in Verdun. He was able to return to Geneva in 1812, and, when the Austrian general Ferdinand Bubna Graf von Litic liberated the city, Francis Duval was chosen to carry the news to Allied HQ at Freiburg-in-Breisgau. He settled in Geneva, retiring at the rank of captain, and marrying his young cousin Henrietta Duval[ccxcvi].

Many rank-and-file were also of Huguenot descent, being subject to the same rules and punishments as British-born

---

[ccxcvi] The Duval Archives.

servicemen, and the vast majority loyally served their adopted country with a true and honest patriotism.

* * * * * *

GUNMAKERS

During the reign of Louis XIV, French gunmakers had taken their art to new heights, but the expertise of some of these artisans was to be a great loss to France. With measures to stamp out Protestantism during the reign of Louis XIV becoming more and more draconian, it left families of gunmakers little choice if they wished to remain Protestant but to leave France and some chose to settle in England.

Amongst such families were two prominent Parisian gunsmiths: Pierre Monlong, who had arrived in 1684 with his wife and two children, and Pierre Gruché, who was to be found working in Compton Street, London as early as 1699. Both chose to settle in Soho, tellingly outside the jurisdiction of the Worshipful Company of Gunmakers. Other Huguenot gunmakers from provincial areas of France likewise chose to settle in London. Their meticulous workmanship and skilful decoration of a wide range of firearms were much prized amongst the nobility.

Second-generation Huguenot gunmakers continued to manufacture guns of the highest quality with intricate engraving on the finished weapons, amongst whom was Henry Delany, admitted to the Freedom of the Gunmakers Company in 1715. He worked in Long Acre, Holborn, and was recorded as a '*maker of fine breech loading sporting guns and silver-mounted pistols*'. Delany died in 1745, but he was followed by the next generation of gunmakers in the persons of Pierre Gandon and Israel Segallas[ccxcvii]

Lewis (Louis) Barbar, a Huguenot from Poitou, came to London in 1688, and was granted naturalisation in 1700. He

---

[ccxcvii] Museum of London, The, *The Quiet Conquest: The Huguenots, 1685-1985* (London, 1985) p223.

became 'gentleman armourer' to both George I and George II. After his death in 1741, his son James succeeded him. Arguably the best gunsmiths of the time, these Huguenots were able to apply a hitherto unknown level of refinement, technical skill and workmanship, which gave a global prominence to London's French-made guns, especially pocket-sized pistols for which there was a huge market due to the personal protection they afforded.

- 26 -

The Quality of the Huguenot Artisan

The highly skilled Huguenot artisan communities that chose to settle in this country raised their individual crafts to a superior level, as is demonstrated below:

GOLD AND SILVERSMITHS

Huguenot goldsmiths were persecuted twice over, firstly for their religious beliefs, and secondly because Louis XIV, in order to finance his wars with Holland, decreed that all gold plate was to be melted down. As a direct consequence, many of the families affected left the towns of Lille, Le Mans, Metz and Rouen to seek a new life in England, taking the artistry of the goldsmith and silversmith to new heights with radical, groundbreaking techniques, much to the loss of their former homeland.

As in all things, fashions also evolve over time: since the time of Charles II acceding to the throne, the style in precious metalwork had been predominantly Dutch, but with the arrival of William III following the Glorious Revolution, such style and form evolved – perhaps rather ironically – from Dutch to French, mainly due to the influx of Huguenots arriving not only directly from France, but also those who had travelled first to Holland, and who then chose to follow William to make their home here,

The Story of the Huguenots – a Unique Legacy

doubtless tempted by the Royal Bounty as a means of helping to alleviate their dire financial circumstances[ccxcviii].

The records held by the Worshipful Company of Goldsmiths provide details of the families and their places of origin; often these were beneficiaries of the Royal Bounty and were elderly or widowed, but their surnames nevertheless reappear in future generations. Surnames of many famous Huguenot gold and silversmiths can be traced back to some of the Royal Bounty entries, such as Louis Mettayer from Poitou, Pierre Harache from Rouen, John Le Sage from Alençon, and David Willaume from Metz. Some of these later Huguenot goldsmiths had never worked in France, but were apprenticed to refugees who had trained in the French style although taught in England. Paul de Lamerie had been apprenticed to Pierre Plantel; another famous name, Augustine Courtauld[262], was apprenticed to Simon Pantin[ccxcix].

During the 1730s and 1740s, two particular Huguenots, Paul Crespin and Paul de Lamerie, produced some of the finest work of that period in the Rococo style[ccc].

As with all sections of refugees in society, for the first two or three generations the families tended to retain ties within their family and friends. Frequently, their sons or their friends' sons would become apprenticed to them.

Paul, son of Daniel Crespin, was born in 1694 in the parish of St Giles, Westminster, and was apprenticed to Jean Pons in 1713 for the standard term of seven years[ccci]. At the end of his apprenticeship[263], Paul Crespin's 'mark[264]' was recorded at Goldsmiths' Hall. Paul became the 2nd Duke of Portland's preferred master goldsmith, producing a wide array of silver

---

[ccxcviii] J. F. Hayward, *Huguenot Silver in England 1688-1727* (London, 1959) p1.
[ccxcix] Ibid, p10.
[ccc] Museum of London, The, *The Quiet Conquest: The Huguenots, 1685-1985* (London, 1985) p229.
[ccci] Jones, Alfred, MA, *Paul Crespin Huguenot Goldsmith.* The Huguenot Society Proceedings, Vol XVI (1939-40) p375.

The Story of the Huguenots – a Unique Legacy

including 181 dinner plates, 23 meat dishes, 12 butter boats, and various salts[265], candlesticks, soup plates and tureens all of which are still carefully maintained at Welbeck Abbey[cccii]. Further examples of his work are preserved at Windsor Castle, including a beautifully crafted early 18th century two-handled cup and cover that had once belonged to Empress Elizabeth of Russia, herself a prolific collector of Huguenot plate.

The very first Huguenot goldsmith to gain admission to the Goldsmiths Company was Pierre Harache. On 21 July 1682, an Order of the Lord Mayor and Council of Aldermen of the City of London was read out, which requested:

> *...that the said Peter Harache shall be admitted into the freedom of this City by Redemption into the Company of Goldsmiths paying to Mr Chamberlain to the City's use forty-six shillings and eight pence.*

A certificate was also presented, which stated:

> *To whom it may concern Peter Harache, lately come from France to avoid persecution and live quietly, is not only a Protestant, but by his Majesty's bounty is made a free denizen, that he may settle here freely with his family in token whereof we have given him this certificate.*

As we have seen several times before, not all indigenous people welcomed either the refugees or their innovations – the London Goldsmiths were petitioned by various freemen on several occasions against the admission of Huguenots to the Goldsmiths Company[ccciii], but fortunately they did not succeed in driving them away.

In 1740, Paul de Lamerie took on an apprentice – Abraham Portal[266] whose grandfather, Jean François Portal, had arrived in

---

[cccii] Jones, Alfred, MA, *Paul Crespin Huguenot Goldsmith*. The Huguenot Society Proceedings, Vol XVI (1939-40) p376.
[ccciii] J. F. Hayward, *Huguenot Silver in England 1688-1727* (London, 1959) p17.

England in 1699[ccciv]. He died in 1705, leaving instructions in his will that if any of his children should convert to Catholicism, they were to be excluded from his will[cccv]. Amongst his eight surviving children were his sons William, Henry[267] and Stephen. William entered the Church in 1722, and two years later he married Mary Magdalen Findlater. Their second son, Abraham, was born at Clowne near Bolsover in Derbyshire on 10 May 1726.

Just after Abraham's eighth birthday, the family moved to London. The close family network no doubt enabled young Abraham to be taken on as apprentice to Paul de Lamerie for a fee of £35, whereupon he was thrown into the noisy, hot, dusty world of the gold and silversmiths. Paul de Lamerie's business premises were situated in Gerrard Street, Soho, not far from Abraham's family home. The master would provide the apprentice with essential clothing, and lodging would be available in the attic rooms, but should he fall sick an apprentice would be expected to meet his medical costs himself [cccvi].

Abraham would have served the usual seven-year apprenticeship and, aged 21, would have then probably continued to work for his employer as a journeyman until he was able to register his own mark as a 'largeworker[268]', which he duly did on 26 October 1749. Abraham was amongst the last apprentices taken on by Paul de Lamerie, who was now approaching retirement.

Abraham applied himself to the precise art of working the precious metals, but his particular fondness was the cutting of jewels, as was demonstrated in the first play he wrote[269].

Abraham had learned his trade well and produced some fine pieces of silverware including those commissioned by the Royal Family. He had married in 1748 and his wife, Eliza Nethersole, bore him a son the following year, who sadly only lived a few

---

[ccciv] Christopher Portal, *The Reluctant Goldsmith* (Somerset, 1993) p7.
[cccv] Ibid, p9.
[cccvi] Ibid, p16.

The Story of the Huguenots – a Unique Legacy

months. Eliza herself died in 1758[cccvii], but Abraham did not remain a widower for long; within a year he had remarried – his bride was Elizabeth Bedwell, whose brother Bernard was to become a lifelong friend of Abraham. By the early 1700s Abraham had his own shop premises at 34 Ludgate Hill, where he formed a business partnership with George Coyte. His success led to him being elected to The Livery in June 1763, a not inconsiderable accolade that also gave him a vote in the elections for City Officers and Members of Parliament, as well as a voice in matters relating to the Goldsmiths Company[cccviii].

He pursued a second career whilst he continued to craft fine objects in precious metals. At varying times, Abraham is described in a variety of trade directories as a *'goldsmith as against silversmith; goldsmith and jeweller and as a jeweller and toyman[270]'*. His craftsmanship as a jeweller often led to commissions including one for an engagement ring ordered by his very good friend and fellow poet the Rev. John Langhorne, who had written to Abraham on 7 February 1762:

> *I desire you would put an Amethyst on the Ring and let this be the motto – sacré à l'amour et l'amitié. It is with the utmost confidence I apply to you on this occasion[cccix].*

Meanwhile, Paul de Lamerie himself merits more than a mention in the story of the Huguenots. He was born on 9 April 1688 in Hertogenbosch in the Netherlands after his parents, whose indigenous married name was De La Merie, had travelled there from France to escape persecution; they eventually chose to leave the Netherlands for London, where they settled in Berwick Street, Soho. When aged 15, Paul was apprenticed to Pierre Platel, who clearly saw Paul's potential as he was known to only very rarely take on an apprentice.

[cccvii] Christopher Portal, *The Reluctant Goldsmith* (Somerset, 1993) p20.
[cccviii] Ibid, p25.
[cccix] Ibid, p63.

Following the registration of Paul de Lamerie's mark with the Goldsmith Company on 4 February 1713, he set up his own premises in Great Windmill Street. He was a charismatic, well-educated man, but also one who often clashed with the authorities of the Goldsmiths Hall[271]. In 1714, he was called before the Goldsmiths Hall Court and fined £20, today the equivalent of £2,653, for failing to 'mark' pieces he had produced.

There were two important reasons why all gold and silver had to be 'marked' – the first was that it was illegal to sell objects that had not been officially converted from one bullion standard to another, such as from Sterling to Britannia[272]; and secondly, without proper hallmarking a piece remained 'off the radar', and therefore the tax due would be avoided. It seems to have been a tax that was even less popular amongst maker and client than amongst most other artisans and customers, and so it became difficult to persuade makers to present their work to the Goldsmiths' assay office for official hallmarking.

Paul felt the fine to be unfair as the court had not fully proven the extent of his guilt and, determined to make a point, he began almost immediately to offer for hallmarking considerable amounts of plain domestic silverware that had been produced by anonymous French silversmiths. He was again called to the court in 1715, this time for presenting foreigners' works as his own before the assay office[273][cccx].

Despite all this, he was appointed goldsmith to George I in 1716 – the same year in which he was again called before the court, as well as once more in 1717 – for the same offence. The officers of the court were in despair, but recognised they needed to employ new tactics in trying to deal with this particular artisan, and it appears Paul was now offered livery status, in other words, admission to the upper echelons, which he accepted.

[cccx] Christopher Portal, The Reluctant Goldsmith (Somerset, 1993) p71.

The Story of the Huguenots – a Unique Legacy

His fame was such that his business went from strength to strength, and like many such businessmen he probably felt he was untouchable; however, he was to experience a dark episode too. In 1722, the King's Bench Court Report recorded that the plaintiff was:

'...a chimney sweeper's boy [who] found a jewel and carried it to the defendant's shop to know what it was, and delivered it into the hands of the apprentice, who under pretence of weighing it, took out the stone, and calling to the master to let him know it came to three halfpence, the master offered the boy the money, who refused to take it, and insisted to have the thing again; whereupon the apprentice delivered him back the socket without the stones'. [cccxi]

As to the value of the jewel, several of the trade were examined to prove what a jewel of the finest water that would fit the socket would be worth; and the Chief Justice directed the jury, that unless the defendant could produce the jewel for examination and prove it not to be of the finest water, they should presume the strongest case against him, and make the value of the best jewel the measure of their damages: which they accordingly did.

As the owner of the shop, Paul de Lamerie was now ordered to compensate the sweep boy with what had to be a diamond of the 'finest and first water[274]' and for it to be of a size to fit into the original jewel setting.

He moved to new premises in Gerrard Street in 1738. At first, his work had been simply designed – Queen Anne-styled tankards and teapots – but by the 1730s he had graduated from plain classical style to a rich rococo that showed not only considerable innovation in style but also his mastery of his craft. Amongst his illustrious customers were the tsarinas of Russia, Anna and

---

[cccxi] GEORGIAN LONDON: INTO THE STREETS by Lucy Inglis (Penguin Books, 2014). Copyright © Lucy Inglis, 2013.

The Story of the Huguenots – a Unique Legacy

Catherine; Sir Robert Walpole; the earls of Ilchester and Thanet, and the Duke of Bedford. The soup tureen is believed to have been a Huguenot introduction into this country. Examples of his work can be viewed at the Victoria and Albert Museum, who believe him to be the finest silversmith to work in England in the 18th century.

He was not a 'bad' person, though, in spite of his endeavours to avoid paying tax on some of his work, and of course in the case of the little chimney sweep; amongst his good qualities are those demonstrated by his benevolence towards James Ray.

James Ray was a silversmith, probably a gilder, which meant he would have been constantly breathing in the fumes of the mercury used in this process (given the constant exposure to these toxic fumes, often it would seriously affect the artisan's mental state over time). One day in 1734, James Ray suddenly left his work and was sighted running through the streets, shouting: "Oranges and lemons!". He was taken to the hospital for admission, but a member of the community was required to stand surety for him in case he spoilt any hospital property or attacked any person. Within the French Hospital records, that guarantor was found to be none other than Paul de Lamerie.

Amongst the wedding gifts that Princess Elizabeth and her husband, Philip, Duke of Edinburgh, received in 1947 was a Paul de Lamerie 1720 two-handled silver cup with cover, now housed in the Royal Collection. Another example of his work is the famous 29-piece Treby toilet service at the Ashmolean Museum, Oxford, ordered by the Rt. Hon. George Treby as a wedding gift for his bride, Charity Hele[cccxii]. Although all the pieces bear the same hallmark, this does not mean that they were all crafted by one individual, but they would all definitely have been produced by one workshop, in this case, de Lamerie's.

[cccxii] J. F. Hayward, *Huguenot Silver in England 1688-1727* (London, 1959) p42.

Gold and silversmiths used pattern books, some of which were brought over from France, to create and style their work. They also used moulds created by pattern makers whose work would not necessarily be exclusively for one gold or silversmith.

In what would appear to be exclusively a man's world, Ann Tanqueray – widow of master goldsmith David Tanqueray and daughter of another master goldsmith, David Willaume, who had originated in Metz – is one of those pleasant exceptions. She ran her own workshop producing fine quality work including eight silver jugs, at least one of which was obtained on behalf of Catherine the Great, Empress of Russia[cccxiii].

* * * * * *

CLOCK AND WATCHMAKERS

Many skilled clock and watchmakers living and working in Protestant strongholds such as La Rochelle and Blois had chosen to become Protestants early on in their working lives. Henry VIII employed several Huguenot clockmakers in the embellishment of Nonsuch Palace, arguably one of the grandest of his many building projects.

The earliest recorded Huguenot clockmaker was Nicholas Urseau[275], recorded as being appointed by Elizabeth I. By 1680, the records of the Huguenot churches listed more than 90 of their flock as watchmakers. The persecution of Huguenots and Walloons in France and the Low Countries respectively made the idea of seeking refuge in a stable Protestant country very desirable, and they were especially drawn to the City of London where wealthy citizens could be tempted to buy their timepieces. However, to work in the City of London they were required to 'buy' themselves into a craft guild. Until 1631, a clockmakers'

[cccxiii] Jones, Alfred, MA, *Paul Crespin Huguenot Goldsmith*. The Huguenot Society Proceedings, Vol XVI (1939-40) p377.

The Story of the Huguenots – a Unique Legacy

guild did not exist, so in order to comply, clockmakers had to join other guilds, such as the Blacksmiths' Guild, although some did take the risk of working just outside of the City in the 'liberties' – beyond the control of any of the guilds, making it extremely difficult to collect subscriptions. Twice, in 1620 and 1622, the skilled Huguenot clock and watchmakers petitioned Charles I asking for permission to form their own guild, but to no avail: eventually, their third petition was granted in exchange for a sum of money.

Earlier, in 1603, the Plague had returned. Areas badly affected were the City of London and also St Anne's, Blackfriars – an area favoured by refugees from the Low Countries. It is believed that up to 670 of the refugee community of clockmakers and their families succumbed[cccxiv]. It seems that the gap left by this tragic mortality was gradually filled with English artisans, but French Huguenots were also swelling the numbers in this trade, so much so that their influx and success led to such a dearth of skilled craftsmen in France that by the 18th century an invitation was sent to clockmakers across the Channel to revitalise the ailing French clock manufacturing in Versailles.

Coterminous with this was of course the inevitability that not everyone welcomed the arrival of the French Huguenot clockmakers; indeed, the newly formed Clockmakers Guild received several complaints from English clockmakers, arguing that they felt *'exceedingly oppressed'* by the arrival of so many skilled French tradesmen.

Not all the fine craftsmanship associated with these timepieces can be attributed to a specific person – a variety of skills were needed to create a timepiece with its delicate mechanisms and casing, but it was estimated in 1842 that the annual number of watches stamped at Goldsmiths Hall, as required by law, were 14,000 gold and 85,000 silver; whilst this does not indicate that all

---

[cccxiv] Sir G. J. White, *The Clockmakers of London* (The Trustees of the Worshipful Company of Clockmakers, London, 1998) p8.

The Story of the Huguenots – a Unique Legacy

these timepieces were made by Huguenots or their descendants, it does illustrate people's high regard for the skill of these particular craftsmen and women, many of whom, it has been proven, were either refugees or of refugee ancestry of whom there are numerous examples to mention:

Henry Lepine, whose ancestors had fled to England and settled in Canterbury in 1685, was listed as a 'Watch and clockmaker, Silversmith and Jeweller in the High Street, Canterbury'. His family had been master silk weavers, but young Henry chose a different career path, and one of his beautifully engraved timepieces can today be viewed in the City of Canterbury Museum. Sadly, in 1850, due to his declining health, he became an inmate of the French Hospital, and remained there until his death 25 years later.

The Debaufre family were highly skilled watchmakers, who first settled in Soho in the 17th century. Peter Debaufre had arrived from Paris, setting up his workshop in Church Street in 1686. He was granted admission to the Worshipful Company of Clockmakers in 1689. Peter's son, Jacob, had also been born in Paris, but both were granted naturalisation in 1703-4. On 6 December 1704, a petition was presented to the House of Commons, beginning with the words *'praying for the continuance to them for a longer term of the sole use of their invention for jewelling and clock and watches*[cccxv]*'*. A patent was granted to the Debaufres and their friend, Nicolas Fatio de Duillier, for jewel-bearing (the application of jewels to the pivot holes of watches and clocks). As soon as the patent was granted, they began advertising and selling extremely elaborate, jewelled watches.

Peter Debaufre later went on to invent a 'dead-beat' – a club-footed, verge escapement, which was eventually used and adapted by several other watchmakers. Jacob had a younger brother, James, who had been born in London in 1691 and who was

---

[cccxv] Museum of London, The, *The Quiet Conquest: The Huguenots, 1685-1985* (London, 1985) p246.

The Story of the Huguenots – a Unique Legacy

admitted to the Worshipful Company of Clockmakers in 1712. Although the Debaufres' family business ceased to trade in 1750, examples of their skill can be found today in the Victoria & Albert Museum, the British Museum and the Worshipful Company of Clockmakers Collection. James' only son married one of the daughters of the famous goldsmith Paul de Lamarie.

Simon De Charmes had escaped to England in 1688 and was admitted to the Worshipful Company of Clockmakers in 1691. Five years later, he married Eliene Dieu at the Huguenot church in Berwick Street, Soho. His immense talent brought wealth with which, in 1730, he was able to build a palatial house – Grove Hall, in Hammersmith, west London. His son, David, succeeded him, and ran the family business until his death in 1783. An exquisite De Charmes watch once owned by the Duke of Bridgewater is now on display at the Clockmakers Museum, which houses some stunning timepieces.

There are many more highly skilled Huguenot watch and clockmakers too numerous to detail in this book, but a few, by way of example, do deserve a mention because of their outstanding contributions to the creation of some very fine timepieces.

Thomas Grignion (maker of the first long pendulum clock in Europe);

John Perigal, whose ancestors came to London from Dieppe, and one of whose descendants, Francis, became a Master of the Clockmakers Company;

The Barraud family, who came from Angoulême, near Bordeaux. Francis Gabriel Barraud married the daughter of Paul Crespin (a goldsmith), and in the will of his mother-in-law dated 1775, he is noted as being a watchmaker of the parish of St Giles, London. Barraud's work, including a very fine musical table clock with a verge escapement (c1797) and this was presented to the Company by Miss Barraud[cccxvi].

[cccxvi] Museum of London, The, *The Quiet Conquest: The Huguenots, 1685-1985* (London, 1985) p252.

The Story of the Huguenots – a Unique Legacy

The Vulliamys, who originated from Switzerland. Justin Vulliamy moved to England around 1730. He was already an accomplished watchmaker when he arrived, and entered into partnership with Benjamin Gray, royal clockmaker to George II. Justin Vulliamy became an extremely competent clockmaker in his own right, he married Benjamin Gray's daughter Mary and their son Benjamin took over the family business, becoming clockmaker to George III. Many fine specimens of Vulliamy clocks still grace the royal palaces. The grandson of Justin, Benjamin Lewis Vulliamy, was also the author of several pamphlets relating to the art of clockmaking including one on the construction of the dead-beat escapement. He was also five times Master of the Company of Clockmakers, who presented him with a piece of plate in recognition of his services in 1849.

And among the lesser known horologists can be found William Dupen, a descendant of John Dupen (indentured as an apprenticed weaver in 1688). William also left England with his family, and they made their home in New York. Before emigrating, William had begun working in the clockmaking industry, and he continued this trade for some years in California, where he successfully applied for a patent for his eight-day alarm clock in 1908[cccxvii].

* * * * * *

ENGRAVING

One of the most famous engravers of all time is without doubt Simon Gribelin. Born in Blois in 1661 of Huguenot parents, he had fled to England a few years before the Revocation, and was granted denization on 8 March 1682. His family were watchmakers and engravers, and he became a member of the Clockmakers Guild in 1686. Five years' later, he married the

---

[cccxvii] The Dupen Archives.

daughter of the minister of the Huguenot church in Spitalfields, having moved into Arundel Street the previous year. His designs were either engraved on copper plates for printing, or were for use as decorative engraving on silver objects. The style and type of silverware engraved was wide-ranging – from large plate to small snuff boxes and watch cases, invariably wrought by fellow Huguenots. He drew his inspiration from the old masters such as the Rubens masterful work adorning the ceiling of the Banqueting House, Whitehall.

Although he produced designs unaided in most cases, he did join forces with fellow Huguenot Paul Van Somer[276] to produce two very noteworthy plates: *The Seven Bishops* of 1688, and – of primary importance to Huguenot history – a portrait of the Duke of Schomberg.

* * * * * *

Isaac Basire, son of a refugee solider from Rouen, was to become the founder of the Basire engraving dynasty. He lived and worked in St John's Gate, Clerkenwell. His specialty was cartography and engraving, and his work included some of the famous maps created by John Rocque; he also produced many maps and illustrations for the publisher John Norse but perhaps his most famous work was the frontispiece of Bailey's Dictionary (1755).

On 24 August 1728, Isaac married Sarah Flavill at St John's Church, Clerkenwell. During their marriage, they were blessed with three children including a son, James (1730-1802), who eventually followed their father's printing and engraving career path. Isaac died on 27 August 1768 and is buried at the church where he had married Sarah. Isaac's grandson, also named James (1769-1822) continued the family engraving business as well as his father's James' appointment to the Society of Antiquarians. The last of the Basire engraving family was the third named James

(1796-1869) who produced several plates of Sussex country houses, but he was less well known than his predecessors.

* * * * * *

HORN CRAFTSMANSHIP

Jean Obrisset came to England as a refugee at the end of the 17th century; he produced some very fine work in a variety of materials including horn, tortoiseshell and silver, and he is known as the premier artisan of horn craftsmanship. Amongst the items he produced were tobacco boxes, which he carved and moulded, the lids of his boxes varying from the formal portrait and equestrian form to mythological and sporting scenes dating from the early years of the 18th century to 1735, the year of his death. One of the box lids attributed to Jean Obrisset is a moulded horn, lidded box with a portrait of Charles I, right-side-facing, in armour. Usually, he would mark his work 'OB'[277], but occasionally, as in the case of the Charles I box, he did not put his mark on it.

It was a highly skilled craft whereby to create the horn, a substance known as 'keratin', being a natural product, had to be heated to a precise temperature in order to form it into the required shapes aided by various metal dies and chemicals to achieve the required colour[278].

- 27 -

Architecture and Creativity

The skilled Huguenot craftsman was able to demonstrate an extremely high level of flair and precision in the realms of style, structural design and the more delicate creations produced in glass.

ARCHITECTURE AND DESIGN
One of the foremost Huguenot architects of his time was Daniel Marot. His paradigm was that everything in a room should be devised by just one person, and this was to be a guiding principle adopted by later famous designers. Daniel had been born in Paris in 1661. His father, Jean, was an engraver and architect who trained his son, but although Daniel's early career was influenced by French architectural style, his Protestant beliefs led him, post-Revocation, to leave his homeland to travel to Holland, where he began working for William of Orange. He designed the *Armistice Chamber* at The Hague as well as the gardens and apartments at Het Loo before coming to England in 1694 to work for William at Hampton Court Palace.

Marot drew designs for the layout of the gardens at the palace and oversaw their execution. True to his ideals, he also drew designs intended for the interior of the palace, and he was much sought after by the owners of several stately houses including Montague House (where he was invited to design panelling for a state drawing room).

But his diverse talent was to extend still further – to the State Coach for William III. The coach was built in The Hague in 1698,

The Story of the Huguenots – a Unique Legacy

but was first used in England after being presented by Queen Anne to the Speaker of the House of Commons, Charles Abbot, and continues in use today to transport the Speaker to the Coronation and to jubilee celebrations[cccxviii]. It was last used by the Speaker to attend the Royal Wedding of Charles, Prince of Wales, to Lady Diana Spencer in 1981; since then, it has had a major refurbishment, and can now be viewed as the centrepiece of the Carriage Museum, Arlington Court, Devon. After such success, Marot seems to have decided to return to Holland in 1698, remaining there until his death in 1752.

Jean Tijou, a refugee ironsmith, had left his home in St. Germain and travelled first to Holland and then onwards to England, where he began working for Christopher Wren as an assistant on the new St Paul's Church. Tijou's grillwork in the choir is a fine testimony to his talent, but this was not the only project he was connected with. Hampton Court Palace also displays some of his intricate work, the fine wrought iron gates of the Fountain Court designed by Tijou are based upon the gates devised for the Palace of Versailles.

A number of artisans blessed with a variety of skills were also encouraged to seek a new life in England by Ralph, Duke of Montague. As Britain's ambassador in France from 1666-78 and again from 1682-5, he spent time in Montpellier, a Huguenot stronghold at that time[279]. It was during this time that he became mindful of French Protestant persecution, which was to have a profound effect on his future actions. After his second return to England, he became patron to a number of Huguenot refugees including wood carvers and gilders John and Thomas Pelletier; stone carver Gideon du Chesne, who worked at stately homes such as Broughton House and Castle Howard; carpenter Peter Rieusset, and upholsterers Remy George and François Lapierre.

* * * * * *

[cccxviii] Museum of London, The, *The Quiet Conquest: The Huguenots, 1685-1985* (London, 1985) p186.

WOODWORK AND FURNITURE

During the early 18th century, new styles of furniture had begun to emerge from skilled woodcarvers of Huguenot origin. Countless families working within the woodcarving and furniture industry relied upon other Huguenot craftsmen who were skilled in designing many of the highly decorative designs so fashionable in that period.

Britain was, at that time, on the verge of global expansion following the defeat of Louis XIV, and the signing of the *Treaty of Utrecht* in 1713, which ended the War of the Spanish Succession. At the start of the century, exports were outstripping imports in many areas, not least in furniture. Huguenot craftsmen excelled in the rococo style, which they had brought to England in the 1740s. Prior to this, the baroque style had been much favoured during the reign of Charles II, and both French and Dutch craftsmen were to have a huge impact on the furniture fashion of the day. For the Huguenot furniture makers who came and worked here, the most productive and profitable period for them was 1660-1714. As with numerous other trades, their clientele would range from monarchy and aristocrats to the lower end of the socio-economic scale, where the humble, lesser-skilled craftsman would struggle simply to earn enough to feed his family.

They often married within other Huguenot families, partly from a shared heritage and partly through financial acumen – to 'keep it in the family'. The catastrophic events of the Plague and then the Great Fire of London swept away many people and buildings with all their contents, but they also heralded the opportunity for new ideas and styles to flourish, which of course was a heaven-sent opportunity for artisans, especially Huguenots, to display their talents for design and craftsmanship.

An official Return dated 1635 lists several hundred Huguenots operating workshops and employing outworkers in Southwark and Westminster, and there are French Church records that indicate

The Story of the Huguenots – a Unique Legacy

that many areas outside the capital were also home to furniture makers; the largest proportion of these were in places such as: Bristol (955), Norwich (575), Plymouth and Stonehouse (142), Southampton (111), Exeter (97), Colchester (86) and Dover (45) – while other individual areas supported up to 20 furniture makers at that time[cccxix].

The Pelletier family were prominent furniture makers. John Pelletier had fled from Paris due to increasing, and eventually unbearable, religious intolerance. He arrived in London with his wife and their two sons, René and Thomas, via Amsterdam, applying for denization status in March 1682. He specialised in the 'high baroque' style of furniture with its intricately carved and gilded designs. His furniture graced the homes of William and Mary following his appointment to the Crown in 1690. Amongst his wide range of furniture are carved and gilded table frames, stands, screens and mirrors. Two sets of candle-stands at Hampton Court Palace are believed to have been made by him, as evidenced in his accounts in 1701: *'For carving and gilding two pairs of large stands— £70'.*

These candle stands can still today be viewed at Hampton Court Palace. He also supplied furnishings for Windsor Castle, together with a substantial order from Ralph Montague, 1st Duke of Montague, for Montague House in Bloomsbury, London.

Following the death of John Pelletier in 1704, his two sons continued the family business as a partnership until they decided to pursue individual careers from 1711 onwards. Thomas, the more prominently successful son, was appointed Cabinet Maker 'in Ordinary' to Queen Anne[cccxx].

We find that among the lesser-known furniture makers working as subcontractors are Jean Pelletier's sons-in-law, John Guilbaud,

---

[cccxix] Goodwin, James, MBA., MA, *The Huguenot Influence on English Furniture 1660-1714*, p7.
[cccxx] Ibid, p8.

and Philip Arbuthnot – the former becoming a reputable cabinet maker, who is recorded as providing two overmantle mirrors to Hopetoun House, Scotland, and two escritoires to William III – and the latter working in the Strand, listed as running a japaning[280] and looking-glass shop[cccxxi]. A Guilbaud cabinet can be viewed at the Geffrye Museum in London.

I have not listed every prominent furniture maker nor all of the pieces they are famous for, but the Huguenot makers' lasting epithet must be the exemplary skill and imagination through which they developed a unique 'English' style in the 18th century at the precise time that Britain's trade was forging ahead.

The development of papier-mâché for decorative purposes was another Huguenot achievement. Peter Babel of St James Street, Long Acre in west London, advertised his skills as a papier-mâché frame and ornament maker in 1763.

* * * * * *

CERAMICS AND GLASS

The fine skills of the Huguenot artisan were much admired, in many areas including ceramics as well as in glass. England was indeed blessed by the creation of a porcelain factory in Chelsea by second generation Huguenots Nicholas Sprimont and Charles Gouyon in 1745. It was the first of its kind in England – able to produce quality pieces on a par with the factories in France. The two men drew much inspiration from the manufacturing areas of Chantilly and St Cloud[cccxxii].

The Derby Porcelain Factory was probably started in 1748 by Huguenot descendant Andrew Planché, a potter and uncle of playwright James Robinson Planché. He had entered into an

---

[cccxxi] Goodwin, James, MBA., MA, The Huguenot Influence on English Furniture 1660-1714, p8.
[cccxxii] Catherine Rawlinson and Isabelle Janvrin, *The French in London: from William the Conqueror to Charles de Gaulle* (London, 2016) p66.

The Story of the Huguenots – a Unique Legacy

agreement with local banker John Heath, and William Duesbury, an enameller from Staffordshire, and the resultant commercial alliance proved to contain the perfect ingredients for a successful business, which in just a short time grew significantly. Soon, large orders were being handled for them by a Mr Williams from his premises in Craig's Court, Charing Cross, London. In fact, by the early 1770s, the company was so profitable that it was able to buy out the Chelsea China Works from Nicholas Sprimont and Charles Gouyon. The china itself was mainly produced at the Derby factory, with the decoration being added following its shipment to the Chelsea works until the premises were closed in 1784.

On 28 March 1775, a Royal Warrant was granted to the business by George III, which gave the owners a reason to design a new 'mark' to recognise the honour that had been awarded to the factory, and so the letter 'D', surmounted by a crown, signified the Royal Warrant.

Many independent enamellers, such as Jean Mussard (who had trained in Geneva) and Anthony Tregent, would have been employed to embellish clock and watch faces. Not all started out as enamellers; often they began their working life as jewellers. James Giles was one such man who had served an apprenticeship as a jeweller before following in his father's footsteps as a high-quality porcelain painter[cccxxiii]. At one point, he was decorating various plates and other items for a Worcester manufacturer before returning to London in 1756. Initially, he had settled in Kentish Town, but by 1763 had moved to Berwick Street, Soho. In 1771, he insured his tools and stock for the then enormous sum of £2,000 with the Sun Insurance Company, which surely demonstrates how successful his career as a painter of quality china had become. James' grandfather, Abraham Giles, had been a cabinet maker and refugee from France.

[cccxxiii] Museum of London, The, *The Quiet Conquest: The Huguenots, 1685-1985* (London, 1985) p267.

- 317 -

GLASS

Glass production had been a relatively small industry before the arrival of the Huguenots. Most of the English glassware had been plain and for many years just a cottage industry stagnating at a level of inability to provide good quality table glassware or glazing, both of which were becoming popular abroad, and would soon become more desirous in England. Any superior glass that might have been commissioned before the arrival of the Huguenots had often been manufactured in either France or the Low Countries. One advantage that the foreign makers were blessed with was a 'guild system' that ensured the glassmaker was of a certain status. Both Normandy and Lorraine were areas well known for good quality window glass. Normandy could boast several families who excelled at window glass production[281], such as the de Caqueray and Le Valliant, whilst families in Lorraine, such as Thiétry and Thysac, produced what was termed 'broad' glass[282]. Table and other small items of glassware were produced by the Massey, Bigault and Bonny families, but it must be noted that high-quality glass was also being manufactured across the border in Antwerp.

One of the earliest glass makers to resettle in England for religious reasons was Jean Carré, born in Arras but who had moved to Antwerp, a prominent glass making centre. He arrived in England in 1567, where he pursued permission for the building in London of a Venetian-style furnace to produce luxury glassware, as well as two furnaces at Fernfold in The Weald (Surrey-Sussex border) to manufacture window glass. Jean Carré died in 1572, but not before he had seen the success of his enterprise.

The later Huguenot glass makers chose to settle more diversely in England than other artisans – usually where there was a plentiful supply of wood for their furnaces and an outlet for their products – yet they were not always welcomed by local people, who witnessed the large quantities of wood felled for this new manufacturing process. Furthermore, these glassmakers from overseas were not protected by powerful guilds as they had been whilst living and working on the continent. Changes had to be made, one of which was the use of coal in their furnaces, instead of wood[cccxxiv].

There are many sites of former Huguenot glass manufacture that occurred between the years 1567-1620, and these include: Newcastle upon Tyne; Wollaton; Kingswinford, near Stourbridge; Ashow, near Kenilworth; Gloucester; Newnham on Severn; Southwark; Knowle; Alfold; Wisborough Green; Petworth and Kimmeridge[cccxxv].

[cccxxiv] Museum of London, The, *The Quiet Conquest: The Huguenots, 1685-1985* (London, 1985) p265.
[cccxxv] Ibid, p264.

- 28 -

The Arts

So many famous Huguenots fall into the categories this chapter is devoted to.

AUTHORS

One of the more well-known names is unquestionably Peter Mark Roget, creator and writer of the world-famous *Roget's Thesaurus*. He was the only son of John Roget, a Genevan pastor at the Threadneedle Street Church, and Catherine Romilly, who made their home in Soho. Tragedy struck the family early in Peter's life when his father became seriously ill with pulmonary tuberculosis. His parents travelled back to Geneva in search of a cure leaving Peter and his younger sister in the care of their maternal grandfather. After his father's death in 1873, his mother returned home to care for her children; several moves later, the family settled in Edinburgh, where Peter attended university, graduating in 1798 aged just 19 years old.

He had been a gifted child – and one who from a young age had shown an interest in lists. He had suffered from depression since childhood, and his lists appear to have been a means of attempting to control his life as far as possible; no doubt his father's illness and his parents' abrupt departure to seek a cure had led to feelings of insecurity in their son. Paranoia had already

The Story of the Huguenots – a Unique Legacy

manifested itself in the maternal side of his family through his mother and his mother's brother, Sir Samuel Romilly, who had become a substitute father figure to Peter after his own father's untimely death[283]. Peter had attempted to write a book of lists whilst still in his mid-twenties, but he did not complete his unique thesaurus until he was in his early seventies.

After university, he had begun his professional life as a physician, but was also engaged as a private teacher in which capacity he travelled extensively across Europe with his students. Apart from his *Roget's Thesaurus*, which has remained continually in print since the first edition was published, his contributions in other fields include his invention in 1815 of the slide rule – an invaluable aid to calculation that was only superseded by the electronic calculator in the 20th century. Another sphere of interest to him was optics, and his work in this field ultimately led to the future development of the motion picture.

The Martineau family had originated from Fontenay les Camps in the Poitou area, but it is believed that the family moved to Bergerac in the Perigord region of Aquitaine so that one of the family could study medicine. The first member of the family to arrive in England after the Revocation was Gaston Martineau, a surgeon, who had undertaken the perilous journey to Calais after leaving behind other family members forced to abjure their faith in order to remain in the land of their birth[284]. Gaston then travelled to England with the Pierre family, settling in Spitalfields; Gaston married Marie Pierre at La Patente church, Spitalfields, before moving to Norwich[cccxxvi].

It was Harriet Martineau, granddaughter of David, who was to become the most famous of the family as an accomplished author. From 1832-4, Harriet published a series of stories related to political economy. More than 6,000 copies were printed, bringing

---

[cccxxvi] The Martineau Archives.

her to literary prominence. She was permitted access to the private papers of Chancellor Brougham, which gave her the opportunity to write at length in defence of the 1834 Poor Law Amendment Act. Despite the nature of much of the subject matter, her style of writing was neither dry nor dull, making her work popular with many[cccxxvii].

Within the Ouvry family's contribution to authorship is Francisca Ingram Ouvry, who wrote the famous *Henri de Rohan,* alternatively known as *The Huguenot Refugee*[cccxxviii].

Further authors, to name just a small selection, who can lay claim to Huguenot descent are: Daphne du Maurier (English author and playwright); George du Maurier (English author and cartoonist); I. D. Du Plessis (South African writer); Theodor Fontane (German novelist and poet); William Larminie (Irish poet); Henry Wadsworth Longfellow (American poet), and Pierre Bayle (French author and philosopher).

* * * * * *

PLAYWRIGHTS

Abraham Portal, who has already come to our attention as a gold and silversmith, had begun writing poetry whilst still apprenticed to Paul de Lamerie. Abraham had his first full-length play, a tragedy entitled *Olindo and Sophronia,* published in 1758. His second play, *Vortimer,* alternatively known as *The True Patriot,* followed in 1762-3, and his last play, *The Indiscreet Lover,* in 1768; this latter play was a comedy whose sole performance was at The Haymarket theatre for the benefit of the British Lying-in Hospital[285]. He also wrote a number of poems, the most famous being in memory of his first wife Eliza[cccxxix].

[cccxxvii] Museum of London, The, *The Quiet Conquest: The Huguenots, 1685-1985* (London, 1985) p152.
[cccxxviii] Ibid. p418.
[cccxxix] Christopher Portal, *The Reluctant Goldsmith* (Somerset, 1993) pp.43-5.

The Story of the Huguenots – a Unique Legacy

Abraham also took a lively interest in both the national and international events unfolding around him and wrote several politically motivated letters and articles related to many pressing social issues of the time. He died in 1809.

James Robinson Planché was born in 1796; during his life, he became a dramatist as well as an antiquarian. His grandfather had been a coffee merchant, one of whose two sons, Andrew, was the gifted clay modeller who helped found the Derbyshire porcelain factory described earlier in this book[cccxxx].

Andrews's brother, Jacques, a watchmaker by profession, in time had a son, James, who, once he had completed his education, became articled to a bookseller; and it was the world of books, particularly writing, that drew his already inclined mind towards this as a career as he hoped this would lead to some of his own work being published one day[cccxxxi]. In 1821, he married, and was eventually blessed with two daughters of whom the younger, Matilda Ann Mackarness, became a successful authoress through her novel *A Trap to Catch a Sunbeam,* proving so popular that over time no less than 42 editions were printed.

James, however, was finding himself drawn to the theatre, and he would often perform as an amateur actor in small provincial theatres; it was here that he began his career as a playwright, writing *Amoroso, King of Little Britain.* The success of this play enabled him to make playwriting his full-time career, but his desire to marry pen and paper also led him to write music as well, one example of which is his first opera, *Maid Marion,* in 1822.

An endlessly talented man, he was instrumental in the development of certain stage props including the 'Vamp Trap', whereby two spring leaves parted under pressure to allow an actor or actress to appear as if from nowhere, and of course as soon as the trap was sprung, it would immediately close again. This prop

---

[cccxxx] Colin, Lee, *James Robinson Planché.* Proceedings of the Huguenot Society, Vol XXVIII (2003) p22.
[cccxxxi] Ibid, p23.

The Story of the Huguenots – a Unique Legacy

was first used in James' version of *The Vampire* hence it being forever known by this name. James died on 30 May 1880[cccxxxii].

* * * * * *

ANTIQUARIANS

A number of antiquities were donated by Huguenots to the British Museum, including those given by Matthew Maty, librarian at the museum and donator of at least 20 artefacts, while William Lethieullier donated several Egyptian antiquities.

Frederic Ouvry (a descendant of Jacques Ouvry) was born in 1814; he studied law, becoming a solicitor in 1837. He was admitted as a partner to the firm of Robinson, King and Ouvry, but later left to become a partner in Farrer & Co. On 24 February 1848, he was elected treasurer of The Society of Antiquaries. He was a keen collector of fine books and a good friend, as well as solicitor, of Charles Dickens, who based his character Mr Undery on his friend in the story *The Haunted House*[cccxxxiii].

Although not strictly classified as an antiquarian, Benjamin Lewis Vulliamy was, on 7 July 1817, given £20 by the Worshipful Company of Clockmakers to buy a suitable and noteworthy piece of furniture for housing the Clockmakers Library and collection[286]. He had been one of the founders of The Clockmakers Library, taking a keen interest in the library until his death, and his enthusiasm for this project encouraged many from within the world of horology to donate books as well as timepieces and other relevant artefacts. The initial meeting of the library committee was held at Vulliamy's own premises, 74 Pall Mall, before moving to the *King's Head* tavern. Having set out to find the handsome piece of furniture that would perfectly display the clockmakers'

[cccxxxii] Colin, Lee, *James Robinson Planché*. Proceedings of the Huguenot Society, Vol XXVIII (2003) pp.23-5.
[cccxxxiii] Ouvry, Johnathan G., *The Ouvry Family in the 19th Century*. The Huguenot Society, Vol XXIV (1988) p478.

treasures, he purchased a second-hand mahogany bureau that had originally been made by Gillows of London in 1795. It was subsequently installed in the *King's Head* tavern, and then fitted with secure intricate locks in order to protect its fine collection.

Within five years, the library contained amongst its treasured possessions 100 books and 48 watches or watch movements. Today, the Clockmakers Library is the oldest surviving collection of clocks and watches in the world[cccxxxiv].

* * * * * *

FREEDOM OF INFORMATION

One final mention relating to the written word must go to the wonderful sources of data that are freely available to the public for research purposes, and which can be found in many archives. The second son of Sir Samuel Romilly, Sir John Romilly, who became Baron Romilly in 1860, is the man we owe our gratitude to for this. He was born in 1802, entering the world of politics at the age of 30 before becoming an MP in 1846, having previously been called to the Bar in 1827. He was appointed Solicitor General (1848-50) and then became Attorney General (1850-1) when he was then chosen for the office of Master of the Rolls, a post he remained in until 1873. It was while he held this office that he decided to campaign for records to be made available to the public so that they could undertake research unhampered by prevailing restrictions that hindered such research; he was not only successful in achieving this, but also ensured that access would be without charge. Today, his statue benignly watches over the great number of people who visit the National Archives in Kew, Richmond, many of whom are likely to be oblivious to the debt we owe him.

* * * * * *

[cccxxxiv] Sir G. J. White, *The Clockmakers of London* (The Trustees of the Worshipful Company of Clockmakers, London, 1998) p38.

THEATRE AND ENTERTAINMENT

The theatre and the arts were, at first, a source of immense disapproval by Calvinists, yet, paradoxically, there would be some later generations of Huguenot refugees who would go on to become famous playwrights and actors. One such descendant was David Garrick, whose grandfather, David Garrie[287], had fled to England from Bordeaux in 1685. David Garrick was born in Hereford on 19 February 1717, the oldest of seven children. David and his siblings were given a strict moral upbringing[288]. The family were of modest means and for some years resided in Gibraltar (David's father, Peter, was a captain in the English army). David, aged 14, wrote home wholly animated letters that perhaps indicated his otherwise unlikely career path for the future.

After the family's return to England, David, now 19, was encouraged to join Samuel Johnson's academy in Litchfield, but within a few months following the failure of this venture he set out for London with his new friend Samuel, together possessing just a few pennies in their pockets. At this point, he did not pursue an acting career – instead he put his name down as a law student at Lincoln's Inn, but fate then intervened in the form of a substantial legacy of £1,000 from an uncle. He and his brother decided to set up a wine merchant company – Garrick & Co. It was this business that took David into the world of entertainment, where he soon made numerous friends.

His first acting role came about when he was asked to take on the part of Harlequin at a small theatre in Goodman's Fields, London, in March 1741 as the original actor had been taken ill. He went on to play several parts in various productions, and, following some success, he applied to Drury Lane as well as Covent Garden – only to be rejected by both. His family were unaware of his thespian career aspirations[289] until the night after he had played the part of Richard III to overwhelming acclaim, when he finally disclosed his chosen vocation to his father.

The audiences loved him. His fresh approach was greatly applauded as he undertook many different acting roles over the next few years, but his overwhelming success did not alter his good character – he appears not to have ever let it go to his head. He was helped by friends to raise the enormous sum, by the standards of the day, of £8,000 – his share of the purchase cost of the lease and furnishings of the Drury Lane Theatre. David's theatre of the future was to be truly innovative as he changed the method of acting, the stage and eventually even the lighting. When he had decided to try to raise capital to purchase Drury Lane, the theatre had been failing, but his vision took the theatre from financial ruin to resounding triumph. That said, he did have his hindrances along the way, such as in November 1755, when his theatre was stormed and wrecked by ruffians.

He was undeniably a man of many talents. When he staged *Harlequin's Invasion* during the Christmas season of 1759, he wrote the lyrics to the music penned by William Boyce, which later became the famous composition *Hearts of Oak*. David Garrick was also an immense admirer of William Shakespeare, and he paid for a small temple on the north bank of the Thames at Hampton to be built in the Bard's memory, which remains a well-maintained local feature even today.

Finally, in 1775, he arranged the sale of his share of the Drury Lane Theatre, and spent the next four years in happy retirement. Following his death in 1779, he was given an honourable burial in Poets Corner, Westminster Abbey.

With large pockets of Huguenots and their descendants living in London, their growing attendance at the 'local' theatres such as those in the Haymarket area gradually but significantly increased the ultimate popularity of French theatre[cccxxxv].

Today, many Huguenot descendants have followed the worthy footsteps of these earlier thespians: Len Goodman (*Strictly Come*

[cccxxxv] Ehrman, Esther, Dr, *Huguenot Participation in the French Theatre in London*. The Huguenot Society, Vol XXIV (1988) p487.

Dancing); Jon and Sean Pertwee, and Lawrence Olivier and Derek Jacobi (English actors); Julia Sawalha (English actress), and Eddie Izzard (comedian and actor). Huguenot descendants in other areas are also well represented, for example: Simon Le Bon (English musician) and Victor Lardent (creator of the Times New Roman font, which has been selected for use in this book).

This selection can be further expanded to include those in other countries: Judy Garland (American actress and singer); Joan Crawford (American actress); Johnny Depp (American actor) Nikolaus Harnoncourt (Austrian conductor) and Jean-Luc Goddard (French film director).

Not all actors followed in the footsteps of their famous Huguenot ancestors; for example, Christopher Cazenove (1943-2010) was a famous film, television and stage actor from the Cazenove family which had previously been involved in the banking profession. Christopher's father had taken up a military career, rising to the rank of brigadier.

* * * * * *

THE ARTS

In 1912, a new resident moved into *Glencairn*, 46 West End Lane, Hampstead, London. His name was Albert de Belleroche. His family were one of the oldest houses in Europe and connected to the royal family of France, but as Huguenots they felt that by 1685 the time had sadly come to depart their homeland to settle in England.

Albert had been born in Swansea in 1864, but, when he was just three years old, his father died. His mother, Alice, a famed beauty, married for the second time in 1871, and Albert's step-father, William Henry Vane Millbank, became a guiding light in young Albert's life. The family had moved to Paris, where his mother lavishly entertained many notable persons including the future Edward VII and Carolus Duran – a distinguished portrait painter, who by chance saw some sketches that de Belleroche had produced, and he was naturally very impressed by the raw talent demonstrated by the young man.

He offered Albert the chance to study at his own studio, but de Belleroche, though mindful of what a wonderful opportunity this was, decided after a short time to leave as he did not want a formal structure to his studies; instead, he felt that art could not really be 'learned' in schools but rather in museums amongst the masters, whose work was there for all to see and study. He did however remain in contact with Duran, and through him met John Singer Sergeant, who became a lifelong friend. De Belleroche and Sergeant shared studios in Paris with the style and technique of each complementing the other.

De Belleroche found lithography his favoured medium, and he was instrumental in progressing the techniques of the time; indeed, his dexterity was so certain that he could draw directly onto the stone without the need for preparatory sketches. By 1904, his work was given such critical acclaim that he had earned the respect of many giants in the art world – including Renoir.

At the age of 45, de Belleroche finally married. His wife was the 28-year-old beauty Julie Emilie Visseaux, and they were wed at All Saints Church, St John's Wood[290]. After two years, the couple moved to 46 West End Lane[291]. At the start of World War II, Albert moved his family to Southwell, Nottingham, where after a long illness he died in 1944[cccxxxvi].

The Courtauld family has already been mentioned in the wider Huguenot story, but mention needs to be made of their contribution to the arts in the form of an unrivalled art foundation: The Courtauld Institute. Samuel Courtauld, the industrialist, was an enthusiastic art collector who, with the help of his friends Lord Lee Farnham (diplomat and art collector) and Sir Robert Witt (art historian) initiated The Courtauld Institute in 1932, which was at

---

[cccxxxvi] Marianne Colloms and Dick Weindling, *West Hampstead Life: The Artist and his stepfather,* (2 February 2003).

the outset furnished with a sizable donation of paintings, the majority of which were French Impressionists such as Manet, Pissarro and Monet, as well as Cézanne and Degas. He made further substantial gifts to the Institute throughout the 1930s as well as a bequest in 1948. Courtauld was not the only founder to make important donations to the Institute, but he was certainly the premier patron and donator of important works of art.

In the years following its inception right up to the present day, there have been numerous other collections donated to this veritable institute, and consequently it now encompasses a wide range of famous works by artists such as Turner, Rubens, Gainsborough and Van Dyke. Since 1989, both the Institute and the Courtauld Gallery, which is open to the public, have been sited in the same building – the North Strand block of Somerset House[292].

1. The Houblon Almshouses, Richmond, London

2. Sealy Fourdrinier

3. Baptismal entry for Catherine Elizabeth Guion, 31 October 1705

4. The Calas family house in Toulouse

5. Portrait of Mary Blaquire

6. Glasses manufactured by Huguenot craftsmen

7. Guilbauld cabinet at the Geffrye Museum, London

8. The document pledging the rebuilding of the Temple at Luneray

9. The rebuilt Temple of Luneray, Normandy

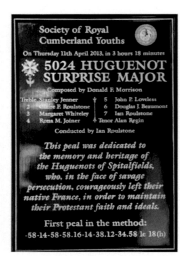

10. Plaque in honour of the Huguenots, Christchurch, Spitalfields

11. Exterior of the French Hospital, Rochester, Kent

12. Interior of the last remaining Huguenot Church, Soho, on the occasion of the service commemorating the 500th anniversary of Martin Luther's Ninety-Five Theses

Part Four

France and England to the Present Day

An entire century of French history had passed, and still the cruel hand of religious repression and punishment was felt across the land by any still resisting. And whilst they could not have known that the tender shoots of enlightenment, was soon to burgeon within society, in their daily lives they must have prayed with all their remaining strength that the God they worshipped would still enable their faith to somehow survive.

But how was this to be achieved? The years that intervened between the *Edict of Fontainebleau* and the French Revolution continued to witness those of the Huguenot faith ruthlessly persecuted through severe restrictions not only in matters of faith but also in their professions as well as areas of their daily life.

In England and other neighbouring Protestant countries, as we have seen, their ethno-religious kinsmen were free to live and worship as all religions were and still are despite deep differences of opinion, yet such freedoms continued to be unequivocally denied in France for years to come. The narrative to their journey to equality is of course incomplete without testimony to their immense suffering highlighted in a number of poignant records referring to many individuals, but few more so than the deeply moving case of Jean Calas.

- 29 -

France – Injustice and Enlightenment

A young woman by the name of Anne-Rose Cabibel returned to France[293] and at 21 years of age married her father's first cousin. Aged 33, Jean Calas was a linen merchant and shopkeeper as well as being a grandson of the master surgeon of Mazamet. Soon after the young couple's marriage they decided they would like to make their home in England, but their plans were thwarted when they were discovered by the authorities before they could reach a safe departure point, and so they returned to Toulouse, where they settled down to what they hoped would be a happy married life[cccxxxvii]. Jean Calas' shop and warehouse were in the Grand Rue Des Filatiers, the main shopping street of Toulouse, and they and their four sons and two daughters lived comfortably in the accommodation above the shop.

The years passed by, the children growing into adults; they were all Protestants with the exception of the third son Louis, who had, to the immense anguish of his parents and siblings, converted to Catholicism, leaving home to live with a Catholic family nearby[cccxxxviii].

The day of 13 October 1761 started like any other, at the end of which, as usual, apart from the Calas' daughters and the youngest

---

[cccxxxvii] Vigne, Randolph, *The Killing of Jean Calas: Voltaire's First Huguenot Cause*. The Huguenot Society Vol XXIII (1980), pp.282-3.
[cccxxxviii] Ibid, p282.

The Story of the Huguenots – a Unique Legacy

son who were not at home, the rest of the family sat down to dinner at 7pm. They had a guest that night, a friend of the second son Pierre, Gaubert de Lavaysse[cccxxxix].

After the meal had ended Marc-Antoine, the eldest son, rose from the table, apparently to meet his friends as he often did to play billiards; he stopped momentarily to speak with Jeanne Viguier[294] in the kitchen, then continued on his way. No one perceived anything untoward about Marc-Antoine that evening except that he remarked to Jeanne Viguier as he left her kitchen that cool October evening that he felt 'burning hot'. Marc-Antoine had become embittered as he resented the injustice of being prevented from being called to the Bar as an Advocat due to his Protestant faith[295]; instead, he had to remain at home running errands for his parents[cccxl].

Later that night, cries rang from the Calas' shop when the body of 28-year-old Marc-Antoine was discovered. Pierre escorted his friend downstairs at the end of the evening, and it was only then that the unusually half-closed door to the shop alerted Pierre and his friend to check if all was well…as they pushed the door open they found the body of Marc-Antoine[cccxli].

At first, the family stated that Pierre and his friend had found Marc-Antoine's body on the floor of the shop, apparently the victim of an intruder. A crowd had quickly congregated outside the shop on hearing the alarm, and shortly afterwards a doctor arrived to examine the body, but he only found a *'livid mark'* upon the neck of the deceased. The doctor's report concluded that *'he had been hanged whilst alive, by himself or others'* – this fatal sentence was to haunt the Calas family for the rest of their lives as the finger of suspicion was now pointed unequivocally towards them[cccxlii].

[cccxxxix] Vigne, Randolph, *The Killing of Jean Calas: Voltaire's First Huguenot Cause.* The Huguenot Society, Vol XXIII (1980) p283.
[cccxl] Ibid p284.
[cccxli] Armstrong, Ken, *Paris Review, 13 March 2015*, pp.3-4.
[cccxlii] Ibid, p5.

The Story of the Huguenots – a Unique Legacy

A capitoul[296] of Toulouse was hastily summoned, and he arrested the Calas family as well as Gaubert, the servant Jeanne, and a nearby neighbour, who had been first on the scene after the discovery of the body. Jean Calas was separated from his family as they were led away to prison, all apparently stating that an intruder must have broken in to the shop downstairs, and that he then killed Marc-Antoine; but 36 hours later, after relentless questioning, Jean Calas and the others admitted that Marc-Antoine had committed suicide. Jean said he had realised that if Marc-Antoine was branded a suicide, his corpse would be dragged through the streets naked and face down on a hurdle to be desecrated and pelted by the crowds, and that, desperately wanting to spare his family this additional anguish, he had tried to cover up the truth. Counterclaims pointing to murder rather than suicide were made by unreliable witnesses, who now unhesitatingly passed on their dubious third-party accounts.

The scale and intensity with which the cause of the death of Marc-Antoine were debated reveal the raw emotions at work in France at that time. With one exception, the Calas family members were all Protestants, still holding out against what must have been overwhelming Catholic discrimination and persecution. Looking back, we can see that it would have been virtually impossible for any Protestant to have received a fair trial for an alleged crime, especially murder, but the change of plea surely did not serve the Calas family well as it could be perceived that they were trying to evade a far greater evil – that of killing one of their own. Consequently, a multitude of malicious suspicions began to fall on Jean Calas, including the unfounded accusation that Marc-Antione had intended to convert to Catholicism against his father's wishes.

The dangerous and damaging wildfire of rumours that swept through the local towns and eventually across France seems to have had a profound effect on his right to 'justice' as French law at that time made no distinction between hearsay and factual evidence. Five months after the night of Marc-Antoine's death,

- 334 -

The Story of the Huguenots – a Unique Legacy

Jean Calas was brought to 'trial'. The verdict, clearly a forgone conclusion was passed – guilty; the punishment – death by burning. But the method of implementation was to be far more barbaric than the sentence implied.

The execution of Jean Calas was to be carried out on 10 March 1762 starting in the Torture Chamber of the prison before transferring to the main square of Toulouse, just one day after judgement had been passed. Murder always carried the death sentence, but the court's ruling for the murder of a family member was as repulsive as the supposed crime itself – it ordered interrogation under torture as part of the sentence to try to elicit a full confession of the 'crime', which he steadfastly and in all innocence refused to make. The crowd watched, mesmerised by each phase of the 'punishment', which culminated with Jean Calas being tied over a cartwheel. His limbs were smashed with iron rods before the executioner strangled him – his body, horrifically shattered, lay still at last, but throughout the violent brutality of his ordeal he had protested his innocence. His corpse lay there mutilated and lifeless before it was removed from the wheel, and then burned until just his ashes remained. With bitter irony, Marc-Antoine, who had died a Protestant, was given a Catholic martyr's funeral.

It was Voltaire[297] who brought the facts of this case to the public's attention, after a meeting with Donat Calas, the youngest son of the Calas family who had been away at the time of Marc-Antoine's death; Voltaire was immediately struck by the young man's gentle disposition and sorrowful defense of his family, he was so impressed by the young man's obvious distress and bearing that he immediately set about raising funds for an appeal against the judgement.

Voltaire's intervention led to international awareness of the plight of Jean Calas, and the unfair treatment meted out to anyone else following the Huguenot faith. Voltaire gained immense support for the Calas family, but this belated defense could not

The Story of the Huguenots – a Unique Legacy

turn back the clock and prevent Jean Calas from being wrongfully found guilty of his son's murder. He had died for a crime he had not committed, but his death was not in vain, the injustice of being treated a lesser person simply because of his faith was now brought fully to the attention of all.

Voltaire spoke against this discrimination reminding people that toleration is not dangerous but can bring enhancement to a nation that practices open-mindedness. Voltaire's [298] intercession was the first collective tentative step towards acceptance of those citizens who chose the Protestant faith, and it eventually led to Lafayette's mediation with Louis XVI in 1785 on behalf of French Protestants[cccxliii]. Public opinion enabled the conviction of Jean Calas to be reviewed and overturned by a panel of 50 judges on 9 March 1765. After the original judgment was overturned, a commemorative plaque exonerating Jean Calas was placed outside the Calas family house in Toulouse, and when I visited the Temple du Salin in Toulouse in 2016, I saw inside a beautiful memorial tablet to this Protestant martyr.

* * * * * *

In 1762, just a month before the execution of Jean Calas, the last Protestant minister in France, François Rochette, paid the ultimate price for his defiant adherence to his faith. He was hanged, but, true to his belief in the psalms he went to the scaffold singing: *'this is the day that the Lord has made; let us rejoice and be glad in it.'* Yet perhaps he had an intuition that told him that the tide would eventually turn towards a more enlightened outlook[cccxliv].

In the early 1760s, a public debate had begun amongst many educated people about the country's attitude towards the

---

[cccxliii] Museum of London, The, *The Quiet Conquest: The Huguenots, 1685-1985* (London, 1985) p50.
[cccxliv] Burdett, Dallas, R; D Min, *Biblical Preaching and Teaching, vol, 2* (USA, 2010) p182.

persecution of Protestants. Ironically, the demands for change were now being encouraged by the Catholic Church itself, which felt that freedom of conscience should in this enlightened era be encouraged[cccxlv]. By bringing the tragic case of Jean Calas to the public's attention, Voltaire[299] had encouraged and fanned the flames of ongoing doubt and uncertainty relating to whether the harsh laws against those who chose to practice the Protestant form of worship should be reviewed. It appears that the barbaric acts of violence perpetrated for so many years were starting to cause serious unease and consternation throughout France – particularly in the more literate strata of society – and the forthcoming policy of greater tolerance can be directly attributed, in part, to this national debate[cccxlvi]. In 1787, just two years before the French Revolution, the *Edict of Toleration* gave remaining Huguenots the right to at last live freely. Although Catholicism was still the sole form of recognised public worship, this significant step must have represented a watershed moment in royal thinking at the time. With discontent in the country growing widely, other factors were rapidly coming into play that would alter not just the course of the plight of the Huguenots, but the destiny of France itself.

[cccxlv] David Garrioch, *The Huguenots of Paris and the Coming of Religious Freedom 1685-1789* (New York, 2014) p271.
[cccxlvi] Ibid, pp.270-1.

- 30 -

The early 20th Century

Within a year of the dawn of the twentieth century, in England, Queen Victoria had died, and her son Edward was now king. Plans for his coronation had begun in minute detail. A modest house in east London was the home of the man who was to become famous for his part in the king's coronation. Its owner, George Dorée, was interviewed by a local newspaper about the velvet material for Edward VII's coronation robes that he had been commissioned to weave. He took the reporter, at his request, into his front room in Alma Road, Bethnal Green, to show where he had fulfilled this historic order – on a simple hand loom.

To give a little appreciation of the delicate and precise nature of velvet weaving, a short explanation of the processes will, I hope, allow some insight into the skill required. In the article by *The London Daily News,* the reporter was taken upstairs to see where the silk used to produce the velvet was spun. The reporter was shown a thread finer than a human hair. To his astonishment, Mr Dorée asked the reporter to look at the 'five' threads. To make the 'pile', brass reeds are used, which are woven into the silk. These reeds are made with a groove in the top over which the silk threads are woven, and then cut by the 'trevat', the divided threads falling evenly apart to form the outside edge, or pile, of the velvet.

The trevat – or little knife – which retains its old French name, is attached to two runners, and is set to the depth of the groove on the reed. The two runners must be perfectly true, or the pile will be unevenly cut with one side being longer than the other. It is essential that the pile is even in its entirety, or its effect is spoilt, and it is in the cutting of the woven thread that the skill of the weaver comes particularly into play. The weaving itself may be quite true, but one slip of the knife and that portion must be started all over again.

Edward VII's coronation velvet was 30 yards long and 20 inches[300] wide. To use the technical expressions of the trade, it was an 1850 thread, 60 wires, 180 shoots and treble pole, with a 'GEORGE DOREE, CITIZEN AND WEAVER OF LONDON 421' two-thread ground. It took six yards of the top cane to make one yard of the pile of the velvet. Speaking generally, it means that Mr Dorée in his work on this particular velvet had to weave in the brass reed 60 times to every inch; nevertheless, the cut of the pile is so true that the grain of the pile cannot be seen at all.

As the *Daily News* remarked at the time: '*There must be a special organ, which biologists should investigate, called ~ 'the weaver's eye'.'*

To each square inch, 33,120 threads stand on end; to each yard, 23,846,400; and therefore 763,084,800 threads in the entire piece, and withal perfect in match and size, so strong that a man could stand on it 'without pressing it down'.

In all, it took George Dorée, who was by then 60 years of age, five months from start to finish to create this work of art for the king's coronation in 1902[cccxlvii]. He also wove the velvet for Queen Alexandra's coronation robes, which were a mere 12 yards long[301]. George was one of the final and most notable weavers of east London, but his wide-ranging and in-depth knowledge of his craft

---

[cccxlvii] Manchee, W. H., *George Doree: Citizen and Weaver of London - The Maker of King Edward VII's coronation robes.* The Huguenot Society Proceedings, Vol XI (1916) p421.

led to his additional expertise as a 'canespreader', which entitled him to display a 'bobbin' outside his house. The 'bobbin' was roughly 18 inches long; a few of these signs can still be seen above the front doors of some houses in Spitalfields. The silk would be conveyed to the canespreader's premises on bobbins for him to comb out and prepare the silk for weaving.

A modest, self-educated man, he clearly took an immense pride in his craft and his 'freedom' of the Weavers Company, which had awarded him a Silver Medal in 1898 in recognition of his outstanding abilities in that era. But George Dorée's only boast, which is an understandable one, was of his Huguenot ancestry. His pride of his origins is amply demonstrated through every press interview that he agreed to – his Huguenot descent is mentioned without exception[cccxlviii].

The surname Dorée had emanated in Picardy, and was first mentioned in England by the diarist Evelyn in 1652, who wrote: '*I inspected the manner of chambletting[302] silk and grograms[303] at one Mr La Dorée's in Moorfields.*'

The Dorées had eventually settled in the Spitalfields area, and over time became wealthy velvet weavers, but a failed lawsuit in pursuit of a claim to lands in France plunged them into poverty – a real-life riches-to-rags story as suddenly the family found themselves in a somewhat hand to mouth existence.

With their subsequent loss of wealth, all the members of the family were pressed into work in order to earn enough to subsist, this being a greater necessity than education at that time. Added to the dire straits of many such families was the additional hardship of food shortages during the period of the Crimean War[304]. However, George Dorée, although denied a structured education, was to rise above adversity through his skilful application of the craft of velvet weaving. It is a complicated and intricate process of

---

[cccxlviii] Manchee, W. H., *George Doree: Citizen and Weaver of London - The Maker of King Edward VII's coronation robes.* The Huguenot Society Proceedings, Vol XI (1916) p425.

The Story of the Huguenots – a Unique Legacy

numerous stages, which George had begun to learn at the age of 11, achieving fame and widespread recognition early in the twentieth century

After George Dorée's death in 1916, his wife continued to teach would-be weavers the art, but with only relatively mediocre results – George Dorée's skills were so unique that he sadly took his expertise to the grave. As he had once said to a reporter: the art of weaving is an almost hereditary instinct[cccxlix].

In Bethnal Green, hand-weaving continued, although as a diminishing trade, into the 1930s. Mrs Stanley Baldwin, wife of the Prime Minister, visited Mrs Mary Waite on 8 April 1930 at her home, 45 Cranbrook Street. Mr and Mrs Waite were both weavers of Huguenot descent. Tragically, the house and many other weavers' houses including George Dorée's were demolished to build the Cranbrook Estate[305].

* * * * * *

World War I (also known as the Great War) was to inevitably bring Huguenot descendants into conflict. The global diaspora of French Protestants, already well established long before 1914, meant that enlistment in many countries could realistically cause two different branches of a Huguenot family to face each other from opposing battle lines.

The call to arms was issued to the people of many nations, including South Africa. Countless descendants of those early Huguenot refugees who had settled at the Cape now joined the first South African Infantry Brigade, and fought one of its most renowned battles on 20 July 1916 in thickly covered woodland near the village of Longueval on the Somme. The fierce fighting between the Germans and a battalion of South Africans is shown

---

[cccxlix] Manchee, W. H., *George Doree: Citizen and Weaver of London - The Maker of King Edward VII's coronation robes.* The Huguenot Society Proceedings, Vol XI (1916) pp.419-25.

The Story of the Huguenots – a Unique Legacy

by all that remained after the battle was over[306] was just one tree, a hornbeam, still standing in defiance of the carnage.

Two years after the Armistice of 11 November 1918, the South African government, mindful of the general clamour for a fitting memorial to its fallen sons of World War I in northern France, agreed that Delville Wood should be purchased by Sir Percy FitzPatrick[307] and given to the nation. Then began the clearing and replanting of the wood, with a suitable memorial to those South Africans who had fallen.

But the saplings that now grow on this site have a special provenance. Franschhoek, near the Cape, had been a settlement for Huguenots, including one family in particular, who in the 1680s had left La Coste near the Luberon mountains in Provence: the Guardiols. Antoine Guardiol and his family set off on the long voyage to the Cape with a pocketful of acorns, but sadly, Antoine died before he reached their destination. His 14-year old son Jean planted the acorns on what became the family farm, *La Cotte*. Jean died childless, but his two sisters inherited the farm. It was a poignant and appropriate tribute to the fallen, especially those of Huguenot descent, that the reforestation of Delville Wood was undertaken with acorns gathered from the Luberon oaks of Franschhoek, which in turn had grown from the acorns that Jean had planted in 1688[cccl].

The Guyon family also sacrificed a member in this first global conflict. George Sutherland Guyon (1875-1916), born in Richmond, Surrey, was one of six children of whom his favourite sibling was his sister Lilian. Their father had been General Gardiner Fredric Guyon, late of the Royal Fusiliers[308], who earlier in his career had been sent on a tour of duty to Guernsey, and his family naturally went with him. On 15 May 1897, aged 22, George Sutherland Guyon joined the family regiment and with the 2nd Battalion served his country throughout the Boer War; he was

---

[cccl] Vigne, Randolph, *A Great War Link with the Cape Huguenots.* The Huguenot Society Proceedings, Vol XXX (2014) p277.

decorated for his bravery and rose through the officer ranks, eventually becoming a major in 1912. He had married three years earlier and his son, John Mervyn (Peter), was born in Jubbulpore, Central Provinces, India in 1910[309].

At the outbreak of World War I, George's battalion and their families returned home on the troopship *SS Dongola*. By 1915, Major George Guyon had become the second-in-command in his regiment when they were despatched to the Dardanelles. Winston Churchill[310], First Sea Lord at the time, counselled the War Cabinet that the Dardanelles Narrows[311] – the gateway to Russia – could be opened up purely through the use of battleships. A concerted attack by British, French and Russian battleships began on 19 February 1915, but, because they proved unable to take the Narrows, troops were ordered into the attack just six days later. They landed on both shores of the Dardanelles straits[312], but were met by well- reinforced defences which they found impenetrable, and the order to withdraw was given at the end of 1915. Following this, the battalion was moved to another front at Sulva, but having failed to capture the ridge, they were evacuated following heavy casualties.

Major Guyon wrote a letter to his family at home, before the landings from *HMS Implacable*, whilst he waited on board the Cunard liner *SS Alaunia*:

> *Altogether we are tremendous pals and they say we are the best soldiers they've ever met; as a rule, they don't like soldiers. During the preliminary bombardment, of course all our men will have to be undercover, so I am going with the Gunnery Lieutenant. It all ought to be vastly interesting and I am looking forward to it tremendously. From what I have just been told by one from HMS Implacable who has just been on board, we are moving across to Tenedos tomorrow if the weather is fine and we shall transfer to HMS Implacable about six in the evening, sleep on board, and start across before daylight next morning: but, of*

- 343 -

course it all depends on the weather. We got half the battalion on board this morning. I had a letter from Lil (his sister) *but haven't had a single word from my Ma since I left. I am sending a snap of our ship. Goodbye my darling. Take the greatest care of yourself and Peter. Ever your loving husband.*

Major Guyon received a light head wound shortly after the landing on the shore. On 20 December 1915, Major Guyon again wrote home to his wife:

I am feeling greatly relieved today. The big operation which has been worrying us so long was finished last night with complete success. The operation was the evacuation of Anzac and Sulva in face of an enemy in many cases only 20 yards away. I can't tell you how we did it as it is against the rules but we spoofed the Turk properly and got off 70,000 men and 200 guns without his knowing anything about it. He was in fact so spoofed that he continued firing on our trenches and bombarding them heavily for five hours after our people were safely at sea. I can safely say it was the biggest operation that has ever been performed in war. We have had the thanks of Government in the highest eulogistic terms, and Sir Charles Munroe has also received a personal wire from the King[cccli].

Major Guyon's division went to Egypt, then on to the Western Front in time for the Battle of the Somme, 1 July 1916. They joined VIII Corps of Fourth Army on the left of the attack opposite Beaumont Hamel. A week before the set-piece attack was due to start, Major George Guyon was transferred to command an inexperienced battalion of Kitchener's New Army, the First Bradford Pals (16 West Yorkshire Regiment), part of 31 Division on the left flank of Fourth Army opposite Serre. The initial British

---

[cccli] The Guion Archives.

bombardment continued for seven days and nights, after which it was confidently felt that very few Germans could possibly have survived, yet some had, and these desperate defenders took a heavy toll in British lives, inflicting casualties and fatalities on a previously unknown scale.

On 14 July 1916, J G Thornton, chaplain to the regiment, with a heavy heart, sat down and wrote a letter to the wife of Major Guyon:

Dear Madam, the Chaplain of 148th Infantry Brigade had written to me asking me to give you any information about Major Guyon. It has been difficult to obtain many details as so many of the officers and men were killed or wounded but luckily Mr Laxton, the Intelligence Officer of the Battalion was only wounded and was able to give me some details of Major Guyon's death. He said that when the advance began on 1 July 1916 Major Guyon came out of the HQ dugout with him and the adjutant and the rest of the HQ staff and that very soon after Major Guyon was hit in the temple by a bullet. He was unconscious at once. They stayed a moment to put a dressing on his wound, but then had to leave him and go on advancing. Mr Laxton said that Major Guyon was evidently dying. As he was unconscious he cannot have suffered any pain. I am very sorry for all those who have been bereaved in these last few days. I do offer to you my most sincere sympathy. Major Guyon had only been appointed a week before to command the battalion. I think he felt very much being taken away from his old Regiment, but he set himself loyally to the task of getting to know officers and men. We so much regret losing an officer of such experience – Yours faithfully, J G Thornton, Chaplain.

The Somme was one of the bloodiest battles in military history, with nearly 60,000 British casualties on the first day. The battle

The Story of the Huguenots – a Unique Legacy

was fought to take German pressure off the French at Verdun, who, it was feared, were in danger of collapse. Post-war, the Imperial War Graves Commission (now the Commonwealth War Graves Commission) collected all known and marked burials into local war cemeteries. There were six war cemeteries at Serre alone. It was decided to build a monument at Thiepval to commemorate all those who fell at the Somme, but who had no known grave. The monument is a huge open archway on 16 pillars, standing on a high point above the village. The names of every known man who fell but has no known grave has been inscribed on a face of the 16 pillars – some 73,000 souls in all. In 1984, Peter and his brother George (the latter born after their father died) visited the memorial. They listened to an address given by a padre (by then 92 years old) who had been at the battle, and they laid a Royal Fusilier wreath. Poignantly, they were able to find their father's name amongst his old regiment, high up on a face of pillar number 16[ccclii].

* * * * * *

Huguenot women also played their parts during the conflict – the Reverend William Cazalet listed 65 in his Huguenot War Record alone[313]. Just over a century ago, society viewed the role of women differently to how women are perceived today, and for this reason the records of those women of Huguenot descent who served their country are quite scarce, in fact quite rare, in comparison to those for men[cccliii].

Women did of course undertake meaningful roles, and a mention of just two of these brave women will help to illustrate the breadth and depth of their courage and self-sacrifice during this period. Upon the outbreak of hostilities in 1914, the Suffragette

---

[ccclii] The Guion Archives.
[cccliii] Finch, K., *Great War Women of Huguenot Ancestry*. The Huguenot Society Proceedings, Vol XXX (2016) p547.

The Story of the Huguenots – a Unique Legacy

movement agreed to halt their campaign for women's rights, and instead actively encouraged women to undertake voluntary war work. A few years prior to the onset of the war, the Voluntary Aid Detachments (VADs) had been formed, which by 1914 possessed a membership approximately two thirds of which were women and girls. The VADs were to be a supportive group for the medical services during wartime, but they also undertook many other ancillary roles including air raid duties[cccliv].

By the spring of 1915, the War Office agreed to the employment of VADs in the large military hospitals at home as much-needed additions to the trained staff already working in these establishments. Not all VADs were employed to serve at home; quite a number were deployed in France, while others were sent further afield to Malta, Serbia, Salonika, Egypt and Mesopotamia.

The first of the Huguenot women I have selected whose bravery and courage is exceptional is Cecilia (abbreviated to Celia) who was the daughter of Charles William Blunt La Touche. On 30 June 1890, she married Walter Norris Congreve at St Jude's, South Kensington, and seemed destined for a comfortable, domesticated life, the lot of many women in that era; however, fate moves in mysterious ways and it now selected Celia for a greater destiny than anyone could have foretold at the time of her marriage.

Celia had left her quiet home in Staffordshire in 1914 to travel to Antwerp, where she worked as a voluntary nurse until the German occupation in October of that year. She was fearless and did not flee or flinch in the face of the aggressor as she was transferred to hospitals at various locations near Paris and the 'Front'[ccclv].

She became 'Infirmiére Principale' with officer rank in the French Army, being awarded the 1914 Star and the Croix de Guerre[314] for her courage and coolness when the hospital area of Nancy was under simultaneous shellfire and air attack. She was

---

[cccliv] Finch, K., *Great War Women of Huguenot Ancestry*. The Huguenot Society Proceedings, Vol XXX (2016), p548.
[ccclv] Ibid, p550.

- 347 -

also awarded the Queen Elizabeth Medal by King Albert of the Belgians in recognition of her exceptional services to Belgium in the relief of its citizens during World War I, and the Médialle de la Reconnaissance Français[315].

Celia was also an authoress, and her touchingly written poem *Lay Your Head* was first published in April 1915 in *Country Life* magazine before its inclusion in the 1915 compilation *The Fiery Cross*; she had been inspired to write this poem after reading an article in *The Times* entitled *Natures' Tears over the Fallen*. Although she had not lost any of her sons at the time she penned the poem, she was to know the heartache and pain of loss the following year when her eldest son, Billy, was killed in action and posthumously awarded the Victoria Cross *'for most conspicuous bravery during the period of fourteen days preceding his death in action*[ccclvi]*'*.

When she had first joined the VADs, she had been asked to teach basic French to the nurses and doctors. Later, when the hospital that became known as the Johnson Reckitt Hospital opened at Ris-Orangis near Paris, Celia had charge of a ward as well as being a member of the committee, and financially contributed towards the hospital. Harold J Reckitt, a co-founder of the hospital near Paris, wrote a detailed account of the hospital's wartime history within which he wrote of Celia:

...how much I owe to her tact and goodwill in smoothing out the little daily difficulties in the Nursing Department I shall probably never know. She brought with her, her youngest boy, John, aged fourteen, a boy scout, who acted as a messenger boy. After a year of devoted work, hearing that many French hospitals were in urgent need of skilled nurses, Lady Congreve left us to go to Revigny[ccclvii]*.*

[ccclvi] Finch, K., *Great War Women of Huguenot Ancestry*. The Huguenot Society Proceedings, Vol XXX (2016) p550.
[ccclvii] Harold J Reckitt, *VR76. A French Military Hospital* (London, 1921) pp.20-2.

The second woman I have included is Elizabeth Courtauld. She was part of the famous Courtauld dynasty, being daughter of George and Susanna Courtauld, and became one of the very few women of World War I to have undergone professional training in medicine in the years beforehand. By 1901, she had qualified as a nurse, but in spite of almost insurmountable obstacles at that time she set her sights on qualifying as a surgeon, and trained as such at the Royal Free Hospital. Once her training was complete, she had to travel to Brussels to obtain her degree as there had never been a degree awarded to a woman in England up until that time.

Just before World War I broke out, she returned to Europe from India to serve in the Scottish women's advance field hospitals in France and Serbia. She was awarded both the Croix de Guerre and the Legion d'Honneur for operating on patients by the light of just one candle whilst under constant shellfire from the enemy[ccclviii].

* * * * * *

The end of the war in 1919 (the Armistice occurred in 1918) left a greatly changed and battle-scarred European continent, but with the arrival of 'peace' so the nations of Europe began trying to rebuild themselves, albeit with some having to accept altered borders and reductions in territory upon the implementation of the peace settlement. Those that had survived the conflict now returned to their homeland, cherishing the hope that never again would there be such a war; indeed, the conflict was at one time famously known as *'The War to End all Wars'*.

Tentative negotiations were even undertaken in 1927 to outlaw war itself, leading to the Kellogg-Briand Pact[316] being signed in Paris on 27 August 1928 initially by the representatives of 15

[ccclviii] Finch, K., *Great War Women of Huguenot Ancestry.* The Huguenot Society Proceedings, Vol XXX (2016) p552.

nations including France, Germany, Great Britain and the United States[317], with all expressing a willingness to prevent further wars and acts of aggression. Looking back, we know this pact was doomed to failure, but at the time it was a new method of trying to maintain peace internationally, and was arguably one which could have worked if all major nations had signed up to its principles.

Huguenot descendants might well have considered this rather forward-thinking strategy a great benevolent leap towards a more tolerant international society – an ideal their ancestors would surely have wholeheartedly embraced.

- 31 -

To the end of the 20th Century

The 1920s gave way to the 1930s, and it was during 1936 that a carpenter made a rare and historically invaluable discovery inside a warehouse in Cutler Street, east London. The warehouse was being refurbished and as the workman began to remove an old window sill he noticed a piece of decaying, screwed up paper fall to the floor. He stared down at the wrinkled ball then slowly bent over, picked it up and carefully began to unfold and smooth it out. To his amazement, he realised he was staring at a song that had been written many, many years earlier – 120 years, in fact. The composer was none other than James Rondeau[318]; his composition had been published and sold by T. Evans of 79 Long Lane[ccclix]. The song's title was *The Failure of the Bill against the Weavers*. At the time that James had written this song, the dire conditions in which many of the silk weavers now had to exist was under discussion by Parliament. The Act of 1773 that had been expected to protect the silk weavers was, in truth, having the reverse effect. The Act was finally repealed in 1824, but the song has an historic resonance that needs to be included to give a flavour of the conditions of that era; how fortunate we are that this carpenter chose to satisfy his curiosity by unfolding that piece of historical paper:

[ccclix] The Rondeau Archives.

The Story of the Huguenots – a Unique Legacy

Brother weavers, cease singing, one moment, sit still
While I move for to leave to bring in a new bill.
Read it over I beg, o'er you drink the next glass,
If it meets not your sanction, why, don't let it pass!
With a fol de rol de, &c.

The chief prop of our nation was nearly thrown down
By they foes to humanity, country and Crown,
Who (shame on their heads) this base Act would have made
To import foreign goods and destroy our home trade.
But they are all Fools, fol de rol de, &c.

Much concern, care and trouble this bill caused us all,
Our hopes, like the stocks would now rise, and now fall.
And tho' every exertion was used in our power,
The case still hung doubtfull our fate seem'd to lower.

At length we found friends to espouse our just cause,
The chief of whom CURTIS still claims our applause,
Who in more than one instance has proved our real friend,
May his memory be blest, and his praise know no end.

Tho' our foes were full crafty, and those not a few,
Yet their vain endeavours they found would not do
For their sorrowful leader no more could be seen,
He'd slip'd slyly home, to old Bethnal Green

Now thank God and good friends, we have gained this just cause,
let none henceforth date to infringe weavers' laws!
None more quiet than us if they let us alone,
But rob us of our Rights and we're up every one!

The Story of the Huguenots – a Unique Legacy

Come fill up a bumper quick, quick let it pass
And Raise your brave spirits by each flowing glass,
The toast shall be this "as we have conquered to day,
Nay conquer for ever, huzza boys huzza!"[ccclx]

The reference in this poem to 'Curtis' points to Sir William Curtis, who brought to Parliament's attention the sad plight of the silk weavers whom he considered to be a most valuable and industrious body of men, and who were exceedingly alarmed at the apparently open-door policy of encouraging the importation of manufactured silk handkerchiefs from India[ccclxi].

* * * * * *

Not long after the discovery of this historic poem, war clouds were again gathering over Europe as History repeated itself once more when the Treaty of Versailles was challenged and then flouted by a new leader of a Germany anxious to recover lost territories and acquire new living space in the vastness of the Soviet Union. The challenge was met with an ultimatum, which was in turn ignored and defied, becoming the spark leading to another world war. As in the previous conflict, the vast numbers of people called upon to fight for their country included some who were knowingly of Huguenot descent.

In France, many Protestant families who had been forced until at least the Act of Toleration to profess the Catholic faith had passed down precious family stories to their descendants, and it was those descendants of fighting age in 1939 who now took up the banner of righteousness. Whilst visiting the Aveyron valley in south west France in 2016, I learnt a little about the people in the villages of this beautiful valley and how many Huguenot families

---

[ccclx] The Rondeau Archives.
[ccclxi] W. Woodfall, *Parliamentary Register: In the course of the first session of the second Parliament 1803 (London, 1803) pp.224-5.*

- 353 -

The Story of the Huguenots – a Unique Legacy

had risked their own lives to protect and assist Jewish families fleeing persecution[319] in a number of areas across France.

There are many individual stories of bravery and compassion in occupied France during World War II, and no less than three villages have been given the prestigious award *Righteous Among The Nations* by Yad Vashem[320] for their determination to assist fellow human beings enduring persecution for their faith – in this case, simply because they were Jewish[ccclxii].

Two of these villages are Le Chambon-sur-Lignon in the Haute Loire in the western foothills of the Cévennes – the very area that had been so active with the brave defiance of the Protestant *Churches of the Desert,* and Dieulefit in the Drôme department, south-eastern France. Remembrance of those brave men and women of centuries earlier who had resisted and remained true to their beliefs led the predominantly Protestant townspeople of Le Chambon-sur-Lignon to follow the words of their pastor, André Trocmé, who urged his congregation on the day after the Franco-German Armistice of June 1940 to resist Nazi rule using *'the weapons of the spirit'*. Eventually, he and another pastor in the village, Édouard Theis, not only refused to sign the oath of loyalty required of them by Marshall Philippe Petain, they also declined to hand over a list of Jews in the area, stating that *'we do not know what a Jew is. We only know men[321]'*.

On his paternal side, Pastor Trocmé was of Huguenot descent. His father had raised all of his ten children along strict guidelines; he was often heard to expound to his children: *'If you always do your duty, then you will never make a mistake'*. The Trocmé children had been born and raised in eastern France in Saint Quentin, just 20 kilometres from the battlefield of the Somme; indeed, André had borne witness to the heavily bandaged and often mutilated soldiers in the town during World War I, so from an early age the harshness of war had dug deep into his psyche

---

ccclxii Chater, K., *The Legacy of the Huguenots in Wartime France.* The Huguenot Society Proceedings, Vol XXX (2014) p181.

The Story of the Huguenots – a Unique Legacy

committing him to a lifelong desire for peace, his pacifism having been reinforced through his friendship with a young soldier billeted with the family, who passed on his own views to the young and impressionable Trocmé[ccclxiii].

André Trocmé was appointed as the local pastor of Le Chambon in 1934 at the invitation of the local parish council. He and his Italian wife Magda and their four children soon settled into their new home[ccclxiv].

By the late 1930s, many communities were looking fearfully towards a very uncertain future, and when Germany launched its successful attack upon France and the Low Countries in May 1940, Pastor Trocmé wrote to a friend of his to ask if he could offer to assist the children in the internment camps; they arranged to meet in Marseille to discuss this idea further, whereupon it was suggested that the village of Le Chambon might be a good place to bring the children to.

Trocmé, assisted by a sympathetic network of individuals and groups, began to rapidly organise an emerging network of people into specific bands to provide shelter and support for the Jewish children. The groups were funded by organisations such as Cimade (Inter-Movement Committee for Evacuees)[ccclxv].

To begin with, the locals offered just passive resistance towards their German occupiers, and stories of dignified defiance pepper these years, such as that of Amélie, a churchwarden, who refused Pétain's order to ring the church bells, stating unequivocally that the bells at the temple were meant to be rung in praise of God and for no other reason[ccclxvi].

The ancient byways and half-forgotten tracks and trails across terrain earlier taken by Huguenots fleeing Louis XIV's

---

[ccclxiii] Caroline Moorehead, *Defying the Nazis in Vichy France* (London, 2015) p113.
[ccclxiv] Ibid, p112.
[ccclxv] Ibid, pp.124-5.
[ccclxvi] Chater, K., *The Legacy of the Huguenots in Wartime France.* The Huguenot Society Proceedings, Vol XXX (2014), p184.

Catholic forces of persecution were once again utilised. Local guides, whose Huguenot descendants had known similar persecution, now led Jewish refugees to places of greater safety, such as Switzerland. But it was not solely the descendants of Huguenots who felt a strong desire to resist the injustice directed towards the Jews, and an example of this should be included. Robert Bach, a Catholic, had been appointed Prefect of the Haute-Loire in June 1941 with his headquarters in Le Puy. Under the Vichy government the prefects were empowered with greater authority, and although Bach was an official of the Vichy government, that should not lead us to assume he approved of all they stood for – indeed, far from it. Whilst travelling around his 'department' he met Pastor Marcel Jennet, who told Bach: '*If, even in France, Jews were to be persecuted, the Protestants would say 'No'!'* Bach's reply was said to have been: '*M Le Pasteur, I am a Catholic, and I too would say 'No'![ccclxvii]*'

Countless Jewish children whose parents had been deported to Auschwitz via French internment camps were quietly collected by farmers and taken to sympathetic homes.

In 1942, the German army swept into the 'free' south of France, leading to fiercer and more urgent resistance by locals as they frantically tried to put as many Jews as possible out of their reach, mostly by means of false documentation[322] and a network of dedicated volunteers[ccclxviii].

But German officers and their men now moved into local hotels. They also ordered the local police to '*keep an eye on the Protestant circles whose memory of the wars of religion had left them attached to the notions of 'liberty and internationalism'.*

Refugees arriving in the area were impressed by the *esprit de frondeur* that united locals from all sections of society into various

---

[ccclxvii] Caroline Moorehead, *Defying the Nazis in Vichy France* (London, 2015), p134.
[ccclxviii] Ibid, p157.

The Story of the Huguenots – a Unique Legacy

forms of resistance. When Trocmé sent messages to people in the local bible study groups, they were usually on postcards with a picture of Marie Durand, who had been imprisoned in the Tour de Constance, Aigues-Mortes, for 38 years in the 17th century, and frequently his message would end with her word *'resister'* to emphasise his point.

Some Jewish children were so successfully concealed among local children that a group of battle-hardened German soldiers convalescing in the local hotels had no idea they were surrounded by Jews[ccclxix].

Both Protestants and Jews were scarred by the events they lived through. Yet, a number of those who carried out the incredibly risky work of saving Jewish young and old were not fortunate enough to survive the war. Some were captured and interned; others were tortured and beaten to death; the heroic village doctor, Le Forestier, who had given a clear message to potential army recruits following the newly instigated National Service law by stating unequivocally that no one should serve the Germans, was apprehended and shot. Despite all the threats issued by the German army, amazingly not one informer revealed the whereabouts of the hidden Jews nor the individuals within the network of their saviours.

Active opposition to Vichy government policy[323] was obviously fraught with immense danger to the local population, but by the end of the war families in Vichy France had actively helped 3,800 Jews to safety. No other region of France was able to assist so many, but this was an area of remote villages that had survived the Wars of Religion, and whose people had founded, through necessity, their own Protestant stronghold here in the 17th century – in this stark mountainous area that for part of each and every year was virtually inaccessible[ccclxx].

[ccclxix] Caroline Moorehead, *Defying the Nazis in Vichy France* (London, 2015), pp.166-7.
[ccclxx] Ibid, p112.

- 357 -

The Story of the Huguenots – a Unique Legacy

In Dieulefit, the leader of the network assisting the Jews was a young woman – Marguerite Soubreyran, a communist who was, ironically, from a local Protestant family[ccclxxi]. Dieulefit, unlike Le Chambon-sur-Lignon, was an industrial town with a long history of pottery as an industry rather than arable, and although its Protestant citizens were in a minority, it was nevertheless known as a Protestant stronghold.

In both towns, supporting the Jews required a great deal of fake documentation, such as identity cards, ration books and clothing coupons. The identity of some of the forgers in Le Chambon-sur-Lignon is known; for example Jacqueline Decourdemanche, the school secretary was blessed with the ability to produce beautiful copperplate script ideal for the eloquent signatures so adored by French officialdom, and ably assisted by Oscar Rosowsky, a young Jewish refugee who volunteered to help her and displayed a talent as a forger; using various pens, inks and tracing paper he began producing a wide variety of 'documents' all urgently needed by Jewish refugees[ccclxxii]. In Dieulefit the forger was 21-year-old Jeanne Barnier, the secretary of the local mayor. Marguerite Soubreyran had originally assigned the job to her, but Jeanne at first had hesitated before asking her local pastor, Henri Eberhard, for guidance. He advised her, as a good Protestant, to consult her bible for therein would lie the answer to her dilemma. She thereupon returned home and opened her bible, whereupon her eyes fell upon Isaiah 58: 6-7:

Loose the bands of wickedness, strip away the ties of servitude, free the oppressed, and that every kind of yoke is broken; share your bread with the hungry and bring into your house the unfortunate that have no shelter. If you see a

---

[ccclxxi] Chater, K., *The Legacy of the Huguenots in Wartime France.* The Huguenot Society Proceedings, Vol XXX (2014) p187.

[ccclxxii] Caroline Moorehead, *Defying the Nazis in Vichy France* (London, 2015) p161.

naked man cover him, and do not turn away from those like you. [ccclxxiii]

By 1940, the Catholic mayor of the town, Justin Jouve, felt he had to stand down from office as his conscience would not permit him to sign the Oath of Loyalty demanded by the Vichy government. His successor, the Protestant Colonel Pierre Pizot, did sign, but seems to have done so with the intention of ignoring the covert activities of his secretary Jeanne Barnier. Neither of them ever spoke of Jewish refugees, but on just one occasion he ordered Jeanne to leave, saying he had had enough of her. She left, taking with her the equipment used to produce forged documents, and travelled to her grandparents' home in nearby Bordeaux. She only stayed ten days before the Mayor recalled her[324].

Tacit approval was given by Catholics in Dieulefit of the activities of their Protestant neighbours. Although the local priest publicly advised his flock to obey the authorities, he never remarked on the activities of the local Catholic secondary school, La Roseraie, run by M and Mme Arcens – sympathisers of the plight of the Jews of whom they sheltered many in the school. Some of the Jewish adults were even employed to teach the children. It has to be said that without the Catholic population's silence, the successful network of people bravely assisting the Jews could not have flourished[ccclxxiv].

These courageous, stout-hearted people, mindful perhaps of how their persecuted ancestors had been aided by a number of Catholics, are thus today remembered with pride by ensuing generations, and rightly so too that they should have held out the hand of kindness and deliverance to people of another faith. France should be justly proud of her sons and daughters who risked their own and their families' and friends' lives in these dark times.

[ccclxxiii] Chater, K., *The Legacy of the Huguenots in Wartime France.* The Huguenot Society Proceedings, Vol XXX (2014) p187.
[ccclxxiv] Ibid, pp.186-9.

The Story of the Huguenots – a Unique Legacy

* * * * * *

Post-war Europe needed time to rise again from the ashes and carnage of a second global conflict in the space of just one generation. Gradually, countries again began to rebuild their war-torn communities and tentatively look forward with hope towards a better future.

Added to the human death toll of the conflict was the incredible scale of financial debt amidst extreme economic fragility. People of the time must have felt this acutely, and rationing of many essential products was to endure for years to come. And so, those same people must have longed for something that would lighten the national mood and lift the oppressively grey skies of war damage. In Great Britain, perhaps this came in the form of the coronation in 1953 of Queen Elizabeth II[325]. Yet most who have seen the film footage of the young queen on her stately progress along the aisle of Westminster Abbey are unaware that the silk of her coronation robes had been woven by Stephen Walters & Sons.

In 1720, a Huguenot refugee by the name of Joseph Walters founded the company at 25 Wilkes Street in Spitalfields. In the early 19th century, the company moved firstly to Bow Lane, just inside the City walls, and then to Finsbury, north London; expansion of the business resulted in leasing another building (in Braintree, Essex) followed by another factory, in Kettering, Northamptonshire, as well as mills in Suffolk from where it still produces the highest-quality silk.

In fact, Walters & Sons were contracted to make silk for two further royal occasions – the marriage of Princess Anne to Captain Mark Philips in 1973 and in 1981 the marriage of Prince Charles to Lady Diana Spencer. The company holds an extensive collection of books containing samples of all the beautiful silks they have produced over the centuries, and often the samples have detailed written information such as the name of the weaver, as

- 360 -

The Story of the Huguenots – a Unique Legacy

well as practical details of the methods used to produce each pattern.

1953 was also the year of another important Huguenot event – the foundation of the Huguenot Society of South Africa took place in March of that year.

Perhaps this is a good point on which to reflect on those early Huguenots who gave us so much. Surely, they would be proud not only of their own achievements but also those of their descendants, who continue in each generation to make significant social, economic and technological contributions, encompassing so many diverse areas of our lives.

- 32 -

Revolution and Recognition, Apology and the Future

The wheel of fortune turns inexorably, and invariably it is influenced by preceding events – thus the bitterly contested French Wars of Religion, the lasting tolerance sought in vain by the *Edict of Nantes,* and ultimately the cruel and uncompromising revocation of that proud edict can all be seen to have directly contributed to the French Revolution of 1789.

A wave of tolerance – relative to the hitherto prevailing levels of discrimination and authoritarianism – had swept across the country as early as 1764 as the tide of both populist and learned opinion began to turn following the horrific case of Jean Calas. Huguenots began to find themselves gradually becoming more accepted in French society; however, it was not until 29 November 1787 that the Revocation was formally annulled, with the signing by Louis XVI of the *Edict of Tolerance*[326]. This was achieved only through the passionate and determined efforts of many well-known public figures including the king's brother, the Comte d'Artois, but although it permitted both civic equality and freedom of worship, crucially it did not allow Protestants to establish their own church or to hold public services.

French nobleman Gilbert du Motier, Marquis de Lafayette, having newly returned from America after the War of

The Story of the Huguenots – a Unique Legacy

Independence, began to voice his support for the Huguenots, even seeking out the head of the Church of the Desert, Pastor Rabault Saint-Etienne, and arranging for him to meet with government minister Guillaume-Chrétien Malesherbes, well-known for his defiant sympathy for the Huguenots, and his strong opinions in favour of legalising civil marriages for Huguenots.

The *Edict of Tolerance* was born out of several papers prepared by various open-minded persons, but it was Minister Malesherbes who penned the paper relating to the civil status of those not of the Catholic faith – a non-religious wedding service would now be permitted before the king's judge or even the priest if he was serving as the local registrar; at the same time, births and deaths were also to be recorded by the person deemed the area registrar, irrespective of their religion.

Following the *Edict of Tolerance,* a great number of Huguenot families now chose to legalise their Church of the Desert marriages and children's births with the formality of registration by the area registrar. Yet this does not mean that all the limitations endured by Huguenots were suddenly swept away – they were definitely not. When Parlement formally registered the *Edict of Tolerance* on 29 January 1788, it did so with the notable caveat that Catholicism would remain the official religion of France, and that anyone not of the Catholic religion would still be barred from public service, and not allowed entry into the vocation of teaching.

If this enlightenment, or attempt at enlightenment, was meant to calm the virulent civil unrest arising from mounting anger at – and hatred of – the ruling classes in France, it was to prove too late. The old monarchic order, entrenched in the falsehood of the divine right of kings, and of its natural social superiority over all others, was to be swept away just 18 months later. The forever momentous day of 14 July 1789 heralded the start of the French Revolution with the storming of the Bastille – the beginning of a veritable storm surge of events that would continue for ten years

The Story of the Huguenots – a Unique Legacy

as radicals and revolutionaries sought to build a better, fairer France.

The wheel of fortune turned once more, and now it was the turn of many French Catholics to flee their homeland with little or nothing, just as many of their Huguenot counterparts had done in the 1680s. Ironically, amidst the chaos and bloodthirstiness of true revolution, a few were given help and comfort by Huguenot descendants.

Mary Magdalen Blaquiere, née Guyon, had lived comfortably for many years in Hampstead, Middlesex. Although her life was financially secure, she practised the virtue of economy in order to assist the less fortunate around her – in particular, these new arrivals from revolutionary France. She had sadly not been blessed with children, but her generous heart and her purse was readily opened to these émigrés.

An article in *The Times* newspaper reporting her death in 1805 observed:

> *...The numerous French emigrants who, during the Revolution, took up their residence in her neighbourhood, were particularly the objects of her kindness and commiseration. For those amongst them who had lost their all and were suffering under the united miseries of poverty and disease; her humanity was actively employed in providing such necessaries and comforts, as they were unable to procure for themselves...*[ccclxxv].

In France, on 27 August 1789, the *Declaration of the Rights of Man and of the Citizen* was signed declaring all French citizens equal in the eyes of the law. This important document, a compound of the basic reasons that had so inspired and led to the French Revolution itself, was contained within 17 articles legally enshrining the belief that '*all men are born and remain free and*

[ccclxxv] The Guion Archives.

equal in rights'. It was a first step towards preparing a constitution for France.

One year later, the French Government offered the right of return to all Huguenot descendants, with the promise of full French citizenship:

> *All persons born in a foreign country and descending in any degree of a French man or woman expatriated for religious reasons are declared French nationals and will benefit from rights attached to that quality if they come back to France, establish their domicile there and take the civil oath.*

For many Huguenot families, the resettling in a new country had given them a chance to start again, but often, as we have seen, future generations of some of these families would witness further migrations of family members, and so it is today that we are in a position of usually being able to discover the far-flung family trees of many of these families – and what a joy it is to embark on this voyage of discovery, reaching back into times past not knowing what we might unearth in our own families and possibly those of others. We must remember that, be they humble or great, they were – by virtue of their beliefs – hardworking and conscientious.

It appears that only a small number of French Protestants decided to accept this historic offer, although we shall never know for sure why, it certainly is a fact that many had already made a life for themselves and their families in a new country to the extent that they were content to remain where either they or their forefathers had settled. They had no doubt either been told of the horrors inflicted on their ancestors or experienced such horrors at first-hand, perhaps their ancestors experiences had engendered such fear that even a slight risk of anything remotely similar was too hideous to contemplate. A well-known phrase Huguenots had lived by during the dark days of persecution in France was *'help yourself and God will be with you'*. Considering how they embraced their new life wherever they settled, this seems the perfect maxim.

The reign of terror that had followed the storming of the Bastille was followed in 1790 by the National Constituent Assembly passing the *Civil Constitution of the Clergy*, which was designed to limit their powers by reorganising the Catholic Church of France, but this proved such a divisive policy that in 1793 it led to all churches and religious orders in France being forcibly closed down, and religious worship suppressed. Partly, this was attributed to a growing feeling that priests and tonsured clerics were surplus to requirements and that they did nothing to enhance the everyday lives of the working people of France.

In 1889, a slight modification was made to the original citizenship law for Huguenots with the formality of a decree as well as the oath.

The 1790 invitation to return to the homeland of their forefathers was to remain open until 1945, when, after over a century and a half, the French Government took the seemingly inexplicable decision to repeal the right to citizenship that had been offered to French Huguenot descendants returning to France. Probably, they felt the offer to be no longer relevant; after all, as so many years – and in some cases, generations – had passed by, the former Huguenots of France were now citizens of other countries to whom they felt their loyalties belonged and to whom they felt a profound gratitude. They knew, in most cases, that their distressed, dejected ancestors had been given succour by them at a time of great need.

It was Napoleon who instigated a thorough and comprehensive review of French laws[327], and in 1804 the first of these laws, eventually to be collectively known as the *Napoleonic Code*, was enshrined in French law. The most significant phrase within the 1804 civil code was the affirmation that *'every French person was equal before the law'*.

Protestant communities had also been heartened by the Concordant Napoleon had signed in 1802, which gave their

The Story of the Huguenots – a Unique Legacy

Church official recognition and permitted those of the Protestant faith to organise their own church affairs.

In 1806, the Protestants of Luneray in Normandy decided to build a new temple. The Consistory, led by Pastor Mordant, approved the construction, which took six years to complete. All the families of the church contributed either by donations of money or materials or simply their time. Within the records are details of both the donors and what materials they willingly gave, and how they raised through subscriptions some of the money needed for the project. The shortfall was raised in the form of a loan by members of the church, and within the list of sponsors can be found Jean Ouvry's signature, a French descendant of Jacques who had left France in 1681 for a new life in England. Currently, a photographic copy of the list can be seen in the Protestant temple in Luneray (the original document is kept safely preserved elsewhere)[ccclxxvi].

After such a huge effort, the enthusiasm and joy of the flock must have been immense, when, on 6 September 1812, the day of the dedication of their temple arrived. The Minutes of this event begin by praising Bonaparte, and recalling that:

This temple is intended to replace two rooms of prayers dedicated to this use since the edit of November 1787 and to revive the memory of that which existed in the town during the Revocation of L'Edit de Nantes.

Pastor Laurent also oversaw the opening of the first French Sunday school in Luneray in 1814[ccclxxvii].

Today, the thriving Protestant community in and around Luneray is testimony to the ties that bind the inhabitants of the area, and to the legacy of their forefathers who suffered so much in the cause of their beliefs, one of so many communities across France.

[ccclxxvi] Pierre Lheureux, *Les Protestants de Luneray et leur Église en pays de Caux*, (Luneray, 1937) pp.50-51.
[ccclxxvii] Ibid, p52.

The Story of the Huguenots – a Unique Legacy

In 1852 in Paris, an important society was founded – the French Protestant Society; the founders' objectives were to search out and gather all published and unpublished papers as well as other documents of the French Protestant Church in order to study them and make the information known publicly. They were so successful that by 1866 they were able to open their own library, and since the Society's inception it has worked tirelessly to encourage genealogical research together with maintaining the memory of the Huguenots.

Yet it was not until 1905 that the French Government finally made the momentous leap towards a modern state by dividing Church and State, thus reversing the infamous words of Louis XIV: *'une foi, un loi, un roi'*. The French monarchy had been abolished back in 1792, but the State and Church had remained as one despite numerous attempts in the ensuing years to change this.

And the 1905 division had itself taken a lengthy time to become reality. 1901 saw the first tentative steps towards the eventual split, with the inception of the law guaranteeing *'freedom of association'* and a limiting of religious influence on education. In 1902, the first draft of a law to separate Church and State was prepared, but there was a great deal of dissent from all interested parties leading to delay and stalemate until three years later when a series of passionate debates had begun – in fact, between March and July of that year no less than 48 very lengthy, drawn out sessions had taken place with heated arguments for and against the divorce of Church and State. Even after 'agreement' was reached with the Council so that the bill could progress to the Senate, a further 21 sessions during November and early December took place before the Law of Separation was ultimately passed on 9 December 1905, embracing 44 Articles within six headings each of which dealt with a specific area of division. For example, and rather tellingly, within Article 1 it states: *'The Republic ensures freedom of conscience. It guarantees freedom of worship limited only by the following rules in the interest of public order...'*

The principal act of separation is contained in Article 2, with the words:

The Republic neither acknowledges, nor pays for nor subsidises any form of worship. Consequently, from 1 January on, after the present law has been publicised, all spending related to worship will be eliminated from the budgets of the State and localities. However, expenses related to chaplaincy and destined to assure the freedom of worship in public education, secondary and primary schools, homes, asylums and prisons, can be presented in the aforementioned budgets.

This Act annulled two earlier Articles of 1801 and 1802, which had given the Church financial support from the State; now, however, all churches were expected to be self-supporting. Within the remaining 42 Articles of the Law of Separation can be found provision for a wide range of legally phrased concepts applying to all areas of religion, and to all religions in the land.

It had taken 220 years from Louis XIV's revocation of the *Edict of Nantes* for this momentous step to be taken, but of course not everyone was delighted – Pope Pious X (1903-14) condemned the law, forbidding Catholics to initiate worship associations, hence the reason why for a few years, most churches built before 1905 became the property of communes, while cathedrals were retained as State property.

Today, the 1905 law is an idiosyncrasy within the European Union because in all other member states the Church is not restricted to the area of worship but is also permitted to plan and carry out social events.

As these momentous changes began to take effect, so The Cult Association of the Reformed Church of Toulouse, noting the relaxing of attitudes towards Huguenots, decided in 1908 to buy the old Treasury of Toulouse[328]. By then, the building was in a bad state of repair. The work to repair and transform the building into a

The Story of the Huguenots – a Unique Legacy

fitting place of worship for Protestants began in 1909 and took two years to complete. Today, the Temple du Salin is one of the most important Protestant buildings in Toulouse.

* * * * * *

In 1985, the United Kingdom commemorated the tercentenary of the revocation of the *Edict of Nantes* with a special service held at St Paul's Cathedral, London, which was well attended by many Huguenot descendants, including David Guyon whose ancestor Guillaume had walked from Montpellier to Geneva to escape persecution and whose grandfather had fought and died at the Battle of the Somme in 1916.

On 6 October 1985, another celebration – a thanksgiving service conducted partly in French – was held at Saint Brelade's, Jersey, and amongst the congregation that day were descendants of those Huguenots who had fled to the Channel Islands. The congregation was reminded during the service that the Jersey Calvinist Church had been founded in the reign of Elizabeth I, and that later Calvinist churches in England had been fashioned from the ideals of this first one; in fact, two Jerseymen of Huguenot descent, Jean Durell and Richard Dumaresq, later became ministers of the Savoy French Church in London[ccclxxviii].

In the meantime, on the other side of the English Channel, or La Manche, during a speech in the same month of that year, President François Mitterrand gave a formal, national apology to all descendants of Huguenots around the world. At the same time, a special postage stamp was released in their honour. The stamp confirms that France **is** the home of the Huguenots: *Accueil des Huguenots*. Finally, their rights were officially fully recognised.

* * * * * *

[ccclxxviii] Syvret, Marguerite. *Huguenot Heritage: 1685-1985. Annual Bulletin of the Société Jersiaise*, vol. 24 (1986) pp.179-81.

The Story of the Huguenots – a Unique Legacy

100 years earlier in the United Kingdom, the directors of the French Hospital had created a society to promote the publication and interchange of knowledge about the Huguenots. The original Huguenot Society of London has since been renamed The Huguenot Society of Great Britain and Ireland, its aim being to form a bond of fellowship amongst those who respect and admire the Huguenots, and who seek to perpetuate their memory. Without a shadow of a doubt, the Huguenots were the one group of people who helped in so many ways to make Britain 'Great'.

Spitalfields is a unique part of London that even today retains a certain charm and 'continental' air about it. During World War II, it too was bombed, and a number of beautiful Huguenot houses in the area were lost to posterity; more still were tragically demolished post-war to expand the Spitalfields Fruit & Vegetable Market. Fortunately, not everyone applauded this self-inflicted destruction, and so in 1976 a group of conservation enthusiasts, inspired by Dr Mark Girouard, founded the Spitalfields Historic Buildings Trust. They successfully lobbied for the remaining Huguenot houses[329] to be preserved, and for the market to be transferred to outer London. We owe them an immense debt, for without their foresight and courageous stance, many – perhaps all – of these precious buildings would have been razed to the ground, inexorably altering the area of Spitalfields. As it is, present and future generations can still enjoy a distinctive and very special part of London, but perhaps they should remember that such valiant preservation was hard-fought and extremely hard-won.

The wooden spools that you see hanging today outside some of the fine dwellings in the streets of Spitalfields indicate houses which were once inhabited by Huguenot weavers. These symbols were placed there in 1985 in commemoration of the tercentenary of the revocation of the *Edict of Nantes*, which brought many Huguenots to London.

Links of friendship and ties of blood are still being forged in modern times. A descendant of the English Agombar family paid

- 371 -

The Story of the Huguenots – a Unique Legacy

a visit to a French village in Picardy – Brancourt Le Grand – where his ancestors had once lived, and, during this visit, he met a woman whose mother's maiden name had been Agombar[330]. The two families were able to piece together, their considerable shared family heritage, thus proving that even 500 years later the history of these remarkable people, the Huguenots, is still being written and revisited by many, curious to know their own heritage[ccclxxix].

The Huguenot Society of Australia was founded in 2003, bringing Huguenot descendants together in that part of the world to research and celebrate the Huguenot families who settled there.

When the Huguenots first arrived in England during Henry VIII's reign, the kingdom had been mostly arable with just fledgling industries located mainly within larger towns, or cottage industries where families produced a variety of goods by hand. During the period 1760-1840, the descendants of those early Huguenot refugees were at the forefront of forging new methods of wealth enabling Britain to take her place on the world stage through such energy of enterprise and rapidly developing technologies.

* * * * * *

The Huguenots' story is a rich and varied one, and undoubtedly deserves continued recognition. 2014 saw the establishment of the first, and so far, the only, dedicated Huguenot museum in the United Kingdom. Based at Rochester in Kent, it is a window on the lives of the refugees who came here – and to whom we are immensely grateful.

The year 2017 was an important one in the Protestant calendar as it contained monthly celebrations of the 500th anniversary since the Reformation began with the previously described brave act of

---

[ccclxxix] The Agombar Archives.

- 372 -

The Story of the Huguenots – a Unique Legacy

Martin Luther; in honour of this momentous event, a Service of Thanksgiving was held at the French Protestant Church in Soho on 10 June 2017, where once again numerous Huguenot descendants, such as David Guyon (Guion), Stanley Rondeau, Victorine Martineau and Mimi Romilly – all of whose ancestors' stories, along with many others, have featured in this book – gathered together to listen to the pastor speak before hearing a discussion of rich Huguenot history; all perhaps unconsciously taking part in the living chronicle that embodies all Huguenot descendants and hopefully will continue to do so down the centuries.

Notably, among those participating were Catholics, who have recently chosen to come to live and work in London – a continuation of our interwoven history – and long may this cycle endure in both faiths and in both nations. Similar services were held throughout the year across Europe and beyond, including numerous towns and villages throughout France, and amongst those celebrating this important anniversary was the little temple at Luneray, like numerous others rebuilt as a testimony to their faith, endurance and beliefs.

A further significant anniversary, this time in 2018, will be the 300th anniversary of the founding of the French Hospital. Both these anniversaries prove a fortitude and durability of faith and charity by Huguenots.

John Calvin wrote on the first page of the first edition of the *Psalms*[ccclxxx] something that is as relevant now as it was then:

> *Dans les temps difficiles, que nous traversons, il est du devoir de tous les Evangéliques de se tendre la main, de erséverer avec courage dans la tâche, qui leur a été confié et s'il est necessaire, de rester seul avec Dieu*[331]

Throughout this book there have been references to either side of the religious divide holding out the hand of friendship towards

---

[ccclxxx] Privat, E.C., *The Huguenots in Germany*. The Huguenot Society, Vol. XXI No2 (1966), p118.

The Story of the Huguenots – a Unique Legacy

their fellow man often at great risk to their own personal safety. Whatever your religious beliefs, perhaps this is best summed up by those words from the Bible that inspired André Trocmé during the dark days of World War II, and which are still as true today, from Galatians 3:28: *'There is no longer Jew or Greek, there is no longer man or woman for you are one in Jesus Christ'*.

Appendices

1. The Edict of Nantes

Including its secret Articles and Brevets

Translated by Jotham Parsons
The French text consulted was that printed as appendix IV to Roland Mousnier, L'assassinat d'Henri IV (14 mai 1610) et l'affermissement de la monarchic absolue (Paris: N. R.F./Gallimard, 1964), 294-335.
The full text by kind permission of the Huguenot Museum of Germany.

Henri, by the Grace of God, King of France and Navarre, to all present and future, greeting. Among the infinite graces which it has pleased God to bestow on us, this is certainly one of the most notable and remarkable: to have given us virtue and strength to withstand the frightful troubles, confusions, and disorders which prevailed at our accession to this kingdom, which was divided into so many parties and factions, of which that which supported the legitimate government was the smallest; and nevertheless to so have strengthened us against this difficulty, that we have at length surmounted it, and have now reached a harbour of safety and repose for this state. For which to Him alone be all the glory, and to us the grace and obligation, that He has deigned to make use of our labour to accomplish this good work, in which He has been visible to all; if we have borne not only what was within our duty and ability, but something more besides, which might not have been at any other time proper to the dignity we hold, we are no longer afraid of exposing it here, seeing that we have so often and so freely exposed our own life. And in this great concurrence of such great and perilous affairs, which could not all be settled at one and the same time, it has been necessary for us to follow this order: first, to undertake those things which could only be settled by force, and rather to suspend and put aside for a time all other things which could and should be dealt with by reason and justice: such as the general differences among our good subjects, and the particular ills of the more healthy parts of the state, which we believed could be much more easily cured after their principal cause had been removed, namely, the continuance of civil war. In which having (by the grace of God) well and

The Story of the Huguenots – a Unique Legacy

happily succeeded, and armed conflict and hostilities having ceased throughout the interior of the kingdom, we hope for equal success in what remains to be settled, and that by this means we shall attain to the establishment of a good peace and tranquil repose for which we have always hoped and prayed, and which is the reward that we desire for the many pains and travails through which we have passed in the course of our life. Among the above-mentioned affairs which have required patience, and among the most important, have been the complaints we have received from many of our Catholic provinces and cities, that the exercise of the Catholic religion was not universally re-established as is stipulated by the edicts hitherto made for the pacification of troubles on account of religion; as well as the supplications and remonstrances which have been made to us by our subjects of the so-called Reformed religion, both in regard to the non-fulfilment of what has been granted them by these edicts, and in regard to what they wished to be added to them for the practice of their above-mentioned religion, liberty of conscience, and the safety of their persons and property; presuming themselves to have just cause for new and yet greater fears because of these latest troubles and disturbances, whose principal pretext and foundation have been their ruin. In regard to which, so as not to take on too much at one time, and also so that the rage of war might not prevent the establishment of the laws, however good they might be, we have always put off seeing to this from one time to another. But now that it has pleased God to have us enjoy a beginning of rather better repose, we could think of no better way to use it than to apply ourselves to what might concern His holy name and service, and to bring it about that He should be worshiped and adored by all our subjects; and if it has not yet pleased Him that this should be by one and the same form of religion, then it should at least be with the same intention, and under such a rule that there should arise no tumult and disturbance on account of it among them, and that we and this kingdom may forever merit and preserve the title of Most Christian, which has been held for so long and for such merits; and by the same means to take away the cause of evil and trouble which may arise on account of religion, which is always the most subtle and penetrating of all troubles. On this occasion, having recognized the affair as one of very great importance and worthy of the very greatest consideration, after receiving the collections of complaints of our Catholic subjects and having also permitted our subjects of the so-called Reformed religion to assemble by deputies and draw up their own, and to bring together all of their remonstrances, and having conferred with them at different times on this matter, and having reviewed the preceding edicts, we have thought it necessary, at this time, to give to all our subjects a general law on all of this, clear, precise, and absolute, by which they might be governed with regard to all such differences as have hitherto sprung up, or may hereafter arise among them, and by which both sides may be contented insofar as the spirit of

The Story of the Huguenots – a Unique Legacy

the times will permit. Having, for our part, entered on this deliberation only through the zeal we have for the service of God, and so that such service may be offered and rendered by all our subjects, and to establish among them a good and most lasting peace; for which we implore and expect from His divine goodness the same protection and favour that He has always visibly bestowed on this kingdom from its birth, and through the entire, long period which it has attained; and that He may give our subjects the grace to understand well that in the observance of this ordinance consists (next to their duty towards God and towards all) the principal foundation of their union, concord, tranquillity, and repose, and of the re-establishment of this whole state in its first splendour, opulence, and strength. For our part, we promise to see that it is strictly observed without allowing it to be infringed in any way. For these reasons, having, with the advice of the Princes of our Blood, other princes and officers of the crown, and other great and notable personages of our Council of State close to our person, well and diligently weighed and considered the entire affair, we have, by this perpetual and irrevocable Edict, said, declared, and ordered, do say, declare, and order:

1. First, that the memory of everything which has occurred between one side and the other since the beginning of the month of March 1585 up to our accession to the crown, and during the other preceding troubles and on account of them, shall remain extinct and dormant as though they had never happened. And it shall not be allowable or permissible to our *procureurs-generaux*, or any other person whatever, public or private, at any time, or for whatever occasion there may be, to make mention of them, or institute a suit or prosecution in any courts or jurisdiction whatsoever.

2. We forbid all our subjects, of whatever estate or quality they may be, from renewing the memory of those things, attacking, resenting, injuring, or provoking one another by reproaches for what has occurred, for whatever cause and pretext there may be; from disputing these things, contesting, quarrelling, or outraging or offending by word or deed; but they shall restrain themselves and live peaceably together like brothers, friends, and common citizens, under the penalty of being punished as infractors of the peace and disturbers of the public repose.

3. We command that the Roman, Catholic, and Apostolic religion shall be reinstated and re-established in all places and parts of this our kingdom and the lands under our obedience where its exercise has been interrupted, that it may be peaceably and freely exercised without any disturbance or impediment. Expressly forbidding every person of whatever estate, quality, or condition they may be, under the above-mentioned penalties, from troubling, disturbing, or molesting ecclesiastics in the celebration of divine service, in the enjoyment and

collection of the tithes, fruits, and revenues of their benefices, and all other rights and duties belonging to them; and that all those who have taken possession of churches, houses, goods, and revenues belonging to the said ecclesiastics during the troubles, and who still hold and occupy them, place the ecclesiastics back in full possession and quiet enjoyment thereof, with such rights, liberties, and security as they had before they were dispossessed. Also, expressly forbidding those of the said so-called Reformed religion from preaching or otherwise exercising that religion in the churches, houses, and habitations of the said ecclesiastics.

4. The said ecclesiastics will have the choice of purchasing the houses and buildings built on un-consecrated land occupied against them during the troubles, or of constraining the possessors of the said buildings to purchase the ground, all according to a valuation made by experts agreed on by the parties; and if the parties cannot agree on them, they shall be appointed by the local judges, preserving to the said possessors all appropriate legal recourse. And if the said ecclesiastics constrain the holders to purchase the ground, the sum agreed on shall not be paid immediately to them, but the holders shall continue to owe it, paying interest at the rate of five percent, until it can be employed to the profit of the [Catholic]Church, which shall be done within one year. And when the said time shall have elapsed, should the acquirer [sic; the seller seems in fact to be meant] be unwilling to continue the said rent, he shall be discharged therefrom by consigning the moneys into the hands of a solvent person with the consent of the judges. In the case of consecrated land, commissioners appointed for the execution of the present edict will give an opinion, so that we may settle the matter.

5. Nevertheless, the land and sites occupied for repairs and fortifications of the cities and places of our kingdom, and the materials used therein, shall not be taken possession of or resold by the ecclesiastics or other persons, either public or private, unless the said repairs and fortifications shall be demolished by our ordinances.

6. And to leave no occasion for troubles and differences among our subjects, we have permitted and do permit those of the so-called Reformed religion to live and dwell in all cities and places of this our kingdom and the lands of our obedience, without being questioned, vexed, or molested, nor constrained to do anything with regard to religion contrary to their conscience, nor on account of it to be searched out in their houses and the places where they wish to dwell, bearing themselves otherwise according to what is in our present edict.

7. We have also given permission to all lords, gentlemen, and other persons, citizens or otherwise, who profess the so-called Reformed religion and have the right of high justice within our kingdom and country, under our authority, or a full fief with military service *[plein fief de haubert]* (as in Normandy) whether

The Story of the Huguenots – a Unique Legacy

as property or usufruct, in whole or half, or one third, to have, in such of their houses of the said high justice or said fiefs as they shall hold themselves ready to name as their principal domicile before our *baillis* or *senechaux*, each in his district, to exercise the said religion as long as they reside therein, or in their absence their wives, their families, or a part thereof. And even if the title of either justice or of full fief with military service should be disputed, the exercise of the said religion may still be undertaken there provided the above-mentioned persons have actual possession of the said high justice as long as our *procureur-general* is a party to the dispute. We also permit them the said exercise in their other houses with high justice or the said full fief with military service as long as they are actually present and not otherwise, both for themselves, their family, their subjects, and others who wish to attend.

8. In the houses of fiefs where those of the said religion shall not hold high justice or full fief with military service, they may not undertake the said exercise except strictly for their families alone. Nevertheless, we do not mean that, should up to thirty persons congregate there, either on occasion of a baptism, or of a visit from friends, or otherwise, that they may be searched out; provided, also, that said houses are not within cities, towns, or villages belonging to Catholic lords exercising high justice (other than ourself) in which the said Catholic lords have their houses. In that case those of the said religion may not undertake the said exercise in cities, towns, or villages except by the permission and consent of the said lords holding high justice, and not otherwise.

9. We also permit those of the said religion to undertake and continue its exercise in all towns and places of our obedience where it had been established by them, and publicly performed at several different times, in the year 1586, and in the year 1587, until the end of the month of August, notwithstanding all decisions and judgments to the contrary.

10. Likewise the said worship shall be established and re-established in all villages and places where it has been or should have been established by the Edict of Pacification made in the year [15]77, by private articles and the conferences of Nerac and Fleix, without the said establishment being hindered in the places and locations of the domain specified by that edict, articles, and conferences, as places for *bailliages*, or which shall be hereafter, even if they have since been alienated to Catholic persons, or shall be hereafter. We do not intend, however, that the said exercise may be re-established in places and locations of the said domain which were formerly possessed by persons of the so-called Reformed religion in which it might have been allowed for personal consideration, or on account of the privileges of their fiefs, if the said fiefs are at present in the possession of persons of the said Roman, Catholic, and Apostolic religion.

The Story of the Huguenots – a Unique Legacy

11. In addition, each of the old *bailliages, senechaussees*, and governments holding, the place of *bailliages*, which are simply and without an intermediate instance under the jurisdiction of the courts of Parlement, we order that in the suburbs of one city, other than those which have been granted to them by the said edict, private articles, and conferences, and where there are no cities, in a small town or village, the exercise of the said so-called Reformed religion may be made publicly by all those who may wish to go there, even though in the said bailliages, senechaussees, and governments there may be several places in which the said exercise may be at present established; the cities in which there is an archbishopric or bishopric are excluded and excepted for the said place in each *bailliage* newly granted by the present edict, although the members of the said so-called Reformed religion shall nevertheless not be prevented from requesting and naming as the place of the said exercise small towns and villages close to the said cities, excepting also the places and lordships belonging to ecclesiastics, in which we must not be understood as allowing the said place of the *bailliage* to be established, these being excepted and reserved by special grace. We wish and understand, under the name of old *bailliages*, to speak to those which in the time of the late King Henri, our most honoured lord and father-in-law, were held as *bailliages, senechaussees*, and governments falling without intermediary under the jurisdiction of our said courts.

12. We do not intend by the present edict to derogate from the edicts and agreements formerly made for the submission of any princes, lords, gentlemen, and Catholic cities of our obedience in what concerns the exercise of the said religion; which edicts and agreements shall be kept and observed in regard to this matter as shall be determined by the instructions of the commissioners who shall be appointed for the execution of the present edict.

13. We expressly forbid all persons of the said religion from making any exercise of it, either of ministry, regulation, discipline, or public instruction of children, and any other kind, in this our kingdom and in the lands of our obedience, in what concerns religion, except in those places permitted and granted in the present edict.

14. And also from performing any public exercise of the said religion in our court and train, and also in our lands and countries which are beyond the mountains [in Italy], and also in our city of Paris, nor within five leagues of the said city; nevertheless, the members of the said religion, dwelling in the said lands and countries beyond the mountains and in our said city and within five leagues around it, shall not be searched out in their homes, nor be compelled to do anything in regard to their religion contrary to their conscience, comporting themselves otherwise according to what is contained in the present edict.

- 380 -

The Story of the Huguenots – a Unique Legacy

15. Nor may a public exercise of the said religion be made in the armies, except at the quarters of the leaders who shall make profession of it, always excepting the quarter where the lodging of our person will be found.

16. In accord with the twelfth article of the Conference of Nerac, we permit those of the said religion to build places for the exercise of it in the towns and locations where it has been granted them, and those which they have hitherto built shall be restored to them, or the sites of them, in such state as they may be at present, even in those places where the exercise of their worship is not allowed, except where they have been changed into other kinds of buildings. In that case there shall be given to them, by the possessors of the said buildings, places and locations of the same price and value which they had before they were built on, or a just estimation thereof according to the word of experts; reserving to the said possessors and proprietors all appropriate legal recourse.

17. We forbid all preachers, readers, and others who speak in public from using any words, discourses, and terms tending to excite the people to sedition; rather we have enjoined and do enjoin them to contain themselves and carry themselves modestly and to say nothing which is not to the edification and instruction of their listeners and for the maintenance of the repose and tranquillity which we have established in our said kingdom, under the penalties provided in preceding edicts. We expressly enjoin our *procureurs-generaux* and their substitutes to bring cases against those who violate them, under pain of answering in their own private persons, and of privation of their offices.

18. We also forbid all other subjects, of whatever quality or condition they may be, from bearing away children of the said religion by force or persuasion against the will of their parents, in order to have them baptized or confirmed in the Roman, Catholic, and Apostolic Church. The same prohibitions are made to members of the so-called Reformed religion, under pain of exemplary punishment.

19. Those of the said so-called Reformed religion shall in no way be constrained nor continue to be obligated by abjurations, promises, and oaths that they have formerly made, or sureties given by them, with regard to the said religion, and they shall not be molested or disturbed on account of these in any manner whatsoever.

20. They shall be required to keep and observe the feasts prescribed in the Roman, Catholic, and Apostolic Church and shall not work, sell, or open their shops on those days; neither shall artisans work outside their shops and in closed rooms and houses, on the said feast days, and other forbidden days, at any trade the noise of which can be heard outside by passers-by or neighbours. Nevertheless, no search shall be made except by the officers of justice.

21. Books concerning the said so-called Reformed religion may not be printed and sold publicly except in the cities and places where the public exercise of the

said religion is permitted. And as for other books which shall be printed in other cities, they shall be viewed and inspected both by our officers and by theologians, as it is specified in our ordinances. We very expressly forbid the printing, publication, and sale of all defamatory books, libels, and writings, under the penalties contained in our ordinances, enjoining all our judges and officers to carry this out.

22. We order that there shall be no difference or distinction made with regard to the said religion in receiving students to be instructed in the universities, colleges, and schools, as well as for the sick and poor in hospitals, sickhouses, and public charities.

23. Those of the so-called Reformed religion shall be required to keep the laws of the Roman, Catholic, and Apostolic Church received in this our kingdom with regard to degrees of consanguinity and affinity in marriages which have been and shall be contracted.

24. Likewise, the members of the said religion shall pay the entrance fees, as is customary, for the charges and offices which they shall be granted, without being required to attend any ceremonies contrary to their said religion; and when they are called to be sworn, they shall only be required to raise their hand and to swear and promise to God that they will tell the truth. Nor shall they be required to obtain dispensation for the oath which they offer in undertaking contracts and obligations.

25. We wish and order that all members of the said so-called Reformed religion and others who have followed their party, of whatever estate, quality, or condition they may be, should be obliged and constrained by all due and reasonable means, and under the penalties contained in the edicts, to pay and discharge tithes to the curates and other ecclesiastics, and to all others to whom they may belong, according to local usage and custom.

26. Disinheritance or dispossession made solely out of hatred or concern for religion, either by arrangement among the living or by testament, shall not be accepted among our subjects either for the past or for the future.

27. In order to reunite the wills of our subjects all the better, as is our intention, and to remove all occasion for complaint, we declare all those making profession of the said so-called Reformed religion capable of holding and exercising all estates, dignities, offices, and public charges whatsoever, royal, seigniorial, or in the cities of our said kingdom, lands, estates, and seigniorships of our obedience, notwithstanding all oaths contrary to this, and to be admitted and received into them without prejudice; and our courts of Parlement and other judges will content themselves with informing themselves and inquiring into the lives, morals, religion, and respectable conduct of those of both religions who shall be provided with offices, without taking from them any oath other than to serve the king well and faithfully in the exercise of their charges and to keep the

ordinances, as has been done for all time. Also, when the said estates, charges, and offices become vacant, for those of which we dispose we shall distribute them indifferently and without distinction to capable persons, as a matter which regards the union of our subjects. We also understand that those of the said so-called Reformed religion may be admitted and received into all counsels, deliberations, assemblies, and functions which are involved in the above-mentioned positions, nor may they be excluded from them or prevented from their enjoyment on account of the said religion.

28. We order, in regard to the burial of the dead of those of the said religion in all the cities and places of this kingdom, that there be promptly provided the most commodious space possible in each place by our officers and magistrates and by the commissioners we shall appoint for the execution of the present edict. And the cemeteries which they have formerly had, and of which they have been deprived on occasion of the troubles, shall be returned to them unless they are at present occupied by structures and buildings of whatever sort, in which case others shall be provided to them free of charge.

29. We expressly command our said officers to see to it that no scandal is committed at the said burials; and they shall be required to provide the members of the said religion a commodious place for the said burials within fifteen days after the requisition which will be made, without putting it off or engaging in delays, under penalty of a fine of five hundred ecus to be paid in their own private persons. It is also forbidden for the said officers, as well as all others, to charge anything for the transport of these dead bodies, under the penalties prescribed for embezzlement.

30. So that justice may be given and administered to our subjects without any suspicion, hatred, or favour, as being one of the principal means of maintaining them in peace and concord, we have ordered and do order that there shall be established a chamber in our court of Parlement of Paris, composed of a president and sixteen councillors of the said Parlement, which shall be named and entitled the Chamber of the Edict [*chambre de l'edit*], and shall have cognizance not only of the cases and suits of those of the so-called Reformed religion who shall be within the jurisdiction of the said court; but also from the territories of our Parlements of Normandy and Brittany, according to the jurisdiction which shall be assigned to them by this edict below, and until a chamber shall be established in each of the said parlements to render justice in that place. We also order that in the four offices of councillors in our said Parlement remaining from the last enlargement made by us, there shall shortly be presented and received to this Parlement, four sufficient and capable persons of the so-called Reformed religion, who shall be distributed as follows: the first to be appointed to the said Chamber of the Edict, and the other three, as they shall be selected, to three of the Chambers of Inquests [*chambres des enquetes*].

The Story of the Huguenots – a Unique Legacy

Moreover, the first two offices of lay councillors of said court which shall become vacant by death shall also be filled by two persons of the said so-called Reformed religion; and these shall be distributed to the other two Chambers of Inquests.

31. Besides the chamber formerly established at Castres for the jurisdiction of our court of Parlement of Toulouse, which shall be continued in the state in which it is now, we have for the same considerations ordered and do order that in each of our courts of Parlement of Grenoble and Bordeaux there shall be likewise established a chamber composed of two presidents, one Catholic and the other of the so-called Reformed religion, and of twelve councillors, of whom six shall be Catholics and the other six of the said religion; which Catholic presidents and councillors shall be taken and chosen by us from the bodies of our said courts. And as for those of the said religion, one president and six councillors shall be newly created in the Parlement of Bordeaux, and one president and three councillors in that of Grenoble, who, with the three councillors of the said religion who are presently in the said Parlement, shall be employed in the said chamber of Dauphiné. And the said offices shall be newly created with the same salary, honours, authorities, and pre-eminences as others of the said courts. And the said chamber of Bordeaux shall sit at the said Bordeaux or at Nerac, and that of Dauphiné, at Grenoble.

32. The said chamber of Dauphiné shall have cognizance of the cases of those of the so-called Reformed religion from the jurisdiction of our Parlement of Provence, without the necessity of obtaining letters of evocation, nor other provisions, except in our chancery of Dauphiné. As also those of the said religion in Normandy and Brittany shall not be required to obtain letters of evocation, nor other provisions, except in our chancery of Paris.

33. Our subjects of the religion under the Parlement of Burgundy shall have the choice and option of pleading in the chamber ordered at Paris, or in that of Dauphiné. And they, too, shall not be required to obtain letters of evocation or other provisions except in the said chanceries of Paris, or of Dauphiné, according to the option which they shall take.

34. All of the said chambers composed as has been said shall have cognizance and judge by decree sovereignly and without appeal, excluding all others, in suits and quarrels filed and to be filed, in which those of the said so-called Reformed religion shall be the principal parties and guarantors, whether plaintiff or defendant, in all matters both civil and criminal, whether conducted in writing or orally. And this applies to cases yet to be filed if it seems good to the said parties, and one of them demands it before the suit is heard. This excludes; however, all matters respecting benefices and the possessory of non-laicized tithes, of ecclesiastical patronage, and cases which concern the rights and duties or the domain of the[Catholic] Church, which shall be treated and judged in the

The Story of the Huguenots – a Unique Legacy

courts of Parlement, without the said chambers of the edict having jurisdiction. So, too, we desire, as to the judgments and decision of criminal cases which shall arise between the said ecclesiastics and those of the said so-called Reformed religion; when the ecclesiastic shall be the defendant, in that case the cognizance and judgment of the criminal case shall belong to our sovereign courts, excluding the said chambers; but when the ecclesiastic shall be the plaintiff, and the defendant is of the said religion, the cognizance and judgment shall belong by appeal and without further instance to the said established chambers. During the vacations, the said chambers shall also have cognizance of the matters assigned to the chambers established for the vacations [thus is, the *chambres des vacations* of the parlements] in the edicts and ordinances, each in its own jurisdiction.

35. Starting immediately, the said chamber of Grenoble shall be united and incorporated with the body of the said court of Parlement, and the presidents and councillors of the said so-called Reformed religion shall be named presidents and councillors of the said court, and considered to be of their rank and number. And, to these ends, they shall at first be distributed among the other chambers and then extracted and taken out of them to be employed and to serve in the one which we newly order; always with the requirement that they shall attend and have voice and seat in all the deliberations which shall take place with the chambers assembled, and shall enjoy the same wages, authorities, and pre-eminences as the other presidents and councillors of the said court.

36. We wish and understand thus the said chambers of Castres and Bordeaux shall be reunited and incorporated into those parlements in the same way as the others, when it shall be necessary, and that the causes which moved us to establish them shall cease and no longer take place among our subjects. And for these ends their presidents and councillors of the said religion shall be named and considered to be presidents and councillors of said courts.

37. There shall also be created and newly erected, in the chamber ordained for the Parlement of Bordeaux, two substitutes of our *procureurs* and attorneys-general, of whom the substitute for the procureur shall be a Catholic, and the other of the said religion, who shall be appointed to said offices at ready wages.

38. All of the said substitutes shall claim no other quality than that of substitutes; and when the chambers ordered for the Parlements of Toulouse and Bordeaux shall be united and incorporated with the said parlements, the said substitutes shall be provided with offices of councillors in them.

39. Documents sent by the chancery of Bordeaux shall be made in the presence of two councillors of this chamber, of whom one shall be Catholic and the other of the said so-called Reformed religion, in the absence of one of the masters of requests of our palace; and one of the notaries and secretaries of the said court of Parlement of Bordeaux, or one of the ordinary secretaries of the chancery,

The Story of the Huguenots – a Unique Legacy

shall make his residence at the place where the said chamber shall be established to sign the documents sent by the said chancery.

40. We wish and order that in the said chamber of Bordeaux there shall be two assistants of the clerk of the said Parlement, one for the civil and the other for the criminal branch, who shall exercise their charges by our commissions, and shall be called the assistants to the civil and criminal clerkship, and yet they may not have their positions taken away or revoked by the said clerks of the Parlement. However, they shall be bound to hand over the revenue of the said clerkships to the said clerks; the said assistants shall be salaried by the said clerks as it shall be determined and agreed upon by the said chamber. Besides these, Catholic ushers shall be appointed, who shall be taken from the said court or elsewhere, according to our good pleasure, besides whom two of the said religion shall be newly created and provided with their positions without charge. And all the said ushers shall be regulated by the said chamber, both in the exercise and conduct [reading 'deportment' for 'department'] of their charges and in the revenues which they should collect. Commissions shall also be prepared for officials to pay the wages and collect the fines of the said chamber, to be filled however it shall please us, if the said chamber is established elsewhere than in the said city; and the commission previously given to the official for paying the wages of the chamber of Castres shall take effect fully and entirely, and the commission for collecting fines of the said chamber shall be joined to the said charge.

41. Good and sufficient revenues shall be assigned for the wages of the officers of the chambers ordained by this edict.

42. The presidents, councillors, and other Catholics officers of the said chambers shall continue in office as long as is possible and as we shall see useful for our service and for the good of our subjects; and when some are released, others shall be provided in their places before their departure, nor shall they be able to depart or absent themselves from the said chambers during the time of their service without the permission of those chambers, which shall be judged according to the cases of the ordinance.

43. The said chambers shall be established within six months, during which (so long as the establishment remains to be made) suits filed and to be filed within the jurisdiction of our Parlements of Paris, Rouen, Dijon, and Rennes, to which those of the said religion are parties, shall be evoked to the chamber currently established at. Paris, in virtue of the Edict of 1577, or else to the grand conseil, at the choice and option of those of the said religion, if they demand it; those which shall be in the Parlement of Bordeaux, [shall be heard] in the chamber established at Castres, or in the said grand conseil, at their choice; and those which shall be of Provence, in the Parlement of Grenoble. And if the said chambers are not established within three months after the presentation which

shall be made there of our present edict, such of our parlements as shall have refused so to do, shall be prohibited from taking cognizance of and judging the cases of those of the said religion.

44. Suits not yet decided, pending in the said courts of the Parlement and *grand conseil* of the above-mentioned quality, shall be returned in whatever state they may be to the said chambers, each in its own jurisdiction, within four months after their establishment if one of the parties of the said religion demands it. And as to those which shall be discontinued, and not ripe for judgment, the said persons of the religion shall be required to make a declaration when it is first indicated and signified to them that they are being pursued; and the said time being passed, they shall no longer be received in demanding the said returns.

45. The said chambers of Grenoble and Bordeaux, as well as that of Castres, shall follow the forms and styles of the parlements within whose jurisdictions they shall be established, and shall sit to pass judgment in equal numbers of the one and the other religion, if the parties do not agree otherwise.

46. All judges who shall be called on to carry out the decrees, the commissions of the said chambers, and letters obtained in their chanceries, as well as all ushers and sergeants, shall be required to place them in execution, and the said ushers and sergeants to undertake all actions of enforcement throughout our kingdom, without demanding *placet, visa,* or *pareatis* [all chancery documents], under penalty of suspension from their estates and of the expenses, damages, and interests of the parties, the cognizance of which shall belong to the said parties.

47. No evocations shall be granted of cases the cognizance of which is attributed to the said chambers, except in cases concerning the ordinances, which shall be sent to the closest chamber established according to our edict. And the suits of the said chambers where the judges divide evenly will be judged in the closest one, observing the proportion and forms of the said chambers from which the suits shall have originated. This except for the Chamber of the Edict in our Parlement of Paris, where such suits shall be resolved in the same chamber by the judges who will be named by us by our private letters for this purpose, if the parties do not prefer to await the renewal of the said chamber. And if it should happen that the same suit should lead to a tie in all of the *chambres mi-parties*, the resolution will be referred to the said chamber of Paris.

48. Recusals which shall be requested against the presidents and councillors of the *chambres mi-parties* may be entertained up to the number of six, to which number the parties shall be required to limit themselves; beyond this, matters will proceed without regard to the said recusals.

49. The examination of presidents and councillors newly created for the said chambres mi-parties shall be made in our conseil prive or by the said courts,

The Story of the Huguenots – a Unique Legacy

each in its own territory, when they shall have sufficient numbers. But nevertheless, the customary oath shall be taken by them in the courts where the said chambers shall be established, and if they refuse, in our *conseil prive*, except for those of the chamber of Languedoc, who shall take the oath before our chancellor, or in that chamber.

50. We wish and order that the reception of our officers of the said religion should be judged in the said *chambres mi-parties* by a plurality of voices, as is customary in other judgments, without the necessity that the votes should surpass two-thirds as the ordinance has it, from which in this regard we derogate.

51. There shall be made in the said chambers those proposals, deliberations, and resolutions which will concern the public peace, the individual state, and the administration of the towns in which those chambers shall be.

52. The article of jurisdiction of the said chambers ordered by the present edict shall be followed and observed according to its form and tenor, even in what concerns the execution and lack of execution or infraction of our edicts, when those of the said religion shall be parties.

53. Subordinate officers, royal or otherwise, whose reception is entrusted to our courts of Parlement, if they are of the said so-called Reformed religion, shall be examined and received in the said chambers; that is, those within the jurisdictions of the Parlements of Paris, Normandy, and Brittany, in the said chamber of Paris; those of Dauphiné and Provence, in the chamber of Grenoble; those of Burgundy, in the said chamber of Paris, or of Dauphiné, at their choice; those in the jurisdiction of Toulouse, in the chamber of Castres; and those in the Parlement of Bordeaux, in the chamber of Guyenne. Nor may any others except our *procureurs-generaux* or their substitutes, and those provided with the said offices, oppose their reception and make themselves parties to the matter. But nevertheless, they shall take the customary oath in the courts of Parlement, which may take no cognizance of their said reception; and if the said parlements refuse to do this, the said officers shall take the oath in the said chambers. After it has been taken, they shall be required to present the act of their admittance to the clerks of the said courts of Parlement by an usher or notary, and to leave a collated copy with the said clerks, who are enjoined to register the said acts, under penalty of being liable for all charges, damages, and interest of the parties. And, in case the said clerks shall refuse to do this it shall suffice for the said officers to report the act of the said summons sent by way of the said ushers or notaries, and to have it registered by the clerks of their said [individual] jurisdictions, to have recourse to it when necessary, under penalty of the nullification of their procedures and judgments. And as for the officers whose reception is not accustomed to be made in our said parlements, in case those to whom it belongs shall refuse to proceed with the said examination and

reception, the said officers shall bring the matter before the said chambers, to be dealt with by them as shall be appropriate.

54. The officers of the said so-called Reformed religion who shall be provided with offices in the future to serve in the bodies of our said courts of Parlement, *grand conseil*, chambers of accounts, courts of aids, bureaux of the treasurers-general of France, and other officers of the finances, shall be examined and received in such places as they are accustomed to be; and, in case of refusal or denial of justice, they shall be admitted in our *conseil prive*.

55. The reception of our officers in the chamber formerly established at Castres shall remain valid, notwithstanding all decrees and ordinances to the contrary. Also valid are the receptions of judges, councillors, elected, and other officers of the said religion made in our *conseil prive*, or by commissioners ordained by us on the occasion of refusals of our courts of Parlement, of aids, and chambers of accounts, just as if they had been made in the said courts and chambers and by the other judges to whom the reception belonged. And their wages shall be allowed by the chambers of accounts without difficulties; and if any have been removed from the records, they shall be reinstated without any other order than the present decree, and without the said officers being obliged to appear for a new reception, notwithstanding all court decrees given to the contrary, which shall remain null and void.

56. Until there shall be means of meeting the expenses of justice of the said chambers on the revenue from fines, a valuable and sufficient assignment shall be provided by us in order to provide for the said expenses, though the same funds shall not be raised again on the goods of the condemned.

57. The president and councillors of the said religion formerly received into our court of Parlement of Dauphiné, and in the Chamber of the Edict [*chambre de l'edit*] incorporated with it, shall continue in office and hold their seats and order therein; that is to say, the presidents, as they have enjoyed them and do enjoy them at present; and the councillors, according to the decrees and provisions which they have obtained on the matter in our *conseil prive*.

58. We declare all sentences, court decrees, procedures, seizures, sales, and decrees made and given against persons of the so-called Reformed religion, living or dead, since the decree of the late King Henri II, our most honoured lord and father-in-law, on account of the said religion and of the tumults and disturbances arising thereafter, together with the execution of the said judgments and decrees, to be broken, revoked, and annulled effective immediately, and we do break, revoke, and annul them. We order that they shall be struck out and excluded from the registers of the courts, both sovereign and inferior. We likewise wish that all marks, vestiges, and monuments of the said executions, books, and defamatory acts against their persons, memory, and posterity, shall be destroyed and effaced; and that the sites where demolitions and razings have

The Story of the Huguenots – a Unique Legacy

been made on such occasions shall be returned in such state as they are to their proprietors, to enjoy and dispose of them as they please. And generally, we have broken, revoked, and annulled all procedures and investigations undertaken for any kind of enterprises [against the state], so called crimes of lese majeste, and others. Which procedures, decrees, and judgments containing the confiscation [of Protestant goods], reunion, and incorporation [thereof into the royal domain] notwithstanding, we desire that those of the said religion, and others who have followed their party, and their heirs, shall re-enter into real and immediate possession of all and each of their goods.

59. All procedures instituted and judgments and decrees given, in any other matter than religion and the troubles, against those of the said religion who have borne arms, or have withdrawn out of our kingdom, or within it to the cities and areas held by them, together with all pre-emptions of instances, legal, contractual, and customary prescriptions, and feudal seizures which have befallen during the said troubles or because of legitimate obstacles deriving from them, and of which the cognizance remains with our judges, shall be taken as not having been made, given, or come about. And we so have declared do declare them, and have made and do make them null, so that the parties cannot in any way make use of them, but rather they shall be put back into the condition in which they were formerly, notwithstanding the said decrees and their execution; and they shall be put back in the possession which they had in these matters. The above will likewise apply to those who have followed the party of those of the said religion, or who were absent from our kingdom on account of the troubles. And as for minor children of the said quality who died during the troubles, we place the parties back in the same condition in which they formerly were, without refunding expenses nor being obliged to return fines. However, we do not intend that the judgments given by presidial judges or other inferior judges against persons of the said religion, or who have followed their party, shall be considered null if they were given by judges sitting in towns which they held, and to which they had free access.

60. The decrees given in our courts of parlement in matters where jurisdiction belongs to the chambers instituted by the Edict of the year 1577, and the articles of Nerac and Fleix, in which courts the parties have not proceeded voluntarily, that is to say, have alleged lack of jurisdiction and moved for dismissal, or which have been given by default or foreclosure, in civil and criminal matters equally, notwithstanding which exceptions the said parties have been compelled to continue, shall, in like manner, be null and of no value. And with regard to decrees rendered against those of the said religion who have proceeded voluntarily and without having moved for dismissal for lack of jurisdiction, those decrees shall remain in force. But nevertheless, without prejudice to their execution, they can, if it seems good, take recourse for [reading 'pour' for 'par']

The Story of the Huguenots – a Unique Legacy

the previous judgments by civil request before the relevant chamber. And until the said chambers and their chanceries shall be established, verbal or written appeals interposed by those of the said religion before the judges, clerks, or assistants charged with executing the said decrees and judgments shall have the same effect as if they were authorized by royal letters.

61. In all inquests which shall be made for whatever cause in civil cases, if the examiner or commissioner is a Catholic, the parties shall be bound to choose an adjunct who shall be of the said so-called Reformed religion, and if they cannot agree on one, one shall be furnished by the authority of the said examiner or commissioner; and the same shall be done when the examiner or commissioner shall be of the said religion, with a Catholic adjunct.

62. We wish and order that our judges may have cognizance of the validity of wills in which persons of the said religion have an interest, if they demand it; and the appeals of the said judgments can be brought up by persons of the said religion, notwithstanding all customs to the contrary, even those of Brittany.

63. To avoid all differences which might arise between the courts of parlement and the chambers of those courts ordered by our present edict, we shall provide a good and ample regulation between the said courts and chambers, such that persons of the said so-called Reformed religion shall enjoy this edict in its entirety; which regulation shall be verified in our courts of parlement, and kept and observed without regard to the previous ones.

64. We prohibit and forbid all our sovereign courts, and other of this kingdom, from taking cognizance of and judging civil and criminal suits of those of the said religion, the cognizance of which is given by our edict to the said chambers, as long as their return [to the chambers] is demanded as is specified in 44, above.

65. We also desire, provisionally and until we have otherwise ordered, that in all suits filed and to be filed where persons of the said religion shall have the status of either plaintiffs or defendants, principal parties or guarantors, in civil cases in which our officers and presidial courts have power to judge without recourse, they shall be allowed to demand that two members of the chamber where the suit is to be judged abstain from the judgment; who, without cause being given, shall be required to do so, notwithstanding the ordinance by which the judges may not hold themselves recused without cause; they meanwhile retaining, besides this, the ordinary legal challenges against the other judges. And in criminal cases in which the said presidial and other judges also judge without recourse, the accused of the said religion may demand that three of the said judges shall abstain from the judgment of their cases without giving cause. And the provosts of the marshals of France, *vice-baillis, vice-seneschaux*, lieutenants of the short robe, and other officers of similar status shall judge vagrants according to the ordinances and regulations previously given. And as

to those with a fixed residence charged and accused in cases belonging to the provosts, if they are of the said religion, they can demand that three of the said judges who may have cognizance abstain from the judgment of their case, and they shall be bound to abstain, without cause being given, unless there shall be found in the company where the said cases are to be judged at least two of the said religion in civil matters, and three in criminal matters, in which case no recusations shall be made without reason being given; this will be allowed in common and reciprocally to Catholics in the manner described above, with regard to the said recusations of judges, where those of the so-called Reformed religion shall be in the greater number. We do not intend, however, that the said presidial courts, provosts of the marshals, vice-baillis, vice-seneschaux and others who judge without recourse, shall in consequence of what is now said, take cognizance of past troubles. And as to crimes and excesses arising from other occasions than the said troubles since the beginning of March 1585 up until the end of the year 1597, where they do take cognizance we desire that there shall be an appeal from their judgments to the chambers ordered by this edict; as it shall be done likewise for Catholic accomplices, and where those of the said so-called Reformed religion are parties.

66. We also wish and order that henceforth in all investigations other than investigations in criminal cases, in the senechaussees of Toulouse, Carcassonne, Rouergue, Loraguais, Beziers, Montpellier, and Nimes, that the magistrate or commissioner assigned to the said investigation, if he is a Catholic, shall be required to take an adjunct on whom the parties shall agree who shall be of the said so-called Reformed religion, and when they cannot agree, one of the said religion shall be selected by the said magistrate or commissioner on his authority. So, similarly, if the said magistrate or commissioner is of the said religion, he shall be required in the same way described above to take a Catholic adjunct.

67. When there shall be a question of instituting a criminal case by the provosts of the marshals, or their lieutenants, against anyone of the said religion with a fixed address who shall be charged and accused of a crime to be tried by provosts, the said provosts, or their lieutenants, if they are Catholics, shall be bound to call to the investigation an adjunct of the said religion, which adjunct shall assist as well in judging the competence of the tribunal and in the definitive judgment of the case; which competence may not be judged except at the nearest presidial seat in assembly with the principal judges of the said seat who shall be found on that place, under pain of nullity, unless the accused requests that the competence be judged in the said chambers ordained by the present edict. In that case, for those domiciled in the provinces of Guyenne, Languedoc, Provence, and Dauphiné, the substitutes of our *procureurs-generaux* in the said chambers shall, at the request of those domiciled persons,

The Story of the Huguenots – a Unique Legacy

cause to be brought into those chambers the charges and informations made against them, in order to decide and judge if the cases are under the jurisdiction of the provosts or not, so that afterwards, according to the quality of the crimes, they may be sent back to the ordinary jurisdiction by the chambers, or judged under the authority of the provosts, as they shall see fit and reasonable to do, observing the contents of our present edict. And the presidial judges, provosts of marshals, *vice-baillis, vice-senenchaux*, and others who judge without recourse shall be bound respectively to obey and satisfy the commands which shall be made to them by the said chambers, just as they have been accustomed to do for the said parlements, under penalty of being deprived of their estates.

68. The proclamations, posters, and auctions of inheritances of which the decree is being pursued shall be made at the accustomed places and times, if it can be done, according to our ordinances, or else in the public markets, if there is a market in the place where the said inheritance is situated, and where there is none, they shall be made at the nearest market within the territory of the court where the matter is to be adjudicated, and the posters shall be placed on the post of the said market and in the entrance to the auditorium of the said place, and by this means the said proclamations shall be good and valid, and one shall proceed to the interposition of the decree without regard to the nullities which may be alleged in this regard.

69. All titles, papers, vouchers, and documents which have been taken, shall be returned and restored, by one side and the other, to those to whom they belong, even where the said papers, or the castles and houses in which they were kept, have been taken and seized, either by special commissions of the late king last deceased, our very honoured lord and brother-in-law, or our own, or by the commands of the governors and lieutenants-general of our provinces, or by the authority of the leaders of either party, or under whatever other pretext there might be.

70. The children of those who have withdrawn from our kingdom since the death of the late King Henri II, our very honoured lord and father-in-law, on account of religion and the troubles, even though the said children have been born outside this kingdom, shall be considered true Frenchmen and citizens; and so we have declared and do declare them, without it being necessary for them to take letters of naturalization or other provisions from us besides our present edict; notwithstanding all ordinances to the contrary, from which we have derogated and do derogate, on the condition that the said children born in foreign countries shall be required to come dwell in this kingdom within ten years after the publication of the present edict.

71. Those of the said so-called Reformed religion, and others who have followed their party, who have leased registry fees or other domains, salt taxes, taxes on fairs, and other rights belonging to us before the troubles, which they

have been unable to enjoy because of those troubles, shall remain not liable, as we now declare them not liable, for [payment for] that which they have not received of the said finances or that they have paid without fraud elsewhere than to the receivers of our finances, notwithstanding all obligations undertaken by them on this.

72. All places, towns, and provinces of our kingdom, countries, lands, and lordships of our obedience shall have and enjoy the same privileges, immunities, liberties, franchises, fairs, markets, jurisdictions, and seats of justice as they did before the troubles, beginning with the month of March 1585, and others preceding, notwithstanding all letters to the contrary and transfers of any of the said seats elsewhere; provided that they have been made solely on account of the troubles. Which seats shall be returned and re-established in the towns and places where they were before.

73. If there are any prisoners who are still held by the authority of justice, or otherwise, even in the galleys, on account of the troubles or of the said religion, they shall be released and set at full liberty.

74. Those of the said religion may not in the future be surcharged and burdened more than the Catholics with any ordinary or extraordinary charges, according to their goods and faculties; and those parties who claim to be excessively charged may have recourse to the judges to whom the cognizance belongs. And all our subjects, both of the Catholic and of the so-called Reformed religion, shall be indifferently relieved from all charges which have been imposed by one side and the other during the troubles on those who were of the opposite party without their consent, together with debts created and not paid and expenses incurred without their consent, without, however, their being able to reclaim the fruits which would have been employed to the payment of the said charges.

75. Nor do we mean that those of the said religion, and others who have followed their party, nor the Catholics who remained in the towns and places occupied and held by them, and have contributed to them, shall be pursued for the payment of tallies, aids, grants, increase, taillon, utensils, reparations, and other impositions and subsidies which fell due and were imposed during the troubles before and up to our accession to the crown, whether by edicts, commands of the late kings our predecessors, or by the advice and deliberation of the governors and estates of the provinces, courts of parlement and others, from which we have discharged and do discharge them, forbidding the treasurer-general of France and of our finances, general and special receivers, their subordinates and agents, and other intendants and commissioners of our said finances, from searching them out, molesting, or disturbing them, directly or indirectly, in whatever way there may be.

76. All leaders, lords, knights, gentlemen, officers, corporations of cities and communities, and all others who have aided and succoured them, their widows,

The Story of the Huguenots – a Unique Legacy

heirs, and successors, shall remain quit and discharged of the payments of all moneys which have been taken and levied by them and their ordinances, both of royal funds, to whatever sum it may amount, and of towns and communities, and private individuals, of rents, revenues, plate, sale of movable goods, ecclesiastical or otherwise, woods with standing timber whether of the royal domain or otherwise, fines, booty, ransoms, or money of any other nature, taken by them on account of the troubles begun in the month of March 1585, and other troubles preceding up to our accession to the crown; nor may those who have been commissioned by them to levy the said funds, or who have put up or furnished them by their ordinances be pursued for them in any way at present, nor in the future. And they shall remain quit, both themselves and their subordinates, for all the management and administration of the said funds in bringing in for full discharge quittances duly issued by the leaders of those of the said religion, or of those commissioned by them to hear and close their accounts, or of the communities of the towns which have had command and authority during the said troubles, within four months after the publication of the present edict made in our court of Parlement of Paris. In the same way they shall remain quit and not liable for all acts of hostility, the levy and conduct of troops, the fabrication and valuation of money made according to the ordinances of the said leaders, the casting and seizure of artillery and munitions, the manufacture of powder and saltpetre, seizures, fortifications, dismantling and demolitions of towns, castles, fortified towns and villages, attacks upon them, the burning and destruction of churches and houses, the establishment of justices and their judgments and the execution of the same, both in civil and criminal matters, administration and regulations made within them, voyages and intelligences, negotiations, treaties, and contracts made with all foreign princes and communities, and the introduction of the said foreigners into the towns and other areas of our kingdom, and generally for all that has been done, overseen, and negotiated during the said troubles, since the death of the late King Henri II, our very honoured lord and brother-in-law, by those of the said religion and others who have followed their party, even though it ought to be particularly expressed and specified.

77. Those of the said religion shall also remain not liable for all general and provincial assemblies made and held by them, both at Nantes and at other places up to the present time, together with the councils established by them and ordered by the provinces, deliberations, ordinances, and regulations made at the said assemblies and councils, establishment and augmentation of garrisons, assembly of troops, raising and taking of our funds, either in the hands of the receivers-general or particular, parish collectors, or otherwise, in whatever fashion it may be, seizure of salt taxes, continuation or erection anew of trade monopolies, tolls, and the receipts from them, even at Royan, and upon the

The Story of the Huguenots – a Unique Legacy

banks of the Charente, Garonne, the Rhone, and Dordogne, armaments and combats at sea, and all accidents and excesses committed to force payment of the said commerces, tolls, and other funds, the fortification of cities, castles, and strongholds, exactions of money and labour, receipts thereof, destitution of our receivers and leaseholders, and other officers, the establishment of others in their place, and of all unions, dispatches, and negotiations made both within and outside our kingdom; and generally of all which has been done, deliberated, written, and ordered by the said assemblies and councils; nor may those who have given their advice, signed, executed, or caused to be signed and executed, the said ordinances, regulations, and deliberations, nor their widows, heirs, and successors be molested for it, now or in the future, even though the particulars of these actions are not fully described here. And perpetual silence about the entire matter shall be imposed on our procureurs-generaux and their substitutes, and on all those who may pretend to be interested parties, in whatever fashion and manner it may be, notwithstanding all decrees, sentences, judgments, investigations, and procedures made to the contrary.

78. Moreover, we approve, validate, and authorize the accounts which have been heard, closed, and examined by the deputies of the said assembly. We wish that these, with the quittances and papers which have been rendered by the accountants, should be taken to our Chamber of Accounts at Paris three months after the publication of the present edict, and placed in the hands of our procureur-general, to be delivered to the keeper of the books and registers of our Chamber, to be consulted on all occasions when it is found necessary without the said accounts being subject to review, nor the accountants bound to any appearance or correction except in the case of the omission of the receipt of a sum, or of false quittances; imposing silence on our said procureur-general with regard to claims which may be made that the surplus is defective, and that formalities may not have been observed. Forbidding the officers of our accounts, both at Paris and in other provinces where they are established, from taking any cognizance thereof in whatever way or manner it may be.

79. And with regard to the accounts which have not yet been rendered, we wish them to be heard, closed, and examined by commissioners who shall be appointed by us, who shall pass and allocate without difficulty the accounts paid by the said accountants, in virtue of the ordinances of the said assembly, or others having power.

80. All collectors, receivers, fiscal leaseholders, and all others, shall remain well and duly discharged of all sums of money that they have paid to the said deputies of the said assembly, of whatever nature they may be, up to the last day of this month. We wish all of this to be passed and allocated in the accounts which shall be rendered at our Chambers of Accounts, purely and simply, in virtue of the quittances which shall be brought in; and if any shall have been

The Story of the Huguenots – a Unique Legacy

expedited or delivered thereafter, they shall remain null, and those who accept or pass them shall be condemned to the fine for fraudulent use. And where there shall be any accounts already rendered in which anything has been struck out or added, in this respect we have excluded and lifted them, and have entirely re-established and do re-establish the said parties in virtue of these present, without there being any necessity for private letters or any other things than the extract of the present article.

81. Governors, captains, consuls, and persons commissioned for the collection of funds to pay the garrisons of places held by those of the said religion, to whom our receivers and parish collectors shall have advanced the necessary funds for the support of the said garrisons by loan on their promissory notes and obligations, either under constraint or in order to obey the commands made of them by the treasurers-general, up to the amount specified by the regulation which we caused to be issued at the beginning of the year 1596 and the augmentation since granted by us, shall be considered not liable and discharged for that which has been paid for the above mentioned purpose, even if no explicit mention thereof is made in the said promissory notes and obligations, which shall be returned to them as void. And to satisfy them, the treasurers-general in each generality shall have the individual receivers of our tallies furnish their quittances to the said collectors, and the receivers-general, their quittances to the individual receivers. For the discharge of which receivers-general, the sums of which they shall have kept account, as has been said, shall be endorsed on the orders levied by the treasurer of the central treasury, under the names of the treasurers-general of our extraordinary revenues for war, for the payment of the said garrisons. And where the said orders shall not amount to as much as is specified in our said regulation granted in the year 1596 with augmentation, we command that in order to supplement it new orders shall be issued for what is lacking for the discharge of our accountants, and the redemption of the said promises and obligations, in such a way that nothing shall be demanded in the future of those who have made them, and that all letters of validation which shall be necessary for the discharge of the accountants shall be issued by virtue of the present article.

82. Also, those of the said religion shall cease and desist immediately from all illicit manoeuvres, negotiations, and intelligence, both within and outside our kingdom, and the said assemblies and councils established in the provinces shall dissolve themselves promptly, and all leagues and associations made or to be made to the prejudice of our present edict under whatever pretext there may be shall be broken and annulled, as we now break and annul them; forbidding our subjects very expressly to make henceforth any assessments and levies of funds without our permission, or fortifications, enrolments of men, congregations and assemblies, other than those permitted by our present edict, and without arms;

The Story of the Huguenots – a Unique Legacy

which we prohibit and forbid them to do under penalty of being rigorously punished, as being in contempt and violation of our commands and ordinances.

83. All seizures which have been made at sea during the troubles in virtue of releases and admissions granted, and those which have taken place on land against those of the contrary party, and which have been approved of by judges and commissioners of the admiralty, or by the leaders of those of the said religion or their council, shall remain dormant under the benefit of our present edict without the possibility of the matter being pursued; nor shall the captains and others who have made the said seizures, their sureties, and the said judges, and officers, their widows and heirs, be searched out or molested in whatever manner it may be, notwithstanding all decrees of our conseil prive and of the parlements and all letters of marque and seizures pending and not adjudged, which we desire to be fully and completely released.

84. Nor, in the same way, shall those of the said religion be searched out for the opposition and obstacles which they previously placed, even after the troubles, in the way of the execution of the decrees and judgments given for the re-establishment of the Roman, Catholic, and Apostolic religion in various places in this kingdom.

85. And as for whatever has been done or taken during the troubles outside the regular course of hostilities, or by hostility against the public and private regulations of the leaders or of communities of provinces which have had command, they may be pursued for them at justice.

86. Nevertheless, since if that which was done against the regulations by one side and the other is indifferently excluded and reserved from the general abolition specified in the present edict and is subject to being pursued, there is no soldier who might not be placed under a penalty, which might lead to a renewal of the troubles. For this reason, we wish and order that only execrable cases shall remain excluded from the said abolition; as, kidnapping and rape of women and girls, arson, murders, and thefts by betrayal and lying in wait, outside the regular course of hostilities, and for the exercise of private vengeance against the duties of war, the violation of passports and safe conducts, together with murder and pillage without command, with regard to those of the said religion and others who followed the party of the leaders who have had authority over them, based on the particular occasions which have led them to so command and order.

87. We also order that crimes and offenses committed between persons of the same party shall be punished if it is not a matter of acts commanded by the leaders of one party or the other according to the necessity, law, and order of war. And as to the levy and exaction of funds, bearing of arms, and other exploits of war made by private authority, and without permission, they shall be pursued at justice.

The Story of the Huguenots – a Unique Legacy

88. In the towns [whose fortifications were] dismantled during the troubles, the ruins and remains of the same may, by our permission, be rebuilt and repaired by the inhabitants, at their cost and expense, and the provisions formerly granted in this regard shall continue and be in force.

89. We order, wish, and it pleases us, that all lords, knights, gentlemen, and others, of whatever quality and condition they may be, of the said religion, and others who have followed their party, shall resume and be effectually preserved in the enjoyment of all and each of their goods, rights, names, consideration, and actions, notwithstanding the judgments issued concerning them during the troubles and on account of them; which decrees, seizures, and judgments, and everything following on them we have to this end declared and do declare null and without effect and value.

90. The acquisitions which those of the so-called Reformed religion, and others who have followed their party, have made by the authority of others than of the late kings our predecessors from the real property belonging to the [Catholic] Church shall have no force and effect. Thus we order, wish, and it pleases us, that ecclesiastics shall immediately and without delay resume and be preserved in the real and actual possession and enjoyment of the said properties thus alienated, without being required to return the price of the said sales, and this notwithstanding the said contracts of sale, which for this purpose we have annulled and revoked. Nor yet shall the said purchasers have any claim on the leaders by whose authority the said goods have been sold. But nevertheless, for the reimbursement of funds disbursed by them truly and without fraud, our letters patent of permission shall be issued to persons of the said religion, to impose and equalize on them the sums to which the said sales have amounted; without the said purchasers being able to pretend any action for their damages and interest for being deprived of enjoyment. But rather they shall content themselves with the reimbursement of the funds furnished by them for the price of the said acquisitions; estimating the said price based on the fruits received by them from the properties in case the said sale shall be found to have been made at an extremely low and unjust price.

91. And so that both our justiciars, officers, and our other subjects, may clearly and with all certainty be informed of our will and intention, and to remove all ambiguities and doubts which may be introduced by means of preceding edicts, from their diversity, we have declared and do declare all other preceding edicts, secret articles, letters, declarations, modifications, restrictions, interpretations, decrees, and registers [of] deliberations both secret and otherwise, made heretofore by us or our predecessors in our courts of parlement or elsewhere, concerning matters of the said religion, and the troubles arising in our kingdom, to be null and of no effect and value; from which, and from the derogations which they contain, we have by this our edict derogated, and do derogate,

The Story of the Huguenots – a Unique Legacy

effective immediately, as for the future we overrule, revoke, and annul them; we expressly declare that we wish this our edict to be firm and inviolable, guarded and observed both by our said justiciars, officers, and our other subjects, without let or any regard to all which may be to the contrary and derogatory to it.

92. And for the greater assurance of the upholding and observance which we desire for this, we will, order, and it pleases us, that all the governors and lieutenants-general of our provinces, baillis, seneschaux and other ordinary judges of the towns of our said kingdom, immediately after the reception of this edict, swear to guard and observe it each in his district, as well as the mayors, *echevins, capitouls, consuls,* and *jurats* [all municipal officials] of the towns, annual or perpetual. We also enjoin our baillis, senenchaux, or their lieutenants, and other judges, to have the principal inhabitants of the said towns, both of the one and the other religion, swear to uphold the present edict, immediately after its publication. Placing all those of the said town under our protection and safeguard, and the ones under the protection of the others, requiring them respectively, and by public acts, to respond in the civil courts for violations which may be made of our said edict in the said towns, by their inhabitants, or else to present and place into the hands of justice the said violators. We order our beloved and loyal people holding our courts of parlement, chambers of accounts, and courts of aids that immediately after having received the present edict they shall, suspending all other affairs and under penalty of the nullity of all acts which they may otherwise undertake, to make the same oath as above, and to cause this our edict to be registered and published in our said courts according to its form and tenor, purely and simply, without using any modifications, restrictions, declarations, or registers of unpublished resolutions, nor waiting for any other order to publish or command from us; and we order our *procureurs-generaux* to request and pursue the said publication without delay.

Given at Nantes, in the month of April, the year of grace 1598; and of our reign the ninth.

Signed "Henri"; and above, "The King, being in his council, Forget." And sealed with the great seal of green wax, over red and green silk ribbons. Read and published, and registered, etc. Signed, "Voysin."

2. The Edict of Fontainebleau (Revocation)

Louis, by the grace of God king of France and Navarre, to all present and to come, greeting:

King Henry the Great, our grandfather of glorious memory, being desirous that the peace which he had procured for his subjects after the grievous losses they had sustained in the course of domestic and foreign wars, should not be troubled on account of the R.P.R. [*Religion prétendue réformée* — "the religion called the Reformed"], as had happened in the reigns of the kings, his predecessors, by his edict, granted at Nantes in the month of April, 1598, regulated the procedure to be adopted with regard to those of the said religion, and the places in which they might meet for public worship, established extraordinary judges to administer justice to them, and, in fine, provided in particular articles for whatever could be thought necessary for maintaining the tranquility of his kingdom and for diminishing mutual aversion between the members of the two religions, so as to put himself in a better position to labour, as he had resolved to do, for the reunion to the Church of those who had so lightly withdrawn from it.

As the intention of the king, our grandfather, was frustrated by his sudden death, and as the execution of the said edict was interrupted during the minority of the late king, our most honoured lord and father of glorious memory, by new encroachments on the part of the adherents of the said R.P.R., which gave occasion for their being deprived of divers advantages accorded to them by the said edict; nevertheless the king, our late lord and father, in the exercise of his usual clemency, granted them yet another edict at Nimes, in July, 1629, by means of which, tranquility being established anew, the said late king, animated by the same spirit and the same zeal for religion as the king, our said grandfather, had resolved to take advantage of this repose to attempt to put his said pious design into execution. But foreign wars having supervened soon after, so that the kingdom was seldom tranquil from 1635 to the truce concluded in 1684 with the powers of Europe, nothing more could be done for the advantage of religion beyond diminishing the number of places for the public exercise of the R.P.R., interdicting such places as were found established to the prejudice of the dispositions made by the edicts, and suppressing of the bi-partisan courts, these having been appointed provisionally only.

God having at last permitted that our people should enjoy perfect peace, we, no longer absorbed in protecting them from our enemies, are able to profit by this truce (which we have ourselves facilitated), and devote our whole attention to the means of accomplishing the designs of our said grandfather and father, which we have consistently kept before us since our succession to the crown.

The Story of the Huguenots – a Unique Legacy

And now we perceive, with thankful acknowledgment of God's aid, that our endeavours have attained their proposed end, inasmuch as the better and the greater part of our subjects of the said R.P.R. have embraced the Catholic faith. And since by this fact the execution of the Edict of Nantes and of all that has ever been ordained in favour of the said R.P.R. has been rendered nugatory, we have determined that we can do nothing better, in order wholly to obliterate the memory of the troubles, the confusion, and the evils which the progress of this false religion has caused in this kingdom, and which furnished occasion for the said edict and for so many previous and subsequent edicts and declarations, than entirely to revoke the said Edict of Nantes, with the special articles granted as a sequel to it, as well as all that has since been done in favour of the said religion.

I. Be it known that for these causes and others us hereunto moving, and of our certain knowledge, full power, and royal authority, we have, by this present perpetual and irrevocable edict, suppressed and revoked, and do suppress and revoke, the edict of our said grandfather, given at Nantes in April, 1598, in its whole extent, together with the particular articles agreed upon in the month of May following, and the letters patent issued upon the same date; and also the edict given at Nimes in July, 1629; we declare them null and void, together with all concessions, of whatever nature they may be, made by them as well as by other edicts, declarations, and orders, in favour of the said persons of the R.P.R., the which shall remain in like manner as if they had never been granted; and in consequence we desire, and it is our pleasure, that all the temples of those of the said R.P.R. situate in our kingdom, countries, territories, and the lordships under our crown, shall be demolished without delay.

II. We forbid our subjects of the R.P.R. to meet any more for the exercise of the said religion in any place or private house, under any pretext whatever excuse it can be, even of real exercises or bailliages, even though the aforementioned exercises would have been maintained by the rulings of our council.

III. We likewise forbid all noblemen, of what condition so ever, to hold such religious exercises in their houses or fiefs, under penalty to be inflicted upon all our said subjects who shall engage in the said exercises, of imprisonment and confiscation.

IV. We enjoin all ministers of the said R.P.R., who do not choose to become converts and to embrace the Catholic, apostolic, and Roman religion, to leave our kingdom and the territories subject to us within a fortnight of the publication of our present edict, without leave to reside therein beyond that period, or, during the said fortnight, to engage in any preaching, exhortation, or any other function, on pain of being sent to the galleys. . . .

V. Let us want that those the aforementioned Ministers who will be converted, continue to enjoy their lasting life, and their widows later them death,

The Story of the Huguenots – a Unique Legacy

whereas they will be in viduity of the same exemptions of size and flat of war people, which they enjoyed while they made the function of Ministers, and besides, we shall charge auxdits Ministers also their lasting life, one pension which will be of a third stronger than the salaries which they got as Ministers, as half of which pension his women will also enjoy after their death, as long as they will live in viduity.

VI. That if any of the aforementioned Ministers wish to be made lawyer or to take the degrees of doctor in law, we want and hear that they are exempted from three years of studies prescribed by our declarations; and that having undergone the common exams, and by these to be considered capable, they are received doctors by paying only half of the rights that we accustomed to perceive for this end in each University.

VII. We forbid private schools for the instruction of children of the said R.P.R., and in general all things whatever which can be regarded as a concession of any kind in favour of the said religion.

VIII. As for children who may be born of persons of the said R.P.R., we desire that from henceforth they be baptized by the parish priests. We enjoin parents to send them to the churches for that purpose, under penalty of five hundred livres fine, to be increased as circumstances may demand; and thereafter the children shall be brought up in the Catholic, apostolic, and Roman religion, which we expressly enjoin the local magistrates to see done.

IX. And in the exercise of our clemency towards our subjects of the said R.P.R. who have emigrated from our kingdom, lands, and territories subject to us, previous to the publication of our present edict, it is our will and pleasure that in case of their returning within the period of four months from the day of the said publication, they may, and it shall be lawful for them to, again take possession of their property, and to enjoy the same as if they had all along remained there: on the contrary, the property abandoned by those who, during the specified period of four months, shall not have returned into our kingdom, lands, and territories subject to us, shall remain and be confiscated in consequence of our declaration of the 20th of August last.

X. We repeat our most express prohibition to all our subjects of the said R.P.R., together with their wives and children, against leaving our kingdom, lands, and territories subject to us, or transporting their goods and effects there from under penalty, as respects the men, of being sent to the galleys, and as respects the women, of imprisonment and confiscation.

XI. It is our will and intention that the declarations rendered against the relapsed shall be executed according to their form and tenor.

XII. As for the rest, liberty is granted to the said persons of the R.P.R., pending the time when it shall please God to enlighten them as well as others, to remain in the cities and places of our kingdom, lands, and territories subject to

The Story of the Huguenots – a Unique Legacy

us, and there to continue their commerce, and to enjoy their possessions, without being subjected to molestation or hindrance on account of the said R.P.R., on condition of not engaging in the exercise of the said religion, or of meeting under pretext of prayers or religious services, of whatever nature these may be, under the penalties above mentioned of imprisonment and confiscation. This do we give in charge to our trusty and well-beloved counsellors, etc.

Given at Fontainebleau in the month of October, in the year of grace 1685, and of our reign the forty-third.

3.   The Huguenot Cross

The Huguenot cross is now the formal insignia of The Huguenot Society of Great Britain and Ireland, and while it is not exclusively the property of the society, it is nevertheless a symbol of recognition for all Huguenot descendants. There have been many models of the cross over the centuries, however; the most recognised form of the Huguenot cross is known as the Cross of Languedoc as it was discovered by the Reverend Andrew Malihet in the region during the 18th century. There does not appear to be a record of when the Huguenots adopted this cross as their own, but it is thought to have become a sign of their faith and recognition to another believer from as early as the 17th century. The first cross was based on the Order of the Holy Spirit insignia that Henri of Navarre wore, and no doubt because he had issued the Edict of Nantes in 1598 to give Huguenots freedom this was the reason the cross was based on this order. The first recorded design and manufacture of a Huguenot cross was by Mystre of Nimes in 1688, and was based on the badge of the Hospitaler Knights of St John of Jerusalem, which had been founded in the 7th century AD.

The cross is symbolic and is composed of four elements:

1.   An open four-petal Lily of France (Fleur-de-lis) as a reminder of the Motherland of France. Each petal is V-shaped, with the four petals pointing north, south, east and west, similar to the Maltese cross. The four petals denote the Four Gospels. On each petal at the point of the V shape are two rounded points indicating the Eight Beatitudes.

2.   The four petals are linked together with four fleur-de-lis, again a reminder of the mother country. Each fleur-de-lis has three petals; thus, the four fleur-de-lis each with their three petals imply the Twelve Apostles.

3.   Between each fleur-de-lis and its adjoining four-petalled lilies is an open-heart-shaped space, a symbol of loyalty, which inclines towards the seal of the great reformer John Calvin, founder of the Huguenot Church.

4.   A dove pendant in downward flight beneath the cross itself is believed to epitomise the 'Sainted Spirit' – the guide of the Huguenot Church.

4.   The Huguenot Refugee's Four-part Song

I tell of the noble Refugee
Who strove in a holy faith,
At the stars of his God to bow,
When the road it was marked with death.

How vain was the flight, in the wild midnight,
To the forest's inmost glade;
When the holy few, to those altars true,
On the greensward knelt and prayed.

When the despot's sword and the bigot's torch
Had driven him forth to roam
From village, and farm, and city and town,
He sought our Island Home.

And store of wealth, and a rich reward,
He brought in his open hand,
For many a peaceful art he taught,
Instead of the foreman's brand.

And boldly he fought for the land he'd sought,
When the battle storm awoke.
In the tented field, or the guarded fort,
Or on board our hearts of oak.

And dear to him now is the red crossed flag
(His ancient hate and fear),
And well does he love his adopted land,
And the friends who've welcomed him here.

Chorus
Hey! For our land, our English land,
The land of the brave and free;
Who with open arms in the olden time,
Received the Refugee.

Tables

Table 1. The population of London c. 1660

The city within the walls	76,000
The liberties 'without' the walls	149,000
Westminster, Lambeth and Stepney	23,000
Total recorded population	**248,000**

The Story of the Huguenots – a Unique Legacy

Table 2. Immigrants requesting entry into the French Church at Threadneedle Street in the year 1681

Total entries for the year	912
Total persons seeking entry	**1111**
Country of origin:	
France	871
Great Britain & N. Ireland	24
Holland	13
Germany	1
Switzerland	1
Unknown origin	201
Total persons seeking entry	**1111**

Table 3. Examples of Huguenot refugees and the ships on which they travelled to Table Bay, South Africa

Surname	First name	Ship	Date of arrival
Des Prez (du Preez)	Hercule	*De Schelde*	June 1688
Fourie	Louis	*Wapen van Alkmaar*	1689
Gauch (Gouws)	Andre	*Spierdijk*	April 1691
Jacob (Jacobs)	Pierre	*De Schelde*	June 1688
Le Roux	Jean	*Voorschooten*	April 1688
Marais	Charles	*Voorschooten*	April 1688
Martin	Antoine	*Wapen van Alkmaar*	January 1689
Mouton	Jacques	*Donkervliet*	July 1699
Roux	Paul	*Berg China*	August 1688
Therond (Theron)	Jacques	*Oosterland*	April 1688

Huguenot Societies

and Corresponding Societies

In Alphabetical Order

AUSTRALIA
The Huguenot Society — P. O. Box 184, Newtown, NSW 2042

BELGIUM
Société Royale d'Histoire du Protestantisme Belge — Av. Adolphe Lacomblé 60/12, B-1030 Bruxelles
Centre de Documentation, Belge — 40, rue des Bollandistes, B-1040, Bruxelles

CHANNEL ISLANDS
La Société Guernesiaise — Hon Sec., F. G. Caldwell, Candie Gardens, St Peter Port, Guernsey, GY1 1UG
Société Jersiaise — Lord Coutanche Library, 7 Pier Road, St Helier, Jersey, JE2 4XW

FRANCE
Les Amitiés Huguenotes Internationales (ex Comité Protestant des Amitiés Françaises à l'Étranger) — 47 rue de Clichy, 75311, Paris CEDEX 09 FRANCE
Société de l'Histoire du Protestantisme Française — 54 rue des Saint-Pères, Paris 75007
Société d'Histoire du Protestantisme en Normandie — 4 rue Auguste Lechesne, Caen 14000

GERMANY
Consistorium der Frazösischen Kirche zu Berlin	Joachim Friedrich Strasse 4, 10711 Berlin 31
Deutche Hugenotten-Gesellschaft	Hafenplatz 9a, D-34385 Bad Karlshafen
Deutsche Wadenservereinigung e. V.,	Henri-Arnaud-Haus, 75443 Otisheim-Schoenenberg
Herzog August Biblioteck,	Postfach 1364, D38299, Wolfenbüttel
J. A. Lasco Bibliotek	Grosse Kirche Emden, Brückstrasse, 110, D-26725, Emden

GREAT BRITAIN
The Huguenot Society of Great Britain and Ireland	PO Box 444, Ruislip, London HA4 4GU

IRELAND
RCB Library	Braemar Park, Dublin 14, Republic of Ireland

ITALY
Società di Studi Valdesi,	Via Roberto D'Azeglio 2., 10065 Torre Pelice, Peidmont

THE NETHERLANDS
Fondation Huguenote des Pays-Bas,	Zacharias Jansestraat 13, 1097 CH Amsterdam

POLAND
Polski Towarzystwo Hugenockie, al, Solidarnasci	76a 00-145 Warsaw

SOUTH AFRICA
Huguenot Society of South Africa	P.O. Box 293, Franschhoek 7690

SWITZERLAND
Société d'Histoire et d'Archéologie de Genève BPU,	Promenade des Bastions CH-1211 Genève 4

UNITED STATES OF AMERICA
The Huguenot Society of America	20 West 44th Street, Suite 510, New York, NY 10036
The Huguenot Society of South Carolina	138 Logan Street, Charlestown, SC 29401-1941

Notes

Introduction

[1] From the French word *réfugié(e)*.

[2] The Channel Islands were almost all that was left of the continental possessions once held by the kings of England. The population, however, although French-speaking were anti-French. Huguenots had begun arriving during the reign of Edward VI (1547-53).

PART ONE
The Beginnings of French Protestantism
Chapter 1 – A Question of Faith

[3] Fundamentally they believed there was a Good God and a Bad God, not dissimilar to the Jehovah and Satan of Christianity, but the Good God was the god of all immaterial things while the Bad God was the god of all material things; this ideal was age-old even in the time of Jesus.

[4] The Inquisition – a group of institutions within the judicial system of the Roman Catholic Church, whose aim was to combat heresy. It started in 13th century France to combat religious sectarianism, in particular the Cathars.

[5] Peter Waldo gave his name to this group of people; he was a wealthy merchant of Lyon and a devout Christian, who, in circa 1179 following denial by his local bishop to his request for permission to preach, took his plea to the Pope, but was refused, and thus began the long quest to confront the Catholic faith and various elements of its doctrine.

The Story of the Huguenots – a Unique Legacy

[6] Henry VIII found the wealth of the monasteries to be of immense help in replenishing his coffers, and he would certainly not have wanted to hand any of this wealth back to the Catholic Church.

[7] Hamelin was one of the earliest Huguenot martyrs in south-west France.

[8] Tuileries is French for 'tile works'.

[9] The construction of the cathedral of St Cécile in Albi, south western France, was begun in 1282, and was intended to make a clear statement following the Albigensian Crusade. Its walls clearly depict the Catholic Church's version of Heaven and Hell as a warning to any who should dare question the Church's teachings.

[10] This was ratified by the Synod of La Rochelle in 1571. Among the signatories was Queen Jeanne de Navarre.

[11] The Parlement in Toulouse did not have the powers to make laws; they were instead charged with ruling on laws already in force.

[12] The Italian Wars (1494–1559) were a series of violent wars for control of Italy. Fought largely by France and Spain but involving much of Europe, they resulted in the Spanish Habsburgs dominating Italy, and consequently shifted power from Italy to north western Europe.

Chapter 2 – The Road to the Wars of Religion
[13] Translates as 'one faith, one law, one king'.

[14] Translates as 'there is no authority except from God'.

[15] As Emperor Charles, he was ruler of Spain as well as the Spanish Netherlands.

[16] Vaudois – the name given to the remaining pocket of Waldensians.

- 413 -

The Story of the Huguenots – a Unique Legacy

[17] The king's opponent in the fateful joust was Gabriel de Montgomery, the captain of his Scottish Guard. The king forgave him before he died, but the queen never did and, following his failed attempt in 1573 to aid the Protestants within La Rochelle, she took the opportunity to have him beheaded the following year.

[18] The age a French king was considered to have attained maturity was 14 years.

[19] The list included all the bibles that had been printed in languages other than Latin.

[20] Although he was a Catholic, he was far-sighted realising that this religious division was not good for the country. He advised a more conciliatory attitude, suggesting the different religions – Huguenot, Catholic, Lutheran and Papist – should be put aside, and that all men should henceforth be known as Christians.

[21] Canterbury Cathedral is the surprising setting for the last resting place of Odet Coligny, one of the three famous Protestant Coligny brothers. Ten years after his conversion to Protestantism, he fled France. Soon after his arrival in England, whilst staying in Canterbury he became ill (perhaps through eating a poisoned apple) and died. His body was placed in a coffin, which was bricked over as a temporary measure whilst awaiting shipment back to France – today, he still lies in the cathedral in Trinity Chapel not far from the tomb of Edward known as the Black Prince.

[22] Daughter of Marguerite, Queen of Navarre, and niece to Francis I, King of France.

[23] Otherwise known as the Edict of St Germain, there was a second Edict of Toleration in 1787, but this was commonly known as the Edict of Tolerance.

Chapter 3 – The First Three Wars 1562-76
[24] In the 16th century, this town was known as Vassy.

- 414 -

The Story of the Huguenots – a Unique Legacy

[25] Middle English from Middle French: administer from *baillir* (from bail jurisdiction) and *age*.

[26] At that time, the Spanish Netherlands were formed of 17 provinces – 14 Dutch and three Walloon. They were also collectively known as the Low Countries as they were mainly below sea level.

[27] When Philip II of Spain succeeded to the throne in 1566 following the abdication of Charles V, his inheritance was, in effect, two kingdoms – Spain and the Spanish Netherlands. The latter was keen to embrace the new Protestant religion. Philip II, a staunch Catholic, would spare no means to root out this 'heresy', and he found a willing partner in the Jesuits and their instrument of power – the Inquisition. The Netherlands, once a rich industrial area, was reduced to ruins as Protestants fled their homeland leaving thousands of people who had relied on these artisans for employment reduced to beggary. The war in the Netherlands lasted six years during which time the Duke of Alva, Philip's commander in the Netherlands, boasted that he had sent 18,000 persons either to the stake or to the scaffold.

[28] The Spanish Road was a military supply and trade route used from 1567–1620 along which soldiers were able to march the 1,000 km (620 miles) from Milan to Flanders.

[29] When the French Wars of Religion began in 1562, Monluc was a strong supporter of the Roman Catholic House of Guise. The victory he achieved at Vergt (9 October 1562) broke Huguenot power in Guyenne. He later became a powerful force within the league of Roman Catholic nobles in the south-west. He was given a reputation for extreme barbarity by his opponents that he may not have fully deserved.

[30] A league of Dutch and Flemish patriots formed in 1566 to resist the introduction of the Spanish Inquisition to the Netherlands.

Chapter 4 – The St Bartholomew's Day Massacre and the Final Five Wars 1572-88

[31] Henri did not attend Mass as he was at that time a Huguenot.

[32] White crosses had been used in earlier conflicts to differentiate Catholics from Huguenots. This symbol would be used again in later battles.

[33] When news of the massacre reached the Vatican in Rome, Pope Gregory XIII celebrated with a jubilee day of public thanksgiving. Guns were fired in salute, and a medallion was struck to commemorate the massacre. Later, the Pope commissioned a mural by Giorgio Vasari of the 'wondrous' St Bartholomew's Day Massacre to hang in the Vatican.

[34] Believed to have been written in both Latin and French by Junius Brutus, a French Calvinist, in 1579.

[35] Their numbers had been swelled with the arrival of a further 1,500 Huguenots fleeing the bloodbath of St Bartholomew's Day.

[36] The Coligny brothers were: Odet de Coligny (1517–71) Count-Bishop of Beauvais and Cardinal of Châtillon; Gaspard II de Coligny (1519–72) Seigneur of Châtillon and an admiral of France; and François de Coligny (1521–69), Seigneur of Andelot and colonel-general of the royal infantry.

[37] *Monsieur* was the traditional title of the next oldest brother to the reigning king.

[38] Meaning 'half room'- or *'part'* was a *room* set up in each parlement, composed equally of Catholic judges and magistrates, and those of the Reformée Protestant Religion (RPR), to try cases of people.

[39] Chamber of the Edict, or Chamber of the Law.

[40] The French Estates-General was a general assembly representing the French estates of the realm: the clergy (First Estate), the nobles (Second Estate), and the common people (Third Estate).

[41] The Salic law in France prevented a female inheriting the French throne, but her husband could ascend the throne in her place.

[42] The Catholic League was especially well organised in Paris; a central committee – 'The Sixteen' – prompted a further Committee on Public Safety, which conducted a reign of terror in a manner similar to the much more famous one that occurred during the French Revolution 200 years later.

Chapter 5 – The Wars of the League 1589-98

[43] Henri III and Henri de Navarre were both descended from St Louis, who had died in 1270.

[44] Following this battle, the town of Arques became Arques la Bataille, and is still known as such today; across the valley is a memorial to Henri IV and the battle.

[45] The Cardinal de Bourbon was the younger brother of Antoine, father of Henri de Navarre. The League proclaimed him their king as he was a Catholic, but he renounced this title in favour of his nephew, Henri de Navarre.

[46] Translates as 'Paris is worth a Mass'.

[47] The French Parlement at that time was still staunchly adhering to the principle of 'one king, one law, one faith'.

[48] Many of the articles within the Edict of Nantes were based upon earlier edicts that had punctuated the years of the Wars of Religion.

[49] Maximilien de Bethune, Duc de Sully, was a French statesman, who, as the trusted minister of Henri IV, substantially contributed to the

The Story of the Huguenots – a Unique Legacy

rehabilitation of France after the Wars of Religion. He had also strongly advised Henri IV to convert to Catholicism for political reasons, but he remained a staunch Protestant himself.

Chapter 6 – From the Edict of Nantes to the Succession of Louis XIV
[50] Often referred to as the 'reformed' faith.

[51] The *Thirty Years War* (1618-48) commenced when Holy Roman Emperor Ferdinand II of Bohemia tried to limit the religious activities of his subjects, sparking rebellion amongst Protestants.

[52] Popular feeling ran high against Charles I and his Catholic Queen (sister to the French king) at the failure of England to effectively aid the French Protestants, and years later these events were recalled at the trial of Charles I.

[53] A *mole* is a marine rampart – Richelieu had one built across the opening of the harbour of La Rochelle so that ships carrying supplies could not pass safely into the port.

Chapter 7 – The Fronde to the Revocation 1648-85
[54] Fronde is the French word for 'sling', part of a children's game played in the streets of Paris during this period in defiance of the civil authorities.

[55] Provincial officials employed by central government.

[56] At the time, these newspaper reports in England filled many with unease as the heir apparent to the throne of England was the Catholic James II.

[57] Often the dragoons were referred to as *The Dragonnades* but strictly speaking they were the king's dragoons – a 'dragonnade' was the forced lodging of dragoons in Huguenot homes.

[58] The billeting of these unruly troops had been tried as early as 1661, but their brutal actions led to furious Protestant uprisings.

- 418 -

The Story of the Huguenots – a Unique Legacy

[59] Although the term *Dragonnade* did not come into official existence across France before 1681, a trial of dragoons carrying out such activity was undertaken in a few areas (see previous note and note 57).

[60] The main direct tax levied on people (*personelle)* and property (*reelle)* was the *taille*.

[61] Madam Maintenon, the king's mistress, wrote to her brother thus: '*I beg of you to carefully use the money you are about to receive. Estates in Poitou may be got for nothing'*.

Chapter 8 – Post Revocation: Persecution and Punishment

[62] The 'Election de Montivilliers' is just one of the lists drawn up across France giving details of properties and their former Protestant owners. As an example, this particular list details several houses in Fécamp which had been owned by Anne Despommare, widow of Malendin (Mallandain).

[63] During the period that Protestant religious services were illegal in France, Huguenots worshipped secretly at these secluded churches.

[64] Only a small number of pastors were ever sentenced to the galleys. Usually they were given the death sentence.

[65] It has often been assumed that all the refugees who left their homeland fled, but in fact, not all did – some were eventually forcibly exiled on the orders of Louis XIV (see note 66).

[66] Jean was left in solitary confinement for five weeks before being moved to a cell with other prisoners, including his erstwhile friend Perigal.

[67] Translates as '*Names of the confessors who by the orders of King Louis XIV were brought from various prisons to the castle of Dieppe in March and April 1688 and embarked by the same order on April 27, to be transported to England – Goderville: Jean Malandain, Marthe Baudouin his wife'*.

Chapter 9 – Decisions and Harsh Realities

[68] Although the boat crossing would often be hazardous, it would be viewed as being a safer alternative to a long journey on foot across country.

[69] From this date any child up to the age of 16 years could be forcibly taken from his or her Protestant parents.

[70] Known alternatively as the *Grace* (or *Peace) of Alais*.

[71] There were a number of prisons across France that held women who had been discovered and consequently arrested for still practising their Protestant faith, the most famous of which is the Tour de Constance, Aigues-Mortes, in the south of France. One woman, Marie Durand, taken prisoner at the age of 15 years old, was held there for 38 years, and is believed to have scrawled the word *'resist'* on the wall of her prison cell.

[72] Some historians have questioned whether this sizable migration of Huguenots from France did in fact have a harmful effect on the French economy. It may not have been as damaging as first surmised, but nonetheless the loss of so many skilled citizens could only have impacted very adversely on the French economy.

[73] Louis XIV had a few years earlier exiled Huguenots who refused to abjure, but now imposed this new law.

[74] *Camisard* – from the word 'camisole', which is a white shirt worn over a person's outer clothes so as to be easily recognised in the dark by comrades. In 1707, a coffee house in St Martin's Lane, London, was named *The Camisards* in support of these valiant men and women.

[75] Following the French Revolution, Protestantism was again practiced without fear of reprisal.

[76] Abraham Mazel and Elie Marion were amongst the four main leaders of the Camisards.

PART TWO
The Exodus and the Way Forward

Chapter 10 – Time to Start Again
[77] Those from the Netherlands who fled during the uprisings of 1572 against the rule of Philip II and his desire to stamp out Protestantism.

[78] A word used to describe people akin to the French but who inhabited the (now Belgian) provinces of Hainault, Namur and Liège together with parts of Luxembourg and southern Brabant.

[79] Arras, once the capital of the county of Artois, was renowned for its skilled artisans whose rich, finely woven pictorial tapestries were much sought after throughout Europe – hence high-quality tapestries becoming known as '*Arras*'.

[80] He was granted naturalisation in 1683.

[81] In that era, the crossing from Dieppe to Dover would have probably taken up to 20 hours depending on the weather and tides at that time of year.

[82] After this order became law, any who tried to hide in the hold in barrels were often suffocated by the fumes.

[83] Montpellier was one of many towns and cities across France that had been designated 'Free Protestant' until the Revocation.

[84] The Louis D'Or was the French currency at that time; it had replaced the livre. One Louis D'Or was worth ten livres.

Chapter 11 – Protestant England's Welcome
[85] Belgium is now roughly the area once known as the Spanish Netherlands.

[86] Failure to prove adherence to the Protestant faith could, and often did, result in forced removal from England's shores.

- 421 -

The Story of the Huguenots – a Unique Legacy

[87] There were of course arrivals through the whole of this period but not necessarily in significant numbers at any one time.

[88] The town had been the sole remaining English foothold in France until it was lost on 23 January 1558 during the reign of Mary I.

[89] Walloon is the name given to people who lived in Wallonia, (now part of southern Belgium) whereas Huguenots came from all areas of France.

[90] Charles Lefevre, a descendant of this same Lefevre family, became Mayor of Canterbury and was a prominent figure during World War II in and around Kent.

Chapter 12 – Assimilation, Integration and Discord during the Tudor and Stuart eras

[91] In that era, Europe was mainly agricultural; in other words, pre-Industrial Revolution.

[92] The overspill of London beyond the city walls with its ancient gates of Aldgate, Bishopsgate, Moorgate, Cripplegate, Aldersgate, Newgate, Ludgate and Bridge Gate were known as '*liberties*', and contained a multi-styled variety of close-knit buildings covering the area from the city walls to the edge of the city ditch.

[93] Large quantities of the bricks used to rebuild London were made from clay dug from the Bethnal Green area, hence a famous thoroughfare eventually being named 'Brick Lane'.

[94] Doctor William Harvey (1576-1657) was famous as the man who discovered the circulation of the blood.

[95] A farthing was one quarter of a pre-decimal penny, and there were 240 pre-decimal pennies to £1.

- 422 -

The Story of the Huguenots – a Unique Legacy

[96] French word used to describe the Catholic party in France during the first half of the 17th century.

[97] Laws that limited private expenditure on food and personal items.

[98] Nethersocks were the precursor to stockings.

[99] They printed onto material that had been originally imported from India.

[100] A political party during the period 1680-1850, which preceded the Liberal Party.

Chapter 13 – England's Huguenot Churches
[101] The original church was destroyed during the blitz of WWII but was rebuilt during 1950-4, and the foundation stone was laid by Princess Irene of the Netherlands.

[102] The church was eventually re-sited in Victorian times to Soho Square in the midst of a well-established French community. Today, this is the sole survivor of the 23 Huguenot churches of London.

[103] Conference.

[104] The king had signed their Charter on 24 July 1550.

[105] The site of the original Threadneedle Street Church could not accommodate any expansion.

[106] It can be noted in these two examples that often there are differences in the spelling of both Christian names and surnames. A frequent, historical error in the precise spelling of names, particularly surnames, can often impede the search for an ancestor.

[107] Named in remembrance of the original 'Patent' granted by King James II.

- 423 -

The Story of the Huguenots – a Unique Legacy

[108] Huguenot French Protestants were also known as Calvinists in acknowledgement of John Calvin bringing Protestantism to France.

[109] *Témoignage* is the French word for Testimony, a declaration and evidence account.

[110] The meaning is that of one who had previously suffered for their faith as a galley slave.

[111] By this officially confirmed renunciation of the Roman religion, a person could be admitted as a member of this church.

[112] The Confirmation Service, whereby the person would 'confirm' their wish to be accepted in the protestant faith.

[113] Founded in 1641 by the Lord of Soubise, this church became the main church for those living in west London.

[114] *Pastor* is the Huguenot equivalent of a Church of England vicar, or a Catholic priest.

[115] Henceforth it became part of the Church of England, but today still hosts events for the Huguenot Society of Great Britain and Ireland.

[116] Although it had originally been set aside for French Huguenots, it eventually was given over to a Dutch congregation, and continued to be used by them until well into the 18th century.

[117] This parliament uniquely lasted for 20 years from 1640-60. Nearly all members of both Houses hotly condemned the non-parliamentary policies of personal rule by the king, and slowly but systematically took apart the edifice of personal rule, which the king was forced to accept.

[118] This Act for the first time allowed for non-religious services to be held in registry offices all over the United Kingdom.

- 424 -

The Story of the Huguenots – a Unique Legacy

[119] The former Huguenot church in Fournier Street, built in 1743-4 as an addition to the Threadneedle Street Church became a Methodist chapel in 1819, but was converted to a synagogue in 1897 before being transformed into a mosque in 1976, and is the only religious building outside of the Holy Land that has been home to Christianity, Judaism and Islam. Today, the Huguenot Sundial above the doorway can still be seen with the date 1743 and the words 'UMBRA SUMUS' ('We are but shadows') inscribed upon it.

[120] John's neighbour, two doors along at 2 Princelet Street, was Anna Maria Garthwaite, the famous silk pattern designer.

[121] A member of the clergy imprisoned for debt would often perform these weddings; in fact, a 'Fleet' wedding was very popular in the first half of the 18th century.

Chapter 14 – England: Aid and Legal Status
[122] The value of this collection today would be £12,030,000.

[123] Although England and Scotland were ruled by one king from 1603, they remained two separate countries until 1 May 1707.

[124] This Bill was an attempt at limiting the powers of the Catholic heir to the throne, the future James II; the alternative was for Charles II to be pressed into a second marriage to produce a Protestant heir.

[125] In 1681, the Threadneedle Street Church recorded 912 entries for 1,111 individuals whereas in 1685 the church listed 578 entries.

[126] This sum would be worth approximately £2,052,000 today.

[127] Lustring was a cloth similar to brocade.

[128] This sum would be worth approximately £2,202,000 today.

- 425 -

The Story of the Huguenots – a Unique Legacy

[129] This sum would be worth approximately £236,500 today.

[130] The Pest House of London was built in 1594 to house those suffering from what were then incurable diseases, such as leprosy or the plague. In 1693, the building was taken over to house sick Huguenot refugees until 1718.

[131] These were not the only funds – just the funds for which records were discovered in the hospital cellars. There were several other major funds including those instigated by Charles II as well as others initiated during the reigns of William and Mary and the reign of Queen Anne whose records are held elsewhere. The remainder of the grants, known as 'briefs', were from Parliament which issued 'letters patent' in the sovereign's name as Head of the Church for the authorisation of collections to be made in churches throughout England.

[132] Charles II's mother was aunt to Louis XIV.

[133] Henri IV, King of Navarre and France.

[134] This became a part of the Home Office in 1836.

Chapter 15 – To Aid One's Fellow Man
[135] Previously known as The Pest House.

[136] The word is derived from the French word '*journee*'; thus, a man seeking a day's work was known as a 'journeyman'.

[137] This record book commenced in 1737, and it gives details of the number of portions, and the type of portion, that were distributed.

[138] This sum would be worth £9.64 today.

[139] Jacques de Gastigny's portrait can still be seen at the French Hospital today.

[140] The term 'outdoor relief' meant the petitioner was seeking financial assistance, not applying for admission

Chapter 16 – London Settlements
[141] Somerstown borders Wandsworth and Merton.

[142] This was the largest bequest they had ever received.

[143] On the site where Ravensbury Mill now stands.

[144] Wandsworth scarlet – the dye was extracted from brazilwood, see note 185.

[145] Also cultivated along the River Thames at Battersea, Chelsea and Putney.

[146] A 'shift' or 'chemise' was a simple garment worn next to the skin to protect clothing.

[147] The church would have been the Ancienne Patente of Soho.

[148] Some fire policy registers are kept at the London Metropolitan Archives.

[149] Although the street these two men lived in was Rosoman, named after Thomas Rosoman (who rebuilt Sadler's Wells), the insurance clerk recorded their address as *Rosamond* Street – a neat illustration of how names could be carelessly misspelt, sometimes just because the scribe was unaware of the provenance, but at other times because the name did not have a recognisable sound, and therefore the spelling would be guessed at.

[150] Houses that were insured would display the insurance company escution so that the fire crews could identify the property that was insured by a specific company – if your property was without this identification it was assumed it was not insured and would therefore, be left to the mercy of the flames.

The Story of the Huguenots – a Unique Legacy

Chapter 17 – Spitalfields and Silk Weaving

[151] The silk for Queen Victoria's wedding gown was also woven by the Spitalfields weavers who lived and worked at no. 12 Church Street (now Fournier Street).

[152] A glossy silk fabric.

[153] A lightweight, glossy silk fabric.

[154] Meaning to 'reinforce'.

[155] A common complaint by the local population was that Huguenots only apprenticed other Huguenots.

[156] Dupon evolved into 'Dupen' for some family members.

[157] Paradoxically, in France, the preference was for English materials and fashions.

[158] French silk was the main rival of Spitalfields silk.

[159] In order to be a member of one of the livery companies, such as the Weavers Guild, you were obliged by law to become a 'freeman' if you were to work in the City of London. This was applicable to most cities within the United Kingdom.

[160] A political movement during the English Civil War (1642-51) which stood for the equality of all men in the eyes of the law, and religious tolerance.

[161] A working-class movement during the period 1838-67, which stood for political reform.

[162] Dr Kay, a Manchester-based doctor, who witnessed first-hand the insanitary conditions prevailing at the time.

- 428 -

[163] Joseph Marie Jacquard from Lyon, France, invented the first programmable power loom; this had an early form of punch cards that enabled many intricate designs to be woven that had previously been hand-woven. The machine was exhibited in 1801 at an industrial exhibition in Paris, and was, in effect, the first computer as it ultimately led to the first punch-card computers.

[164] Five shillings (5s) was one quarter of a pound; in decimal coinage the equivalent would be 25p.

[165] It must be noted that not all of the silk weavers in the area were of Huguenot descent. There could also be found an Irish population of weavers in Spitalfields and beyond.

Chapter 18 – Huguenot European Migration
[166] Ireland was at that time an unequal mixture of Gaelic and English settlements, but was also divided by religion.

[167] This treaty concluded the war between William III's forces and the Jacobites following the siege of Limerick.

[168] The Huguenot church in Portarlington kept its records in French until 1816.

[169] Arlington House was one of these schools; it had been founded in the building that had previously been the home of Col. de Petit Bosc.

[170] As in many sizable cities, parts of the city were often named for historical reasons, and the district where the Huguenots settled and worked in is still known as 'Picardy'.

[171] A Scottish acre equals 54,760 square feet, whereas the English acre is 43,560 square feet.

The Story of the Huguenots – a Unique Legacy

[172] After having persuaded Francis Bouchard and Claude Paulin, who had settled in London, to travel on with him to Scotland.

[173] This sum would be worth approximately £38,500 today.

[174] Prussia at the time of the *Thirty Years War* was an area comprising the Duchy of Prussia and the Margraviate of Brandenburg; it became the leading state of the German Empire in 1871, and Wilhelm I, King of Prussia from the Hohenzollern dynasty was proclaimed the German emperor.

[175] Within the family archives, as with many other families, there are several different spellings of Dupont, but for clarity I have chosen to use just one in this book.

[176] Tenant.

[177] Southern Belgium's inhabitants are still primarily French speaking, no doubt due to the influx into the area of so many Huguenots from France.

[178] Johan de Witt was a prominent republican in the Netherlands.

[179] Approaching Geneva from the north-west, the Cornavin Gate would probably have been the travellers' point of entry to the city. Today, *Geneva* Gare Cornavin train station, often simply called *'Cornavin',* is *Geneva's* central railway station, located in the north-western part of the city.

[180] Theriac was an ancient multi-ingredient preparation; originating as a cure for the bites of serpents, mad dogs and wild beasts, it later became an antidote to all known poisons. The name *'theriac'* (treacle), (Greek: *theriake,* Latin: *theriaca,* French: *theriaque)* was derived from the Greek for wild beast - *theriakos*. The first formula was created by Mithridates VI, King of Pontus, a skilful ruler but a monster of cruelty, who, living in such a fear of being poisoned, took a great interest in toxicology.

The Story of the Huguenots – a Unique Legacy

[181] He was the first Christian to obtain the rank of Pasha in the Turkish army without converting to Islam.

Chapter 19 – To Explore the Furthest Reaches

[182] This was a fairly common practice despite the risk that the owner's bible itself could suffer from the baking process; a 'baked' bible can be viewed at the Huguenot Museum, Rochester, Kent.

[183] The fifth ship that left the Netherlands with French refugees on board.

[184] Ironically, given the crime for which Samuel had been convicted, the Bank of England was persuaded by her to donate £25 towards the cost of the family's passage.

[185] The United States of America was founded on 4 July 1776; before then it was a colony of the United Kingdom.

[186] René Laudonniere later wrote a first-hand account of the three attempts to found a French colony in America.

[187] Becoming part of New Jersey and also New York, and previously known as New Amsterdam.

[188] The Huguenot settlers named the area as a tribute to Die Pfalz, the region in Germany where they had first settled. The literal translation of Die Pfalz is 'The Palatinate'.

[189] Jean was one of the founders of New Paltz.

[190] Canada did not officially exist as a country until 1 July 1867; before then it was a group of colonies that included New Brunswick, Canada and Nova Scotia.

[191] In 1621, James I, King of England, renamed Acadia to *'Nova Scotia'* (Latin for 'New Scotland').

The Story of the Huguenots – a Unique Legacy

[192] The Mallandains were a much-travelled family, who at one point left England to return to France for a few years before once more returning to England.

[193] From Gaspard de Coligny's line, many royal lines of Europe are descended including the current British royal family.

[194] Pau-Brasil was a highly valued durable wood that eventually gave its name to the country (see note 144).

[195] Villegaignon was a Catholic, but for a time he did feel some empathy towards the Calvinist teachings.

Chapter 20 – Riots, Justice and Retribution
[196] Weaver's assistant who sat at the loom to lift the heavy warps for the weaver. Until the invention of the Jacquard loom, all looms needed two people to operate and produce the material to the required design.

[197] A person employed to wind the weft thread onto a quill.

[198] A form of printed linen that had become very fashionable.

[199] The medieval Palace of Westminster, which housed Parliament, stood on this site until a fire in October 1834 largely destroyed it. Old Palace Yard was part of this complex. The current Houses of Parliament were built to replace the old medieval buildings.

[200] The first Calico Act of 1700 banned the importation of this material, whereas the second Act confirmed the ban on importation as well as the sale and use of cotton (calico).

[201] A person who twists silk fibres into thread.

The Story of the Huguenots – a Unique Legacy

[202] The weavers had prepared a large book detailing prices for all the different types of silk and the variously-skilled persons employed in the production of the finished articles.

[203] Now known as Boundary Street, Bethnal Green.

Chapter 21 – The Glorious Revolution and the Huguenot Regiments
[204] His older brother, Charles II, insisted that although James had converted to Catholicism he was to continue taking the Anglican sacrament.

[205] The two kingdoms became one on 1 May 1707.

[206] William had been first in line to the thrones of England and Scotland by virtue of his wife Mary Stuart, but the birth of the male heir James Francis had pushed Mary and her husband's claim into second place. William was also the son of Charles I's eldest daughter Mary.

[207] His wife and two of his children were ultimately reunited with de Bostaquet, but a number of his female relatives were incarcerated – in several instances for life – in convents.

[208] His last act of defiance as he fled England was to toss the Great Seal into the Thames.

[209] Yale Law School, *Avalon Project, Documents in Law, History and Diplomacy.*

[210] The 1689 Act of Toleration did not give the same rights and privileges to Catholics.

[211] Known today as Parliamentary Privilege.

[212] The area is now known as County Donegal; it had been an old Gaelic kingdom, was staunchly Catholic, and therefore keen to see James II regain his throne.

- 433 -

213 Schomberg greatly favoured Huguenots; he even told William that Huguenot soldiers were worth twice the number of any other troops.

214 The elderly Marquis de Ruvigny had been a good friend to De Bostaquet, and he had even stood godfather to De Bostaquet's 19th child. A month later, however, he was dead, and he lies buried in the Savoy Church in the Strand. Ruvigny had raised the three Huguenot cavalry regiments, but following his death in 1689, the command of these regiments was taken up by his two sons: Henry, the second Marquis, who assumed overall command, and Pierre, later known as *La Caillemotte*, who, together with Cambon and La Melonière, led each of the regiments.

215 His invasion of Ireland met with the approval of Pope Alexander VIII, who was part of the Grand Alliance against Louis XIV's ambitions to dominate Europe. Whilst the war in Ireland was aimed at consolidating William's kingdom, it was also about halting the French monarchy in its attempt to rule much of Europe. And so it was not simply Protestants fighting Catholics because both armies were a mix of both faiths. The Irish Jacobites, however, considered it to be for religious and ethnic reasons as they wanted to regain Catholic toleration and the restoration of land ownership, both of which had been swept aside under Oliver Cromwell along with the right to hold public office, practice their religion and sit in the Irish Parliament.

216 These Ulster Protestants chose the epithet '*Enniskilleners*', but they were often known as 'Scots-Irish' as many had previously left Scotland to settle in Ireland.

217 This was the date of the battle according to the Julian calendar, which was replaced by the Gregorian calendar in 1752, but with the adoption of the new calendar the date of the battle became 11 July; paradoxically, the battle has been celebrated for over 200 years on 12 July.

218 The Battle of the Boyne was the beginning of the end of the fight for control of Ireland that was to conclude just two years later.

The Story of the Huguenots – a Unique Legacy

Chapter 22 – Citizenship, Faith and Loyalty
[219] Named for George Fournier of Huguenot descent.

Chapter 23 – French Inheritances
[220] A celebrated preacher of his time also on a visit to Geneva.

[221] Their elder son, Peter Thomas, married Jane Anne Romilly whose daughter, Catherine, married John Roget, father of Peter Roget.

[222] A term derived from the 'silk' gowns worn by a Queen's Councillor (QC).

[223] Due to the recurring problem of the spelling of French names, not to mention their similarity in some cases, this family's surname is written in either format.

PART THREE
Huguenot Enhancement of Life in the United Kingdom – A Legacy

Chapter 24 – Commerce, Benevolence and The Word
[224] Huguenots contributed up to ten percent of the capital put forward to enable the establishment of the Bank of England.

[225] A London merchant and a member of the Merchant Taylors' Company, Paterson's proposal was to utilise public debt as a means of borrowing from a bank.

[226] Today, there are blue plaques indicating where both coffee houses once stood.

[227] In 1984 this company became the first City stockbroker to be granted a coat of arms.

[228] There is some ambiguity over the date the society was formed as it is also noted as being founded on 29 January 1720.

- 435 -

The Story of the Huguenots – a Unique Legacy

[229] A term used by Gilds as well as Huguenots referring to the funds paid in.

[230] This was the name of the French almshouses on the corner of Black Eagle Street and Grey Eagle Street.

[231] On the corner of Fournier Street and Brick Lane, Spitalfields.

[232] The same decision was taken in 1776 by the other church schools in west London for the same reasons.

[233] The Briefs were forerunners to the Royal Bounty.

[234] John Mallandain senior was a professional musician, but also earned his living as a sugar refiner and grocer.

[235] These two men would have had close family links with the Mallandains to have recommended young John, as it was rare for someone of the lower classes to be accepted as a cadet.

[236] Paul's apprenticeship was to Bernard Picart, specialising in architecture and portrait illustrations for books.

[237] Jemima became the mother of John Henry Newman (February 1801 - August 1890). He had first become an Anglican priest, poet and theologian, and later a Catholic cardinal, before he developed into an important yet controversial figure in the religious history of England in the 19th century.

[238] The Fourdriniers ultimately became known as the first 'wholesale stationers'.

[239] Charles Fourdrinier and Mathew Towgood built up the wholesale stationery business at Sherbourne Lane, selling paper products that Mathew Towgood manufactured at the St Neots Mill.

The Story of the Huguenots – a Unique Legacy

[240] After many years of trying to obtain the annual fees due to them, Henry and his daughter travelled to St Petersburg, remaining there for a year in a vain attempt to persuade the Imperial Court to settle the debt owed.

[241] Now known as the Royal Botanical Gardens, Kew.

Chapter 25 – Science and Service
[242] Both of William's sons were confusingly named Peter, but to differentiate them, one was known as Peter the Elder and the other as Peter the Younger.

[243] A Dutch mathematician, who also laid the foundations for mechanics and worked on astronomy and probability.

[244] The results of these experiments were published in 1674; some of these had included attempts at food preservation in a vacuum following his construction of an air pump.

[245] The Royal Society was begun in 1645 when a group of scientists began to meet regularly to discuss their ideas and experiments. It is the oldest independent scientific academy and was founded to promote high standards of scientific research.

[246] Pressure cookers were first known as digesters.

[247] Due to radiational cooling on the surface of the earth.

[248] The Copley medal is the Royal Society's oldest and most prestigious award. It is presented annually for outstanding research achievements in any area of the sciences.

[249] Lenses that transmit light without separating it into constituent colours.

[250] Although it merged with Boots the Chemist in 2009.

[251] A large watertight chamber, open at the bottom, from which the water is kept out by air pressure, and in which construction work may therefore be carried out under water.

[252] And remained so until 1917.

[253] This was during the War of the Spanish Succession 1701-4 into which England was drawn in 1702.

[254] This honour was only ever given on the battlefield.

[255] When the last Hapsburg king of Spain, Charles II, died childless, several candidates came forward resulting in a power struggle across Europe.

[256] Much earlier, Geneva had been part of the Dukedom of Savoy, but the dukedom gradually fell apart resulting in the Swiss declaring Geneva an independent republic in 1535. This independence was challenged several times until final independence was achieved by the Genevans in 1602 when they repelled an invasion by the Duke of Savoy. This final repulsion is celebrated annually in the city.

[257] William of Orange was hailed the saviour of his people when he expelled the Catholic army of Louis XIV from nearly all of the Dutch Republic.

[258] There were disputes between France and some of her neighbours on her northern, eastern and south-eastern borders, which resulted in a series of summer campaigns. These wars lasted from 1688-97.

[259] An early type of portable gun supported on a tripod or a forked rest.

[260] As many had been, following William's victory in Ireland.

[261] Henri de Massue, 2nd Marquis de Ruvigny, was the 2nd Earl of Galway.

Chapter 26 – The Quality of the Huguenot Artisan

[262] Augustine's grandson, George, became an apprentice silk weaver, who went on to establish the Courtauld empire. He introduced silk-throwing into Essex.

[263] An apprentice would usually serve a term of seven years, at the end of which his 'binding' to his master would be broken; thus, he would be deemed a 'freeman' and therefore a free member of the Guild.

[264] The goldsmith would register his own mark with Goldsmiths Hall, and he would be obliged to stamp each piece of his work with his unique mark.

[265] Salt was a condiment that was used a great deal in flavouring dishes far more than we do in society today. Often a special receptacle for salt was manufactured for use by diners. Frequently, a person's station in life would be determined by their position at the table – hence the term 'above or below the salt', or even 'worth his salt'.

[266] The story of the Portals' daring escape from France, according to Christopher Portal; page 6 of his book *The Reluctant Goldsmith* relates to another branch of the family – second cousins who remained in France, and who reluctantly converted to Catholicism. Although the escape is well documented in Samuel Smiles' book, perhaps Christopher Portal's version is the more factual.

[267] Henry became the wealthiest of the Portals having founded a successful paper-making business in Hampshire.

[268] Gold and silversmiths' work was divided into two groups until the 20th century. A largeworker produced more substantial items, such as tureens, baskets and dishes.

[269] *'The precious jewel hides its peerless lustre; In a coarse, rugged coat, with pain removed; But well rewarding all the pain it gives.'*

The Story of the Huguenots – a Unique Legacy

270 A toyman was a person who produced a wide range of silver miniatures, as well as retailing trinkets fashioned from materials such as mother-of-pearl and/or papier-mâché or tortoiseshell; products would also have included items such as snuff boxes.

271 Once you had become a 'freeman' you would be expected to register your mark with the Goldsmiths Hall. You had to apply your mark to each piece of work and send it to the Goldsmiths Hall to be 'hallmarked'. If they did not feel a submission was up to the required standard they would have it destroyed in order to maintain the high standards expected of them.

272 In this period, the Britannia standard was higher than Sterling.

273 Paul de Lamerie was not the only Huguenot silversmith to be brought before the Court for this, but no one else flouted the rules as much as he did.

274 A term used in the jewellery trade to describe a gem of the 'highest quality'. The greater the translucence, or purity, of a jewel – such as is found in a drop of clean water – the better the quality.

275 Also spelt *Oursiau*.

276 A pioneer of mezzotint – the production of a print made from an engraved copper or steel plate the surface of which has been scraped and polished to give areas of shade and light respectively. The technique was much used in the 17th, 18th and early 19th centuries for the reproduction of paintings.

277 Artisans always marked their work with the first two letters of their surname as their 'hallmark'.

278 The term 'greenhorn' comes from the overheating of horn by an apprentice – causing discolouration.

- 440 -

The Story of the Huguenots – a Unique Legacy

Chapter 27 – Architecture and Creativity

[279] He chose to settle there for a time in order to wait for any adverse consequences from his alleged collusion in Popish plots.

[280] A type of finish used to imitate Asian lacquer work.

[281] The glass produced in Normandy became known as a 'crown' – a globule of molten glass attached to a tube which a glass blower would blow down and spin continuously.

[282] A technique well used in Lorraine whereby the glass-blower would blow long cylinders of glass that were then cut open lengthways and flattened into sheets.

Chapter 28 – The Arts

[283] Sir Samuel Romilly had been a lawyer and member of the flourishing reform movement of Regency England, but his own mental instability led to his suicide following his wife's death, which his nephew and physician Peter witnessed, and who, despite frantic efforts, was unable to save his uncle's life.

[284] One of the Martineau family descendants, who had remained in France, eventually moved to England, and amongst the current family descendants is Victorine Martineau.

[285] The British Lying-in Hospital was the second maternity hospital in London. It was established in 1749 in Brownlow Street, but moved to new premises in Endell Street in 1849. Not everyone welcomed the maternity hospital, and indeed the debate about male midwives and forceps continued for many years. The hospital itself closed in 1913.

[286] His family had themselves donated various examples of their own timepieces, actively encouraging other watchmakers to follow suit.

[287] Within two generations, this was to change from Garrie to Garrick.

The Story of the Huguenots – a Unique Legacy

288 Their mother, Anne Cough, was the daughter of a vicar.

289 The acting profession at that time was not held in high regard.

290 His mother had returned to England after the death of her second husband, and Albert decided to follow her because his mistress had been very angry when news of his forthcoming marriage became known, and vengefully tried to come between the couple.

291 This house was destroyed by a V1 flying bomb in June 1944.

292 In 1933, Samuel Courtauld's younger brother Stephen took out a 99-year lease from the Crown for Eltham Palace, the agreement being that he restored the Great Hall to its former state; as there were no other restrictions, the palace indeed re-surfaced, but not this time as a medieval edifice – instead it would be a fine example of an art deco mansion.

PART FOUR
France and England to the Present Day

Chapter 29 – France – Injustice and Enlightenment
293 Anne-Rose Calas had been born in Spitalfields before the family returned to France a few years later.

294 Jeanne Viguier was the sole maid in the household – and a staunch Catholic. It was forbidden for Huguenot families to employ more than one servant, who had to be of the Catholic faith.

295 Certain professions were barred to Protestants; a certificate confirming they were of the Catholic faith would be required from a priest. Marc-Antoine had apparently tried to obtain one in order to achieve his chosen career path, but a woman in the local Catholic church had spoken out that he was the son of Protestant parents, who furthermore had tried to leave the country years before because of their faith.

[296] Police detective, prosecutor and magistrate best describes this role. There were at that time eight capitouls of Toulouse. The capitoul who attended the Calas family was David de Beaudrigue, said to be particularly fanatical, who made the arrests without the warrants that were necessary under prevailing French law, and it was he who issued the call for witnesses. He immediately believed members of the Calas family had carried out the murder of Marc-Antoine.

[297] Widely considered one of France's greatest Enlightenment writers, Voltaire, as he later became known, was born François-Marie Arouet to a prosperous family on 21 November 1694 in Paris. He was a prolific writer of a wide diversity of literature including his famously acclaimed philosophical work *Dictionnaire Philosophique*, an encyclopedic dictionary that embraced the concepts of Enlightenment, and, significantly, rejected the ideas of the Roman Catholic Church.

[298] It was Voltaire's sustained campaign that led to the posthumous exoneration and pardon of Jean Calas.

[299] Voltaire's intervention – along with others including the brother of Louis XVI – was to finally bring about a change in the law towards Protestants with a new edict.

Chapter 30 –The early 20th Century
[300] 27.432 metres by 50.8 centimetres.

[301] He undertook one further substantial order in 1904 for the Raj of Jhalawar whose requirements were the same as the king's except for being 12 yards longer.

[302] A technique used to produce a marbled or watered effect.

[303] A cloth produced from a mix of silk and wool.

[304] October 1853 – March 1856.

305 The Cranbrook Estate opened in 1963, it consists of six tower blocks that were each named after towns twinned with Bethnal Green at that time.

306 4,648 South Africans died on the Western Front; a large percentage of these fatalities occurred during this battle at Delville Wood, and there were also a number of Southern Rhodesians who died during this battle.

307 A South African author, politician, mining financier and pioneer of the fruit industry.

308 He was the sixth generation from Guillaume Guyon.

309 Extraordinarily, 38 years later, the post-war British Labour Government ruled that Peter and all the other children born in India of British parents were henceforth to be known not as British but Indian as that had been their place of birth.

310 Winston Churchill could claim Huguenot descent through his maternal line, the Jeromes.

311 Known as 'The Narrows' because just 1,600 metres of heavily mined waters separated the two shores.

312 The Straits – 65km in length and 7km in width (aside from The Narrows) – were overlooked by vertiginous, heavily fortified cliffs rising sharply out of the strong swirling currents making navigation challenging: to the north-west lies the Gallipoli Peninsula with the coast of Asia Minor to the south.

313 This list was published in the Huguenot Society's Proceedings of 1920 Vol 12, No 4, pp 290-320.

314 An honour rarely bestowed upon a woman.

315 *La Croix de Guerre* – a French military decoration awarded from 1915, often awarded to foreign military allies. The *Médialle de la*

- 444 -

Reconnaissance Français was first issued in 1917, awarded to civilians in gratitude of their heroism.

[316] In an attempt to persuade the United States to become part of a peace-keeping alliance after WWI, it was the French foreign minister, Aristide Briand, who first suggested a bi-lateral non-aggression pact to U.S. Secretary of State Frank B. Kellogg.

[317] A further 47 nations later signed the pact.

Chapter 31 –To the End of the 20th Century

[318] James Rondeau had studied teaching; a wordsmith by both inclination and profession, he wrote two weighty tomes as well as a pamphlet on the untimely death of George IV's only child, Princess Charlotte, in 1817. Published by Hatchard's of Piccadilly, and Lackington, Allen & Co of Finsbury.

[319] The fact that some Catholic families had felt pity and compassion for the Huguenots, and thus aided them in their times of need, has been documented earlier in this book.

[320] The Holocaust Centre in Jerusalem is Israel's official memorial to Jewish victims of WWII, and also to non-Jews who aided them.

[321] A biblical reference which can be found in Galatians 3:28 or Romans 10:12; roughly speaking, both these quotations state that race is unimportant, and that being human is what truly matters.

[322] German orders stated that all Jews in France would need to carry identity papers stamped with a 'J', hence the need for false papers.

[323] At his trial in 1947, an SS officer commented, "We found no difficulty with the Vichy Government in implementing Jewish policy."

[324] It is highly likely that the mayor felt her to be in danger, and this was why he sent her away.

[325] The Queen is a Huguenot descendant through her ancestor, Sophia Dorothea, granddaughter of the Marquis D'Olbreuse, a Huguenot nobleman.

Chapter 32 – Revolution and Recognition, Apology and the Future
[326] Alternatively known also as the Edict of Versailles.

[327] Prior to this time, not all the laws of France were the same across its domains; many laws were still only identified with specific regions rather than the entire country. Napoleon wanted to give the French people universal laws that were legally binding no matter where in France they lived. Today, the *Napoleonic Code* forms the basis of many legal systems within Europe. Napoleon, when living in exile, expressed a desire that he would forever be remembered for his Code.

[328] A 13th century building much altered over time that once housed the Royal Treasury until it was broken up during the French Revolution, the building becoming State-owned.

[329] Today there are a little over 100 of these grand old houses in Spitalfields.

[330] The spelling she gave was *Agombart*, but we have learnt that names have been frequently misspelt over the centuries.

[331] Which translates as: '*In the difficult times that we have to pass through, it is the duty of all the Evangelicals to extend their hand, to persevere with courage in the task which has been entrusted to them, and if it is necessary, to remain alone with God.*'

BIBLIOGRAPHY OF HARD-COPY (non-online) BOOKS

Albion: *The Proceedings of Conference of British Studies at its Regional and National Meetings: Vol 8 No 3, 1976.*

Barker, Dr S. K., *Protestantism, Poetry and Protest: The Vernacular Writings of Antoine de Candieu (c1534-1591).* (Ashgate Publishing Limited, Farnham, 2009.)

Benedict, Philip, *Graphic History: The Wars, massacres and troubles of Totorel and Perrissin.* (Librarie Droz, Geneva, 2007.)

Bersier, Eugene, *The earlier life of the great Huguenot,* translated by Annie Holmden. (Hodder and Stoughton, London, 1884.)

Birnie, Arthur, MA, *The March of History: The early nineteenth century to the present day (retrospect 1760-1832).* (McDougall's Educational Co. Ltd., Edinburgh.)

Burn, John Southerden, *The History of the French, Walloon, Dutch, and Other Foreign Protestant Churches* (London, 1846).

Boyle, John, *Portrait of Canterbury.* (Robert Hale, London, 1974.)

Burdette, Dallas R., D. Min., *Biblical Preaching and Teaching,* volume 2. (Xulon Press, USA, 2010.)

Carpenter, Audrey T., *John Theophilus Desaguliers: A Natural Philosopher, Engineer and Freemason in Newtonian England.* (Continuum International Pubishing Group, London, 2011.)

Carsten F.L., T*he New Cambridge Modern History: Volume 5, The Ascendancy of France 1648-88.* (Cambridge University Press, London, 1961.)

Church of England Council for Christian Unity, *Called to Witness and Service*: *The Reuilly Commons Statement, with Essays on Christ, Eucharist and Ministry.* (Church House Publishing, 1999.)

Churchill, Winston, Sir, *A History of the English-Speaking Peoples: Vol 2 The New World.* (Weidenfeld and Nicolson, London, 1974.)

Clarke, Jack A., *Huguenot Warrior: The Life and times of Henri de Rohan 1578-1638.* (Springer Science & Business Media B.V., 1966.)

Costella, John, *Walk with Me Charles Dickens.* (AuthorHouse UK, 2014.)

Cox, Jane, *Old East Enders.* (The History Press, Stroud (Gloucs) 2013.)

- 447 -

Cruickshank, Dan, *Spitalfields: The History of a Nation in a handful of Streets.* (Windmill Books, London, 2017.)

Cunningham, William, *The Growth of English industry and commerce in modern times.* Vol. 1. (Frank Cass & Co., London, 1968.)

Currer-Briggs, Noel, and Gambier, Royston, *Huguenot Ancestry.* (Phillimore, Chichester, 1985.)

Davies, Norman, *Europe: A History.* (Pimlico, London, 1997.)

Derek H. Davis (ed.) and Elena Miroshnikova (ed.), *The Routledge International Handbook of Religious Education.* (Routledge, London, 2013)

Dodd, G., *London,* edited by Charles Knight. (Charles Knight & Co., London, 1842.)

Duffy, Christopher, *Siege Warfare: The Fortress of the early modern world 1494-1660.* (Routledge, London, 1996.)

Fransman, Laurie, QC, *Fransman's British Nationality Law* (3rd edition.) (Haywards Heath, Bloomsbury Professional, 2011.)

Garnier, A. J., Revd, *The Huguenots in Britain with special reference to their settlements in Canterbury.* French Huguenot Church, The Crypt, Canterbury. (Canterbury, 1965.)

Garrioch, David, *The Huguenots of Paris and the Coming of Religious Freedom, 1685–1789.* (Cambridge University Press, New York, 2014.)

Goodwin, James, MBA, MA, *The Huguenot Influence on English Furniture 1660-1714.* (Birkbeck College University of London, 2003; also available in PDF.)

Greengrass, Mark, *France in the Age of King Henri IV: The struggle for stability.* (2nd edition.) (Routledge Taylor and Francis Group, London, 1995.)

Greengrass, Mark, 1983. *The Anatomy of a Religious Riot in Toulouse in May 1562.* The journal of Ecclesiastical History Volume 34, Issue 3. (Cambridge University Press, 1983.)

Gwynn, Grace L., M.A., *Le Lien - The Huguenot settlements in London.* (Special edition.)

Gwynn, Robin D., *Huguenot Heritage: The History and contributions of the Huguenots in Britian.* (Routledge & Kegan Paul, 1985.)

Hayward, J. F., *Hugenot Silver in England 1688-1727*. (Faber and Faber Limited, London, 1959.)

Heathcote, T. A., *The British Field Marshals: 1736-1997: A Biographical Dictionary*. (Pen and Sword Military, Barnsley, 2012.)

Holt, Mack P., *The French Wars of Religion, 1562–1629* (2nd edition). (Cambridge University Press, New York, 2005.)

Hylton, Raymond, *Ireland's Huguenots and Their Refuge 1662-1745*. (Sussex Academic Press, 2005.)

Inglis, Lucy, *Georgian London: Into the Streets*. (Penguin, London, 2014.)

Jenkins, Cecil, *France: People, History, and Culture*. (Constable & Robinson Ltd, London, 2011.)

Joby, Christopher, *The Dutch Language in Britain: (1550-1702) a social history of the use of Dutch in early modern Britain*. (Brill, Leiden Boston, 2015.)

Kershen, Anne, *Strangers, Aliens and Asians: Huguenots, Jews and Bangladeshis in Spitalfields 1660-2000*. (Routledge, Abingdon, 2005.)

Knecht, R J., *French Renaissance Monarchy: Francis I and Henri II*. (Routledge, Abingdon, 2014.)

Knecht, R.J., *Hero or Tyrant? Henri III, King of France, 1574-89*. (Routledge Taylor & Francis Group, London, 2014.)

Koenigsberger, H.G., Mosse, George L., *A General History of Europe: Europe in the Sixteenth Century*. (Longman, London, 1971.)

Lheureux, Pierre, *Les Protestants de Luneray et leur Église en pays de Caux*. (Luneray, 1937.)

Lindsay, Thomas M., MA, *A History of the Reformation in 2 volumes*. (Wipf & Stocks, Orgeon, 1999.)

Linebaugh, Philip, *The London Hanged: Crime and Civil Society in the Eighteenth Century*. [Verso, London, 2006.]

London, Museum of, *The Quiet Conquest: The Huguenots, 1685-1985*. (Museum of London, London, 1985.)

Lublinskaya, A. D., *French Absolutism: The Crucial Phase 1620-1629*, translated by Brian Pearce. (Cambridge University Press, New York, 2008.)

The Story of the Huguenots – a Unique Legacy

Luria, Keith P., *Sacred Boundaries: Religious Coexistence and Conflict in Early-Modern France.* (Catholic University Press of America, Washington, 2005; also available in PDF.)

Margolf, Diane C., *Religion and Royal Justice in early modern France - The Paris Chambre de l'Edit 1598-1665.* (Truman State University Press, Missouri, 2003; also available in PDF.)

Marriot, John, *Beyond the Tower: A History of East London.* (Yale University Press, London, 2012.)

Macartney, C A., *The Hapsburg and Hohenzollern Dynasties in the 17th and 18th Centuries.* (Harper and Row, London, 1970.)

McLynn, Frank, *Crime and Punishment in Eighteenth Century England.* (Psychology Press, London, 1999.)

Montague, E.N., *Ravensbury Mitcham Histories.* (The Ravensbury Print Works, 2008.)

Moorehead, Caroline, *Village of Secrets: Defying the Nazis in Vichy France.* (Penguin Random House, London, 2015).

Nash, Robert (ed.), *The Hidden Thread: Huguenot Families in Australia.* (The Australian Huguenot Society, Newtown (New South Wales), 2009.)

Norris, Clive Murray, *The Financing of John Wesley's Methodism c1740-1800.* (Oxford University Press, Kettering, 2017.)

Onnekink, David, *War, Religion & Service: Huguenot Soldiery 1685-1713* edited by Matthew Glozier. (Ashgate Publishing Limited, Aldershot, 2007.)

O'Shea, Stephen, *The Perfect Heresy - The Life and Death of the Cathars.* (Profile Books, London, 2001.)

Plank, Ezra Lincoln, Dr (of Philosophy), *Creating perfect families: French Reformed Churches and family formation, 1559-1685.* (Thesis, University of Iowa, Iowa, 2013.)

Plummer, Alfred, *The London Weavers Company 1600-1700.* (Routledge (part of Taylor and Francis Group) London, 1972 reprint 2006.)

Portal, Christopher, *The Reluctant Goldsmith.* (Mendip Publishing, Somerset, 1993.)

Rawlinson, Catherine, and Janvrin, Isabelle, *The French in London: from William the Conqueror to Charles de Gaulle.* (Wilmington Square Books, London, 2016.)

- 450 -

Reaman, G. Elmore, *The Trail of the Huguenots in Europe, the United States, South Africa and Canada*. (Fredrick Muller Ltd, London, 1983.)

Reckitt, Harold J., RVR76. *A French Military Hospital.* (William Heinemann, London, 1921.)

Rondeau, Stan, *The Rondeaus of Spitalfields, An everyday Story of Huguenot Folk.* (Rondeau archives, London, 2014.)

Schneider, Robert A., *Public Life in Toulouse 1463-1789.* (Cornell University Press, New York, 1989.)

Scouloudi, Irene (ed.), *Huguenots in Britain and their French Background 1500-1800.* (Macmillan, London, 1987.)

Sharma, Simon, *A History of Britain 1603-1776.* (BBC Worldwide Ltd, London, 2001.)

Shaw, Caroline, *Britannia's Embrace: Modern Humanitarianism and the Imperial Origins of Refugee Relief.* (Oxford University Press, Oxford, 2015.)

Sider, Sandra, *Handbook to Life in Renaissance Europe.* (Facts on File Inc., 2005.)

Smiles, Samuel, *The Huguenots - Their settlements, churches and Industries in England and Ireland (1889).* (Kessinger, MT, 2008.)

Spicer, Andrew, and Mentzer, Raymond (editors) *Society and Culture in the Huguenot World 1559-1685.* (Cambridge University Press, New York, 2002.)

Stow, John, *A Survey of London: written in the year 1598.* (Sutton Publishing Ltd, London, 2005.)

Tapié, Victor Lucien, *La France de Louis XIII et de Richelieu,* translated by D. McN. Lockie. (Cambridge University Press, New York, 1984.)

Thomas, P., Shaw, R.A., Gwynn, R.D., *Huguenots in Wandsworth.* (Wandsworth Borough Council, London, 1985.)

Treasure, Geoffrey, *The Huguenots.* (Yale University Press, London, 2014.)

Trevelyan, G.M., *English Social History: A Survey of six centuries - Chaucer to Queen Victoria.* (Book Club Associates by arrangement with the Longman Group, London, 1973.)

The Story of the Huguenots – a Unique Legacy

Tulchin, Allan, *That Men Would Praise the Lord: The Triumph of Protestantism in Nimes, 1530-1570.* (Oxford University Press, Oxford, 2010.)

Watson, Robert, *The history of the reign of Philip the Second, King of Spain,* seventh edition. (Thomas Tegg, London, 1839.)

White, George, Sir, *The Clockmakers of London.* (The Trustees of the Museum and Educational Trust of the Worshipful Company of Clockmakers, 1998.)

White, Jerry, *London in the 18th Century - A Great and Monstrous Thing.* (Cambridge Massachusetts, Harvard University Press, 2013.)

Wilson, Derek, *A Brief History of The English Reformation.* (Constable & Robinson Ltd, London, 2012.)

Woodfall, W., and assistants, *Parliamentary Register: in the course of the first session of the second Parliament 1803.* (T. Gillet, London, 1803.)

Wylie, James Aitken, *The History of Protestantism.* (Virginia, 2002.)

ONLINE BIBLIOGRAPHY

The Huguenot Society

Anthony Springall, 'A Huguenot community in Scotland: the weavers of Picardy', *The Huguenot Society*, XXVII (1) 1998.

C. F. A. Marmoy, 'La Masion de Charité de Spitalfields', *Proceedings of the Huguenot Society,* XXIII (3) 1979.

Colin Lee, 'James Robinson Planche', *Proceedings of the Huguenot Society* XXVIII (1) 2003.

Denis Desert, 'The Stranger Community and the Established Church', *The Huguenot Society,* XXVIII (1) 2003.

Durand (family), 'The Durand Family Archive', *The Huguenot Society,* Huguenot Library, ref. no. M/16; and UCL Special Collections, miscellaneous copy letters, ref. no. 1769.

E. Alfred Jones, MA, FSA, 'Paul Crespin, Huguenot Goldsmith', *The Huguenot Society*, XVI (3) 1939-40.

- 452 -

The Story of the Huguenots – a Unique Legacy

E. C. Privat, 'The Huguenots in Germany', *The Huguenot Society,* XXI (2) 1966.

E. H. Fairbrother, (Miss), 'A French Protestant Prisoner of War', *The Huguenot Society* X (2) 1912.

E. H. Varley, 'John Rocque, the Map-maker and his Huguenot associations', *The Huguenot Society Proceedings,* XVII (5) 1945-46.

Esther J. Ehrman, Dr, 'Huguenot Participation in the French Theatre in London', *Proceedings of the Huguenot Society*, XXIV, 1988.

Francis H. W. Sheppard, Ph.D., FSA, 'The Huguenots in Spitalfields and Soho', *The Huguenot Society,* XXI (4) 1968.

George R. Beeman, 'Notes on the City of London Records dealing with the French Protestant Refugees', *The Huguenot Society* VII (1) 1901-02.

G. H. Overend, FSA, 'Strangers at Dover Part 1 1558-1644', *The Huguenot Society Proceedings,* XI (3) 1889.

Isaac Dumont de Bostaquet, 'Memoirs of Isaac Dumont de Bostaquet: A Gentleman of Normandy', edited by Dianne W Ressinger, *The Huguenot Society,* 2005.

John S. Powell, 'The French Church Portalington - after the French', *Huguenot Society Proceedings*, XXVII (4) 2001.

Jonathan Garnault Ouvry, 'The Ouvry family in the 19th Century', *The Huguenot Society,* XXIV (6) 1988.

Katherine Chater, *'The Legacy of the Huguenots in Wartime France'*, *Huguenot Society Journal* XXX (2) 2014.

Keith Finch, 'Great War Women of Huguenot Ancestry', *The Huguenot Society Proceedings,* XXX (4) 2016.

Keith Le May, 'Charity Schools provided by the French Protestant institution in London 1682-1931', *Proceedings of the Huguenot Society,* XXVII (I) 1998.

Philip Marland Rambaut, 'The Rambaut family: astronomy and astronautics', *The Huguenot Society,* XXVII (1) 1998.

Randolph Vigne, 'The Killing of Jean Calas: Voltaire's First Huguenot Cause', *The Hugenot Society*, XXIII (No 84 issue 5) 1980.

Randolph Vigne, 'A Great War link with the Cape Huguenots', *The Huguenot Society Proceedings,* XXX (2) 2014.

Susan Minet, 'Notes on the War of the Cevennes', *The Huguenot Society,* 43, XVI (3) 1939.

W. H. Manchee, 'George Doree: Citizen and weaver of London, b1844 d1916: The maker of King Edward VII's coronaton robes', *Huguenot Society Proceedings,* XI (3) 1916.

W. H. Manchee, 'Huguenot Soliders and their Conditions of Service in the English Army', *The Huguenot Society,* XVI (2) 1938/9.

William Chapman Waller, 'Early Huguenot Friendly Societies', *The Huguenot Society,* VII (3) 1900.

Winifred Turner, BA Lond., 'The Archives and Library of the French Protestant Church, Soho Square, formerly Threadneedle Street', *The Huguenot Society Proceedings,* XIV (4) 1932-3.

Quarto Series, The, *The Huguenot Society*, LI, 1974; LIV, 1979; LVI, 1983; LII, 1977.

References to electronic sources

Bristol Radical History Group, *The Spitalfields Silk Weavers: London's Luddites?* 2012.
https://www.brh.org.uk/site/articles/bold-defiance/ [Accessed 1 March 2017.]

Britannica, The Editors of Encyclopædia, *Dutch War.* Encyclopædia Britannica 24 July 2014.
https://www.britannica.com/event/Dutch-War. [Accessed 18 October, 2017.]

Britannica, The Editors of Encyclopædia, *Conspiracy of Amboise.* Encyclopædia Britannica 25 July 2015.
https://www.britannica.com/event/Conspiracy-of-Amboise [Accessed 13 April 2016.]

Britannica, The Editors of Encyclopædia, *Daniel Marot.* Encyclopædia Britannica 27 December 2006.
https://www.britannica.com/biography/Daniel-Marot. [Accessed 13 October 2017.]

Britannica, The Editors of Encyclopædia, *Edict of Nantes.* Encyclopædia Britannica 22 March 2016. https://www.britannica.com/event/Edict-of-Nantes. [Accessed March 2017.]

Britannica, The Editors of Encyclopædia, *Edmund Bonner.* Encyclopædia Britannica 20 July 1998. https://www.britannica.com/biography/Edmund-Bonner. [Accessed 20 April 2015.]

Britannica, The Editors of Encyclopædia, *Eighty Years' War.* Encyclopædia Britannica 29 February 2016. https://www.britannica.com/event/Eighty-Years-War. [Accessed 31 December 2017.]

Britannica, The Editors of Encyclopædia, *Frederick Herman, Duke of Schomberg.* Encyclopædia Britannica 21 January 2011. https://www.britannica.com/biography/Frederick-Herman-duke-of-Schomberg. [Accessed 25 December 2017.]

Britannica, The Editors of Encyclopædia, *Huguenot.* Encyclopædia Britannica 3 August 2016. http://www.britannica.com/print/topic/27500. [Accessed 6 August 2016.]

Britannica, The Editors of Encyclopaedia, *Jean Calas.* Encyclopædia Britannica 4 November 2011. https://www.britannica.com/biography/Jean-Calas. [Accessed 1 March 2016.]

Britannica, The Editors of Encyclopædia, *Kellogg-Briand Pact.* Encyclopædia Britannica 22 July 2016. https://www.britannica.com/event/Kellogg-Briand-Pact. [Accessed 24 December 2017.]

Britannica, The Editors of Encyclopædia, *Paul de Lamerie.* Encyclopædia Britannica 1 September 2017. https://www.britannica.com/biography/Paul-de-Lamerie. [Accessed 4 April 2017.]

Britannica, The Editors of Encyclopædia, *Peace of Cateau-Cambrésis.* Encyclopædia Britannica 13 March 2014. https://www.britannica.com/event/Peace-of-Cateau-Cambresis. [Accessed 31 December 2017.]

The Story of the Huguenots – a Unique Legacy

Britannica, The Editors of Encyclopædia, *Sir Samuel Romilly.* Encyclopædia Britannica 10 January 2011. https://www.britannica.com/biography/Samuel-Romilly. [Accessed 13 December 2017.]

Britannica, The Editors of Encyclopædia, *The Fronde.* Encyclopædia Britannica 5 February 2014. https://www.britannica.com/event/The-Fronde. [Accessed 19 May 2015.]

Britannica, The Editors of Encyclopædia, *Act of Toleration.* Encyclopædia Britannica 18 July 2016. https://www.britannica.com/event/Toleration-Act-Great-Britain-1689. [Accessed 27 March 2017.]

Churchmousec.wordpress.com, *Huguenot Settlements.* (page not in existence at time of print). http://churchmouse.wordpress.com/2013/08/2the-huguenot-settlements. [Accessed March 2017.]

Churchmouse Campanologist, *When the Huguenots Finally Became part of French Society.* 22 August 2013. http://churchmouse.wordpress.com/2013/08/22/when the huguenots finally became part of French society. [Accessed 10 January 2017.]

Churchmouse Campanologist, *Huguenot Clockmakers.* 26 August 2015. https://churchmousec.wordpress.com/2015/08/26/huguenot-clock makers-in-england/ [Accessed 31 May 2017.]

Churchmouse Campanologist, *The Huguenot Settlements in 16th Century Brazil.* 23 August 2013. https://churchmousec.wordpress.com/2013/08/23/the-huguenot-settlements-in-16th-century-brazil/ [Accessed 24 October 2016.]

Ed.ac.uk, *Peter Mark Roget.* The University of Edinburgh 22 January 2016. http://www.ed.ac.uk/ alumni/services/notable-alumni/alumni-in-history/peter-mark-roget. [Accessed 2 May 2017.]

Gracesguide.co.uk, *British Industrial History - Courtaulds.* 21 April 2016. http://www.gracesguide.co. uk/Courtaulds. [Accessed 14 June 2017.]

Gracesguide.co.uk, *Henry Fourdrinier.* n.d. http://www.gracesguide.co.uk/Henry Fourdrinier. [Accessed 30 June 2017.]

The Story of the Huguenots – a Unique Legacy

HistoryLearningSite.co.uk, *Cardinal Richelieu and the Huguenots.* n.d. http://www.historylearningsite .co.uk/france-in-the-seventeenth-century. [Accessed 31 March 2017.]

HistoryofWar.org, *Surprise of Meaux, September 1567.* 19 January 2011. http://www.historyofwar.org/articles/surprisemeaux.html. [Accessed 10 May 2016.]

Home.RootsWeb.Ancestry.com, *Huguenot Wars of France.* n.d. http://www.rootsweb.ancestry.com/wggerman/map/huguenotwar. htm. [Accessed 31 March 2017.]

Horners.org, *The Craft of the Horner.* 22 January 2016. http://www.horners.org.uk. [Accessed 6 September 2017.]

Mackey's Encyclopaedia of Freemasonry - Masonic biography. *John Desangliers.* n.d. http://www.masonicdictionary.com/desaguliers.html. [Accessed 12 June 2017.]

MapForum.com, *Rocque biography.* n.d. http://www.mapforum.com/ 05/rocque.htm. [Accessed 14 February 2017.]

MuseeProtestant.org, *The Eight Wars of Religion.* n.d. http://www.museeprotestant.org/en/notice/the-eight-wars-of-religion. [Accessed 10 January 2017.]

MuseeProtestant.org, *Pastors of the Church of the Desert.* n.d. https://www.museeprotestant.org/en/notice/pastors-of-the-church-of-the-desert/ [Accessed 10 January 2017.]

MuseeProtestant.org, *The First Canadian Colony: Acadia.* n.d. http://www.museeprotestant.org/en/notice/the-first-canadian-colony-acadia/ [Accessed 5 June 2017.]

MuseeProtestant.org, *The Eight Wars of Religion.* n.d. http://www.museeprotestant.org/en/notice/the-eight-wars-of-religion. [Accessed 10 January 2017.]

MuseeProtestant.org, *The Dragonnades 1681-1685.* n.d. http://www.museeprotestant.org/en/notice/the-dragonnades-1681-1685. [Accessed 9 November 2015.]

MuseeProtestant.org, *The Law of 1905.* n.d. http://www.museeprotestant.org.en.notice.the-law-of-1905. [Accessed 27 March 2017.]

The Story of the Huguenots – a Unique Legacy

MuseeProtestant.org, *The Edict of Fontainbleau or the Revocation (1685).* n.d.
http://www.museeprotestant.org/en/notice/the-edict-of-fontainbleau-or-the-revocation(1685). [Accessed 28 March 2015.]
New World Encyclopaedia, *Huguenot.* 26 March 2014.
http://www.newworldencyclopedia.org/p/index.php?title=Huguenot&oldid=979492. [Accessed 23 October 2017.]
Page, William, *Industries: Clock and Watch-making* in *A History of the County of Middlesex: Volume 2, General; Ashford, East Bedfont With Hatton, Feltham, Hampton With Hampton Wick, Hanworth, Laleham, Littleton,* Victoria County History, London, 1911.
BritishHistoryOnline.ac.uk.
http://www.british-history.ac.uk/vch/ middlesex/vol2/pp158-165. [Accessed 15 April 2018.]
Page, William, *Industries: Silk-weaving in A History of the County of Middlesex: Volume 2, General; Ashford, East Bedfont With Hatton, Feltham, Hampton With Hampton Wick, Hanworth, Laleham, Littleton.* BritishHistory.Online.ac.uk.
http://www.british-history.ac.uk/vch/middx/vol2/pp 132-137. [Accessed 25 May 2016.]
Parliament.uk, *The Law of Marriages - UK Parliament.* 2017. (Contains Parliamentary information licensed under the Open Parliament Licence v3.0.)
http://www.parliament.uk/about/living-heritage/transforming society. [Accessed 11 June 2017.]
Richard, J., *The battle of St Dennis - 10 November 1567.* 24 January 2011.
http://www.historyofwar.org/articles/battlesstdenis.html. [Accessed 22 Janaury 2016.]
Rickard, J., *Peace of Bergerac, 14 September 1577.*
http://www.historyofwar.org/articles/peacebergerac.html. [Accessed 21 December 2017.]
Rickard, J., *First War of Religion 1562-63.* 13 January 2011.
http://www.historyofwar.org/articles/warsfirstwarreligion.html. [Accessed 10 May 2016.]

The Story of the Huguenots – a Unique Legacy

SAHistory.org, *South African History Online.* 28 March 2012. http://www.sahistory.org.za/topic/arrival-jan-van-riebeeck-cape-6-april-1652. [Accessed 30 December 2017.]

Simpson, Peter, *The Forgotten Fourdrinier: The life, times and work of Paul Fourdrinier Huguenot Master Printmaker in London 1720-1758.* (e-book, AuthorHouse, Bloomington, 2017.)

StephenWalters.co.uk, n.d. http://stephenwalters.co.uk/history. [Accessed 24 December 2017.]

Worshipful Company of Apothecaries, The, *Origins.* n.d. http://www.apothecaries.org/charity/history/our-history. [Accessed 21 March 2017.]

Yale Law School, *Avalon Project, Documents in Law, History and Diplomacy.* n.d. http://avalon.law. yale.edu/ [Accessed 27 December 2017.]

Archival Sources

Agnew, David C. A., Revd, *Protestant Exiles from France in the reign of Louis XIV, or The Huguenot Refugees and their Descendants in Great Britain and Ireland* (second edition, 1886). n.d. (Contributor: Princeton Theological Seminary Library, Princeton, Edinburgh.) https://archive.org/details/protestantexiles01agne0. [Accessed March 2017.]

Archive.org, *The Dutch Church Registers, Austin Friars, London 1571-1874.* 15 November 2009. https://archive.org/details/cu31924029785445. [Accessed March 2017.

BritishLibrary.uk, *The Burney Collection.* The British Library. https://www.bl.uk/collection-guides/burney-collection. [Accessed 31 March 2017.]

BritishLibrary.uk, *Newspaper report of the Gordon riots, 1780.* The British Library. https://www.bl.uk/collection-items/newspaper-report-of-the-gordon-riots-handbill-1780. [Accessed 30 December 2016.]

The Story of the Huguenots – a Unique Legacy

BritishMuseum.org, 2017. *Isaac Basire - Printmaker*. British Museum. Ref. no. 133182. http://www.britishmuseum.org./research/ search_the_collection_database/termdetails.aspx?bioId=133182. [Accessed 1 March 2017.]

CityofLondon.gov.uk, *Huguenot Clerkenwell*. 29 September 2017. https://www.cityoflondon.gov.uk/ things-to-do/london-metropolitan-archives/the-collections/Pages/huguenot-clerkenwell.aspx. [Accessed 1 March 2018.]

LondonMetropolitanArchives.org, *Huguenots of Clerkenwell*. n.d. https://www.cityoflondon.gov.uk/things-to-do/london-metropolitan-archives/the-collections/Pages/huguenot-clerkenwell.aspx. [Accessed March 2017.]

Parliament.uk, *The Glorious Revolution - Bill of Rights 1689*. https://www.parliament.uk/about/living-heritage/evolutionof parliament/parliamentaryauthority/revolution/collections1/ collections-glorious-revolution/billofrights [Accessed 1 March 2017.]

PensionsArchive.org, *Research Guide to LMA's collections published April 2013. Huguenot Friendly Benefit Societies*. LMA Collections. http://www.pensionsarchive.org.uk/31/?form_19. reply ids=36 [Accessed 31 March 2017.]

Special Collections and Archive Research Centre. *Treasures of the McDonald Collection*. Oregon State University Special Collections. http://scarc.library.oregonstate.edu/omeka/exhibits/show/ mcdonald/incunabula/gutenberg/ [Accessed 31 March 2017.]

Miscellanea, *A French Protestant Prisoner of War*. Miscellanea, vol X, no. 17, issue 2.

LondonMetropolitanArchives.org, *Details taken from the LMA records relating to the case of the Gasherie, Gashry and Hanrott families*. (Based on research from personal visits.)

The Story of the Huguenots – a Unique Legacy

Citation of Articles

Anne M. Oakley, 'Strangers in Canterbury 1590-1790: The Huguenots follow the Walloons', *French Canterbury,* 1992. www.frenchchurchcanterbury.org.uk [Accessed 2 April 2017.]

Clive Emsley and Tim Hitchcock and Robert Shoemaker, 'Old Bailey Records', *Old Bailey Proceedings Online.* http://www.oldbaileyonline.org/static/huguenot [Accessed 25 August 2015.]

Dorothea Scarborough, 'The Huguenots - Their Faith, History and Impact', 23 January 2013. *The Reformation Society.* http://reformationsa.org/index.php/reformation/121-the-huguenots-their-faith-history-and-impact [29 May 2017]

Ellen White, 'The Great Controversy', *EllenWhite.info*, pp. 120-125. http://www.ellenwhite.info/future-of-protestantism-3a.htm. [Accessed 1 March 2017.]

G. Goyau, 'Louis XIV', 1910. *NewAdvent.org.* http://www.newadvent.org/cathen/09371a.htm. [Accessed 23 March 2017.]

Geoffrey W. Bromiley, 'Huldrych Zwingli,' *Encyclopædia Britannica,* 3 August 2016. https://www. britannica.com/biography/Huldrych-Zwingli [Accessed 5 August 2016.]

Gov.uk, Government summary of the naturalisation acts. 2017. https://www.gov.uk/government/uploads/system/uploads/attachment_data/file/267913/britnatsummary.pdf [Accessed 2 May 2017]

Howard Roberts and Walter H. Godfrey, (editors) 'Lambeth: South Bank and Vauxhall in Westminster Bridge Survey of London, volume 23. *BritishHistoryOnline.* http://www.british-history.ac. uk/survey-london/vol23 [Accessed 12 June 2017.]

James D. Tracy, 'Desiderius Erasmus', *Encyclopædia Britannica,* 16 December 2016. https://www.britannica.com/biography/Desiderius-Erasmus. [Accessed 20 December 2016.]

- 461 -

The Story of the Huguenots – a Unique Legacy

James McDonald, MA, MSc, 'Cathars and Cathar Beliefs in the Languedoc', *Cathar.info*, 8 February 2017.
http://www.cathar.info [Accessed 1 March 2017.]
Jean Marteihle, 'Life in the galleys - the memoirs of Jean Marteihle'. 21 June 2016.
http://rodama1789.blogspot.co.uk/2015/06/life-in-galleys-memoirs-of-jean.html [Accessed 10 August 2016.]
J. H. Thomas BA, 'Hampshire and the Company of White Paper Makers'.
http://www.hantsfieldclub.org.uk/publications/hampshirestudies/digital/1960s/vol26/Thomas.pdf
John Stacey, 'John Wycliffe', *Encyclopædia Britannica,* 18 December 2016.
https://www.britannica. com/biography/John-Wycliffe [Accessed 20 December 2016.]
Ken Armstrong, 'Paris Review,' *ParisReview.org.*
https://www.theparisreview.org/blog/2015/03/13/broken-on-the-wheel/ [Accessed 13 March 2015.]
Marianne Colloms and Dick Weindling, 'West Hampstead Life: The artist and his stepfather', *West Hampstead Life,* 2 February 2013.
http://westhampsteadlife.com/2013/02/02/the-artist-and-his-stepfather/5087. [Accessed 1 March 20017.]
New World Encyclopedia contributors, 'The Battle of the Boyne', *New World Encyclopedia*, 20 May 2016.
http://www.newworldencyclopedia.org/p/index.php?title=Battleof_the_Boyne&oldid=996097. [Accessed 7 June 2017.]
Rachel Cole, 'Peter Carl Faberge', *Encyclopædia Britannica* 20 June 2013.
https://www.britannica.com/ biography/Peter-Carl-Faberge. [Accessed 4 June 2017.]
Robin Gwynn, 'England's 'First Refugees', Vol 35, Issue 5 (May 1985). *HistoryToday.com.*
http://www.historytoday.com/robin-gwynn/englands-first-refugees. [Accessed 1 February 2015.]
Srta.hu/wp, 'John Calvin's presence in the Hungarian Reformed Church, 17th - 18th century', *The Reformed Theological Academy of Sárospatak,* online paper 2017.
srta.hu/wp-content/uploads/ 2015/02/Calvin.pdf. [Accessed 26 April 2017.]

The Economist, 'Fournier Street: One roof, many histories. Changing Shadows', *The Economist,* 18 December 2003. https://www.economist.com/node/2281603. [Accessed 1 March 2017.]

W. Carlos Martin, 'A History of the Huguenots', *The American Tract Society (1866).* http://illuminati-bg.bg/holy_bible/History-and-Archaeology/A-History-of-the-Huguenots-1866--W. Carlos-Martin.pdf. [Accessed 7 November 2017.]

William Bouwsma, 'John Calvin', *Encyclopædia Britannica* 15 November 2017. https://www.britannica.com/biography/John-Calvin. [Accessed 31 December 2017.]

References to Digitized Books

Bank of England, The, *The Bank of England: History and Functions.* (Bank of England Printing Works, Loughton, 1970, available in PDF.)

Bishop, Paul A., *Martin Luther and the Protestant Reformation.* 2017. http://www.hccfl.edu/media/173616/ee2luther.pdf [Accessed 7 November 2017.]

Christian Library, The, *The Reformer John a Lasco (1499-1560).* n.d. http://www.christianstudy library.org/files/pub/20120763%20-%20Faber%20R%20-%20The%20Reformer%20John%20%C3%A0%20Lasco .pdf. [Accessed 18 November 2017.]

Gutenberg.org, *Letters of John Calvin by Dr Jules Bonnet Vol I.* 1858. http://www.gutenberg.org/files/45423/45423-h/45423-h.htm#F Nanchor206206. 2014 [e-book ref. #45423]

Miller, J., *The Glorious Revolution: Contract and Abdication Reconsidered.* The Historical Journal, 25(3), 541-555. doi: 10.1017/ S0018246X0001178X. (1982.)

Orange Order of Scotland, The, *The Battle of the Boyne.* www.orangeorderscotland.com/The%20Battle%20of%20The%20 Boyne.pdf.

Richmond Charities, *Houblon's Almshouses.* www.richmondcharities.org.uk/almshouses/houblon-s-almshouses. *(Downloadable pdf.)*

Sturdy, David J., *Richelieu and Mazarin: A Study in Statesmanship* (kindle version). (Palgrave McMillan, London, 2003.)

Syvret, Marguerite, *Huguenot Heritage 1685-1985*. n.d. Société Jersiaise. *Annual Bulletin of the Societe Jersiaise* (vol. 24 (1986) p179-181). [Accessed 14 February 2017.]

Index

A

Abjuration, certificate of · - *99* -
Act of Toleration 1689, England ·
  - *247* -
Affair of the Placards · - *13* -, - *22* -
Agombar, Pierre · - *109* -
Agombar, Solomon · - *208* -
A'Lasco, Johannes · - *140* -, - *142* -,
  - *143* -
Alba, Duke of · - *33* -, - *37* -
Albigensian Crusade · - *7* -
Alderney, Channel Islands · - *199* -
Aldgate, east London · - *130* -
Ales, Languedoc · - *71* -
Ales, Peace of · - *71* -, - *98* -
Alexander III, Czar of Russia · - *219* -
Alfold, Surrey · - *327* -
Aliens Act 1793 · - *164* -
Almshouses · - *278* -
Amboise, Conspiracy of · - *27* -
Amboise, Edict of · - *32* -, - *33* -, - *35* -,
  - *36* -
Ammonet, Mary · - *226* -
Amsterdam · - *212* -, - *213* -, - *228* -
Andrée, Doctor · - *289* -
Angers, Loire Valley · - *31* -
Anne I, Queen of England · - *255* -
Anne of Denmark, Queen of England ·
  - *131* -, - *291* -
Annuities and life assurance · - *292* -
Antoine, King of Navarre · - *26* -, - *29* -,
  - *31* -
Arques-la-Bataille, Seine-Maritime ·
  - *54* -

Ashow, nr Kenilworth · - *327* -
Austin Friars, London · - *140* -
Australia · - *225* -

B

Babel, Peter · - *324* -
Bank of England · - *264* -
Barbar, Louis · - *304* -
Barnier, Jeanne · - *366* -
Barraud, Francis Gabriel · - *316* -
Basire, Issac · - *318* -
Basle, Switzerland · - *215* -
Bearn, south-west France · - *57* -,
  - *65* -, - *66* -, - *68* -, - *82* -
Beaufort, Francis · - *296* -
Beaugency, Loire Valley · - *31* -
Beaulieu, Edict of · - *47* -
Belleroche, Albert · - *336* -, - *338* -
Bergerac, Peace of · - *49* -
Berlin, Prussia, Kingdom of · - *210* -,
  - *211* -
Bermondsey, south London · - *130* -
Berne, Switzerland · - *215* -
Bethlo, Issac · - *230* -
Bethnal Green, east London · - *130* -,
  - *132* -, - *183* -, - *186* -, - *191* -,
  - *241* -, - *242* -, - *270* -, - *273* -,
  - *346* -, - *349* -
Beuzeville, Mary · - *227* -
Beza, Theodore · - *27* -
Bion, Jean · - *89* -, - *276* -
Birds, Huguenot love for · - *273* -
Bishopsgate, east London · - *130* -
Blackfriars, east London · - *108* -, - *314* -

- 465 -

The Story of the Huguenots – a Unique Legacy

Blois, Loire Valley · - *31* -, - *48* -, - *52* -
Bonner, Edmund, Bishop of London ·
  - *120* -
Bordeaux, south-west France · - *96* -,
  - *110* -
Boston, Massachusetts · - *229* -
Bouchard, Francis · - *204* -, - *205* -
Bourbon, Cardinal, uncle, Henri Prince
  of Navarre · - *52* -, - *54* -
Bourges, Gironde · - *31* -
Boyne, Battle of · - *251* -, - *253* -
Brandenburg, Prussia, Kingdom of ·
  - *208* -, - *210* -
Brazil, Huguenot settlements in · - *232*
Bresson, William, loom broker · - *195* -
Brevets · *See* Nantes, Edict of
Brie, northern France · - *92* -
Bristol, Avon · - *141* -
Brohier, Thomas · - *274* -
Bucer, Martin · - *140* -
Buzeau, Abraham · - *226* -

C

Cabrieres, Luberon · - *92* -
Caen, Normandy · - *92* -
Cahors, Lot, south-west France · - *18* -,
  - *49* -
Caillemotte La, Pierre, son of the
  Marquis de Ruvigny · - *253* -
Caisse des conversions · - *80* -
Calais, northern France · - *31* -, - *123* -,
  - *124* -
Calas, Jean · - *339* -, - *340* -, - *342* -,
  - *343* -, - *344* -, - *370* -
Calas, Jean, execution of · - *343* -
Calico · - *137* -, - *138* -, - *176* -, - *235* -
Calvin, John · - *13* -, - *15* -, - *24* -, - *26* -,
  - *27* -, - *33* -, - *122* -, - *143* -, - *233* -,
  - *381* -
Camisards, rebellion · - *102* -, - *103* -,
  - *104* -

Canada · - *230* -, - *232* -
Canterbury weaving school · - *125* -
Canterbury, Kent · - *108* -, - *124* -,
  - *126* -, - *141* -
Cape of Good Hope, South Africa ·
  - *222* -
Carre, Jean · - *326* -
Carrickfergus, Northern Ireland · - *250*
Carrick-On-Suir, Ireland · - *200* -
Casimir, Jan · - *46* -, - *47* -, - *48* -, - *51* -
Castaing, John · - *266* -
Castres, Languedoc · - *70* -, - *82* -
Cateau-Cambrésis, Peace · - *18* -
Cathars · - *7* -
  Rebellion · - *21* -
Catholic League · - *51* -, - *52* -, - *54* -
Cavalier, Jean, Camisard leader · - *104*
Cazenove, Bernard · - *267* -
Cazenove, Christopher · - *336* -
Cazenove, Philip · - *267* -
Cecil, William, Lord Burghley · - *123* -
Chamberlen, family · - *289* -
Chamberlen, Hugh · - *290* -
Chamberlen, Peter · - *290* -
Chamberlen, William · - *290* -
Chambre Ardente · - *24* -
Chambre L'Edit · - *47* -, - *58* -
Chambres mi-parties · - *47* -, - *48* -
Champagne, north-eastern France ·
  - *92* -
Channel Islands · - *198* -, - *229* -
Chapelizod, Ireland · - *200* -
Charenton, Temple of · - *91* -, - *211* -
Charity schools · - *274* -, - *275* -, - *277* -
Charles I, King of England · - *69* -, - *131* -,
  - *150* -, - *157* -, - *200* -, - *314* -
Charles II, King of England · - *132* -,
  - *134* -, - *157* -, - *161* -, - *228* -
Charles IX, King of France · - *33* -, - *35* -,
  - *41* -, - *42* -, - *43* -, - *46* -
Charles V, Holy Roman Emperor · - *22*
Charlestown, south Carolina · - *228* -
Chartres, Eure-et-Loir · - *92* -

- 466 -

The Story of the Huguenots – a Unique Legacy

Chassereau, Robert · - *180* -

Chateaubriand, Edict of · - *25* -

Chauval, Charles · - *227* -

Chauvet, Lewis · - *240* -, - *241* -

Chauvin, Pierre · - *230* -

Chayla, Father · - *101* -, - *102* -

Chelsea, London · - *275* -

Christchurch, Spitalfields · - *146* -

Churches of the Desert · - *88* -, - *103* -, - *362* -, - *371* -

Churchill, Winston, Sir · - *351* -

Clement VIII, Pope · - *60* -

Clement, Jacques, assassin of Henri III King of France · - *53* -

Clerkenwell, east London · - *178* -, - *179* -

Clockmakers and associated trades · - *178* -

Clockmakers Guild · - *314* -

Clonmel, Ireland · - *200* -

Clovis, King of France · - *20* -

Cognac, Charente, south-west France · - *38* -

Colbert, Jean-Baptiste · - *74* -, - *75* -

Compton, Henry, Bishop of London · - *244* -

Condé, Henri, Duc de · - *51* -

Condé, Henri, Prince of · - *43* -, - *47* -, - *50* -

Condé, Henri, Prince of · - *46* -

Conde, Louis
Prince of · - *35* -

Condé, Louis, Prince of · - *26* -, - *27* -, - *30* -, - *31* -, - *32* -, - *35* -, - *37* -

Congreve, Cecilia, nee Blunt La Touche - *355* -

Coronation robes, Elizabeth II, Queen of England · - *368* -

Court of the Grand Jours · - *64* -

Courtauld business · - *192* -

Courtauld Institute · - *338* -

Courtauld, Augustine · - *306* -

Courtauld, Elizabeth · - *357* -

Courtauld, George · - *191* -

Courtauld, Samuel · - *338* -

Cranmer, Thomas, Archbishop of Canterbury · - *119* -

Cranmer, Thomas, Archbishop of Canterbury, Kent · - *140* -

Crespin, Paul · - *178* -, - *306* -, - *316* -

Cromwell, Oliver · - *134* -

D

d'Albon de *Saint-André,* Marechal de France · - *29* -

D'Albret, Jeanne, Queen of Navarre · - *29* -, - *38* -, - *41* -

Dassauville, Anne · - *207* -

Dassauville, Nicholas · - *206* -

de Boisragon, Louis, Lieutenant Colonel - *301* -

de Bostaquet, Issac, Dumont · - *245* -, - *246* -, - *248* -, - *251* -

de Cardonnel, Adam · - *281* -

De Charmes, Simon · - *316* -

de Coligny, Francois, d'Anderlot · - *44* -

de Coligny, Gaspard, Admiral · - *25* -, - *32* -, - *35* -, - *37* -, - *38* -, - *41* -, - *42* -, - *43* -, - *232* -

de Coligny, Odet, Bishop of Beauvais · - *28* -

de Goullainiere, Charles , Major · - *301*

de la Bouchetière, Charles Janvre, Lieutenant Colonel · - *301* -

de Lamerie, Paul · - *178* -, - *306* -, - *307* -, - *312* -, - *316* -

de Ligonier, Jean Louis · - *298* -

de Moivre, Abraham · - *292* -

de Vaux, Gerald · - *282* -

Deal, Kent · - *123* -

Debaufre, Peter · - *315* -, - *316* -

Debrecen, Hungary · - *215* -

- 467 -

The Story of the Huguenots – a Unique Legacy

Declaration of the Rights of Man and of the Citizen 1789 · - *372* -
Delany, Henry · - *303* -
Delftware · - *204* -
Delville Wood, northern France · - *350*
Denization · - *162* -, - *164* -
Denmark · - *211* -
des Gallars, Nicholas · - *143* -
Desaguliers, John Theophilus · - *293* -
Deschamps, forename unknown · - *204* -
Deschamps, John Anthony · - *180* -
Dieppe, Seine-Maritime · - 54 -, - 92 -, - 93 -, - 94 -, - 176 -, - 230 -
Dieulefit, Auvergne-Rhone-Alpes · - *362* -, - *367* -
Dolland, John · - *294* -, - *295* -
Dolland, Peter · - *294* -, - *295* -
Dominican Friars · - *7* -
Doree, George · - 346 -, - 347 -, - 348 -
Dover, Kent · - 123 -, - 124 -, - 141 -
Dragonnades · - 80 -, - 81 -, - 82 -, - 83 -, - 84 -, - 91 -, - 92 -, - 110 -, - 157 -, - 245 -
Dreux, Eure-et-Loir · - *32* -
Drummond, Patrick, Conservator of Scottish Trade · - *204* -
du Chesne, Gideon · - *322* -
Du Faur, Freda · - *227* -
Du Toit, Francois · - *224* -
Du Toit, Gabriel · - *224* -
Du Toit, Gerhardus Johannes · - *225* -
Dublin · - 200 -, - 201 -, - 203 -
Dublin, Ireland · - *250* -, - *253* -
Dubuison, Peter · - *177* -
Duillier, Nicholas Fatio · - *315* -
Dupen, John · - *186* -
Dupen, William · - *317* -
Dupin, Nicholas · - *281* -
Dupont, Nicholas · - *211* -
Dupont, Philipp · - *211* -
Dupont, Philippe · - *212* -

Durand, Anne · - *92* -
Durand, Anthony, Col · - *97* -
Durand, Daniel Francois · - *199* -
Durand, Francois · - *199* -
Durand, Francois Guillaume · - *92* -
Durand, Guillaume · - *97* -
Durand, Marie · - *365* -
Dutch East India Company · - *221* -, - *222* -, - *232* -
Dutch Reformed Church · - *106* -
Duval, Alexander Edward - xi
Duval, Etienne - 214 -
Duval, Francis - 302 -
Duval, Henrietta - 303 -
Duval, Jean-Pierre - 168 -
Duval, Louis David -218 -
Duval, Louis Jean - 168 -
Duval, Peter - 168 -
Duval, Thomas - 302 -

E

East India Company · - *176* -, - *177* -, - *234* -, - *277* -
Ecouen, Edict of · - *25* -
Edict of Nantes, Revocation of · - *124* -
Edinburgh, Scotland · - *205* -, - *206* -, - *207* -
Edward VI
    King of England · - *140* -
Edward VI, King of England · - 11 -, - 119 -, - 120 -, - 141 -, - 143 -, - 150 -, - 198 -, - 277 -
Elizabeth I, Queen of England · - 27 -, - 31 -, - 32 -, - 37 -, - 38 -, - 51 -, - 120 -, - 123 -, - 124 -, - 127 -, - 129 -, - 150 -, - 198 -, - 200 -, - 313 -
Elizabeth II, Queen of England · - *145* -
Erasmus, Desiderius · - *11* -
Estates General · - *48* -, - *52* -, - *55* -

- 468 -

The Story of the Huguenots – a Unique Legacy

F

Fabergé, Peter Carl · - 218 -, - 219 -
Farel, Guillaume · - 15 -
Finsbury, north London · - 180 -
Fleix, Peace of · - 49 -
Flemings · - 107 -
Fort Coligny, Brazil · - 233 -
Foubert, Solomon · - 277 -
Fourdrinier, Charles · - 285 -
Fourdrinier, Henry · - 283 -, - 284 -
Fourdrinier, Sealy · - 284 -
Francis I, King of France · - 15 -, - 21 -, - 22 -, - 25 -
Francis II, King of France · - 25 -, - 27 -
Frankfurt-am-Main, Free City of · - 210
Franschoek, South Africa · - 222 -, - 224 -, - 225 -, - 350 -
Franzosischer-Dom Cathedral, Berlin · - 211 -
Frederic IV, King of Denmark · - 211 -
Fredericia, Denmark · - 211 -
Fredrick William, Elector of Prussia · - 207 -
French Chapel, Wandsworth, south London · - 175 -
French Committee · - 159 -, - 160 -
French Hospital · - 160 -, - 165 -, - 167 -, - 168 -, - 169 -, - 170 -, - 379 -, - 381 -
French Revolution 1789 · - 370 -, - 371 -
Friedrich II, Landgrave · - 208 -
Friedrichsdorf, Hesse, Germany · - 208 -, - 210 -
Friendly Societies · - 267 -, - 268 -
Fronde, The · - 73 -, - 74 -
Fulham, London · - 107 -
Furneaux, Lewis · - 180 -

G

Galleys sentence · - 88 -, - 89 -, - 90 -, - 91 -
Gandon, Pierre · - 304 -
Gardening Societies · - 272 -
Garnault, Margaret · - 260 -
Garret, Nicholas · - 176 -
Garrick, David · - 100 -, - 334 -, - 335 -
Garthwaite, Anna Maria, Silk pattern designer · - 109 -, - 196 -
Gashry/Gascherie/Chesneau, family names · - 261 -
Gasquel, Louis · - 189 -
Gaucheron, Anne · - 272 -, - 273 -
Gaucheron, Charlotte · - 169 -
Gaucheron, Louis · - 158 -
Geneva, Switzerland · - 24 -, - 112 -, - 114 -, - 215 -, - 216 -, - 232 -
George III, King of England · - 160 -
George Rose Act 1793, Friendly Societies · - 268 -
George, Remy · - 322 -
Germany · - 207 -, - 217 -
Giles, Abraham · - 326 -
Giles, James · - 325 -
Glasgow, Scotland · - 190 -, - 207 -
Glastonbury, Somerset · - 141 -
Gloucester, England · - 327 -
Goldsmiths Hall · - 306 -, - 310 -, - 315
Gordon Riots · - 257 -, - 261 -
Gouyon, Charles · - 324 -
Governorship of the Bank of England · - 283 -
Great Exhibition of 1851 · - 280 -
Great Fire of London, 1666 · - 129 -, - 143 -, - 154 -, - 265 -
Great Yarmouth, Norfolk · - 123 -, - 141 -
Greenwich, London · - 131 -, - 173 -, - 174 -, - 275 -
Grenoble, Auvergne-Rhône-Alpes · - 96 -

- 469 -

The Story of the Huguenots – a Unique Legacy

Gribelin, Simon · - *318* -
Grignion, Thomas · - *316* -
Gruché, Pierre · - *303* -
Guardiols, family name · - *350* -
Guernsey, Channel Islands · - *199* -,
   - *350* -
Gueux, Revolt of the · - *37* -
Guise, Francois, Duc de · - 25 -, - 30 -,
   - 32 -, - 33 -, - 43 -
Guise, Henri, Duc de · - 49 -, - 50 -,
   - 51 -, - 52 -, - 55 -, - 56 -
Guise, Marie, mother of Mary Queen of
   Scots · - *25* -
Gutenberg, Johannes · - *9* -
Guyon (Guion), Blaquiere, Magdalen ·
   - *372* -
Guyon (Guion), David · - *378* -, - *381* -
Guyon (Guion), George Sutherland,
   Major · - *350* -, - *351* -, - *352* -
Guyon (Guion), Guillaume · - *110* -,
   - *201* -, - *203* -
Guyon (Guion), Richard Debaufre ·
   - *216* -

H

Halstead, Essex · - *141* -
Hamburg, Prussia · - *210* -
Hamelin, Philibert, early Huguenot
   martyr · - *13* -
Harache, Pierre · - *306* -, - *307* -
Harwich, Essex · - *123* -
Henri II, King of France · - *24* -, - *25* -,
   - *198* -, - *232* -
Henri III, King of France · - 46 -, - 48 -,
   - 49 -, - 50 -, - 51 -, - 52 -, - 53 -
Henri IV, King of France · - *55* -, - *57* -,
   - *59* -, - *60* -, - *65* -, - *132* -, *See*
   Navarre, Henri,
Henri, d'Anjou · - *42* -, - *45* -, - *50* -
Henrietta Maria, Princess of France ·
   - *132* -

Henrietta Maria, Queen of England ·
   - *150* -
Henry VII, King of England · - *123* -
Henry VIII, King of England · - *12* -,
   - *119* -, - *141* -, - *256* -, - *313* -
Hercule, Duc d'Alencon · - *47* -, - *48* -
Hessen-Cassel · - *208* -
Holland · - 212 -, - 213 -, - 264 -
Honiton, Devon · - *107* -
Houblon, James and Abraham · - *265* -
Houblon, John, Sir, · - *265* -
Houblon, Rebecca · - *278* -
Houle, Arthur · - *180* -
Huguenot chapel, Canterbury, Kent ·
   - *141* -
Huguenot regiments · - *248* -
Hungary · - 215 -, - 216 -

I

Innocent III, Pope · - *7* -
Inquisition (Papal) · - *7* -, - *8* -, - *37* -
Ipswich, Suffolk · - *158* -
Ireland · - 200 -, - 249 -
Isambert, Catherine · - *274* -
Islington, London · - *275* -

J

James I, King of England · - 123 -, - 130 -,
   - 131 -, - 133 -, - 150 -, - 200 -, - 291 -
James II, King of England · - 143 -,
   - 157 -, - 243 -, - 244 -, - 246 -,
   - 249 -, - 250 -, - 251 -, - 253 -
Jamestown, America · - *229* -
Jarnac, Poitou-Charentes · - *37* -
Jersey, Channel Islands · - *199* -
Jewell, John, Bishop of Salisbury · - *122* -
Joinville, Treaty of · - *50* -
Joubert, Pierre · - *224* -
Joucas, Luberon · - *92* -

- 470 -

The Story of the Huguenots – a Unique Legacy

Jourdan, Jean · - *224* -
Jourdan, Pierre · - *224* -
Joyeuse, Duc of · - *51* -

K

King's Lynn, Norfolk · - *141* -
Kingswinford, nr Stourbridge · - *327* -
Knowle, West Midlands · - *327* -
Knox, John · - *10* -, - *123* -
Konigsberg, Prussia, Kingdom of · - *210* -

L

L'Hopital, Michel, Chancellor · - *28* -
La Charite-sur-Loire · - *38* -
La Motte, Franschoek · - *224* -
La Patente, Spitalfields, London · - *144*
La Rochelle, Charente-Maritime · - *36* -,
    - *37* -, - *38* -, - *45* -, - *65* -, - *66* -, - *69* -,
    - *72* -, - *84* -, - *96* -, - *211* -, - *213* -,
    - *229* -, - *232* -, - *261* -, - *293* -, - *313* -
La Rochelle, siege of · - *70* -
La Rochelle, Treaty of · - *46* -, - *69* -
La Trobe, Charles · - *227* -
Labelye, Charles · - *295* -, - *296* -
Lacoste, Luberon · - *92* -
Lafayette, Marquis of · - *344* -, - *370* -
Lambeth, south London · - *129* -, - *130*
Lamerie, Paul de · - *306* -, - *309* -, - *311*
Lapierre, Francois · - *322* -
Laporte, Roland, Camisard leader ·
    - *104* -
L'Artillerie, L'Eglise · - *146* -
Laud, William, Archbishop of
    Canterbury · - *150* -, - *151* -
Laudonniere, Rene · - *227* -
Laune, Gideon de · - *291* -
Lausanne, Switzerland · - *215* -
Law of Separation of Church from State
    1905 · - *376* -

Le Blon, Jacob Christophe · - *279* -
Le Chambon-sur-Lignon, Auvergne-
    Rhone-Alpes · - *362* -, - *366* -
Le Chambon-sur-Lignon, Auvergne-
    Rhone-Aples · - *363* -
Le Havre, Seine-Maritime · - *92* -
Le Mans, Pays de la Loire · - *305* -
Le Renaudie, (Perigord nobleman) ·
    - *27* -
Le Roux, Paul · - *222* -
Le Sage, John · - *306* -
Le Tellier, Francois-Michel, Marquis de
    Louvois · - *75* -
Le Tellier, Francois-Michel, Marquis de
    Louvois · - *81* -
Le Tellier, Francois-Michel, Marquis de
    Louvois · - *82* -
Lefevre, George · - *168* -
Lefevre, Jacques · - *14* -
Leicester Fields L'Eglise, Orange Street
    Chapel · - *149* -
Lekeux, Peter, Col · - *289* -
Leman, James · - *196* -
Leo X, Pope · - *22* -
Lepine, Henry · - *315* -
Ligonier, John, Sir, Lieutenant Governor
    of Guernsey · - *199* -
Lille, Flanders · - *305* -
Longjumeau, Peace of · - *36* -
Lorraine, Cardinal of · - *25* -, - *33* -, - *37*
Louis XII, King of France · - *20* -
Louis XIII, King of France · - *60* -, - *61* -,
    - *65* -, - *66* -, - *67* -, - *68* -, - *70* -, - *72*
Louis XIV, King of France · - *61* -, - *72* -,
    - *73* -, - *74* -, - *75* -, - *76* -, - *79* -, - *82* -,
    - *87* -, - *89* -, - *92* -, - *94* -, - *96* -, - *97* -,
    - *98* -, - *111* -, - *157* -, - *161* -, - *162* -,
    - *169* -, - *199* -, - *200* -, - *212* -, - *213* -,
    - *244* -, - *248* -, - *299* -, - *303* -, - *305* -,
    - *322* -, - *364* -, - *376* -, - *377* -
Louis XV, King of France · - *205* -
Louis XVI, King of France · - *344* -
Lourmarin, Luberon · - *92* -

- 471 -

The Story of the Huguenots – a Unique Legacy

Luneray, Normandy · - *108* -, - *375* -,
- *381* -
Luther, Martin · - 10 -, - 13 -, - *208* -,
- 215 -, - 381 -
Ninety-Five Theses · - *21* -
Lyon, Auvergne-Rhône-Alpes · - *31* -,
- *113* -, - *185* -, - *188* -

M

Magdeburg, Prussia, Kingdom of ·
- *210* -
Maidstone, Kent · - *107* -, - *141* -
Maintenon, Madame de · - *87* -
Maison de Charitie · - *166* -
Malan, Jacques · - *224* -
Mallandain, David · - *169* -
Mallandain, Elizabeth · - *169* -
Mallandain, Jean · - 93 -, - 94 -, - 95 -,
- 159 -, - 255 -
Mallandain, John · - *232* -, - *277* -
Mallandain, Peter · - *180* -
Manakin, Virginia, America · - *230* -
Manchester, England · - *190* -
Marguerite, Princess of France · - *38* -,
- *41* -, - *60* -
Marguerite, Queen of Navarre · - *21* -
Market gardens · - *272* -
Marot, Daniel · - 204 -, - 320 -, - 321 -
Marriage Act 1753 · - *152* -
Marriage Act 1836 · - *152* -
Marseille, Bouches du Rhone · - *90* -,
- *91* -
Marteihle, Jean · - *90* -, - *91* -
Martineau, family name · - *329* -
Martineau, Harriet · - *329* -
Martineau, Victorine · - *381* -
Mary I, Queen of England · - *120* -,
- *198* -
Mary, Queen of Scots · - *25* -, - *37* -,
- *121* -
Marylebone, London · - *146* -, - *275* -

Masion de Charitie · - *165* -, - *167* -
Massachusetts, America · - *229* -
Mauvillain, Peter · - *177* -
Mayerne, Theodore, Sir · - *291* -
Mazarin, Cardinal · - *73* -, - *74* -
Meaux, Seine et Marne · - *12* -, - *24* -,
- *34* -, - *92* -
Medici, Catherine · - 25 -, - 29 -, - 31 -,
- 32 -, - 33 -, - 34 -, - 38 -, - 41 -,
- 42 -, - 47 -, - 58 -
Medici, Marie · - *60* -, - *65* -
Méreaux (gift) · - *147* -, - *153* -
Merindol, Luberon · - *92* -
Merzeau, Peter · - *191* -
Mettayer, Louis · - *306* -
Metz, Lorraine, eastern France · - *305* -
Migault, Jean · - *83* -, - *84* -
Mile End, east London · - *130* -, - *183* -
Molnar, Albert Szenci · - *216* -
Moncontour, Vienne · - *37* -
Monlong, Pierre · - *303* -
Montauban, midi-Pyrenees · - 36 -,
- 38 -, - 46 -, - 70 -, - 71 -, - 82 -, - 91 -,
- 110 -
Montmorency, Anne, Duc de · - 13 -,
- *25* -, - *29* -, - *36* -
Montmorency, Henri Duc de · - *46* -
Montpellier, southern France · - *36* -,
- *82* -, - *92* -, - *260* -, - *321* -
Morden, London · - *177* -
Mortlake, London · - *107* -
Mount Nod, Huguenot Cemetery ·
- *175* -

N

Nantes, Brittany · - *92* -, - *96* -
Nantes, Edict of · - 18 -, - 57 -, - 58 -,
- 59 -, - 61 -, - 62 -, - 63 -, - 64 -, - 67 -,
- 68 -, - 71 -, - 75 -, - 79 -, - 87 -,
- 106 -
Napoleonic Code · - *374* -, - *375* -

- 472 -

The Story of the Huguenots – a Unique Legacy

National (royal) Briefs · - 157 -
National apology to the Huguenots
1985 · - 378 -
Naturalization · - 164 -
Navarre, Henri, Prince of · - 38 -, - 41 -,
- 43 -, - 45 -, - 47 -, - 49 -, - 50 -,
- 51 -, - 53 -
Navarre, Marguerite · - 21 -
Negrepelisse, Massacre · - 66 -, - 67 -
Nemours, Treaty of · - 51 -
Nerac, Treaty of · - 49 -
Netherlands · - 36 -, - 37 -, - 212 -,
- 213 -, - 216 -, - 221 -, - 222 -,
- 229 -
New England, America · - 229 -
New France Company · - 231 -
New Oxford, America · - 229 -
New Paltz, America · - 228 -
New York · - 228 -
Newcastle upon Tyne · - 327 -
Newham on Severn · - 327 -
Nice, Cote d'Azur, southern France ·
- 96 -
Nimes, Languedoc · - 35 -, - 36 -, - 46 -,
- 70 -, - 82 -, - 113 -, - 189 -
Nismes, Languedoc · - 103 -
North America · - 227 -
Norton Folgate, east London · - 130 -
Norwich, Norfolk · - 190 -
Noyon, northern France, birthplace of
Calvin · - 15 -

O

Obrisset, John · - 319 -
Orléans, Edict · - 28 -
Orléans, Loire Valley · - 31 -, - 36 -, - 44 -
Ouvry, Francisca Ingram · - 330 -
Ouvry, Frederic · - 332 -
Ouvry, Jacques · - 108 -
Ouvry, James · - 154 -, - 257 -
Ouvry, Jean · - 375 -

Ouvry, John · - 109 -, - 257 -
Ouvry, Moyise · - 145 -
Ouvry, Peter · - 109 -

P

Paisley, Scotland · - 190 -, - 207 -
Palissy, Bernard · - 13 -
Palma, Duke of · - 55 -
Pantin, Simon · - 306 -
Papin, Dennis · - 208 -, - 292 -, - 293 -
Paris · - 34 -, - 35 -, - 42 -, - 43 -, - 52 -,
- 53 -, - 55 -, - 56 -, - 74 -, - 80 -
Paris, Parlement · - 73 -
Paul IV, Pope · - 26 -
Paulin, Claude · - 204 -, - 205 -
Pelletier, John · - 323 -
Pelletier, Thomas · - 322 -
Pellisson, Paul · - 80 -
Perigal, Francis · - 316 -
Perigal, Jean · - 93 -
Perigal, John · - 316 -
Pest House · - 160 -, - 167 -, - 179 -,
- 276 -
Peter the Great, Czar of Russia · - 217
Petworth, West Sussex · - 327 -
Philip II, King of Spain · - 31 -, - 34 -,
- 37 -, - 50 -, - 55 -, - 56 -, - 121 -
Pious X, Pope · - 377 -
Plague · - 128 -
Planché, Andrew · - 325 -
Planché, James Robinson · - 331 -
Plantel, Pierre · - 306 -
Plymouth, Devon · - 141 -
Poitiers, Vienne · - 31 -
Poitou, Nouvelle-Aquitaine · - 229 -
Pons, Jean · - 306 -
Poor Men of Lyon, also known as
Waldensians · - 8 -
Poor Relief · - 153 -
Port Royal, South Carolina, America ·
- 227 -, - 228 -

- 473 -

The Story of the Huguenots – a Unique Legacy

Portal, Abraham · - *307* -, - *308* -, - *330*

Portal, family · - *110* -

Portal, Henry · - *282* -, - *283* -

Portal, Jean Francois · - *307* -

Portarlington Calvinist Church · - *203* -

Portarlington, Ireland · - *201* -, - *202* -, - *203* -

Potsdam, Edict of · - *209* -

Prioleau, Elias · - *228* -

Privas, Languedoc · - *70* -

Privat, family name · - *208* -

Protestant Regiment · - *299* -

Protestant temples, destruction of · - *76* -, - *79* -, - *91* -, - *108* -

Prussia, Kingdom of · - *207* -, - *208* -, - *210* -

Puritans · - 150 -, - 216 -

Q

Quebec, Canada · - *231* -

Queensland, Canada · - *226* -

R

Rambaut, Edmund · - *297* -

Rambaut, Jean · - *296* -

Rambaut, Paul · - *297* -

Rambaut, William Hautenville · - *296* -

Ravaillac, Francois · - *60* -

Raw Silk Company · - *181* -

Revocation of the Edict of Nantes · - *87* -, - *88* -, - *91* -, - *94* -, - *98* -, - *99* -, - *100* -, - *106* -, - *123* -, - *125* -, - *136* -, - *142* -, - *154* -, - *173* -, - *200* -, - *205* -, - *208* -, - *214* -, - *217* -, - *229* -, - *244* -, - *280* -, - *329* -, - *339* -, - *375* -

Rhode Island, Narragansett · - *229* -

Ribault, Jean de · - *227* -

Richelieu, Cardinal · - 62 -, - 67 -, - 68 -, - 69 -, - 70 -, - 71 -, - 72 -, - 231 -

Riebeeck, Jan · - *221* -, - *222* -

Rieusset, Peter · - *322* -

Riots, Spitalfields · - *238* -

Riots, Spitalfields, London · - *234* -, - *235* -, - *236* -, - *238* -, - *239* -

Riviere, Robert · - *280* -

Rochette, Francois · - *344* -

Rocque, Jean · - *286* -, - *287* -

Roget, Peter Mark · - *328* -, - *329* -

Rohan, Benjamin, Duc de · - *65* -, - *67* -

Romilly, Catherine · - *328* -

Romilly, Etienne · - *259* -, - *260* -

Romilly, John, Sir · - *333* -

Romilly, Mimi · - *381* -

Romilly, Samuel, Sir · - *260* -, - *329* -

Romorantin, Edict of · - *27* -

Rondeau, James · - *359* -

Rondeau, Jean · - 153 -, - 154 -, - 155 -

Rondeau, Stanley · - *381* -

Rosay-en-Brie · - *34* -

Rouen, Seine-Maritime · - *31* -, - *92* -, - *94* -, - *176* -, - *305* -

Roux, Paul · - *224* -

Royal Bounty · - 158 -, - 159 -, - 160 -, - 306 -

Royal Lustring Company · - *158* -, - *185* -, - *234* -

Russia · - *217* -

Russian Revollution · - *219* -

Ruvigny, Henry, Viscount Galway · - *201* -, - *202* -, - *203* -

Ruvigny, Marquis de · - *170* -, - *173* -

Rye, Kent · - *124* -, - *141* -

Ryswick Peace of · - *202* -

S

Sandwich, Kent · - *124* -, - *141* -

Sark, Channel Islands · - *199* -

Savoy Chapel, London · - *142* -, - *149* -, - *150* -, - *152* -

Savoy, Duke of · - *215* -, - *299* -

The Story of the Huguenots – a Unique Legacy

Savoye, Catherine · - *274* -

Saxay, David · - *275* -

Schomberg, Friedrich 1st Duke of · - *299* -

Schomberg, Meinhard, Colonel · - *248* -, - *251* -

Scotland · - 203 -, - 206 -

Segallas, Israel · - *304* -

Shoreditch, east London · - *130* -, - *144* -, - *183* -

Silk production line · - *235* -

Six, James · - *293* -

Sixus V, Pope · - *50* -

Soho Square Huguenot Church · - *145*

Soho, London · - 178 -, - *276* -, - *286* -, - *303* -, - *328* -

South Africa · - 221 -, - *222* -, - *223* -, - *225* -, - *349* -

South Carolina, America · - *227* -, - *229*

Southampton, Hampshire · - *124* -, - *141* -

Southwark, south London · - *130* -, - *131* -, - *327* -

Spanish Armada · - *121* -

Spanish Netherlands · - *33* -, - *56* -, - *121* -

Spanish Road · - *34* -

Spitalfields Acts · - *189* -, - *190* -

Spitalfields Historic Buildings Trust · - *379* -

Spitalfields, London · - 108 -, - *132* -, - *138* -, - *144* -, - *145* -, - *146* -, - *154* -, - *158* -, - *159* -, - *165* -, - *166* -, - *173* -, - *176* -, - *178* -, - *183* -, - *184* -, - *185* -, - *188* -, - *191* -, - *193* -, - *195* -, - *196* -, - *234* -, - *240* -, - *241* -, - *247* -, - *257* -, - *258* -, - *271* -, - *272* -, - *276* -, - *294* -, - *329* -, - *348* -, - *368* -, - *379* -

Sprimont, Nicholas · - *178* -, - *324* -

St Bartholomew's Day Massacre · - *41* -, - *44* -, - *45* -, - *121* -

St Germain, Peace of · - *38* -

St Martin's Le Grand, Church · - *145* -

St Michael's Day · - *34* -

St Petersburg, Russia · - *217* -

Stepney, east London · - *129* -

Stonehouse, Gloucestershire · - *141* -

Sully, Duc de · - *59* -

Sumptuary Laws · - *135* -, - *137* -

Switzerland · - *214* -

Synod, First of French and Dutch churches · - *142* -

T

Tanqueray, Ann · - *313* -

Tanqueray, David · - *313* -

Temoignage · - 147 -, - *148* -, - *157* -

Templeux · - *205* -

The Foreign Protestants Naturalisation Act 1708 · - *255* -

Theis, Edouard · - *362* -

Thorpe-Le-Stoken, Essex · - *141* -

Threadneedle Street Church · - 141 -, - *142* -, - *143* -, - *145* -, - *147* -, - *149* -, - *152* -, - *157* -

Tijou, Jean · - *174* -, - *321* -

Tolerance, Edict of · - *370* -, - *371* -

Toleration, Edict of · - *29* -, - *345* -

Tollin, Henry, Doctor · - *211* -

Tonnet, Nicholas · - *174* -

Toulouse, Riots, south-western France · - *16* -

Toulouse, south-western France · - *62* -, - *76* -, - *340* -, - *344* -

Toulouse, Temple du Salin · - *378* -

Tours, Loire Valley · - *31* -, - *188* -

Tower of London · - *132* -

Trades and manufacture of Huguenot refugees · - *176* -

Trocme, André · - *362* -, - *382* -

Troyes, Peace of · - *32* -

Turkey · - *217* -

U

Urseau, Nicholas · - *313* -
Utenhove, John · - *143* -
Utrecht, Peace Treaty of, 1713 · - *322*
Uzes, Languedoc · - *70* -

V

Valline, John · - *240* -, - *241* -
Van Somer, Paul · - *318* -
Vauloue, James · - *295* -
Vermallet, Jean · - *276* -
Vervins, Treaty of · - *56* -
Villegaignon, Nicholas Durand · - *232* -
Villion, Francois · - *222* -
Voltaire, François-Marie Arouet · - *343* -, - *344* -, - *345* -
Voting · - *138* -
Vulliamy, Benjamin · - *317* -
Vulliamy, Benjamin Lewis · - *332* -
Vulliamy, Justin · - *317* -

W

Waite, Mary · - *349* -
Waldensians, also known as the Poor Men of Lyon · - *8* -
Walloons · - 107 -, - 124 -, - 125 -, - 228 -, - 313 -
Walsingham, Francis, Sir · - *120* -, - *127* -
Walters, Joseph · - *368* -

Wandsworth, south London · - *174* -, - *176* -, - *177* -
Wapping, east London · - *144* -
Wassy, Massacre · - *30* -, - *35* -
Waterford, Ireland · - *200* -, - *202* -
Weavers Company · - 130 -, - 136 -, - 176 -, - 188 -, - 197 -, - 236 -, - 348 -
Weaving · - 134 -, - 136 -, - 138 -, - 183 -, - 184 -, - 185 -, - 186 -, - 188 -, - 189 -, - 192 -, - 193 -, - 204 -, - 206 -, - 207 -, - 348 -, - 349 -
Westminster, London · - *129* -
Westphalia, Peace of · - *207* -
Whitechapel, east London · - *130* -, - *183* -
Willaume, David · - *306* -, - *313* -
William III, King of England · - 159 -, - 201 -, - 202 -, - 212 -, - 213 -, - 249 -, - 250 -, - 251 -, - 253 -, - 300 -
William, Duke of Orange · - *36* -, - *244* -, - *245* -
Winchelsea, Kent · - *141* -
Wisborough Green, West Sussex · - *327* -
Wollaton, nr Nottingham · - *327* -
Worshipful Company of Apothecaries · - *291* -
Worshipful Company of Goldsmiths · - *306* -
Wurttemberg, Germany · - *208* -
Wycliffe, John · - *8* -, - *9* -

Z

Zurich, Switzerland · - *215* -